THE ALL-ROUND MAN

The All-Round Man

SELECTED LETTERS OF
PERCY GRAINGER
1914–1961

Edited by

Malcolm Gillies and David Pear

CLARENDON PRESS · OXFORD

1994

Oxford University Press, Walton Street, Oxford OX2 6DP

Oxford New York
Athens Auckland Bangkok Bombay
Calcutta Cape Town Dar es Salaam Delhi
Florence Hong Kong Istanbul Karachi
Kuala Lumpur Madras Madrid Melbourne
Mexico City Nairobi Paris Singapore
Taipei Tokyo Toronto

and associated companies in
Berlin Ibadan

Oxford is a trade mark of Oxford University Press

Published in the United States
by Oxford University Press Inc., New York

British Library Cataloguing in Publication Data
Data available

Library of Congress Cataloging in Publication Data
Grainger, Percy, 1882–1961.
[Correspondence. Selections]
The all-round man: selected letters of Percy Grainger, 1914–1961
/ edited by Malcolm Gillies and David Pear.
p. cm.
Includes index.
1. Grainger, Percy, 1882–1961—Correspondence.
2. Composers—Correspondence. I. Gillies, Malcolm.
II. Pear, David. III. Title.
ML410.G75A4 1994 786.2'092—dc20 [B] 94–12799
ISBN 0-19-816377-0

Set by Hope Services (Abingdon) Ltd.
Printed in Great Britain
on acid-free paper by
Biddles Ltd.
Guildford & King's Lynn

TO OUR MOTHERS,

BELLE AND MARGARET

ACKNOWLEDGEMENTS

ALL letters and illustrations in this volume have been prepared from materials held in the Grainger Museum at The University of Melbourne, Australia. For permission to include letters and illustrations in this volume, and for much advice, we are grateful to the Baillieu Library and Grainger Museum of The University of Melbourne, Stewart Manville (White Plains, New York), Maurice Lowe (Surrey, British Columbia), Storm Bull (Boulder, Colorado), Thomas Armstrong (Olney, Buckinghamshire), Burnett Cross (White Plains, New York), and Wendell Holmquist (St Peter, Minnesota). For technical reproduction of photographs we are indebted to the photography section of the Centre for the Study of Higher Education, The University of Melbourne. Initial translations from the Danish were undertaken by Philip Grigg (Melbourne), to whom we are indebted. Further translation of passages in various Scandinavian languages and Dutch was provided by Erik J. Jensen, John Martin, and Gary Ekkel (all of Melbourne) and Manfred Jurgensen (Brisbane).

We are also grateful to the following for advice or information which has furthered our research: the Australian War Memorial (Canberra), Ann-Marie Baker (Melbourne), The British Library (London), Frank Callaway (Perth), Clarence S. Crooks (Barstow, California), the Danish Music Information Centre (Copenhagen), Eileen Dorum (Melbourne), Kay Dreyfus (Melbourne), Gabrielle Emery-Reece (Brisbane), Myron R. Falck (St Peter, Minnesota), Rosemary Florrimell (Melbourne), Richard Fowler (Melbourne), Katherine H. Graffam (Portland, Maine), Jennifer Hill (Melbourne), the Hollywood Bowl, John Hopkins (Sydney), The International Percy Grainger Society, Paul Kildea (Oxford), the Library of Congress (Washington, DC), the Library of the University of California at Berkeley, Sandra McColl (Melbourne), the Music and Architecture Library at The University of Queensland, the National Library of Australia (Canberra), the National Library of Scotland (Edinburgh), Kathleen Nelson (Sydney), the New York Public Library, Jane O'Brien (Brisbane), Barry Ould (Aylesbury), Margaret Pear (Tottington, Lancashire), the Percy Grainger Society (UK), Simon Perry (Brisbane), John Poynter (Melbourne), the Queen Elizabeth II Army Memorial

Museum (Waiouru, New Zealand), Rolf Stang (New York), Edith Thorstensson and the archives of Gustavus Adolphus College (St Peter, Minnesota), Louise Wright and the archives of Trinity College School (Port Hope, Ontario), Elinor Wrobel (Sydney).

We acknowledge the financial assistance afforded by the Australian Research Council during 1990–1 which has allowed this project to reach fruition. A grant to assist publication of this volume, and in particular its illustrations, is gratefully acknowledged from The University of Queensland. To the staff of Oxford University Press we express thanks for expert and sympathetic advice over the years of this volume's gestation.

We further acknowledge the considerable assistance to our study from the specialist literature about Frankfurt Group composers by Stephen Lloyd, Stephen Banfield, and Ian Parrott, and about Grainger by Teresa Balough, John Bird, Eileen Dorum, Jane O'Brien, Thomas P. Lewis, Wilfrid Mellers, and, in particular, Kay Dreyfus, to whose collection *The Farthest North of Humanness: Letters of Percy Grainger, 1901–1914* this present volume is intended as a sequel.

M.G.
D.P.

CONTENTS

LIST OF PLATES

CHRONOLOGY

1882   Born George Percy Grainger in Brighton (near Melbourne), Victoria, 8 July.

c.1886   Starts formal education, at home.

c.1888   Commences piano lessons with his mother.

1890   His parents separate.

c.1891   Starts to study acting, painting, and drawing.

c.1892   Commences piano study with Louis Pabst in Melbourne; becomes acquainted with Icelandic sagas.

1894   First appears in public as a pianist. His parents seek support for him to study abroad.

1895   Commences studies at the Hoch Conservatory in Frankfurt, with James Kwast (piano) and Iwan Knorr (composition, theory); develops over following years deep friendships with British students Balfour Gardiner, Roger Quilter, and Cyril Scott, and the Dane Herman Sandby.

1897   First reads Whitman and Kipling works.

1898   Begins his Kipling settings (continued until late 1950s).

1899   Starts to teach piano. His mother's health declines.

1900   Visits France, Britain, and Holland variously with his parents; presents first solo public recital in Frankfurt.

1901   Moves with his mother to London, where he appears in many 'society' concerts as accompanist or assistant artist (averaging about fifty concerts per year, to 1904); commences his *Marching Song of Democracy*, inspired by Whitman.

1902   Undertakes first regional tours in Britain; gains his first concerto appearances, in Bath; makes initial arrangement of *Irish Tune from County Derry*; completes first setting of *Hill-Song* No. 1.

1903   Studies with Busoni in Berlin; undertakes extended concert tour of Australasia and South Africa with the contralto Ada Crossley (to May 1904).

1904   Tours Denmark with Sandby; meets Karen Holten (later Kellermann), his girlfriend until 1912.

1905   Starts serious collection and arrangement of English folk music; gains more concerto engagements, but most concert appearances are as associate artist (averaging about seventy-five concerts per year, to 1909).

1906 Forges friendship with Grieg; first uses the phonograph to record folk-songs; composes *Brigg Fair* setting.

1907 First meets Delius; holidays with the Griegs in Norway; presents memorial performances of Grieg's piano concerto in Britain and Denmark; first sets *Molly on the Shore*.

1908 Publishes a controversial article about the use of the phonograph in folk-music collection; makes first gramophone recordings; departs on second Australasian tour with Crossley (to May 1909).

1909 Is greatly taken with Polynesian and Maori culture in New Zealand; starts to present his compositions more in public; completes *Father and Daughter* setting of Faeroe Islanders' music.

1910 Establishes himself as a solo recitalist and orchestral soloist (averaging about one hundred concerts per year, to 1914, the majority in continental Europe). *Mock Morris* and *Molly on the Shore* are premièred, in Copenhagen.

1911 Changes his professional name to Percy Aldridge Grainger; completes initial settings of *Shepherd's Hey*. Schott (London) starts to publish his compositions.

1912 Hears many of his works performed at the first Balfour Gardiner concert series, in London; holds first public concert solely of his own works; suffers minor nervous breakdown during German concert tour; completes *Handel in the Strand*.

1913 Participates in second Gardiner series; is briefly engaged to his piano student Margot Harrison; starts to compose his 'imaginary ballet' music *The Warriors*.

1914 Postpones or cancels concert engagements when war is declared, August; moves out of London; sails to the United States in September, ostensibly out of regard for his mother's health; contracts with New York music publisher G. Schirmer; first appears in New York, playing the piano part in *Shepherd's Hey*.

1915 Gives recital and concerto débuts in New York, with stunning success; contracts with Duo-Art Company to make piano rolls (to 1933); undertakes first American tour.

1916 Collaborates with Melba in recitals in support of the Allied war effort; completes *The Warriors*, dedicated to Delius. Première of *In a Nutshell* suite.

1917 Enlists in a US Army band learning oboe and soprano-saxophone; makes first gramophone recordings with Columbia (to 1931); starts relationship with Mrs Lotta Mills Hough (to 1922). Premières of *The Warriors* and *Marching Song of Democracy*. Grainger's father dies, in Melbourne.

1918   Expects to be sent with the band to France and makes many recordings of unfinished works; is, instead, appointed a band-music instructor near New York; takes American citizenship; completes his most famous piece, *Country Gardens*.

1919   Is discharged from the US Army; first teaches at the Chicago Musical College (intermittently to 1931); completes *Children's March*, for band.

1920   Undertakes long concert tours of the American Far West and Cuba; makes first attempts at 'elastic scoring' with an arrangement of his *Irish Tune*.

1921   Moves with his mother to their final home, 7 Cromwell Place, White Plains, New York; rescores a number of his early works.

1922   His mother's mental state deteriorates, and she commits suicide, April; he cancels most performing engagements, and sails for Scandinavia, where he collects folk music with Evald Tang Kristensen in Jutland. Première of *The Bride's Tragedy*.

1923   Lives for half a year in Frankfurt, where he assists Delius; arranges production of a memorial volume to his mother; further collects folk music in Jutland. Publication of his *Guide to Virtuosity*.

1924   Arranges concerts in Carnegie Hall, New York, in memory of his mother and in honour of Delius; sails via Polynesia to Australia, where he visits relatives and presents recitals; adopts vegetarianism.

1925   Arranges New York concerts devoted to his own and other recent chamber music; collects further folk music in Jutland.

1926   Travels to Australia for a concert tour; meets in Hobart the linguist Robert Atkinson, who restores his interest in 'Nordic' (or 'Blue-eyed') English; comes to know the Swede Ella Ström, his future wife, while returning to America.

1927   Undertakes final folk-music expedition in Jutland; proposes to Ella Ström; starts to write the long essay 'The Love-Life of Helen and Paris', his first major writing in 'Nordic' English.

1928   Marries Ella Ström in the Hollywood Bowl, Los Angeles; composes *Australian Up-country Song*. Première of *To a Nordic Princess*.

1929   Visits Europe with his wife; organizes performances of 'Frankfurt Group' compositions at a festival in Harrogate; outlines his views on 'elastic scoring' and orchestration in preface to *Spoon River*.

1930   First associates with the National Music Camp, Interlochen, Michigan. Orchestral première of *Spoon River*.

1931   Attends Haslemere Festival in Surrey, organized by Arnold Dolmetsch, heightening his interest in early music; starts to adopt a more

(1931) promotional approach (such as reduction in his fee) to encourage performances of his own compositions. Première of *Tribute to Foster*.

1932 Takes first steps towards building a museum at The University of Melbourne; accepts a year-long appointment as associate professor and music departmental head at New York University, where he delivers a series of twenty-nine lectures entitled 'A General Study of the Manifold Nature of Music'.

1933 Travels from Copenhagen to Australia with his wife aboard the sailing-ship *L'Avenir*; writes 'The Aldridge-Grainger-Ström Saga' while on board.

1934 Mounts his most comprehensive concert and broadcast tour of Australia and New Zealand (to late 1935); arranges concerts and writes articles in memory of Delius; presents twelve lectures entitled 'Music: A Commonsense View of All Types' for the Australian Broadcasting Commission, including the première of his first 'Free Music' work.

1935 Supervises building of the first stage of the Grainger Museum in Melbourne.

1936 Travels to Britain, where he attends Haslemere Festival and undertakes first BBC broadcast, conducting his own works.

1937 Writes *Lincolnshire Posy*, for immediate premièring in Milwaukee; begins annual teaching at Interlochen summer camp (to 1944).

1938 Revisits Australia to supervise building (with Gardiner's financial assistance) of his Museum's second stage and to arrange its exhibits; clarifies his ideas about 'Free Music'.

1939 Visits Europe, returning just before outbreak of war; composes *The Immovable Do* and arrangement of *'The Duke of Marlborough' Fanfare*; begins glossary of his 'Nordic English'.

1940 Employs Henry Cowell as his 'musical secretary' for one year; copies his correspondence and important musical items, fearing invasion of America; moves to Springfield, Missouri (to 1945).

1941 Travels widely giving many concerts for the Red Cross and troops (to 1945).

1942 Attends a Grainger festival in Madison, Wisconsin. Première of *Kipling 'Jungle Book' Cycle*.

1943 Completes *The Power of Rome and the Christian Heart*; underwrites costs of production of *False Foundations of British History* by James Mackinnon Fowler; writes essay 'The Specialist and the All-Round Man'.

1944 Starts a series of recordings with Decca; starts the slow reduction in his concert commitments (to 1960). His favourite aunt, Clara Aldridge, dies in Adelaide.

1945   Comes to know the scientist Burnett Cross, with whom he will work on his 'Free Music' projects; collaborates with Stokowski in Hollywood Bowl concerts.

1946   Undertakes first post-war visit to Scandinavia. Première of *Youthful Suite*.

1947   Hears brilliant performance of his *Hill-Song* No. 1 with West Point Band; writes his 'Bird's-Eye View of the Together-Life of Rose Grainger and Percy Grainger'; presents his first piano recitals in Britain since 1914.

1948   Embarks upon his last formal concert tour in America, although continues to perform frequently, mainly for educational institutions.

1949   Commences his collection of 'Anecdotes' (to 1954); writes essay about his *Hill-Song* No. 1, outlining his early compositional innovations; starts to make new arrangements of several of his popular pieces for a Stokowski recording.

1950   Suffers increasing problems with his hearing. Balfour Gardiner dies.

1951   Constructs the 'Estey reeds tone-tool', with Cross, for playing 'Free Music'.

1952   Invents, with Cross, the 'Kangaroo-pouch' machine.

1953   Undergoes operation for prostate cancer in Aarhus, Denmark, recovering only slowly. Roger Quilter and Karen Kellermann die.

1954   Undergoes further operations for cancer; is awarded Saint Olav medal for services to Norwegian music.

1955   Travels to Australia, for the last time, to work at his Melbourne Museum (to 1956).

1956   Returns mid-year to New York from Australia.

1957   Presents one of his last major performances, in Aarhus; gives only television appearance, with the BBC in London; starts to suffer from occasional mental disorders affecting speech and coordination; undergoes a further cancer operation.

1958   Visits Britain where he meets with many folk-music acquaintances, including Benjamin Britten.

1959   Travels to Britain, for the last time; considers adding another storey to his Melbourne Museum; draws up his final will leaving the bulk of his artistic legacy to his Museum.

1960   Completes final 'Free Music' machine; gives last concert, in Hanover, New Hampshire; further deteriorates mentally and physically.

1961   Writes his last letters; dies of cancer in White Plains Hospital, 20 February.

Biographical Register of Letter-Recipients

ALDRIDGE, CLARA (1856–1944), Grainger's spinster aunt (his mother's elder sister), who lived in Adelaide with her mentally retarded younger brother Frank (1867–1931). After his mother's death, Grainger looked upon her as the strongest link with his mother's family. For many years he even planned to turn her home into an Aldridge–Grainger museum. (Letters **28**, **44**.)

ARMSTRONG, THOMAS (b. 1898), English organist, conductor, and music educator. From 1933 to 1955 he was organist of Christ Church, Oxford, and for the following thirteen years principal of the Royal Academy of Music in London. Between the wars he became a good friend of Balfour Gardiner, through whom he occasionally met Grainger. In 1958 he authored one of the most significant studies of the 'Frankfurt Group' of composers, based partly on his correspondence with Grainger. (Letters **71**, **72**.)

ATKINSON, ROBERT (1872–1950), Yorkshire-born accountant, music critic, and linguist, resident in Austria, then Tasmania, and from 1937 in Melbourne, where he ran a school of modern languages. In August 1926 Grainger had met Atkinson in his capacity as a music critic on the *Mercury* in Hobart, but they soon discovered a shared passion for 'Nordic English'. Their friendship spurred Grainger to renew his own linguistic experiments and also to subsidize Atkinson in his attempts to develop an English free from Mediterranean influences. Atkinson did not, however, complete the book *Our Mothertongue*, which Grainger had intended that he write on the subject. (Letter **26**.)

BARRETT, JAMES (1862–1945), Australian ophthalmologist and educator. After a distinguished medical career Barrett in 1931 became vice-chancellor of The University of Melbourne, then from 1935 to 1939 was its chancellor. Grainger dealt with him in both capacities concerning his Melbourne museum. Sir James Barrett was a keen amateur musician, an able pianist, and a powerful supporter of orchestral music in the city over a forty-year period. (Letter **35**.)

BAX, ARNOLD (1883–1953), English composer, Master of the King's Musick from 1942. He was a prolific composer of music in all major genres. Grainger appears to have known better his companion, the pianist Harriet Cohen. (Letter **57**.)

BRISTOW, ELSIE (ELSA), née FAIRFAX (1909–84), illegitimate daughter, often portrayed as niece, of Ella Grainger. In 1934 she married Robert Bristow, a British army officer stationed in India. She lived in India until its independence in 1947, then returned to Britain. Her letters to the Graingers from India provide a vivid picture of expatriate domestic life late in the Raj. Grainger became particularly close to his stepdaughter during the 1950s; his letters to her are one of the richest sources for his final decade. (Letters **61**, **62**, **74**, **75**.)

BRISTOW, ROBERT (*c*.1895–1982), British soldier, rising to the rank of brigadier. He served in the Dogra Regiment of the Indian Army from 1919 until Indian independence in 1947, when he returned to Britain. His experiences are described in his volume *Memories of the British Raj* (London: Johnson, 1974). In 1934 he married Elsie Fairfax, Ella Grainger's daughter. (Letters **61**, **75**, **76**.)

BRITTEN, BENJAMIN (1913–76), English composer, renowned for his operas and vocal works. With the tenor Peter Pears he made some of the leading recordings of Grainger's folksong settings. (Letter **68**.)

BULL, AGNES, née BULL (1885–1951), and BULL, EYVIND (1882–1949), mother and father of the American pianist Storm Bull. Norwegian-born Agnes was, during her earlier years, a singer and actress. American-born Eyvind, an engineer by training, was for some years an editor and critic for the *Music News* journal of Chicago. (Letter **38**.)

BULL, ELLEN, née CROSS (b. 1915), linguist, author, and editor, from 1941 wife of Storm Bull. (Letter **41**.)

BULL, STORM (b. 1913), American pianist, professor (now emeritus professor) at the University of Colorado at Boulder. During the late 1920s he was a student of Grainger at the Chicago Musical College; later, he studied with Lazare Lévy in Paris and Béla Bartók in Budapest. Because of Bull's Norwegian background Grainger was particularly interested in his development, although Bull's family rarely concurred with the racial advice Grainger gratuitously offered. (Letters **33**, **38**.)

CONDER, WALTER (1888–1974), Australian entrepreneur. After managing a hospital and a prison, he joined radio in the mid-1920s. In 1933 he was appointed general manager of the Australian Broadcasting Commission, in which capacity he came to know Grainger during the composer's Australian tour of 1934–5. Conder left the ABC in 1935 in the face of numerous allegations, including taking private commissions from ABC artists. In later life he managed variously a circus, some hotels, and a New Zealand lottery. (Letter **31**.)

COWELL, HENRY (1897–1965), American composer of over one thousand works, including twenty symphonies and many compositions showing innovative uses of percussion instruments and ethnic music. In his academic career he worked at Stanford, Columbia and at the New School for Social Research in New York. When he was jailed in 1936 following a morals conviction Grainger started to agitate for his release. In 1940 Cowell was released into Grainger's charge and spent a year working as his 'musical secretary' in White Plains. (Letter **36**.)

DELIUS, FREDERICK (1862–1934), English composer, resident in France from 1888. Grainger met him first in 1907, in London, and immediately appreciated his great talents, particularly as heard in his symphonic music. In subsequent decades Grainger promoted many performances of Delius's music in America and Australia, notably of the Piano Concerto. During the 1920s and 1930s as Delius's health declined Grainger supported him more personally, spending over five months with the Deliuses in Frankfurt in 1923, visiting him frequently at his home in Grez-sur-Loing, and assisting or planning for him to visit Scandinavia and America. (Letter **10**.)

DETT, R. NATHANIEL (1882–1943), Canadian-born composer, conductor, and pianist. From 1913 to 1931 he was music director at the Hampton Institute, Virginia, where he developed an internationally acclaimed choir, and in 1919 was a founder of the National Association of Negro Musicians. Grainger came to know his music soon after arriving in America and frequently performed his 'Juba Dance' from the piano suite *In the Bottoms*. (Letter **20**.)

DOLMETSCH, ARNOLD (1858–1940), French-born musician and instrument-maker. He is best known for his role, from the 1880s onwards, in encouraging interest in early music in England. In 1917 he settled in Haslemere, Surrey, where he founded a workshop, and from 1925 mounted annual festivals at which music was performed on instruments and in styles suitable to the period. Grainger first attended the festival in 1931 and became an immediate convert to Dolmetsch's cause. (Letter **29**.)

FORNANDER, SIGURD (1865–1945), masseur, son of the Swedish sculptor Anders Fornander. Grainger and his mother met Fornander in 1899, when they were all staying in the same pension in Frankfurt. He regularly massaged Rose Grainger during her times of ill-health in 1899–1901 and became attached to both mother and son. After his mother's death, Grainger gained much consolation from Fornander, whom he thereafter supported financially. (Letter **49**.)

FOSS, HUBERT J. (1899–1953), British publisher and composer. In 1921 he joined Oxford University Press, the London music department of which he headed between 1923 and 1941. Although zealously promoting the music of many of Grainger's British contemporaries, Foss was not seriously interested in Grainger's works. (Letter **27**.)

FOWLER, RICHARD (b. 1910), Australian museum curator. From the 1930s he worked for the Science and Technology Museum in Melbourne, becoming its director in the early 1960s. With his wife Dorothy (1911–75) he also curated the Grainger Museum part-time, from its opening in 1938 until 1962. (Letter **69**.)

GARDINER, H. BALFOUR (1877–1950), English composer of the 'Frankfurt Group', educated at Charterhouse, Oxford University, and the Hoch Conservatory in Frankfurt, where he met Grainger. He came from a wealthy family, which allowed him to indulge his own and his friends' musical interests, notably through his series of concerts at the Queen's Hall, London, in 1912–13. As a composer he was always reticent and highly self-critical; by the mid-1920s he had given up composition completely to devote himself to rural pursuits. It was to Gardiner that Grainger turned first at the time of his mother's death. (Letters **15, 40**.)

GRAINGER, ELLA VIOLA, née STRÖM (1889–1979), Swedish-born artist and poet, Grainger's wife from 1928. In 1907 she moved from Sweden to London, where during the war years she studied fine art at The Slade School. She later also took classes in wood carving and ceramics, exhibiting her work of the latter in London during November 1925. The following year Ström followed her lover Iyemasa Tokugawa from London to Sydney, where he had been appointed Japanese Consul-General. She met Grainger during November 1926 aboard a ship traversing the Pacific Ocean, and married him two years later. The Graingers lived permanently at White Plains, New York, although they frequently visited Britain and Scandinavia, and travelled several times to Australia. During the Second World War they resided temporarily in Springfield, Missouri. Ella Grainger's poetic interests are represented in two volumes, *The Pavement Artist and Other Poems* of

1939 and *A Wayward Girl* of 1941. She frequently played the bells in Percy Grainger's concerts and composed several tunes, such as 'Love at first sight' (1944), which her husband then arranged. In 1972 Ella Grainger married the Grainger archivist Stewart Manville, who still resides in White Plains. (Letters **22, 23, 24, 42, 43, 46, 60, 65, 73**.)

GRAINGER, ROSA (ROSE), née ALDRIDGE (1861–1922), Grainger's mother and constant companion for his first forty years. She was born in Adelaide but moved to Melbourne soon after marrying John Grainger in 1880. While in Germany during the late 1890s she started to suffer from serious physical and mental problems—the effects of syphilis—and became increasingly dependent upon her son materially and emotionally. In London, and then from 1914 in New York, she managed many aspects of Grainger's career. By the early 1920s she was seriously debilitated and in April 1922 committed suicide by leaping from a New York skyscraper. The relationship between mother and son was intense, even stifling, and suspected by many of being incestuous. In 1954 Grainger wrote: 'I was afraid of her anger, & helpless to oppose her will—except secretly.' (Letters **3, 4, 7, 8, 9, 11, 12, 13, 14**.)

HANDS, E. C. (1885–1940), general manager of the New Zealand Broadcasting Board from 1932 to 1936. He dealt with arrangements for Grainger's tour of New Zealand in October–December 1935. (Letter **32**.)

HARRISON, MARGOT, a London piano student of Grainger, daughter of the painter L. A. (Peter) Harrison. During the summer of 1913 she became engaged to Grainger, an arrangement which was amicably terminated after barely a month. Her father cited the closeness of Grainger to his mother as the reason for the break. Margot Harrison married three times, living variously in Massachusetts, South Africa, Colorado, and California, but remained in correspondence with Grainger until his death. (Letter **2**.)

HEINZE, BERNARD (1894–1982), Australian conductor and music academic. Sir Bernard Heinze was professor of music at The University of Melbourne from 1925 to 1957 and concurrently conductor of the city's symphony orchestra. He then assumed the directorship of the State Conservatorium of Music in Sydney, where he remained until 1966. Heinze came to know Grainger well during the composer's visits to Melbourne in the 1930s to establish his museum, and, through his conducting, championed Australian performances of many of Grainger's works. (Letter **53**.)

HOLTEN, KAREN. See Kellermann, Karen.

IRELAND, JOHN (1879–1962), English composer and pianist, educated and later teaching at the Royal College of Music in London. His mature output was strongly rooted in the Romantic traditions of English lyricism. Grainger knew him only slightly, and appears to have been more interested in the colour of his eyes than in his music. (Letter **56**.)

JAMES, F. CYRIL (1903–73), British-born economist and educator. In 1939 he was appointed principal and vice-chancellor of McGill University in Montreal, in which capacity he dealt with Grainger. (Letter **47**.)

KELLERMANN, KAREN, née HOLTEN (1879–1953), girlfriend and occasional piano student of Grainger. She met him in Copenhagen during October 1904 at the home of his friend Herman Sandby; they soon established an intimate relationship, which lasted until 1912. In 1916 she married, but remained in close contact with Grainger through correspondence (mainly conducted in Danish) and their occasional meetings in Denmark. (Letter **21**.)

KRISTENSEN, EVALD TANG (1843–1929), Danish ethnologist and teacher, collector of Jutish folksongs and tales from the 1860s until his death. Early in his London years Grainger came to admire the many published collections of Tang Kristensen, whom he considered 'the greatest of folksong collectors'. Their plans for joint collecting expeditions using the phonograph were thwarted by the War, but eventually realized in Grainger's four tours of Jutland during the 1920s. (Letter **1**.)

LEGGE, ROBIN (1862–1933), London music critic working on *The Times* from 1891 and the *Daily Telegraph* from 1906 to 1931. For most of Grainger's London years Legge was keenly supportive, admiring particularly his pianism, but he withdrew that support midway through the First World War when he concluded that Grainger was shirking his patriotic duty by staying in America. During 1916 and 1917 he criticized Grainger publicly in his *Daily Telegraph* column, mocking especially his *Marching Song of Democracy*. (Letter **6**.)

LOWE, MAURICE (b. 1902), British-born Canadian composer, pianist, and teacher living in British Columbia. Apart from studies with the Winnipeg pianist Leonard Heaton in 1919–20 he was largely self-taught as both performer and composer. Between the wars he appeared as composer-pianist in several recitals in Vancouver and

Seattle; his compositions, mostly written for voices or pianos, remain unpublished. (Letter **25**.)

MADDY, JOSEPH E. (1891–1966), American music educator, professor of radio music instruction at the University of Michigan. In 1928 he founded the National Music Camp at Interlochen, Michigan, where Grainger regularly taught during the summers of 1937–44. (Letter **45**.)

MASON, DANIEL GREGORY (1873–1953), American composer and academic. From 1905 to 1942 he taught at Columbia University, where he was MacDowell Professor for his final thirteen years. Mason's compositional style was conservative, looking to Austro-German and, to a lesser extent, French precedents. As a scholar he was prolific, writing at least eighteen books, including a volume of reminiscences, *Music in my Time* (1938), in which he expressed his gratitude to Grainger for so keenly advocating his music at a time when few others cared for it. (Letter **51**.)

MASTERS, EDGAR LEE (1869–1950), American writer. His *Spoon River Anthology* greatly influenced Grainger, who established a personal contact with Masters soon after its appearance in 1915. In 1919–22 Grainger arranged a tune called 'Spoon River', passed on to him by Masters, as the first of his *American Folk-Music Settings*; in 1926 Masters dedicated his *Lee, A Dramatic Poem* to Grainger. (Letter **54**.)

MORGENSTIERNE, WILHELM MUNTHE DE (1887–1963), Norwegian representative in the United States, holding various positions between 1910 and 1958. From 1942 he served as Norwegian ambassador in Washington, DC and subsequently as dean of the diplomatic corps. (Letter **67**.)

NYGAARD, KAARE K. (1903–89), Norwegian-born American doctor and sculptor. He became Grainger's doctor in White Plains in 1953, although he had known him as a performer since a 1913 recital in Nygaard's hometown of Lillehammer. For the remaining eight years of Grainger's life Nygaard was his friend, confidant, and sponsor, as well as medical adviser. (Letter **66**.)

PARKER, D. C. (1885–1970), Scottish music critic writing for Glasgow and Edinburgh newspapers. His musical tastes were catholic, resulting in a voluminous correspondence with leading musicians of his day, a biography on Bizet in 1926, several dozen journal articles, and a substantial booklet on Grainger, published by G. Schirmer in 1918. Because of Parker's long-term dedication to promoting Grainger's music their correspondence is especially revealing of the composer's opinions and musical plans. (Letters **5**, **30**.)

QUILTER, ROGER (1877–1953), English composer of the 'Frankfurt Group', son of the brewer, politician, and arts patron Sir Cuthbert Quilter. In Frankfurt Quilter took composition lessons from Iwan Knorr, Grainger's teacher, but was more in sympathy with Knorr's aims than was Grainger. Quilter is best known for his vocal music, in particular settings of Shakespeare, Tennyson and Herrick. An opera, *Julia*, was performed in London in 1936. Perhaps because of his homosexuality, Quilter was disinclined to match the baring of souls which Grainger sought of him. (Letters **17**, **37**.)

RESTA, FRANCIS E. (1894–1968), Italian-born American clarinettist, pianist, and bandmaster. From 1934 to 1957 he led the Military Academy band at West Point. He first met Grainger in 1917 at Fort Hamilton, when both were recruits to army bands, and gave occasional duo piano concerts with him in subsequent years. (Letter **48**.)

SANDBY, ALFHILD, née MYHR (1876–1961), Norwegian-born musician and writer, partly educated in the United States. Around 1909 she married Grainger's Danish friend Herman Sandby. Alfhild Sandby's relationship with Grainger was frequently tempestuous, as she refused to accept many of his interpretations of his past life, in particular his portrayal of his relationship with his mother. (Letter **50**.)

SANDBY, HERMAN (1881–1965), Danish composer and cellist. He was a student friend of Grainger in Frankfurt, where he kindled Grainger's fascination with all things Danish. During the following three decades they frequently performed together in Scandinavia, in Britain, and in America, where Sandby lived between 1912 and the mid-1920s. He then returned to Europe, where he received a state stipend to compose from the Danish government. Among his compositions are three symphonies, a cello concerto and a considerable body of chamber music. In later years Grainger considered Sandby his 'best friend', but found their relationship ever marred by the 'psychologizing' of Sandby's wife Alfhild. (Letters **34**, **64**.)

SCOTT, CYRIL (1879–1970), English pianist and composer of the 'Frankfurt Group', who studied in that city periodically during the 1890s. He became best known in the years before the First World War for his short piano pieces, of which his *Lotus Land* (1905) is perhaps the most famous, but did also write significant works in most other genres.

Although firm friends for nearly seven decades, Scott and Grainger often engaged in intense, at times accusatory, debate in their correspondence. Scott's interest in the occult and his 'English' lack of self-promotion were ready irritants to the more down-to-earth Grainger. (Letters **16**, **39**, **63**, **70**.)

SHARP, CECIL (1859–1924), English collector of folk music and dances. At the turn of the century he realized the huge potential of English folksong and quickly became the leading pioneer in the field, eventually collecting nearly five thousand tunes. Grainger came to know him in about 1905 through his own activity in collecting songs and membership of the Folk-Song Society. A number of Grainger's most popular folk-music settings, including *Shepherd's Hey* and *Country Gardens*, used tunes collected by Sharp. (Letter **18**.)

STOKOWSKI, LEOPOLD (1882–1977), British-born conductor, resident in the United States from 1909. From 1912 to 1938 he conducted the Philadelphia Orchestra. During the 1940s and 1950s he collaborated with Grainger in concerts of the Hollywood Bowl Symphony Orchestra and New York Symphony Orchestra, as well as on recordings. (Letter **58**.)

STRÖM, ELLA VIOLA. See Grainger, Ella Viola.

VAUGHAN WILLIAMS, RALPH (1872–1958), English composer, probably best known for his orchestral music, which includes nine symphonies, and his vocal works. His interest in the early years of the century in collecting and arranging folk music coincided with that of Grainger, whom he saw occasionally from that time until the 1950s. (Letter **55**.)

Introduction

Dum loquimur, fugerit invida
aetas: carpe diem, quam minimum credula postero.

Horace, *Odes*, I, xi. 7–8

Although despising the very language in which these lines were written, the pianist-composer Percy Grainger would certainly have sympathized with their sentiment—'Even while we talk Time, hateful, runs a mile. | Don't trust tomorrow's bough for fruit. Pluck this, here, now.'[1] Grainger is one of the twentieth century's outstanding *carpe diem* figures. His frenzied life, kick-started by a domineering mother and maintained by her memory, shows the 'pluck this, here, now' mentality carried to an extreme of long-term career sacrifice and possibly even fragmentation of personality. For sixty years Grainger lived the 'slave-life' of professional pianism, performing in over three thousand concerts, fearing to trust the allures of tomorrow for fear that today's failure might make him yesterday's man. Although he would often grumble about how 'the treadmill of earning one's living' was 'so unremitting',[2] he clung tenaciously to concert life and only stopped performing in public when senility finally forced him out, at the age of 77 after many 'retirements'. His enthusiasms, however, ranged far beyond the bounds of music, and, there too, were pursued with remarkable gusto. He aimed to be the 'all-round man', able to accomplish the widest range of human activities with reasonable competence.[3] To his 'Frankfurt Group' friend Cyril Scott he wrote in later life: 'I am in the Walt Whitman business: trying to relish & tally the myriad attractiveness of a million different arts & expressions.'[4] In his final two decades, in particular, Grainger enthusiastically preached this creed of anti-specialization. A return to the all-roundedness practised in traditional Scandinavian or outback colonial communities was, he believed, the only antidote to modern-day 'experts' and provided the basis for a return of dignity and happiness to the individual man.[5]

[1] Trans. of James Michie, in *The Odes of Horace* (Harmondsworth: Penguin, 1967), 39.
[2] Letter to Edgar Lee Masters, 28 Mar. 1948 (letter **54** in this vol.). All letters referred to are held in the Grainger Museum, University of Melbourne.
[3] See letter to Cyril Scott, 10–11 Dec. 1951 (letter **63**).   [4] 19 Nov. 1947.
[5] See Grainger's essay 'The Specialist and the All-Round Man', in *A Birthday Offering to C[arl] E[ngel]*, ed. Gustave Reese (New York: G. Schirmer, 1943), 115–19.

The All-Round Man is the sequel to Kay Dreyfus's edition of Grainger's letters from his 'London' years entitled *The Farthest North of Humanness*.[1] In this second volume we present the texts of seventy-six letters written during Grainger's 'American' years, 1914–61, although because of the highly retrospective turn of his mind in later years these letters effectively survey his entire life. Our selection represents a minute fraction of the extant correspondence—the nine letters to his wife Ella found here, for instance, were chosen from 2,338 such letters—but, none the less, attempts to touch upon both the range and the depth of Grainger's activities, exposing the heights of his musical professionalism as well as his unapologetic (and sometimes ludicrous) amateurism in many other endeavours.

As is outlined in the Chronology, Percy Grainger's life falls neatly into four geographically oriented periods: his childhood in Australia, 1882–95; his youth as a music student in Germany, 1895–1901; his early professional years in Britain, 1901–14; his years of full maturity in the United States, 1914–61. These American years also fall naturally into their phases. First were the years of his zenith on the New York concert scene and as composer of his greatest 'hit', *Country Gardens*. This phase ended abruptly with his mother's suicidal leap from a New York skyscraper while her son was on tour in 1922. The next stage, to the outbreak of the Second World War, saw his pianistic and compositional careers falter and then, once he had married in the late 1920s, stabilize, but at a lower level of status. He started to broaden his non-musical interests and to become more retrospective during this second phase, leading to the establishment of his Museum in Melbourne during the 1930s. The 1940s were a curious 'Indian summer' decade for Grainger. He capitalized on the opportunities presented by the war to revitalize his concert career and then, increasingly, to mount performances of his own compositions; his letters bubble with a sense of excitement and conviction not seen since his mother's death. Finally, the 1950s present a man frustrated at the havoc which age and illness were wreaking upon his multitude of plans. This ultimate Grainger looks naggingly back to the past, often writing, it seems, more for the benefit of his Museum's users of later times than for his immediate correspondents. But he also looks to the future with his 'Free Music' of gliding tones and, well before his time, warns of the dangers of population growth, wood-pulping, pollution, and meat-eating. 'Nature will

---

[1] (Melbourne: Macmillan, 1985).

have to teach man a cruel lesson', he prophesied in 1950, on the verge of his old age.[1]

Grainger's many thousands of letters from these four-and-a-half decades are of three types: the intimate letters to family and old friends, letters to more casual acquaintances, business letters. Despite his residence from 1921 onwards in White Plains, New York, none of his correspondents in the first, intimate category was an American. His most trusted correspondents were his British student companions from Frankfurt days (Balfour Gardiner, Roger Quilter, Cyril Scott), and the Dane Herman Sandby, as well as his closest relations: his Australian mother Rose, his Swedish wife Ella, and his British stepdaughter Elsie Bristow. Grainger travelled so incessantly—not just across North America, but quite regularly to Europe and half-a-dozen times to Australia—that, leaving aside the issue of inclination, he seems simply not to have had the time to establish any truly deep bonding with his new countrymen.[2] Even in the second category, of less intimate correspondents, Americans are not very strongly represented, and many of these were fellow composers, such as Daniel Gregory Mason and Nathaniel Dett, whose music interested Grainger more than their personalities. The myriad business letters, on the other hand, dealing with such routine, day-to-day matters as concert programming, publications, royalties, and travel itineraries, were predominantly addressed to Americans. Because of their less sustained interest to posterity they are only occasionally found in this selection.

To the reader of the 1990s Grainger's more intimate letters are certainly unusual; their superficial reading can encourage an interpretation of eccentricity, if not mental instability. They are *long*, sometimes approaching the length of book chapters, and are full of an immediacy and informality of utterance which can alarm today's more censored minds. These letters are best understood as rambles, excursions embarked upon for the fun of going, just like Grainger's musical 'Rambles'; they are similar to today's telephone calls to close friends, which rarely stand up to logical scrutiny when the tabloids flaunt their written form. Grainger was an immensely fluent and practised letter-writer, regularly putting aside time early in the morning when he would squat on the floor with a letter-block upon his knee. Often regardless of spelling and grammar ('a bad wont stepping in between a

---

[1] To his wife, 5 Mar. 1950.

[2] Grainger himself noted, in writing to Balfour Gardiner on 27 Sept. 1941 (letter **40**): 'I who have lived 27 years in USA without forming a single close friendship, without ever opening my lips or ears in tone-talk.'

man'),[1] he would play joyfully with his topics, tossing them this way and that. Where others might think through ideas beforehand, Grainger would simply start writing. This spontaneous approach accorded with his refreshing, open-air view of life. As he wrote to his wife in 1941: 'Nakedness is life's richest gift to men—nakedness of flesh, nakedness of feelings, thots, records.'[2] Important, also, was Grainger's distinction between opinions and loyalties, on the one hand, and whims, fondnesses and tastes, on the other. With all honesty did he write to Cyril Scott on 10–11 December 1951:

> my artistic life is a matter of constantly changing attractions & whims—altho I never change my OPINIONS & LOYALTIES. I dont need to. All my opinions (for instance politically) always turn out to be right; so I have no need to change them. With my FONDNESS it is quite different. I believe in spreading my fondness over as many fields as possible, since life is so short . . .[3]

Despite the frequent repetition of ideas and a long-windedness which would have made even Wagner blush, we present here only entire letters, resisting the temptation to clothe Grainger's rambling nakedness, to tidy up his 'constantly shifting & veering tastes' for those who prefer packaged intellectual tours, or to disguise his perversity.

Stylistically, too, Grainger's letters are highly distinctive. He was a verbal artist, writing in a peculiarly crunchy English (occasionally in other languages, too, notably Danish, but there no less crunchily), resulting from his dislike of words of Graeco-Latin origin. This tendency became a veritable obsession from the mid-1920s as he developed his own 'Nordic', or 'Blue-eyed', English. Universe became 'all-world', intimacy 'close-mood', compared 'side-meted', piano-practising 'keyboard-swinking'; fortunately, Grainger usually gave the more customary 'dark-eyed' alternatives in double parentheses within his correspondence. There was more than just play in these long-lasting linguistic experiments. Grainger hated the growing pollution of English, which he dated back to 1066 with its influx of Continentals, and swore that 'I would do everything to make English uncouth, ungetatable, clumsy, *queer*, & hard for outlanders to master. I would try & keep its howth as a very queer, cut-off, islandy speech.'[4] Whether or not using his made-up 'Nordic' English, Grainger was particularly to the fore as verbal artist in his Round letters, those more polished circulars which he intermittently distributed to friends and relatives. In

---

[1] Letter to his wife, 12 Nov. 1944 (letter **46**).   [2] Letter, 26 Jan. 1941.
[3] Letter **63**.
[4] Letter to fellow 'Nordic' English enthusiast Robert Atkinson, 1 Apr. 1939. 'Howth' = 'quality'.

this volume, three Round letters are presented, describing a visit to Tahiti (letter **19**); his great joy at finally hearing one of his works performed over four decades after its composition (letter **52**); and his grumbles about his health, but happiness at hearing so many of his own works played (letter **59**). Grainger's considerable talents as visual artist, well attested by the illustrations in this volume, also show through in his letters' many unexpected images. Who else would write to his newly wedded wife, 'You are my sluice, my gutter, my dredger, my vacuum cleaner'?[1]

Notable, sometimes even hard to stomach, are many of the views which Grainger presented in his letters. His feelings of the moment led him head first into knotty clusters of controversial social or political issues. Often these feelings underpinned his highly idiosyncratic musical stances, as well. Of this abundance of viewpoints those most commonly misunderstood, or most sensationally presented by latter-day commentators, concerned race, nationality, and sex. We now attempt to present a summary context for these views.

Was this man, on balance, more a cosmopolitan or more a bigot? The reader of Grainger's letters must soon confront this question. From Grainger we gain the most wonderful and progressive statements of musical universalism:

> The worth-whileness of all races & all cultures is proved by all the world's music, & to delay needlessly a drenching of ourselves in all this glorious 'exotic' music is simply (in my opinion) to criminally postpone the dawn of inter-racial worldwide understanding & brotherhood.[2]

The title of his Australian Broadcasting Commission series of radio talks in 1934–5, 'A Commonsense View of All Music', wonderfully reflects the catholicity of his musical tastes in mid-career.[3] He had travelled to all continents bar South America and had found aspects of culture about which to enthuse in so many different settings. Yet his intolerance of things non-Nordic and belief in the superiority of musical Nordicism cannot be disguised.[4] He disliked the sonata, symphony, and orchestral music in general, he stated, because of their 'middle-class nature'[5] and South-influenced Germanness. And beyond issues of music he was much less racially tolerant. Despite his fostering of a

---

[1] 2 Oct. 1929. [2] Letter to Bernard Heinze, 3 Dec. 1947 (letter **53**).
[3] See John Blacking, *'A Commonsense View of All Music': Reflections on Percy Grainger's Contribution to Ethnomusicology and Music Education* (Cambridge: Cambridge University Press, 1987).
[4] See, e.g., his 'The Superiority of Nordic Music', *Quest*, 8/2 (Nov. 1937), 7–8.
[5] See letter to Herman Sandby, 25 Oct. 1952 (letter **64**).

superficial interest in 'primitive races' (in 1919 he referred to himself as a 'Scandinavian–British–American–Negro–Polynesian'),[1] Grainger was, at root, a racial bigot of no small order, and not one to be excused simply as an unwitting victim of the widespread supremacist racial views of his day. He lauded the restrained individualism of the Nordics, which he considered a *sine qua non* for tolerance in any society, and abhorred the intolerance, mass action, and militaristic tendencies of 'Southerners'. He disliked racial intermarriage, even looking upon himself as flawed through the contamination of his maternal Nordic heritage by the blood of his 'dark-eyed' father. For many of non-European origin he had very little sympathy, in the fateful year of 1939 castigating his friend Roger Quilter for showing pity to the 'round-skulled' Jews caught in the Nazis' web:

And I have to imagine you welcoming ugly, fat, self-indulgent, family-loving, art-loving, *food*-loving, reasonable, cultured, *normal* Jews to the shores of Britain. Or welcoming equally normal, family-loving, *natural*, civilised, *plausible* Germans or Greeks. . . . It is hard when the princes of the world are set to street clean the muck of slaves.[2]

This, too, is the Grainger who could congratulate himself on foreseeing Hitler's arguments for racial cleansing before the dictator himself, and in 1938, within weeks of the Munich Agreement, still be claiming Hitler as a gifted man of 'PURE GOODNESS'.[3]

By the 1930s race was the essential and dominating factor in Grainger's interpretation of his world, now well surpassing gender: 'George Moore says that there are few women a man would wish to meet in Paradise. I know nought of such sex differentiation. With me *it is the race*, not the sex, that matters. . . . If *the race* is right, & *the land* is right, I am in heaven.'[4] Even the knowledge of atrocities committed during the Second World War would only mute his more extreme racial outbursts.

The sub-theme of nationality also runs through hundreds of Grainger's letters of the American period. Particularly popular are depictions of the strengths and weaknesses of the four countries of Grainger's own residence. He looked upon himself as a better, but still flawed, example of a bad stock, the Australians, a 'careless, slovenly, mind-blind, lazy, ignorant, self-indulgent, unhealthy' people, who, notwithstanding, retained the happiness and kindliness characteristic of

[1] Letter to his mother, 8 June 1919.   [2] 25 Feb. 1939 (letter **37**).
[3] Letter to Lewis Slavit, 4 Sept. 1938 (see also letter **37**).
[4] Letter to Herman Sandby, 9 Dec. 1937 (letter **34**).

Pacific-rim peoples.[1] Despite their frequent Nordic ancestry the Australians were unable to realize anything really well, but waded through life relying on an amateurish all-roundedness forced upon them by their vast colonial environment and their natural suspicion of hierarchies of any kind. In turning down an honorary doctorate offered by McGill University in 1945, Grainger gave his democratic Australianness as the reason why he refused any distinctions.[2] So, too, he frequently claimed, was his dislike of soloism in music a product of his democratic Australian background. What the world, and Australia, needed in music was fewer concertos and more 'get-together-ness', more large chamber music, more practical musicality rather than specialized cultivation of technique.[3] It was for these solid, democratic reasons that he devised the many 'elastic scorings' of his own and others' works, thereby allowing as many or as few players as desired—and not just the elect—to take part in his music. Although Grainger frequently looked with hope to Australia's musical future,[4] he whinged for nearly forty years about how his musical 'innovations' (such as irregular barring, imaginative large chamber combinations, use of wordless syllables, promotion of British folk music internationally)[5] had never been credited to Australia. He was, he maintained, the only Australian composer to have 'somewhat captured the world's ear',[6] yet, nearing death, was still lamenting that 'no one will give Australia credit for anything in music'.[7]

Grainger found Germany an uncomfortable nation because of its racial bifurcation, with Nordics predominating in the North and Alpine or Mediterranean races in the South. Austria, and most Austrian music, he casually dismissed as frivolous, alleging an excessive Italian influence. Yet he recognized that that musical professionalism which earned him his daily bread was built on the solidly Germanic foundations laid during his years at the Hoch Conservatory in Frankfurt. It was, indeed, this mania and respect for the well-trained specialist which engendered the Germans' periodic undoing. They lacked the common sense of the 'all-rounded' peoples to their North; they worshipped 'professional skill subordinated to the behests of a

[1] Letter to Lewis Slavit, 4 Sept. 1938.
[2] Letter to F. Cyril James, 24 Apr. 1945 (letter **47**). Note, however, his acceptance of the Saint Olav medal of Norway in 1954 (letter **67**).
[3] Letter to Bernard Heinze, 3 Dec. 1947 (letter **53**).
[4] See letter to Daniel Gregory Mason, 24 Jan. 1947 (letter **51**).
[5] Letter to William A. Laver, 25 Apr. 1934.   [6] Letter to D. C. Parker, 23 Sept. 1951.
[7] Letter to Thomas Armstrong, 21 Oct. 1958 (letter **72**).

ruling intellectual class (whether it be professional or military, or the domination of modern "masters" or of past masters such as Beethoven)'.[1] In short, the Germans could be too easily led.

Towards the British Grainger was, like so many Australians, ambivalent. These people were kin, but their society was split by an apparently unchangeable class system and was racially a hotchpotch. Grainger believed this land was 'the "unmelting pot" with a vengeance'. He elaborated:

England, with its wild strain of poachers, its outstanding perverts, its oldest Germanic cultures (Beowulf), its sickly Christianity, yet its wild determination to victory, is a queer medley of inharmonious & unreconciled gifts.[2]

In addition to its class and racial problems, relations between the sexes were thoroughly unhealthy because of the 'game' erected upon life by British women, a game of prejudices, ambitions, and prides determined according to fixed rules of 'mob-morality', in which nature played no part.[3] Through constant contact with his upper middle-class British contemporaries in Frankfurt and later in London, however, so much of Grainger's musical persona had become British. It was, after all, through settings of English folk music that he had scored his greatest public triumphs. Although he could never accept the appalling lack of gumption in so many of his closest British friends, he did come to recognize their common stylistic roots. To Balfour Gardiner he wrote in 1941 that 'Yr & my tone-arts, whatever their flaws, are as English as cricket, football, horseracing,'[4] and he was anxious in later years to forge closer associations with such other 'blue-eyed' composers as William Walton, Vaughan Williams, John Ireland, and Arnold Bax.[5]

America, the real 'melting pot', initially impressed Grainger. His first experiences there were very happy.[6] He relished the tolerance of this multi-cultural society, its substantial acceptance of its Black populations and the spiritual attitude of its people. When writing in 1917 to the British critic Robin Legge he really does seem to have believed that the Americans were the 'most tolerant, most expansive, most gentle, most generous, most trustful, most peace-loving, most unprovocative people I have yet come in contact with'.[7] They were a wonderful embodiment of all that was best in 'Anglo-Saxonism'; Grainger and his mother do appear willingly to have taken American citizenship soon

---

[1] Letter to his mother, 12 Mar. 1919 (letter **8**).   [2] Letter to his wife, 27 Jan. 1951.
[3] Letter to his mother, 12 Mar. 1919 (letter **8**).   [4] 27 Sept. 1941 (letter **40**).
[5] See letters **55–7**.   [6] See letter to Evald Tang Kristensen, 27 June 1915 (letter **1**).
[7] Letter to Robin Legge, 6 May 1917 (letter **6**).

afterwards. This rosy view darkened as he kept criss-crossing the country over the following decades. He came to appreciate the crassness of American materialism, and, as his own earnings declined, the less attractive face of capitalism. As already mentioned, he found himself unable to gain close American friends, despite the superficial openness of the population. The American woman he came particularly to dislike, stereotyping her as a formidable matriarch,

> with the men poor prunes & the women school-marming & nurse-maiding them around. I say nothing against such tactics—if folk like it. But I DONT like it & will have nothing to do with it. I myself dont want to boss women round &, also, dont want to be bossed round myself by women. It is the American woman's tactics to salvation-army the men—to make them admit their weaknesses & then REFORM them.[1]

Among those American men least able to help themselves were the composers whom Grainger used his earnings to support or whose music he tried to promote: Arthur Fickénscher, Daniel Gregory Mason, Henry Cowell, Nathaniel Dett, John Alden Carpenter. So often he came to feel that his support was little appreciated[2] and would gradually let slip his efforts to promote their music.

Grainger's greatest notoriety, however, lies in the domain of unconventional sexual activity. He was one of the century's more practised flagellants, equally at home in giving or receiving the lash. In some notes about 'whip-lust', which he wrote on 24 December 1948 while on a visit to Sweden, he traced the origin of the practice to his mother's whippings of him as a boy, often because of his bed-wetting.[3] With the onset of puberty, while in Frankfurt, he started to associate the whippings with sexual pleasures, consequent upon acts of cruelty to women. What is remarkable in Grainger's case is that he then could directly associate these practices with broader personality traits of cruelty, exhibitionism and 'life-wildness', from which he saw his own music emerging. His notes on 'whip-lust' of 1948 continued:

> [One of the] dream-sights of my mid & late teens was of sticking 2 fishhooks, slung on pulleys, one into each of a woman's breasts, & then pulley-raise the fishhooks till the weight of the woman's body caused the fishhooks to rip thru the breast-flesh. Rather, were not such stirs just an outcome of the vast wildness of my nature—the same wildness that made me walk from one 3rd storey window to another along a 2-inch strip of moulding on the house's

---

[1] Letter to Alfhild Sandby, 25 May 1946 (letter **50**). [2] See letter **20**, e.g.
[3] See also the letter to his wife, 12 Nov. 1944 (letter **46**).

outer wall, to scare old women below; the same wildness that led me to burn myself on hot stoves; the same wildness that fills my Hillsongs & English Dance?

Grainger's fancy for flagellation was further refined in about 1910, when he discovered a shop in Amsterdam specializing in 'whip-lustful books' and came to realize the extent of the practice in society.[1] Perhaps it is from that time that he gained the fascination for visual documentation of his highly athletic acts, which led him to take a large number of explicit photographs (deposited after his death in the Grainger Museum). His desire, too, for 'sadic' stories is well evidenced in dozens of his letters, one of which, that written to his wife-to-be on 23 April 1928, is included in this selection.[2] There Grainger was very explicit, laying out for his intended the things that gave him the most acute sexual pleasure and even prioritizing the parts of the body according to his enjoyment in visualizing them being beaten. Surprisingly, Grainger did not consider his sexual urges at any time compulsive. Sex was, he claimed, just a liberating, joyful experience, but one, none the less, of great importance to him. Faced in his late sixties with prostate trouble he confessed:

All the same, the one [thing] I least willingly would do without is sex. I would much rather give up tone-art [music]. But I have joy-quaffed sex for about 55 years now & I look upon that as the sweetest gift fate could bestow. One would be a glutton if one did not say that it is enough—at a pinch.[3]

The texts of the letters have been prepared from holdings of the Grainger Museum at The University of Melbourne, nearly all either from original letters or from copies made by Grainger himself, his stepdaughter Elsie Bristow or occasional other transcribers. Where letters exist in more than one form, which is frequently the case, the autographed original has been preferred. The letters for which only copies exist can usually be identified in this volume by the lack of a final signature and, occasionally, lack of opening salutations. All letters are presented in their entirety, including musical examples. Other correspondence mentioned in the notes or editorial introductions is held in the Grainger Museum, unless otherwise stated.

Apart from the complete letters presented in translation from the Danish, Grainger's original texts have been transcribed, including passages in foreign languages. For those passages, translations and lan-

---

[1] See letter to Cyril Scott, 20–1 July 1949.   [2] Letter **24**.
[3] Letter to Cyril Scott, 20–1 July 1949.

guage identification are provided in the notes. In general Grainger's idiosyncrasies of spelling, punctuation, and grammar have been preserved, although obvious typing errors or simple slips of the pen have been corrected without comment. Computer checking of Grainger's spelling in some six hundred letters has helped to distinguish these unintentional slips from deliberate spelling idiosyncrasies or just bad spelling. Grainger's English spelling was certainly awkwardly caught between English, Australian, and American usages, with additional complications arising from his experiments with 'Nordic' English and his occasional practice of spelling phonetically. Words fairly regularly spelled unusually are exagerate, corage, lovliness, tho, altho, thoro. Other common words, such as argu(e)ment, accom[m]odate, and words with -(al)ly suffixes can exist in two or more forms. Words frequently abbreviated include yr (your), shld (should), cld (could), and & (and). The possessive and contractive apostrophes, and certain other subtleties of punctuation, were often beyond Grainger's care, but we have not remarked on these unless a significant ambiguity of meaning arises. Likewise, Grainger's failure to provide all the ingredients of an English sentence has gone unnoted unless the meaning is in doubt. The precise representation of Grainger's markings of emphasis posed considerable problems. He loved to underline words anything up to five times, and would break into sustained writing in various sizes of capital letters to emphasize a point (or, simply, if aboard an unsteady train). In this edition Grainger's capitals have been maintained but in a uniform size; his various grades of underlining have all been levelled to italics. His use of double parentheses (( )), indicating the more customary English synonym of a 'Nordic' word or phrase, has been reproduced, and extended occasionally to similar examples where Grainger had used single parentheses or square brackets. Diagrams have sometimes only been verbally described, as, unfortunately, have the quaint train drawings found at the start of several letters.

For discussion of various other aspects of Grainger's letters and a note on his use of Danish the reader is referred to the 'Editor's Note' and 'Translator's Note' on pages xviii–xxiii of *The Farthest North of Humanness.*

1914–1922

'My Adorable, Adoredest Mum'

[On 4 August 1914 Britain declared war on Germany. Within barely a fortnight Grainger and his mother had moved out of their London home, stored many of their possessions, and postponed the coming months' engagements. Early in September they left 'for a short trip to America, to give mother a change', as Grainger wrote to his Uncle Frank. The Graingers, however, would never return to reside in Britain. Within months of his arrival in the United States Grainger had established himself in the first tier of New York's concert life, advancing considerably on his London status.]

1 [In Danish]   *To Evald Tang Kristensen*

C/O Concert Direction Antonia Sawyer | June 27, 1915

Dear Mr Kristensen.

On June 1, I sent you 35 Kroner by 'mandat de poste international' and I hope that the money, which shall meet the amount you were so kind to lay out for me for the cylinders, reached you safely.[1] *But what haven't you thought of me, that I didn't send the money before?*

I think myself that it is *quite unforgivable* that I didn't send the money before, and I can't understand it myself, but there were so many difficulties to get through in the beginning, and I was so concerned about my mother's bad health, that everything else was pushed aside or forgotten. My mother suffered much from bad eyes last winter, but she is much better now in every way, and we are both very well here in America, which daily we love more and more.

When we came over here in September I was rather unknown to the public (because it was our first visit to America), had no impresario, and because of the war only a little cash. But I knew that it was absolutely necessary for my mother's health that we leave England and come to this country, where everything is relatively peaceful and free from the war. Then it turned out, luckily, that 3–4 of my compositions

[1] Phonograph cylinders, to be used during Grainger's collecting tour of Jutland with Kristensen, planned for 3–5 Aug. 1914. This tour was abandoned because of the threat of war and Rose Grainger's ill-health.

13

for orchestra were performed by chance (not because of my presence here in this country) by the greatest orchestras in different places, and these *very* successful performances, made me very famous at a blow.[1] Then I was requested to appear as a piano virtuoso in many places, found an excellent impresario, and also a very good publisher for the compositions.[2] I have never been more successful anywhere than here, both as a composer and pianist, maybe *nowhere* as successful as here. Next winter is already fully booked with the very best concert engagements, and I can assure you that America is a good country for a popular artist!

It is nice to be successful in a new country, but even nicer to *be happy* in *the country itself*, quite apart from one's personal experience, don't you agree? I fell in love with Denmark at once, when I came there for the first time, and before I had played there; and in the same way I liked Boston and N. York very much before I decided to perform here. The Americans are so good-natured, warm-hearted, democratic and talented. The country is teeming with art everywhere. First and foremost the abundance of folk music. The Negroes, the Red Indians, Cowboys (in the West), 'Mountain Whites' in the mountains in the South (W. Virginia, etc.)—they all have their own special, typical art, and even the 'cultured' modern population has great artistic interests and talents.

Many Europeans are (in my opinion) quite wrong as regards the inhabitants here. The Americans seem most of all to me to be spiritual. Most of all we love the Negro people. What a beautiful soul these people have, and so thoroughly entertaining and artistic they are.

When the war is over and we see Europe again, shall we then do our contemplated 'Folk-song-hunt'? I am really longing to do that. I hope that you and yours are as well in dearly beloved Denmark as we are over here. What luck that Denmark didn't enter the terror of the war![3]

Kindest regards to Mrs Kristensen, yourself and your son, from my mother and yours very sincerely,

Percy Grainger

[1] *Molly on the Shore, Irish Tune from County Derry*, and *Shepherd's Hey* were performed in a concert of the New York Symphony Orchestra on 4 Dec. 1914. Grainger's first performing appearance in New York involved playing the piano part of the third piece.

[2] Grainger's recital début in New York took place on 11 Feb. 1915; his concert agent was Antonia Sawyer (1863–1941); his new publisher was Rudolph Schirmer (1859–1919) of G. Schirmer, Inc.

[3] Denmark was to remain neutral throughout the war.

2   *To Margot Harrison*

The Southern | 680 Madison Avenue | N. York City. USA[1]
Dec 25, 1915

Dear little Margot.

I rejoiced to get yr letter. And I take my first free evening for weeks
& weeks for the joy of sending you a few lines. Fancy your dear little
brother a soldier. I hate to think of the heartrending anxieties your
dear mother & you all must be feeling for him, brave & determined
though you are.

It is wonderful what you are all doing in England. You English are
always full of criticalness & you love to find holes in your national deeds;
but to us, reading from afar, it seems as if England had *never* in the past
carried out such huge undertakings with such accuracy & looking-ahead.
But I am not surprised. I have had much dealings with English musicians & orchestras, & judging from them, I would expect wipe-the-floor
excellence from the race. You know my feelings about Germany of yore,
as you wrote. I have always looked upon the Germans as a kindhearted
but stupid & unthoro people & always looked upon the English as a
somewhat cool-hearted but *jolly clever* & thoroly thoro lot.

And naturally my sympathies have always been with the latter. Why
do you fall into the popular error of writing about the Germans as if
they were 'intellectual' & 'efficient'? This whole war proves them to
the whole world to be the hopeless muddlers & uncritical enthusiasts
that they always seemed to me in my young years among them. No
average English or American or Scandinavian schoolboy would be so
hopelessly unintellectual & hotheaded to bring so needlessly upon himself the *unending* calamity that the poor stupid old Germans are bringing upon themselves & all the rest of us as well. Of course NOONE
brought up in Germany & *also a student of the Danish sufferings under
Germany in Sønderjylland* (Slesvig),[2] as I am, could fail to have expected *it
all* for the last 15 years. And I can tell you my first years (from 1900,
on) in England were made bitter in seeing the careless English gentle
attitude towards Germany, where I had so recently witnessed such
very different attitudes & *emotional preparations.*

[1] The Graingers used this hotel as their base from mid-1915 until 1918, and also in 1920–1.
[2] In 1863 Denmark had enacted a new constitution incorporating Schleswig (Slesvig); the following year Austro-Prussian troops invaded first Schleswig, then Denmark. These actions finally
led to the Peace of Vienna in Oct. 1864, whereby Denmark ceded Schleswig, Holstein, and
Lauenburg to Austria and Prussia.

Still, on the whole England evidently knew what she was about after all, & after generations of Germans talking & thinking big, every second phrase beginning in 'world' (Weltkrieg, Weltreisender,[1] etc) what do we find: That Germany has been thinking *too small* all along! Germans were busy proclaiming that nowadays small nations were too small to exist—only Empires sufficed. She now wakes up to find that even 2 or 3 'Empires' are a parochial matter compared to the *world*—for that is what England means. As I see it England means *very nearly* the whole world today & Americans feel & see it & are willing & eager to form part of that world. People in England write about looking askance at America. How do we know whether USA *can* go to war today on our side? Would it be wise to send troops away with so many Germans & ½ Germans here. They cldn't intern their German Americans, how would they know where to begin & end? Why did not England prevent Germany & Austria bullying Denmark in 1864 or whenever it was?[2] *Perhaps she couldn't see her way to it at that particular moment.* Anyway I dont think Australia has held back in any way. I believe Australia has sent more troops per population than any part of the Empire.[3]

I have 4 cousins fighting now, 2 of them wounded, & one of them an only child. I literally hardly know of any young or youngish Australians not fighting or serving in some way.

What England has done seems to me hardly short of miraculous. I would not easily have believed that a fairly small population like the Un. Kingdom could raise anything near 5 million *free-willingly.* It surely is gorgeous.

I am trying to do what I can. It cost me about £1000 to begin business here, but now as I begin to earn I begin to use my earnings for the Cause. Melba & I are doing a joint concert for Allied Ambulance funds shortly,[4] I am giving £50 to the Pittsburgh Red Cross Allied Ambulance, £40 to Hamilton (Canada) Red Cross funds, & as I earn more I will do increasingly on the same lines, to England, Australia, etc.

[1] = world war, globetrotter (German).

[2] Through Lord John Russell Britain had convened the London Conference on the Danish Question in Apr. 1864, but it had been effectively scuttled by Bismarck in June of that year. The war had then resumed.

[3] Through the First World War Australian fighting troops comprised 11.2% of her population, as against 8.9% for Canada and 5.0% for Britain.

[4] The soprano Nellie Melba (1861–1931) had known Grainger since his boyhood in Melbourne, and had occasionally assisted the development of his career in London. On 17 and 20 Jan. 1916 they gave their only two joint concerts, in Boston and Pittsburgh, respectively.

From Australia I have very sad news. My father can neither move his legs or arms, & will never be able to again, has heavy doctors bills & must have a trained nurse always. As he is an architect & not ever a 'saver' it is tragic for him, poor man, & I am thankful indeed that my huge success over here puts me in a position to help him.[1]

Fancy if my mother had not been ill a year & a half ago & we had stayed in Europe. Where would we be now, & what good could I have rendered anybody or anything in a monetary way? It was lucky indeed & we are properly thankful & *adore* being here.

Hundreds of performances of my things are taking place here. Of course I have *not a moment's* time for composing now, I play 4 & 5 times a week & have big journeys (like Australia) and next summer I hope to do a heap. You write as to the possibility of my making music that really expresses *me*.

It is so hard for me to judge, dear Margot. I am not very conscious of 'personality' in art, perhaps so much contact with folkart has blunted that side of my artistic consciousness. I must say that parts of Delius, Cyril Scott, Grieg, Bach, etc seem to *me* to express my soul quite as *personally* as my own music. I dont feel personality strong in music, that's what it is [*sic*]. Other yearnings take all my attention, & keep me busy—*and happy*. I felt British folkmusic was neglected in the International world of music. I tried to bring British & Scandinavian folkmusic (thro my arrangements) to the world ken, & if programs in Russia, Spain, America, etc, prove anything, I have somewhat succeeded. But that is only one little matter. When I get more powerful I wish to help Negro composers (such as W. M. Cook, Dett, Diton,[2] etc) forward & do for negro folkmusic what I've tried to do for British etc. Then I want to bring the beauty of native music (African, Polynesian, etc) home to the ear of all the world.

Then there is my special P.G. mission: the making possible of music without *any* regularity of rhythmic durations.[3] This I began in 1899 or 1900. Have you seen my article, 'The impress of personality in unwritten music' & would you like to see it, or are you too busy just now?[4]

[1] John H. Grainger (1855–1917) had emigrated to Australia in 1877 and soon established a reputation as a leading architect of public buildings in the Australian colonies and New Zealand. In 1880 he had married Rosa (Rose) Aldridge, who bore their son, George Percy, on 8 July 1882; in 1890 John and Rose Grainger separated. John Grainger contracted syphilis in the mid-1880s, and thereafter became increasingly incapacitated by the disease.

[2] Will Marion Cook (1869–1944), writer of musical comedies, often using idioms taken from Negro folk music; Dett, see Biographical Register; Carl Rossini Diton (1886–1962), pianist and singer.   [3] Part of Grainger's concept of 'Free Music'. See letter **62**.

[4] *Musical Quarterly*, 1 (1915), 416–35.

How funny that I met your betrothed's parents. I was not conscious of the fact, alas, because I never know the names of the many people I meet, & have not known (until yr last letter) the name of yr betrothed! As it happens I am not conscious of knowing anyone in this country that knows you. You see my life is a *purely public* one here, as it has always been in all countries except England. I dash about, play at concerts, meet conductors, publishers & business folk, & do my work, & have no time or appetite for any thing social. In England musicians have to work in more 'social' fields because the public musical field in Gt Britain is so limited (not artisticly but businessly.)

3   *To Rose Grainger*

Enclose checks from Hamilton & Buffalo. I got no check in Toronto.

Trinity College School, | Port Hope, Ontario, Canada.
Saturday, Feb 12. 1916.

O, my own Mumsey

It is dull lacking letters from you, but it is also glorious being in Canada. Surely these American years are the happiest yet in our lives, surely they hold more seed of future doings & chances ahead than we've ever enjoyed elsewhere? It is a lovely thing to meet such support as I am all the time. Not even in Norway, maybe, have I felt such a wonderful gladness at my art & response to my aims, as I am meeting on this present trip, both USA, & Canada. England was never hothearted enough for me, & the European Continent never *quite* echoed or trusted or followed my compositional sympathies. But on this continent I find all I want of both. I feel more & more that in USA & Canada lies a very lovely future for me as composer, pianist & creature, perhaps the fairest, after all.

Not that I could ever settle, or feel myself at one with English-speaking life, but artisticly & actively it is pretty perfect for me. After all, they are yearning for just the *very* things I have to give, & to empty oneself out, in art or sex, is the acme of all life. Constipation, of all kinds, is the root of all downheartedness! All your worst hopes are fulfilled, my adorable adoredest mum. I have speechified! And I can foresee a future in which you tremble, not for my silence, as in

Norway, but for the unending resonance of my public tongue. In Toronto I 'said a few words' at Dr. Vogt's lunch for me.[1]

In Hamilton, lunching at the Rotary Club, (a business man's club!) I was definitely called upon to reply to Carey's speech & did so.[2] Worst of all, I on my own bat hatched the idea of speeching at the Hamilton concert. Two of Lucas's compositions were down on program & after my 1st solo (big Bach-B) followed Dett's 'Listen to the lambs.'[3] Noone I had met seemed to know Dett was Canadian, & I felt stirred to do something for him, & focus attention on his composition, so during the Bach applause I held up my hand & said:

> 'I cannot tell you what a joy it is to me to hear Mr Carey conduct your glorious "Elgar choir" tonight, & as an Australian I am natu-
> rally particularly interested to hear the works of Canadian com-
> posers. Of course Clarence Lucas is famous throughout the whole
> English speaking musical world, but perhaps you do not all know
> that R. Nathaniel Dett is also a Canadian (cheers). I think he was
> born near Niagara Falls. He is a Negro, a great friend of mine, & a
> highly gifted musician & composer. He is head of the music at
> Hampton Institute, Virginia, & is doing magnificent work. It is
> lovely for me to have this opportunity of hearing these works here.'

This drew attention to Dett's chorus, which was perfectly given by Carey & his *very lovely* choir, & the work had a *huge* success, & you will see how the press liked it. A robust Grainger clap thrown into the lessening forces of applause every now & then had its old-time effect, & you would have writhed in agony if present, darling comrade! (Not really.) Dett's chorus, when well sung, is one of the most poetic things going, I have written him about it, sending him programs, criticisms (as enclosed) & am writing Schirmers about the success of 'Listen to the lambs', which they've published. Carey is a 3rd generation Canadian of originally Irish stock, a tall, broad, highly handsome, manly, muscular Viking, with noble brave features & a Greek forehead & nose.[4] He is a born chorus conductor, a born leader anyhow, shivering with noble passion & desperation as he conducts, a lovely

[1] Augustus Stephen Vogt (1861–1926), Toronto organist and conductor of the city's Mendelssohn Choir from 1894 to 1917.

[2] Bruce Anderson Carey (1876–1960), born in Hamilton, Ontario. In about 1908 he founded the ninety-nine-voice Elgar Choir.

[3] Clarence Lucas (1866–1947), Canadian composer, born in Niagara; he conducted the Philharmonic Society of Hamilton in the early 1890s, although later lived in London and New York. The 'Bach-B' was Busoni's piano transcription of Bach's Prelude and Fugue in D major for organ. Nathaniel Dett's 'Listen to the lambs' was published by Schirmer in 1914.

[4] Grainger included a few pen strokes here in illustration of Carey's features.

primeval figure to behold as he shakes his choir like a dog a rat, charmingly mannered & lovable in his ways though splendidly churned up within, never rude but always electrifying. Young & the very symbol of health, & very proud of his pretty sister. They gave a stirring rendering of 'We have fed our seas',[1] helped by my thundering out the accompaniment as well as their ordinary accompanist more mildly engaged on a 2nd grand. I *believe* they have a really *glorious* performance of the 'Irish Tune', but I can't really tell. Sex is a stronger lure than art in my case.

I saw that the stage the women of the choir were standing on was a built up affair.[2] The Irish Tune offered a splendid chance & I made my tour of the Contraltos & Sopranos & was highly delighted. At this game I was seen by one of the men who look after the Opera House, who, I expect, took me for a German intent on blowing up the Elgar Choir (in which were several khakied soldiers) with a bomb. So I had to pretend I was deep in music instead of deep.[3] Life is certainly full of divers delights. Here at Orchard's school[4] one shivers, not with excess of sexual delight, but at the utterly freezing temperature of an Englishly non-warmed establishment.

The English idea of home should be felt in a Canadian winter to cull the choicest blossoms of nose-drops. The tip of ones nose is *never* dry under Orchard's roof, he himself is blowing when he is not coughing & he confided to me at breakfast that with him 'one cold in the head simply makes room for the next.' Why not, indeed?

He asked in some friends to enjoy me in addition to his boys last night (the boys evidently have my secret of clapping technic) & it was screaming to note his English embarrassment at the fulsomeness of Canadian praise, which need not blush for itself alongside of American. When someone said 'Well, I surely never enjoyed an evening like this evening. I've heard a lot of piano playing but never anyone with your "punch". Why, Paderewski can't hold a candle to you. Your fingers sure must be made of iron,' etc etc, Orchard would try to switch off with: 'The piano is certainly a most attractive instrument' & that sort of stuff, calculated to relieve me from any *undue*

[1] 'We have fed our seas for a thousand years', the second of Grainger's Kipling settings, composed 1900–4, published for chorus and piano in 1912.

[2] Grainger had originally written, 'the women of the choir were standing on a built-up affair with gaps between the woodwork, through which I, crouching below, could look up their legs', but later crossed much of this out.

[3] Grainger had originally finished this sentence with 'in their skirts'.

[4] The Revd Dr F. Graham Orchard (d. 1943), headmaster of Trinity College School from 1913 to 1933.

20

sense of over-personal responsibility for the evening's pleasures.[1] To meet an exaggerated Englishman like him & his 'carefully chosen staff of teachers, all English except one' in the midst of Canadians & Americans, is *fierce farce*.

War or no war, submarines or no submarines, he has just sent his little *Canadian born* son to an English School (in England) because he noted the beginnings of a Canadian accent! I leave late tonight for *Ottawa*, am invited to lunch at Government House tomorrow (Sunday) & play to their Royal Highnesses the Duke and Duchess of Connaught.[2]

I shall wire you if this comes off as planned. If so, maybe you might like to write a par. for musical papers, which Sawyer can copy & send round to the 3, also maybe to dailies.

'*Percy Grainger's sensational success in Canada*' Saying no pianist for years & years has made such a sensation, 'won 18 recalls at Toronto Recital', was called 'The Elman of the piano',[3] & compared with Paderewski, Patti, Sarasate, Wilhelmj as a sensational occurrence.

Mention the success of Hamilton concert, the big Opera House *entirely sold out, my gift to Red Cross?*, the great success of 'Irish Tune' & 'We have fed' by the Elgar choir (but not of my tours of Sopranos & Contraltos) & giving my speech at Hamilton concert in full, mentioning Clarence Lucas (who is Mus. Courier critic in N. York you know) & R. Nathaniel Dett. Also my Royal Command to play before the Connaughts. You will note the 'Toronto World' criticism of *Toronto* concert enclosed, as well as ditto of Hamilton concert. Orchard could only afford $100.00 to play for his boys, but it is on the way to Ottawa, & saves hotel bills. I arrive Hotel Fremont, Fremont, Ohio, Monday night. Yes, lets accept Swedish Club. Fondest love, beloved one. Wish you were with me.

---

[1] The recital, held in the school's Dining Hall, was described in the *Trinity College School Record* (19/1 (May 1916), 42). Grainger was acknowledged as 'an old friend of the Headmaster'.

[2] HRH Arthur William Patrick Albert, first Duke of Connaught and Strathearn (1850–1942), third son of Queen Victoria, was Governor-General of Canada from 1911 to 1916. His wife was a Prussian princess.

[3] Mischa Elman (1891–1967), Ukrainian-born violinist.

4   *To Rose Grainger*

Buffalo → Cleveland | Monday, Feb 14, 1916. | 2.p.m.

It is delightful to be back in the States again. The security of actual arrival at Buffalo was much appreciated. I look upon it as no longer safe to tour Canada any more, as they are already debating National Registry (see enclosed) & might hold up British subjects on border at any moment, as they already do in Australia & N. Zealand.[1]

I think the Canadians will be a very beautiful race; the men are very markedly tall & broad, with lovely fresh skins, & suprizingly many of them with that smooth round full Greeklike muscular formation so common to Norwegians, very much so in the good looking man in Elverum, do you remember?

I think the Canadians are very trustworthy, open, truthful, good-natured, kindhearted; sturdier than any British breed except the Scotch & the N. Zealanders, but probably sturdier than these too. Lacking the yielding sweetness and brainy humorousness of the Americans, but happy & confident & *enthusiastic* like they. To meet Englishmen alongside them seems like a breath of evil, something sly & distorted & ignoble by comparison. The Canadian speech is fairly close to American only still more countryfied & sonorous than most of the American accents we meet.

I cannot understand you would mind my being an American citizen. I don't care about such things, but if I did, I should feel a real pleasure in having put British citizenship behind me.

Every ideal of theirs, everything they are striving for ,er mig meget imod.'[2] The sound of their speech is utterly sickening to me, I like almost *every* other speech in the world better, I am meaning refined English speech of course, the English dialects are just as sympathetic as Australian, American or Canadian.

All races are full of many qualities at the same time, & sometimes one bosses & sometime another. The past of the English holds great sweetness but the later master-types of England loom as poisonously before me as any German menace could. These men lack *real inner* power too. It is the non-refined parts of the English speaking world,

---

[1] Grainger's fear of compulsory registration for British subjects was real. After long and acrimonious debates Canada did pass the Compulsory Service Act in 1917, as earlier did New Zealand. In Australia the issue of compulsory service was rejected twice in referenda during 1916–17.

[2] = is very contrary to my beliefs (Danish).

Ireland, America, Australia etc that sprout the real humane priceless talents, men who foreshow the world's real betterment. Out of the art of G.B. Shaw, George Moore, W. Whitman,[1] me, looms real hope for the future. There may be *too little* art in the States & Australia, but at least the *feeling* of what there is is sympathetic to me. The Bulletin is so, the comic pictures here are, Norman Lindsay is, McCubbins pictures are.[2] We non-refined English are at least full of *hope & trust*, & if I cared for 'citizenships' at all, I would sooner ally myself to a country not continually exposed to the cynical supercilious maudlin poison of English upperclass influences & schemings. At tea at Government House yesterday was a nice little Australian miniature paintress from Melbourne, doing a very pretty miniature of Princess Patricia.[3] She & her husband are in N York doing well, & liking USA greatly. I gathered they dont hanker any for war service. There was nothing goody goody about her but just practical businesslike traits, & she pretty & softformed, reminding me pleasantly of old impressions in Australia, & awakening the old thought so often thought: 'Australian women might be possible & pleasant to make love to'.

We are not going to be a puritanical race, & maybe my unbridled mental licentiousness foreshadows a future freedom & pleasurableness of the race. The feeling at the Connaughts is very charming & human. ('Dead easy' Doc would say.) She seems just German with a German accent & he is a rather sympathetic type of Jew, rather like a Dutch Jew. Princess Patricia seems simpler & better mannered than most refined English young woman types, & I enjoyed myself there.

I enjoyed the whole day. At lunch (alone in Hotel 'Chateau Laurier') I gave myself up lock stock & barrel to the enjoyment of a 'deep dish apple pie' (20 cents; the ordinary apple pie—without the 'deep dish'—being only 15 cents) with lots of sugar & cream, washed down by hot malted milk, my favorite Hotel and railroad drink. This was so thoroly overwhelming that I gave myself up to a long afternoon sleep, undressed, in bed—in fact I was a *few minutes late* for the tea at Gov. House! But what a thing it is to be really happy. And I can

[1] During 1902 Grainger had attended lectures given by Shaw (1856–1950) and read several of his books; he had come to know the Irish writer George Moore (1852–1933) around 1911; Walt Whitman (1819–92), the American poet, exerted perhaps the strongest intellectual influence upon Grainger, who had first read his *Leaves of Grass* in 1897. See esp. letter **5**.

[2] The *Bulletin*, Australian weekly literary magazine, founded in 1880; Norman Lindsay (1879–1969), Australian artist and writer; Frederick McCubbin (1855–1917), Australian painter, with whom Grainger had studied drawing as a boy in Melbourne.

[3] (1886–1974), daughter of the Duke and Duchess of Connaught and Strathearn, from 1919 Lady Patricia Ramsay. The name of the 'paintress' is unknown.

really say I am that. As I lie on my back in the upper berths, as I sit for hours in the train, I am conscious of feeling filled to the brim with thorough content & well being, glad of my life with you, feeling comfortably abreast of my artistic aims & problems, glad of the war (sure it is a fine thing & for the best) pleased with my career & free from all nervousness as a performer.

In fact my most reposeful moments are on the platform. After looking after baggage, after interviews & always people who talk & talk I feel the empty loneliness of the stage as a real haven of rest & quiet. After the 'heating up'[1] before going on & the effort of the big Bach B is past I sink into a half-unconscious dreamy carefree drowsiness, filled with business thoughts, thoughts of you, thoughts of Karen[2] & other friends, licentious thoughts, which even brilliant passages do not rouse me out of, as a rule. It is a great boon, to enjoy an hour's perfect repose & silence every day like that, & I appreciate it very much. Orchard was a terrible reminder of the horrors of England. I always used to feel this horror at remeeting English folk when returning to Harwich from Denmark, & I also felt it on return from S. Africa, but it was formerly always lessened by the fact of *your* being in England in all those cases.

Orchard is the head of 'Trinity College School' the biggest boarding school in Canada. His aim is to turn wholesome nice minded Canadians into priggish quasi England gentlemen. Luckily, there is not the faintest chance of his succeeding, & his boys seemed to me utterly unEnglish in every way & thoroly happy & sympathetic. Orchard seems utterly ignorant on all subjects we talked about, but as he himself said, when I asked him about his teaching, he is there chiefly for 'disciplinary considerations'. In his jargon 'plin' in 'disciplinary' rhymes with 'mine.' His views on the tiniest subjects are grave to browwinckling & headshaking such as Mrs Teague delights in. The tone of voice in which he told me that 7 of the elder boys were once discovered at midnight in a Chinese Restaurant was pretty rich. 'It wasn't the act in itself I so much deplored, it was the utter flaunting of authority.' He expelled those boys, whom the whole school 'sang off' ('for he's a jolly good f') as they left. 'I felt myself compelled to cane the entire school, & I did, though it took me 3 days to do it, and it made me several years older. The sense of responsibility was over-

---

[1] i.e. beating his hands against his thighs.
[2] Karen Kellermann (née Holten), see Biographical Register.

whelming.'[1] I did not tell him that quite other feelings would have overwhelmed me, which would not have made me any years older. I hardly expect he is a Sadist, certainly not a conscious or optimistic one.

He says he feels it very keenly that he is not 'doing his bit.' He says his little son may say to him later on in life: 'What were you doing in 1916, father'? Why wasn't father fighting? He who is ready to sacrifice the health of the poor to the refinement of the rich is also ready to sacrifice himself for the voice of society, vocal in his son, that he has himself planted there. A beautiful circle of Christian feeling indeed. Beware of the religious. They are *the* worst. I think I shall be home by breakfast on Friday, but do not wait for me, lovey darling. I wish you had been with me on some of this trip.

    With the lovingest thoughts
            Percy.

5   *To D. C. Parker*

[On the recommendation of his London publisher, Willy Strecker of Schott, Grainger had soon contracted with the New York firm G. Schirmer; these two firms would remain his chief publishers until his death. By 1916 such was the demand for Grainger's music and performances in the United States that Schirmer commissioned a small book about him. The task fell to D. C. Parker, whose *Percy Aldridge Grainger: A Study* appeared two years later.]

            680 Madison Avenue, New York City. | August 28th, 1916.

My dear Mr Parker:–

    Mr Sonneck of 'The Musical Quarterly' has just written me that you are providing him with two articles.[2] That is *charming news*, and I shall keenly look forward to reading what you have to say. I shall

---

[1] At this time the school numbered about one hundred boarding students. In a memoir which appeared in the *Trinity College School Record* (47/4 (Apr. 1944), 8–17) a former student and master of the school J. D. Ketchum wrote of Orchard's 'mask of austerity, rigid self-control, unchallenged authority, utter inflexibility. . . . School, like life itself, was always a battlefield to Dr. Orchard, and this terrifying manner was his most powerful weapon.' (p. 11.)

[2] Oscar (George) Sonneck (1873–1928), also chief of the Library of Congress's music division. Parker's articles were 'Exoticism in Music in Retrospect' and 'A View of Giacomo Puccini' (*Musical Quarterly*, 3 (1917), 134–61 and 509–16, respectively). In the former article Parker considered Grainger extensively, concluding: 'He is continually sweeping away the cobwebs of obscurantism, and on account of his searches for new colour effects and striking harmonic combinations is entitled to rank as one of the most successful opponents of Doctor Dry-as-dust.' (p. 158.)

always continue to cherish your strongly individual witty and generous article on me with a special joy.[1] The time has now come for me
to jot down the details you so kindly asked me for some time ago in
connection with a possible article on me. I take the freedom of jot-
ting down all sorts of odds and ends, thoughts, opinions, tendencies,
out of the jumble of which you will so excellently know what to use
and reject. Anyhow, I take it, what you are wanting is simply a mass
of data on which to base, or with which to garnish, your possible
article.

The strongest factor of my artistic life is my mother. Altho herself
not coming from an artistic family, she has clearly all her life been in
love with art; a hungry musician, a greedy reader of poetry, prose and
fairy tales from a very young girl, and more than all this, all her life
long instinctively imbued with an adoration of art, a marked predilection for people showing creative powers, and the yearning to foster,
further and protect, the creative sproutings, wherever and however
shown. Thus art has always been close at hand with me—art has
always been an easy abetted act with me—my thoughts have never
been turned away from it, and I have never failed to get artistic support, criticism and the instinctive insight of a born artist from my
mother. It is my strong belief that every born creature is artistic. All
birds and animals seem to me artistic. They give way to expressing
their feelings, their bodily states and moods in a splendid way, and seldom choose to be silent and inartistic. Savage primitive mankind also
seems almost unfailingly artistic. Birds, beasts and savage races *have
time* to be artistic. A bird in a cage, a beast in a yoke cannot be such a
slave as a civilized man, because you can't *enslave his mind.* A civilized
wage slave not only has laughably little time to be artistic, but he is
held back from the natural unreasoning self abandonment of art by a
1000 and one ideals, ideas, rights and wrongs. Even if he likes 'art'
well enough to devote himself to it, to look at it, hear it, 'go in for it,'
he is still held back from the true full fearless self-confession of art by
ideas of 'good art' and 'bad art' and by a (to me) unexplainable never
failing *wish* to like the good rather than the bad art. I can't see why a
being impelled to such a random untrammelled untamable affair as art
at all shall still have about him this queer timid goody-goodiness.

Personally, I do not feel like a modern person at all. I feel quite at
home in South Sea Island music, in Maori legends, in the Icelandic

---

[1] 'The Art of Percy Grainger', *Monthly Musical Record*, 45 (1915), 152–3.

Sagas, in the Anglosaxon 'Battle of Brunnanburh',[1] feel very close to Negroes in various countries, but hardly understand modern folk at all. I do not dislike modern people, but simply can never learn to understand their reason for being, can never get a true insight into their ways of feeling and acting, and feel among them as among kind but very strange strangers with whom I will take a mighty long time to get acclimatized. I do not tell you this in order to appear 'funny', but in order to throw light on the well-springs of my music. Art with me arises out of the longing to escape out of the (to me) meaningless present into the past, which to me is full of meaning, or into some imaginary world full of keenness and exaggerated excitement. I shall not go into the question of whether my preferance for thinking of the past is unreasonable or justified, nor shall I try to find what foolishness it is in me that makes me turn instinctively away from modern clothes to naked races, from modern morals to the self-controlled individualistic fitness of Icelandic manners of the 10th century, etc. The instinct and the prejudice are there, unuprootably, and I think my music arises to a big extent out of it. When a boy, I read Freeman's 'Anglosaxon history' with passion.[2] The Anglosaxons have always stirred me beyond all reason. The knowledge that the Battle of Hastings had *really happened* was for years one of the bitterest experiences of my life. As a boy, I longed to some day compose music that would seem to me 'really Anglosaxon' full of the sweet even flowing sturdy good humor I thought I saw in that race, music in which I could feel the more dramatic, tense, harsher mentality of the Norman race would seem to be lacking [*sic*]. I wished to 'make good' for Hastings musically. Even nowadays, again and again, I instinctively ask myself, 'Is "Mock Morris" perhaps somewhat Anglosaxon; is it closer to Beowulf than to Malory;[3] am I really carrying out occasionally what I yearned to do as a child?'

Anglosaxon (the tongue) has always drawn me (I am studying it now) and the old Norse tongue and their tales and their view of life has always been a beacon light to me. I love their fearless readiness to try all things, yet cautiously and without foolhardiness. They were the least foolhardy race thinkable. Many races believe in ghosts and are terrified by them and show it in a lot of ways. The old Scandinavians

[1] Poem in the *Anglo-Saxon Chronicle*, depicting the battle fought between the English and the Danes in 937.

[2] The studies of the Norman conquest by E. A. Freeman (1823–92) appeared between 1867 and 1880.

[3] Sir Thomas Malory (d. 1471), author of *Le Morte d'Arthur*, a cycle of Arthurian legends.

were afraid of ghosts too, but that did not hinder them from breaking open a ghost-ridden barrow if they thought there was anything inside they'd like to have. I do not admire courage in itself particularly, but I do think inquisitiveness should exceed fear if there is to be much fun and freedom in the world. It was my boyhood's wild and ignorant adoration of old Norse things that took me to modern Scandinavia, that made me study Danish before I went to Denmark, and has made me learn other Scandinavian languages and dialects, so that I can now speak or read Danish, Swedish, Jutish, Norwegian landsmaal,[1] old Icelandic, Faroese. In modern Scandinavia, I have found life more lovely than elsewhere yet, though I have fond hopes of finding a haven of joy in the South Seas. I was drawn to Scandinavia by my old love of the old Norse, but I soon grew to love the modern North for its own sake too. They still have the old fearless free ways of going about things, and all the old canny cautiousness too.

They dash into divorce just as their forebears dashed into a haunted barrow. No doubt they are afraid, but they are more inquisitive than afraid. I love woman to hold a free place in the world, to walk a free path in all ways unquestioned. 'Votes for women', easy divorce, Selma Lagerlöf and Ellen Key come painlessly and effortlessly to races whose womankind *from the dimmest past* onwards has always been a free sex and an obstreperous sex.[2]

The Northern races are platonic in the splendid sense that they are chiefly interested in *all things* rather than in a very few things.

The Scotch border-ballads have been another strong and never waning influence and delight. I have a big choral work on 'The lads of Wamphray' (unperformed), an already performed setting for voice and eight solo strings of the 'The twa Corbies,' one of my favorite unperformed things of my own is Swinburne's 'The Bride's Tragedy' (Scotch words) (for double chorus and orchestra) then there is my song in Scotch, Swinburne's 'A reiver's neckverse,' etc. In fact, with the exception of many Kipling settings (a few published, a host still unfinished) my only settings of English poems are in Scotch![3]

My favorite book is 'The Saga of Grettir the strong' (in Icelandic).[4]

---

[1] 'Country' Norwegian, based on rural dialects.

[2] Selma Lagerlöf (1858–1940) and Ellen Key (1849–1926), both Swedish writers. Grainger had read Key's *Love and Marriage* in 1911.

[3] Grainger worked on some forty Kipling settings between 1898 and the late 1950s. Kipling's writings also directly inspired five of his early instrumental works.

[4] Grainger came to know this saga originally from Sir George Dasent's *Romances of the Middle Ages*.

Otherwise my favorite literature is Icelandic Sagas, Faeroe folk poems, Danish folk poems collected by Evald Tang Kristensen, Scotch border ballads, Walt Whitman, Hans Christian Andersen, J. P. Jacobsen's novels (Danish), Mark Twain, Walt Whitman and Kipling. Kipling's verse had more artistic influence on me (between the age of fifteen and twenty five) than the art of any other single man,[1] but Walt Whitman is to me the most ideal artist and artist type I know anything about. I really adore Walt Whitman, artistically and personally, though I am not modern enough in my feelings or instincts to share his beliefs and to hope his hopes. I am, personally, far closer to Grettir than to Walt Whitman, but I envy Walt more than I do Grettir; but would not change all the same.

I would like my music to breathe something I see in Grettir and in the Maori proverb 'Die like the shark, fighting to the last gasp.' A spider does not need hope, or consolation, or encouragement, or 'moral support.' When a spider is in a tight place he just does the best he can, like Grettir, like 'Niels Lyhne' in Jacobsen's novel of that name,[2] like most characters in Ibsen, and like the shark in the Maori proverb. It is not necessarily hope or 'uplift' or ideas that keep us going, I feel, but largely just the force of life itself. Chesterton once made fun of Shaw calling sex 'The Life Force' and then imploring humanity to rally to its assistance.[3] Chesterton said something about that he would expect anything called by such a name to forage for itself.

Some force like that, a force not of beliefs, morals, ideals and ideas, but the bodily force of life itself, is what I always long to invest my music with. I wish to leave the uplifting ennobling work to others, but wish in my art to try and voice the unbeatable freshness and undowned every-trying, ever-daring life instinct of men and beasts, the stubbornness of the spider, the tough endurance of Grettir, in 'The Bride's Tragedy' a couple not upset by disaster by trying their best as long as the machinery lasts, etc.[4]

The solid, even (unheroized) vigor of the Faeroese tunes and texts

---

[1] Grainger was introduced to the works of Rudyard Kipling (1865–1936) in 1897, when his father sent him several of Kipling's volumes to prevent him becoming too 'Germanized'. For a general comparison of the two see Teresa Balough, 'Kipling and Grainger', *Studies in Music*, 11 (1977), 74–108.

[2] Jens Peter Jacobsen (1847–85), Danish writer; his novel *Niels Lyhne* appeared in 1880.

[3] G. K. Chesterton (1874–1936), English essayist, in his vol. *George Bernard Shaw* (London: John Lane, 1909).

[4] Writing to Alfhild Sandby in 1936 about *The Bride's Tragedy* (1909–13; premièred 1922), Grainger stated: 'That work was my personal protest against the sex-negation that our capitalistic world . . . offered to young talents like me.'

(such as in 'Father and Daughter' for instance) strike a deep chord in me, and I am sketching a 'Death song for Hjalmar Thuren' (the Dane who collected the lovely Faeroe tunes) on one of the staunchest of the Faeroe tunes.[1]

Apart from the vigor of the folk dances, and the tragic heroism of rhythmic verse such as the border ballads, Scandinavian ballads, Kipling's and Swinburne's heroic ballads, what stirs me to music most is nature, and walking in nature.

My 'Hill-Song' (performed at a Balfour Gardiner concert) is one of my favorite of my own compositions.[2] Barren, treeless, greenless nature I like best, like our Australian deserts, like barren hill-country, flat heather-land like in Jutland, or the sea. My love for the sea is so strong that life feels to me only half-lived on land. Since a boy, I have longed to write 'Sea Songs' for orchestra (or chorus and orchestra), very many-voiced, utterly irregular in rhythm, with no rhythmic 'beats' at all, each voice going its own way. Longing for the rhythmic irregularity of beatless music needed for these 'Sea Songs' made me develop the *irregularly barred* rhythmic scheme of my Hill-Song, Marching Song of Democracy, Train Music, Song of Solomon sketches, etc. The 'Marching Song of Democracy' voices Australian democratic yearnings close to W. Whitman in type, and is a semi-religious composition, a sort of modern and Australian version of the 'Gloria' of a mass.[3]

My favorite composer is Bach and the strongest influence on my compositional style. Chopin I admire deeply as a formist and an instinctive polyphonist, and Wagner, Grieg and Delius are especial admirations.

My strongest musical instinct is for many-voicedness, harmony is the next strongest instinct, while an instinct for melody was never properly stirred until my contact with English folksongs, which, as regards the strength and variety of their resources in 'pure line', seem to me, personally, almost unequally amongst the folktunes of the world. Bach appeals to me also in a Democratic sense. Bach composed music practically as popular as Tipperary and music as abstract (as suited for the 'special few' of study and a lifetime's devotion) as Reger's worst and C.

---

[1] Hjalmar Thuren (1873–1912), Danish folklorist, whose collection of Faeroese folksongs appeared in 1908. Grainger's setting, for baritone, mixed chorus, and orchestra, dates from 1916–17 and appears not to have been published.

[2] *Hill-Song* No. 2 was performed on 25 Feb. 1913 at the sixth Balfour Gardiner concert in London.

[3] For mixed chorus, organ and orchestra (1901–15, scored 1915–17), dedicated to 'my darling mother, united with her in loving adoration of Walt Whitman'.

Franck's best (I don't mean anything against Reger by that). If Bach were living today, I feel he would include Ragtime, Schönbergism, Musical Comedy, Strauss and all the grades in between. As an Australian, I hate to see any art limited to any class. It pains me to think that the ragtime class can't enjoy Bach or Debussy fully or that the classical class cannot enjoy ragtime fully. Music, surely, belongs to all, to birds, to savages, to over-civilized folk, to the over-refined, to the vulgar, all alike. As long as a being feels, why should he not have his special art? He always has. Then why not admire it all, enjoy all types and learn from all types? Artisticly speaking, it seems to me just as necessary and desirable that a vulgar man's art is vulgar, that a so called decadent man's art is decadent, as that Bach's art is, like himself, cosmopolitan, subtle but lusty. Just as I feel towards every class, so do I feel towards every race. I feel that I, as a modern composer, have just as much to learn from Chinese or Zulu music as from Schönberg or Scarlatti. I feel that genius is everywhere. No life no talent, also— no talent no life, a creature without talent would soon snuff out. A creature with talent enough to live six months can generally be relied upon to be some sort of an artist.

Almost my strongest artistic feeling is a motherly artistic instinct. I hate to think of the world being constantly full of artistic outpourings, in every land, in every class, and most of it going to waste for lack of an artistic motherly instinct. Artistic infanticide is to me no better than any other. When we are more cultured, I feel, a Fiji song, a Burmese orchestra, a Javanese Gamalan will mean to us what far Eastern color prints do now. I feel it is only the artistically undeveloped ones that see such a vast gulf between the stone scratchings of the Bushmen and a Rembrandt, such a gulf between Beethoven and a Maori Haka.[1] To prove to you my own great artisticness (!), I may tell you that no lesson in polyphony (not Bach, Wagner, Strauss) has ever been so deeply instructive, so fruitful as the polyphony of the improvised part singing of Rarotongan natives from the South Seas.[2] I long to spend years collecting native musics in Africa, the South Seas, etc. I feel that to be the deepest duty I know. Those natives still create quite unconsciously, or comparatively so. Once we know musical notation, this blissful

[1] = posture dance for welcome, war or amusement. In a letter of 18 Feb. 1909 to Karen Kellermann (then Holten) Grainger wrote: 'To perform a haka must give more joy than to perform any other art I know, almost. For one not only shouts wild bold words, with the rhythmic pulse of a lot of fellow hakamen floating one along, but accompanies the chanting with desperate violent wanton abandoned movements of the whole body! Musical football.'
[2] In the Cook Islands.

31

unconsciousness dwindles or vanishes. I do not think it better to be unconscious than conscious, but it is different, and both states have golden messages. I would like to see at least some small portion of the *unconscious* musical products garnered in before this musical state disappears altogether.

As a democratic Australian, also as a lover of the natural and the universal, I long to see everyone somewhat of a musician, not a world divided between musically abnormally undeveloped amateurs and over-developed professional musical prigs. Therefore, I long to write for the amateur to help to build up a 'home music', a 'room-music', similar to Haydn's in his time, only more varied as to color. I turn, therefore, willingly to instruments (such as guitar, mandolin, whistling, singing, percussion instruments such as the marimba-phone, bells, Nabimba,[1] etc) that amateurs can readily learn; instruments that encourage artistic pleasure in performances rather than yearly labors of preparation for finally joy-poor performances. To me, music is not only, not chiefly, in *how it sounds*, but almost equally in *how it plays*. How music sounds to the takers-part is nearly (if not quite) as serious a question to me as how the music sounds to drone-listeners. Before I die, I hope to leave behind a goodly sheaf of stuff that may give pleasure in this way, music in this respect closer to the musical origin of African or American Negro music than to the origin of Schönberg's (whom I intensely admire and am grateful to) music. I think that is a lesson that the study of primitive music helps to teach one, and a perusal of modern musical conditions points the same story.

May I be allowed to add a few words as to what seem to me the salient characteristics of my compositional style? It always seems to me that the 'texture' (the actual distribution of notes in chords, the critical or unconscious choice of invertions—whether they are close or spread; in short the *weft of the fabric*, the actual *stuff* (sonority) produced by the polyphony or by a 'chordy' style of writing) of a composer is the determining factor of his work, at least to other composers, at least, so it seems to me. The unmusical hearers speak of 'structure' (as if music were a subway or a building) of 'form' of 'development' (I haven't the faintest idea what is meant by this latter means) of 'clarification' (Verklärung); but the composer (so it seems to me) asks first, or asks early; 'What is the texture?' 'Is it sodden texture like linoleum, or a

[1] Grainger had first experienced these 'Deagan' percussion instruments in Chicago during Mar. 1915: steel and wooden marimbaphones (like bass glockenspiels and bass xylophones), Swiss staff bells, and Nabimbas (five-octave marimba-like instruments sounding something like clarinets).

bright hard-shell texture like Chinese porcelain, is it transparent texture like Bach, Debussy and Chopin, or muddy texture like —— and ——?[1]

Music seems almost to have a 'surface', a smooth surface, a grained surface, a prickly surface to the ear. All these distinguishing characteristics (roughly hinted at in the above silly similes) are to me the 'body of music,' are to music what 'looks,' skin, hair are in a person, the actual stuff and manifestation whereby we know it and recognize it— 'though is there more behind' (as Chevy Chase has it). Rightly or wrongly, a composer stands or falls by his 'texture' as far as I am concerned. Is not the beauty of Chopin two-thirds texture? That means to me that he is an essentially *musical* musician, the sort of musician I would like to be. I would know Chopin's greatness by two or three chords out of any of his pieces, just the mere distribution of notes proclaims his sensitive ear, his individual choice of sonorities.

Two or three chords at random from almost anything of C. Scott's[2] would convince me of the presence of an *exquisitive creative* musician, a few chords (torn from their fellows before and behind) out of Delius's Seadrift or Dance Rhapsody would bring me into the presence of one of the most transcendental geniuses of all time.[3] Bach's texture is as fresh today as it ever was, baffling, supreme. Fine, personal texture never ages, nor does even performance on another instrument destroy its individual message, as a rule! This is a long subject, however! As I see myself, if anything in my art is of any worth, means anything, then it is my texture. By it I would like to stand or fall. Folk say my 'Irish Tune from County Derry' is poetic or sad; 'Molly on the Shore' is merry, folk talk of my 'vitality.' All that may be true. I cannot judge of such things. To me the question [is] 'How does such a chord, such a passage tickle, or grate upon, or smooth out my ear when I listen? How do the ant-like armies of polyphonous parts move as they go about their business? Can one trace their paths, or are their movements hid in fog? Do their movements jostle and rub and irritate one another (I love my parts to jostle and rub and irritate) or do they glow together (like glorious passages in Wagner and Brahms) or do they flow sweetly harmoniously, yet somewhat tamely side by side as in Mendelssohn (whom I dearly love)?'

We hear of perpendicularists (Grieg, Debussy, Scott, Delius) and of

---

[1] These exx. were omitted.   [2] See Biographical Register.
[3] *Sea Drift* (1903–4), *Dance Rhapsody* No. 1 (1908). Grainger would transcribe the latter for two pianos in 1922.

horizontalists (Strauss, Schönberg, etc). I believe that any originality that may exist in my 'texture' can be brought home to the particular blend of horizontal and perpendicular that has always been my fate from my earliest childhood's composing beginnings. The whole life-giving element in my music comes from the *flow of my parts* (rather than from my melodic invention or my rhythmic impulses as some believe) but my critical influence is always applied horizontally. My chords grow out of the moving paths of my polyphony, but I listen to the result as a *chordal result* rather than as a *polyphonous result.* I would not tolerate good part-writing that did not produce the particular *harmonic* color I want at each moment, nor would I for long be satisfied with successions of chords that *did not arise* out of *wandering parts.* When my part-writing produces dischords and collisions it is not because my mind is so centered on polyphony that I ignore the harmonic result; on the contrary, I instinctively choose part-writing that will result in a *harmonic clash*, because that is what my ear yearns for, and yearns for *harmonically.*

Delius and C. Scott are two of the most subtle and marvelous per-pendicularists I know, and they get their precious results by thinking *chiefly* (not always of course) on chords. Strauss gets some of his most magnificent sweeping swirling effects by thinking from left to right and ignoring the up and down results. Think of the opening of Helden-leben!

Well, I think my special style, if I have any, arises out of having a craze for part-writing that is always gadding about like traffic at Hyde Park Corner, combined with an ear which is only critical *perpendicularly.* In other words, I like a musical Hyde Park corner traffic but I enjoy each moment for its momentary proportions, for the patterns created by the movements rather than I enjoy following the continued path of any particular vehicle.

I don't especially value 'originality' in art, as I consider the commu-nal development of folksongs is no whit inferior to the original achieve-ments of a great outstanding 'original' genius. It is the *universal* that pulls me in all matters and I am more thrilled by those points that all people have in common than in the special achievement and special-nesses of individuals. Nowadays, an artist has to be 'very artistic' (very untaught, very free, very rebellious) because modern life constantly tries to make a mental and moral slave of everybody, and because the artist sees on all hands the bulk of humanity submitting to utterly needless and useless drudgery and servility, and wishes to avoid this anti-art at all costs. But I would like all men and women to be free in mind and body, which would mean that they would all of them be artists, and I would like art to be largely a communal shared activity. For instance, I would love to write a work jointly with C. Scott and hope I shall some day. He has much that I lack, I have much he lacks. Later on, I hope to publish my sketch books with free permission to anyone to use my themes, chords, ideas, etc. I should like to see every man tinkering with every other man's art; what kaleidoscopic multitudinous results we should see! I enclose a musical example or two giving typical instances of my ½ horizontal ½ perpendicular polyphonic chord-style. No one has written of my texture yet, or of the relation between chordishness and many-voicedness in my stuff. I shall also be sending you other matter. If any of the information in this letter seems usable to you in an article on me, please use it, either as a statement of fact without referring to me, or by quoting me, whichever you prefer.

All heartiest greetings and best wishes,
from,
Yours cordially,[1]

6   *To Robin Legge*

[The United States joined the war on 6 April 1917. On 12 April Robin Legge wrote a 'final letter' to Grainger, accusing him of avoiding his patriotic duty and alerting him to the very strong feelings in Britain towards 'those who pitted a paltry £.s.d. against the blood of their contemporaries'.]

May 6, 1917

It is indeed a cruel blow to receive so harsh a letter as yours of April 12th from one who has been to me so true a friend as you have been; from one to whom I shall never cease to be deeply grateful.

Yet I do not wonder that you feel harshly towards me when I think of that Philadelphia interview, so utterly unrepresentative of my real thoughts and feelings, so fatal in its nauseating flippancy; so *terrible* to me in *every* way.[2]

---

[1] As with so many of the copies Grainger himself made of his letters to others, this letter copy was unsigned.

[2] This interview, with Constance Drexel, had appeared in the *Public Ledger* of Philadelphia on 31 Jan. 1917, under the title 'Percy Grainger holds life too dear to lose in battle: Rebels at

You may ask why I did not promptly write and repudiate it, instead of preferring to let it sink into the oblivion it deserves. My reasons for not doing so were these: As a pacifist (in every sense) I do not desire to stir up strife of any kind, nor attempt to 'right' myself at the expense of others. But chiefly because I consider myself partly guilty of the failure of that interview to voice my true feelings, and in the following manner: As you know, it is a great problem for a continually-interviewed artist to avoid sometimes being misleadingly quoted, and I have hitherto tried to overcome this danger by preparing, in the case of interviewers unknown to me, a little paper stating the subjects to be mentioned, and a rough, but guiding, outline of my views on those subjects. In Philadelphia, however, I had only a few minutes before catching a train, and unwisely (as it proved) abandoned my usual precautions & just spoke a few words with the young lady without giving her any written guidance.

As I no longer subscribe to any American press cutting bureau, I did not see the interview until some weeks after its appearance and would probably not have seen it then had not a lady in Philadelphia enclosed it in a letter to me. It was a terrible moment to read those horrible and ridiculous words as coming from my lips—a real tragedy to me.[1]

You ask under which flag I propose to sail. I wish to become an American citizen as soon as a sufficient length of residence in this country enables me to be one, having taken out very first papers 'declaring my intentions' of becoming a United States citizen during the summer of 1915.[2]

I wish to become an American because I admire and revere the spirit of this country and people more than any words can tell, and because I wish to live my life here.[3] Though I felt an immediate impulse to live my life in America shortly after our arrival here in 1914, I did not take the first step towards becoming naturalized before I had

thought of spending years for career and then having it cut short by Britain's foes'. Grainger's most contentious reported statement appeared in the article's first paragraph: 'Let those who don't like life and want to be killed, go'.

[1] In his reply of 31 May 1917 Legge wrote that he had discussed Grainger's position with several friends and still found him guilty of 'being willing to benefit in everything you most value by sacrifices you are unwilling to share'.

[2] Grainger's formal registration of intention to become a US citizen was dated 7 July 1915.

[3] Grainger took formal steps for naturalization in June 1917, and was received as an American citizen one year later, on 3 June 1918. By the time of the Second World War Grainger was reviewing his residency and citizenship. In a letter of 12 Nov. 1944 he wrote to his wife Ella Grainger of various eventualities 'if I become an Australian again', but he did remain an American citizen and resident, although never gave up public claim to being an Australian.

been here nearly a year, as I did not wish to 'declare my intentions' without the absolute conviction that such a step was dictated by the deepest and truest promptings of my moral, emotional and artistic life.

For a time my mother, although loving this Country from the first, could not quite reconcile herself to the thought of my ceasing to be an Australian, as she cherished hopes of our again settling in our native land. But our stay here has, I rejoice to say, gradually influenced her to my way of thinking.[1]

In wishing to become an American I do not love Australia less, its incomparable scenery, its glorious ultra-democraticness, its myriad nature appeals to me. It is because I am such an ultra-democratic, ultra Colonial Australian, I think, that I find in America such intense satisfaction, such a realisation of my inborn ideals. I am filled with ecstacy at the thought of wonderful parent Britain, bearing within itself (centuries ago no less than today) a new message of freedom and toler-ance for the whole world, flowing forth in streams of colonisation to all these American, Australian and African lands, in all lands taking the risks of new experiments, new independantnesses, and in each land carrying the original British ideals to new and *always individualistic* blos-somings.

It is, for me, proof of the innate unconquerable greatness of the des-tiny of the British breed, proof of its divine mission to humanity that America became what it is, and that in Australia, New Zealand etc., everywhere new types, *new attitudes*, constantly arise.

An exaggerated Anglosaxon like myself might reasonably see in Gr. Britain the most intense realization of his personal Anglosaxon ideals, or he might see it in America, or Australia, Africa, etc. Personally, *I happen* to *see it in America*, because tolerance is, for me, the key-note of Anglosaxon freedom and idealism, & because the Americans seem to me the most tolerant, most expansive, most gentle, most generous, most trustful, most peace-loving, most unprovocative people I have yet come in contact with. Their wonderful cosmopolitanism (in no way accompanied by any weakness of their own moral concepts) & *inborn pacific gifts, instincts and aims* (before & during war, & in their avowed war-aims) are, for me, *personally* the most touching and glorious vindi-cation of the entire Anglosaxon race I can imagine.[2]

[1] Rose Grainger, too, became an American citizen, in 1920.
[2] In his reply Legge asked, 'are you so sure that American feeling will not be somewhat different after the war than before? *Closeness* to the war makes a mountain of difference in our mental attitudes'.

The pacific instincts I allude to are not shown merely in political creeds, but equally in the affairs of every-day life, in the treatment of foreigners, in business dealings, in a thousand sweet & friendly brotherly manifestations.

Not every Australian, no doubt, would see his Australian ideals realised in America to the same degree that I do. Personal temperament, & the accident of associations make me unusually likely to feel myself 'at home' here. It was largely American songs that my mother sang to me as a child, 'Saint Nicholas' was the child's book I read,[1] & later it [was] Walt Whitman who influenced my philosophy most, though, of course, Kipling, Mark Twain, folk-literature, & Scandinavian literature all were strong influences in their way.

But W. Whitman was certainly my strongest single influence, bringing me, as he did, to Christianity & Oriental philosophy and I imagine it was his wondrous and complete embodiment of everything most spiritual and mystical in this strangely spiritual & mystical race that made me a ready-made American before I even thought of coming here.

To me Christianity is no light matter; not a thing one can half feel, half endorse, half follow. I cannot, personally, reconcile Christianity with any form of strife or hatred, & though I revere and admire from the depths of my being those noble and heroic men who sacrifice all & go forth & fight when their consciences bid them do so, I cannot hide the fact that my personal individual conscience, as a Christian, forbids me to fight, just as conclusively as it bids me throw any talents I may possess with all possible intensity into the task of alleviating as much as I can of the suffering caused by the war.[2] It is to this end that I have set aside, for the time being, all composing, all 'art for art's sake', & have arranged all my pianistic concert works with the view of serving the Allied Red Cross & War Relief funds, giving concerts for specific objects, & apart from that turning over to such funds my entire concert earnings, except such sums as are necessary for the living expenses of my mother, father & self, & for the carrying on of my tours. I feel this to be 'my bit', the work that my talents, temperament & conscience enable me to do best, & which I therefore hope I may be per-

---

[1] The *Saint Nicholas* magazine for children was published between 1873 and 1939.

[2] Legge's reply asked: 'If, again, as a peace-loving Xtian, you feel bound to take no active part in the war, are you not therefore bound also to wish that everyone else is equally clear-sighted and conscientious, and so impelled to take your cause? If this be true, what becomes of all "the original British ideals" and "always individualistic blossomings"??' For an alternative view of Grainger's own stand towards Christianity, see letter **53**.

mitted to continue. In Canada alone I have 20 concerts pending from which I shall be able to hand over to Canadian Red Cross a really substantial sum, while the amazing prosperity of the United States & the vast scale of its concert life seems to me to make my activities along these lines more efficacious here than they could possibly be elsewhere at the present moment.

For me this war is one of *conscience* against *force*. And I cannot see how any member of the British Empire or of America can remain inwardly true to the cause we all espouse unless his religious & moral conscience remains his guide.

Great Britain, Australia, America & Canada, all seem to me to *recognize this fully* in their war measures (as far as I know & understand them), thereby, it seems to me, taking a typical Anglosaxon stand before the rest of the world, & remaining true to the individualistic ideals that have been fostered in us from baby-hood, whether we grew up in Australia, England, America, Canada or Africa; for, deserting the imperious dictates of conscience *I know not how we should fare; I know not how we should still remain real Britons, Colonials, Americans.*

P.S. Will you not help me in what I feel to be my present duty? If, in your heart, you love me still, as I do you, I am sure you will. Will you not give the enclosed fifty pounds (£50.0.0.), for which I enclose draft, to whatever war charity you think to be in most need of it; not, however, to the British Women's Hospital, as I am already dealing with them direct?[1]

If, in memory of our old friendship, you would do this for me from time to time, I could send you further cheques as my concert receipts come in & I can afford to.

7   *To Rose Grainger*

[The pressure grew for Grainger to enlist. In June 1917, after investigating joining the Canadian forces, he quietly enlisted in the 15th Band, Coast Artillery Corps, of the US Army. By the end of the war he had reached the rank of Assistant Band Leader.]

The mosquitos are no less imødekommende[2] than the bandsmen!

---

[1] Legge sent on the cheque to the Belgravia Workrooms, run by his wife, where splints were made for the wounded.
[2] = obliging (Danish).

Fort Totten, LI | June 12, 1917 | 8.p.m.

My dearest darling

A new life has begun, a nightmare removed. You can guess I was glad when the doctor told me I had passed the physical test, & when I was sworn in.

You should address letters

George P. Grainger
Private
15th Band. C.A.C.
Fort Totten. Long Island.

Meals are fine. Each man has his own pewter mug, plate, & dish, which he keeps always, & washes up himself when he is thru with the meal. It all suits me down to the ground. I shall sleep in a big airy room with 12 others tonight.

Have already had my 1st lesson in the oboe from a charming Spaniard Comulado who unluckily leaves tomorrow to form the Sandy Hook band. I shall not find the oboe especially hard, I think. One of the Danes knows my name as a pianist from Denmark, was born in Frederikshavn, Jylland,[1] & lived in Aalborg, knows Svinkløv,[2] & read of my new work at Norfolk,[3] last week.

My sergeant is a nice kind refined good looking man, not a trace of coarseness that I see yet. Resta is a good & graceful conductor, very Italian, full of fine contrasts.[4] Real hospitality most of the men have shown to me, fetching plates, bread, lending me washup towels. It is assuredly not in the poorer classes than one finds the hardness & coldness of life. Perhaps in a place like this one would learn better to understand a Walt Whitmanish love of humanity, not an abstract, but a personal enjoyable love of public humanity. Everything is public here, even the rears have no doors! No shades to the windows, only blinds, & breezes, real breezes, blowing thru all the time.

I long for the time when I can blow my oboe well enough to play in the band.

Perhaps I shall become a real musician after all. Dear one, so sweet

[1] Jutland.
[2] Village in NW Jutland, well known to Grainger through holidays there in 1904–12 with Karen Holten.
[3] *The Warriors* (1913–16), 'Music to an imaginary ballet', had been premièred at the Norfolk Festival on 7 June, conducted by Grainger.
[4] Rocco (Robert) Resta, Italian-born American conductor, brother of Francis E. Resta (see Biographical Register). See plate No. 7. Rocco Resta continued to conduct Army bands into the 1930s, and later also directed municipal orchestras in Long Beach and San Pedro, California, where Grainger occasionally performed with him.

to get yr wire tonight. Please thank dear Lotta for all her goodness.[1] Without her monetary support of you I would not have been able to get on. When the programs of June 23 are out send me a few so I can try & get off for it, ditto June 30. My own poppinjay. I do not say anything of you & yr feelings but I think the more. Yr grateful

Percy

8   *To Rose Grainger*

[Many of Grainger's letters to his mother were more statements of opinion for posterity than personal communications of the moment. In later years his wife Ella was also to receive (and complain at receiving) such 'Museum letters'. This letter, written two months after Grainger's discharge from the army, was his most comprehensive statement to date of his racial views, in particular 'Anglosaxonism'. His mother felt no need to reply.]

Lewiston-Waterville[2] | Wednesday morn | 8.30
[12 March 1919]

Luggage is really quite a problem on these smaller town trips in US, just as it was in Australia. There is no such thing as a porter on any of the stations, neither at Boston when I arrived yesterday morning, nor at Portland where I changed trains, nor at Lewiston. Not that I care, only I'm glad my suitcases are light & easy to handle.

I am looking forward very much to reading you some of 'Frŭ Danmark',[3] about which I have been thinking since I left. After all, it is very worth reading, & what he seems to omit to say at one place he says in another. And then, of course, there is this absolute chasm between Anglosaxon thinking & Scandinavian thinking, & no book, presenting the North *to Anglosaxon readers* would be fulfilling its object unless it made this chasm most clearly felt. It really is true that a great deal of the spirituality that a Britisher looks for in life is lacking in Denmark, but I ask myself: is it not *only the combative side* of spirituality that is missing, the combat between the ideas of good & evil, the combat between desire & morality, the combat between man's stallionishness & woman's

---

[1] Mrs Lotta Mills Hough (Mrs Williston Hough), American pianist, and Grainger's girlfriend from 1917 to 1922. She acted as assistant to Grainger during his earlier years of teaching the piano at the Chicago Musical College.

[2] In Maine.

[3] By the Anglo-Irish writer Shaw Desmond (1877–1960). The book appeared in Danish in 1917 and in English during the following year under the title *The Soul of Denmark*.

shy-mare-ishness, the combat between Danishness & the outer world. Desmond makes it quite clear that all these combativenesses are absent in Denmark, & also adds 'The Dane is the only true pacifist in Europe'. Why is this, & why are the following facts as they are: the Englishman loves the idea of freedom as much as the Dane, yet in Denmark freedom is actual, in England only *a tendency*, very influential no doubt, but outside the realms of actuality. The Englishman is full of a doctrine of restraint, yet in practice (under stress) he is unrestrained & unaccountable, while the Dane is actually restrained & reasonable without having a doctrine about it. The Britisher believes in the idea of unionism (i.e. unity, & sacrifice of the individual for the whole) & compromise, but is only able to accomplish it in each individual life (almost each Englishman sacrifices his individual welfare, on every point, to consideration for 'society' & the world at large) never in larger amalgamations, never in communities or politics (the strong antagonisms between the various Protestant churches in England, between England & Ireland now, between England & America in the past, are instances).

I explain all this to myself as follows: With the possible exception of the Chinese, there has only appeared in the world one naturally restrained, instinctively freedomloving race—the Northern fair race of Scandinavia & the coasts of the North Sea (Friesland, the North German Coast, Jutland, etc). Probably an individualisticly operating sea-life, or life in a wideflung rather barren country such as Norway (where population is space, and each man & woman has to work & fend for themselves, & the gain from work is too frugal to permit the growth of a luxurious caste founded on slave labor) may have moulded the instincts of the Northern race in this manner. Let us not go into this. Enough to acknowledge that wherever the Northern race is found (whether in overweighing proportions as in Norway or Scotland, or in more blended proportion as in Ireland & England & Finland & the coast cities of Russia) we get, unmistakably, this tendency towards *naturally restrained individualism*; and we find this tendency *in no other race*. Every non-Northern race uses its power *when it has it*, quickly, every other race is restrained by circumstances rather than by the results of its own individual wisdom, every other race allows some spiritual, or superstitious, or religious, or moral *non-personal outside* influence to step in between the individual & *rationalness*. The old vikings believed in ghosts, but did not allow their superstitions to influence their actions, which were governed by *rationalness*. The French and Irish (both with an admixture of Northern blood) do not allow their Catholicism to govern them as do the Spaniards, the South Germans, the Italians, the Mexicans, etc. I think the lonely life of the ancient Northerner made him *an amateur*, made specialisation impossible. Each man had to be simultaneously warrior, cook, boatsman, poet, politician, priest. (We can read this in the actual lives portrayed in the sagas.) There could be no 'statisten (ciphers) unter ihre Pulte';[1] their life could not afford such luxuries. Consequently they could afford no 'girl-wives', no 'womanly women'. Every woman had to be a man when occasion demanded, just as the men had to be able to act womanly too, as often as not, & cook & sew, etc.

It would not have paid to keep their women in subjection, needing the masculine in them so often as they did; consequently they made equals of them very long ago, very long before the age of the first sagas or of the events they record. With this *sex inequality removed*, the corner stone of *general equality* was laid, for there is nothing that leads so readily to class inequality as sex-inequality. The woman, if regarded as inferior & weaker, must have slaves to wait upon her, thereby emphasising the power of the male (who provides the slaves thru his strength) as against the female (whose weakness acknowledges need of assistance), whereby the foundations of a slave society are reared. As each ancient Northerner was now cook, now poet, now warrior, now nurse, as occasion demanded, it could never 'fall him in'[2] to rate one trade or job much higher or lower than another. Did he not see, in his own personal life, the equal, or nearly equal, need for each?

Out of all this grew *instinctive restraint*, not restraint for fear of the law or for fear of his 'superiors', but a restraint emanating from the manysidedness of his personal life. The poet element in the old Northerner had to put a curb on itself in order to allow the cook element *its share*, or else the poet element would go unfed, etc, etc. Consequently all elements in the old Northerners tended to be developed, & *all tended to be restrained from within*, not from outside non personal influences, but from the operation of the many influences arising from a many-sided amateur non-specialising mode of life. Thus the whole life of the Northerner was a constant compromise (between the various parts of himself), a constant restraint so complete & untiring as to have become 2nd nature. In such human soil freedom & 'individualism' could run fecund riot without any danger of bolshevistic hatreds of one part for the other part. Minds so manysided operating in

---

[1] = lowly figures beneath their desks (German).
[2] Grainger is thinking of the Danish 'falde ham ind', meaning 'occur to him'.

43

natures so controlled faced no need for 'paternal' governments or 'paternal' religions. Just as specialisation breeds narrowminded skill so does amateurishness breed a kind of clumsy yet sagacious broadminded-ness proof to the 'putting-over' tactics of wiley priests & sly rulers. A man who can control himself as well as control the waves of the sea & the cows of his farm & the grazing of his pasture is no[t] an easy victim to king or church. He is apt to respect the spirit of the law while he turns his back on the letter of the law; for the law is mainly in his own heart & brain, fed by a manifold wisdom-evoking life of wide scope. Thus we find Anglosaxon England (several centuries before protes-tantism) calmly casting off Rome, at a time when English monks were in the forefront of European learning & of higher standing than most any-where. Thus we find drinking cups unstolen on the public roads thruout Anglosaxon England, because that same broad free Northern life did not stoop to bring forth the shrivelled undernourished mind of the petty thief. Thus we find in the sagas each littlest actor upon the stage of the story portrayed with *equal detail*, with *equal* concentration. Those tale-tellers knew that the whole was but a conglomeration of small separate parts, that the strength of the chain was its weakest link.

But the non-Northern parts of Europe knew none of these things with like clearness. Roman Catholicism could easily enslave the offspring of the celts & Latins & Greeks, from time long ago always submitting to priest rule & oracle superstition. Goths & Romans & Vandals & Huns swept in waves over each other, all of them grown up in schools of militarism, all of them *yielding as individuals*, all of them *merciless in the mass*, none of them naturally restrained, none of them breathing the sweet compromise of freedom, none of them following the *idea of equality*, wherein individuality has its health.

Therefore all religions that come from the South were moulded for mobs, not for individual men. They built their faith on the bible, yet the bible itself was withheld, forbidden. They sanctioned the horrible legal rape called marriage & punished with fire & death the individual choice of the North, called fornication & later 'free love'. Race, the natural consciousness-of-the-blood, that lovely fact, was blotted out in the bloodbaths of 'nationality', that artificial importation of non-Northern rulers, who could (trained in master-&-slave thought) never imagine an individualistic prosperity founded on work, but only a prosperity founded on conquest. That is the root of the whole matter; the whole Northern freedom is based on the idea of individualistic *work* (& this Desmond brings out well in his book, in treating of Danish sex equality) but differs therein from the modern German worship of work in that the German worships professional skill subordinated to the behests of a ruling intellectual class (whether it be professional or military, or the domination of modern 'masters' or of past masters such as Beethoven) while the northern instinct for freedom lays more emphasis on thought than on skill, more emphasis on individuality than on perfection of so-called 'form'.

To go back to the past: We know how Britain (even Ireland) was swamped by the Norman militarists, how Holland blood was mixed with the Catholic Spanish soldiery, we know how the Platt-German[1] became the underling of the High German-speaking Emperors & aristocrat-warriors & statesmen, so that no North-Sea Coast German soul can be said to have been able to raise its voice in Prussia even (until perhaps today in the case of the Spartacide sailors).[2] And we know how the Northerner in England fought the Norman barons & later the king under Cromwell, & the Norman Catholicism, & how the Anglosaxonised lowerdog has at all times held his own (but without substantial victory either way) against the Normanised upperdog in England. We know how the Northern-race Hollander fought for nearly a century against Spanish Catholicism, how even the Swede fought 30 years against Southern German Catholicism, tho *out of his own land*, which is a great difference. Only Denmark, Norway, Iceland & the Faeroes can be said to have been fairly free from this struggle of Northern individualism against Southern mob-religion, mob-morality, mob-militarism; & of these Denmark was, of course, the least free. Thus in Britain & in Holland & even in Germany the *longing for freedom* became *inseparable* from the *fight for freedom*, so that effortless unchallenged freedom no longer seemed to the Northern mind in those countries as the real MacCoy. Also the Britisher gradually fell a prey to the *idealism* (that is; mob-intellectualism) of the slavish Southerner & lost, thereby, his original Northern *interest in ideas*, which is quite a different thing. *Actual freedom* no longer attracted the Britisher as it had the pre-Norman Anglosaxon, because he never experienced it after the establishment of Norman-brought inequalities for one thing, & for another thing because he had lost his taste for actuality in his obsession by *ideals*, just as a drunkard can only imbibe nourish[ment] thru drink & loses his taste for real food. All this, & the continual wars that came

[1] The Low German dialect.
[2] The Communist (Sparticist) *putsch* had taken place in Berlin during 5–11 Jan. 1919. It was led by Karl Liebknecht and Rosa Luxemburg, who were subsequently shot.

with Normanism, turned the pacifistic Anglosaxon into a veritable fighting cock. Neither Norman nor Saxon would quit, & neither could win, with the result that neither race knew any longer what peace meant, or *could mean*. The enjoyment of woman gave place to the struggle for woman, the prosperity of work was swamped in the *struggle to possess the fruits* of work, the benefit to be derived from ideas was exchanged for 'the fight for one's ideals', the art of thinking was abandoned for the art of arguement, the art of agriculture was gradually superceded by a habit of colonisation that was half sword-hilt, half ploughshare. The Scandinavian love of non-combative sport (ski-ing, skating, swimming, bodily culture) was gradually Southernized into the combative & bloody bullbaiting, boxing, fox hunting, shooting, big game hunting, cockfighting, football, & the heartsdescise-producing [*sic*] sprinting, sculling, etc.

So that, finally, when we hear of 'Votes for Women', or 'Conscientious objectors' or the like in England it always settles down into some death-fraught violent blood-stained struggle such as hunger-strikes & forcible feeding in prisons, leaving the original idea-issue, & all its latent possibilities of good & betterments forgotten & far far away.[1] British *idealism* would not be so very much worse than *the appetite for ideas* if it were not so poisonously impregnated with the *idea of sacrifice*. All freedom loving, individualistic & self-restrained & compromise-actuated folk are inclined to distrust the passion for sacrifice, because they see in it mob-hysteria (like the Dervishes who gash & maim themselves) & the relic of druidism & of all that unintellectual Southern godfearingness that could imagine no benefit to mankind without some great ill demanded therefore in payment by some inhuman enslaving god. Christianity itself was never able to graft the idea of sacrifice upon the Scandinavian mind, because that mind had been too long steeped in *individualistic rationalism*. That is why the Scandinavian eshews mob-feeling or mobjudgement in moral & religious & emotional matters, yet is a *furious co-operative-ist* in economic matters, such as dairying & export, insurance, sanatoriums & stipendiums for art-study. He feels (like Yeats) that 'things are always the same under the hand', that money, & butter, & railways tickets & the need for hospital treatment are much the same whether one be a hater or lover of the church, or of sex, or of art. Therefore he considers cooperation *in material questions* a practical & fruitful thing, *in no wise hampering* his per-

---

[1] Reference to the British suffragettes, esp. Emmeline Pankhurst (1858–1928), who died in the year that the right to vote was finally extended to all adult British women.

sonal individuality of judging & feeling in the realms where he considers individualism at home; that is, the realms of feeling & thought. The Scandinavian resents any interference in his personal attitude towards sex, or morality, or nationality just [as] keenly as the Britisher resents any show of personal freedom in dealing with these same questions, because (for the Britisher, only very partially emerged from the tyrannic religious influence of the Catholic church, & hardly at all released from the 'King & Country' sway of his kings & barons) these questions fall within the realms over which mob-morality, mob-religiosity, & mob-vindictiveness still exercise full & dire control. Against this mob-tyranny only the idealistic blind instinct for self-sacrifice lifts its head, in its turn as hysterical, as irrational as the mob itself. Should an anti-militarist leave England during the war in order to carry on, from elsewhere, a campaign against conscription, the English would at once refute him with: 'Why does he not stay & face the music?' meaning, why does he not prove his sincerity & worth by the only qualities we are able to admire; *an act of selfsacrifice.* The English seem unable to understand that the way to further *an idea* is to stick to the idea & avoid being *lead away* from the idea itself & the calm exploitation of the idea by a vain commotion of conflict & selfsacrifice; they cannot understand that he who enters into a conflict with the enemies of an idea or who sacrifices himself on behalf of an idea is playing foolishly into the hands of the enemies of the idea he is fostering, for there is nothing more favorable to the enemies of an idea than that the promoters of the idea shall step aside from calm concentration upon the idea & its explanation into the turmoil of strife—for in strife all pure ideas get forgotten & selfsacrifice only advertises the *champion* of the idea, not the idea itself. The history of England is full of heroic personages & heroic sacrifices made for ideals, Chatham on Pitt dying on the floor of Parliament in the heat of the American problem,[1] men burned for translating the bible, picturesque poets dying of disappointment or drowning, & English hero after hero dies with mission unfulfilled, leaving a deathless life behind & an unregenerated unholpen race. The hero's duty is to *help the race*, not to die a sacrificial hero. What is heroic death, in most cases, but the lack of the strength needful to face life & actualities *victoriously for the idea one espouses?* Think of Sturla Sturlason. They tried to assassinate him some 14 times, yet

---

[1] Reference to J. S. Copley's painting of the collapse of the elder Pitt while addressing the House of Lords in 1778. Pitt only died some six weeks later, but Copley clearly based his representation on Benjamin West's painting of the death of General James Wolfe in Quebec.

he survived & managed to collect & put to paper the entire verse Edda & prose Heimskringla.[1] If there was 'sacrifice' in that life, it must have been on the part of his opponents! That somewhat staring expectancy that Desmond notes in the face of the young English girl & misses in the Danish girl, I'll tell you what it looks to me like: the expectation of sex *conquest* in the young Englishwoman, plus the hysteria & hardening-of-the-mental-arteries by mob-morality. She is torn at by natural life on the one side, but cannot respond, because she is pulled this way & that by prejudices & ambitions & prides that she would rather die than give up. She does not desire life itself, but a 'game' built upon life, a game in which the rules & nets & balks & bunkers & goals are all determined by book in advance. She does not mind losing life itself as long as she does not lose '*the game*' erected by her strange companions upon life, & she does not feel the loss of life because she has never seen it in its naked form, but only in its dished-up form in 'the game', which goes on all round & over & under her.

I assert, if what Desmond thinks is true spirituality (& what I consider to be mainly spiritual 'combativeness' without any clearly divined goal) in England really were so, we could not fail to notice it in the laws of the country, in the freedom from censorship, freedom from capital punishment, in the freedom of the marriage laws, in the freedom from Mrs Grundyism,[2] in the highminded tone of the international policy of the land, in the appreciation & carrying out of the ideas of the great men of the race, in the activity & effectiveness of the race in sport & commerce, science & art. If England is really more spiritual than Denmark, more imaginative, more religious & more temperamental, we ought to see England over 12 times as productive & successful as Denmark, the British Empire some 18 to 20 times more so, on a per capita basis. We would have to find 15 phoneticians to replace Jespersen,[3] 15 Thurens, 15 Evald Tang Kristensens, and so on. But it will be argued: A big country can not be pitted against a small on a per capita basis. If so, what is that, in this connection, but an admission that Denmark, because a small country, has a higher spiritual productivity? But I am going astray.

---

[1] *Edda* was a 13th-cent. Old Norse poetic manual written by the Icelandic chieftain Snorri Sturluson (1179–1241). He also wrote *Heimskringla*, a history of Norwegian kings.

[2] Conventional propriety and prudery, as represented in a character from Thomas Morton's *Speed the Plough* of 1798.

[3] Otto Jespersen (1860–1943), professor of English at Copenhagen from 1893 to 1925, a pioneering figure in linguistics and phonetics.

All I am seriously wishing to emphasize is this: that I see the 2 races as follows:

England: democratic & freedom loving in its instincts, but unable to realise these ideals (or its ideal of self-control) because of its obsession by the prejudices & mob-intellectuality of the Southern European mob-Empire-rule of the Middle Ages.

Denmark: democratic & freedom loving in its instincts like England, but able to realise these instincts in actual practice because its mental & moral training is along lines in harmony with the instinctive freedom of the race, & resulting in *individualism* in intellectual & emotional matters, & in *co-operation* in economic matters.

If we are pacifists it seems to me idle & wicked of us to judge results & achievements only from the taking of the belicose temperature of the race, regarding a high belicosity as high virtue.

I personally am a genuine pacifist as well as an avowed one, & really judge by results & not by the amount of heat expended in the pursuit of the result. To find poverty alleviated, to find folksongs rescued, to find sex a pleasure & not a tragedy, to find talent & genius plentiful & appreciated, to find sanatoriums & cooperative endeavors undertaken & *used*, to find experimental ideas tried out & carried *into effect*, to find books printed that could not be printed elsewhere, to find marriage early & divorce general, to find internationalism and accomplished fact in the face of a persistant racial note, to find dialects honored instead of sneered at, to find peace & selfcontrol & cunning & compromise in place of war & passion & simplicity & stubbornness;— these things are enough for me. I admire, & I try to acquire, to imitate, such qualities, such results. And I do not ask for *pride*, for *grace*, for *brilliance*, for *wit*, if I fear they will cost coldness & combativeness & a beclouding of the issues.

I think I am a survival of those Anglosaxon–Scandinavian preNorman British qualities that the foreign anti-Saxon aristocratic educational & religious systems have so systematically fought to destroy, but not wholly successfully, for they (the truly Northern qualities of mind) still abound in England itself, & on them the greater part of the British colonies & America is builded.

But tho many have felt truly Saxon & acted truly Saxon, I pride myself that few have sensed the *origin* & the *issue* of it all so cleanly, & so early in life, as I. Consequently few are able to stand so completely cured of the Norman disease as do I today. I consider that I stand as true a type of Northern thought & feeling as any Scandinavian, not because I am Scandinavianised, but because the original undiluted Anglosaxon has been gradually extricated from southern foreign stifling creeperlike growths. I do not espouse this Northernness out of racial or non-rational impulse. It is because I see in the selfcontrolled platonic rationalistic natureloving Northern type *the only line of thought* before us today that will lead us away from war, violence, cruelty, & the continuance of stifling injustices. But none of us are Northern enough, in any respect. The Northern outlook is young in its world-wide application, no empire, or cooperation of states has ever been formed on it yet, & since most of our culture & education & influences (religions & morals) are Southern, or Jewish or Oriental, we must be very jealous of its growth, very motherly in our fostering of its health. That is why I try to solve all my own problems along these Northern lines. That is why I do not wish to apply Southern abhorance & intolerance to my own sadism or to any aspect of life, but wish to accomidate all things along friendly lines, thru compromise, *by means of patience & untiring explanations* & unlimited literary openness & wholehogishness. I am sure there is *no force in nature we need to look askance at*, & I am sure that a spirit of patient compromise can meet each & every problem & difficulty, tho I am far from saying that patience & compromise are the only methods.

But I believe in them.

9   *To Rose Grainger*

Sept 1, 1920

Mother darling,

I shall ring you up from Lotta's but as the Schirmer news is confidential I dont want to tell it over the wire. They want me 'movied' while playing Country Gardens, Molly & Shepherd's Hey ('published by G. Schirmer' to appear on the film) & it will be used over the *whole country* as *weekly news*.[1] Isn't it grand? To make it interesting I'm going to feature my sustaining pedal action (have feet 'closed-up'ed), fist on black note chords, & glissando action. *They* want it to

---

[1] Black & white 16mm Schirmer publicity silent film. A copy is held in the Grainger Museum, Melbourne.

get a big sale on my pieces. Isnt America the jolliest business place?

Changed my shoes, had the wires in my teeth X rayed, etc, etc.

10   *To Frederick Delius*

[In early May 1921 Grainger and his mother settled in White Plains, a com-
muter suburb North-east of Manhattan. Despite a love-hate relationship with
their big, rambling house there, Grainger would retain 7 Cromwell Place as
his permanent address for the remaining forty years of his life. Soon after the
move Rose Grainger's health started a further stage of decline. Their friend
Delius, too, was suffering a physical decline, also brought on by syphilis,
which had caused his wife Jelka to have him admitted to a sanatorium in
Wiesbaden in January.]

Bellingham, Wash. | March 28, 1922.

Darling Frederick:

Most deeply distressed to hear from Balfour Gardiner that you are
having such a bad time, trouble with lameness etc. My heart goes out
to you in this matter and wishes you speedy recovery. You recovered
so well from your last trouble in 1912 or 1912 [*sic*], have been so
prolific since and given the world of arts so many immortal works that
I am hoping that you will soon have this trouble behind you also.
Nervouse troubles are terrible while they last. I have seen so much of
them and all the agony they cause but the recoveries I have seen from
the worst of them are remarkable and I wish this to be the case with
you dear friend and revered genius as I hardly need tell you. When
you are ill you must think of how much you mean to many of us and
how your noble and touching compositions stand out above the ruck
of the most talented work of the day as true greatness and depth
stands out from littleness and superfi[ci]ality; you must remember how
many souls you have touched to the core, how many Artists souls you
have gladdened and helped by your inspirations and how many hearts
you have wormed your way into to comfort them and to uphearten
them personally. You know that your art is as close and as personal to
me as my own art and life are and there are many like myself all over
the world that love you deeply for yourself and for your art and to
whom any suffering that falls upon you falls as a personal blow upon
them also.

If my dear Mother were with me now she would join me in all

51

these loving wishes but she is still very ill at home, though slightly better, and unable to join me in California as we had hoped. With the fondest of best wishes.

Your loving and admiring friend,

11   *To Rose Grainger*

> New Hotel Rosslyn, Los Angeles, Cal.
> Friday. early morn. [28 April 1922]

Mother dearie

How terrible all this new strain upon you whatever it is.[1] I am so so sorry. No wire from Lotta has come as my wires to you already have told you. Must leave for S. Barbara now but return early tomorrow. Have enquired 2ce at Western for Lotta's wire but nothing there yet, so it seems no use my getting you long distance before L's wire arrives.

In great distress,

> Lovingly
>> Percy

12   *To Rose Grainger*

> [Los Angeles, 29 April 1922]

REST EASY BELOVED MOTHER TRUST IN GOD & MY LOVE AM WIRING DEAREST FRIEND BEGGING HER FORGIVE WHATEVER IT WAS NO WIRE FROM HER MADE FULLEST INQUIRY LONGING CLASP YOU IN MY ARMS[2] CONCENTRATE ON RECOVERY DEVOTEDLY *PERCY*.

---

[1] The tensions had been mounting between Lotta Hough and Rose Grainger for some time. During the last days of Apr. 1922 Rose Grainger had been in a distraught state. In a torn-up letter which Grainger later reconstructed Rose Grainger had written: 'I asked L. over the phone if you had told her if I had any improper love for you. I didn't want to say this, and knew it was untrue, but couldn't help saying it . . . I have accused myself of something I have never thought of . . . I am insane.'

[2] Grainger later worried about this choice of words, in view of the circulating rumours of incest. Writing in his 'Anecdotes' during May 1954 he confided: 'It may be that those last words of mine seemed to her dangerous in view of the Blodskam rumor. Or it may be that sleeplessness, & the fear of going out of her mind & being a burden to me, drove her to suicide.'

13   *To Rose Grainger*

[This was the first of several letters Grainger wrote to his mother, which
arrived after her death. On its envelope he afterwards wrote 'Too late'.]

New Hotel Rosslyn, Los Angeles, Cal.
Ap. 29, 1922 | Saturday afternoon.

Beloved mother

Returning at noon from Santa Barbara today I found your wire
explaining Lotta's wire, which latter, however, has not arrived, tho I
made searching inquiry at the Central Western Union office. Beloved
mumsie, I can so readily understand how this terrible illness would
lead one to say 'unaccountable things' as you put it, especially after
being so long & cruelly tried by worries. We must realize that these
terrible thing come out of the illness itself & that the only way to cure
them is by *curing the illness*, thru rest, absence of worry, etc. But that is
well nigh impossible with worries at hand. I realize that so well, angel
mumsie, & just long to be back home again & try to take some of the
weight off you, dearie.

I know that to have said anything to hurt our dear friend must be a
special trial & added worry to my beloved mother, longing for my
happiness as she always does.

As far as humanly possible you must try to dismiss these worries &
pray to God for recovery & our future happiness—so dear to me.

We will go & stay wherever you like as long as you like, remember.[1]

Your adoring son,
Percy.

Much of yesterday (Friday) I spent with Mrs Koehler,[2] being the guest
of her friends at the wonderfully beautiful hotel shown on these cards.[3]
It is one of the most exquisite spots imaginable, the flowers, trees,
buildings all having the most entrancing tints, forms, textures. Mrs
Koehler has been doing painting lately & had one sketch with her that
was very lovely & had much the same beauty & distinction her jewelry
had. She is the charming creature she always was & a true artist. She

[1] Grainger had written frequently in his letters to his mother in the past months that he
intended to take a year off performing and to accompany her on a rest-cure abroad.
[2] Florence Koehler (1861–1944), American painter, jeweller, and amateur pianist, whom the
Graingers had known well during the second half of their years in London.
[3] The Samarkand, Persian Hotel, in Santa Barbara. This continuation of the letter was written
on the back of three different picture postcards of the hotel.

sent you the most loving wishes & sympathy having suffered herself (during the past few years) so acutely from *spinal* trouble & nervous prostration.

The evening meal I took with the Dielmans (Susan Herter that was). The husband seems greatly improved, paints portraits with a look of 'likeness' to them, & I saw one of their 3 children, a dear.

They also sent all sorts of loving messages to you. How I wish you & I could be quietly in Hotel Samarkand for some weeks or months.

Lovingly,

Percy

14　　　　　　　　　*To Rose Grainger*

New Hotel Rosslyn, Los Angeles, Cal. | Sunday Ap. 30, 1922

Dearest mother

Got wire this morning from Lotta saying that she had not wired at all & that I will understand when I come. I shall know no peace till I reach you & hold you in my arms, mother darling; the thought of these intervening days is a real torment.

Let us be full of faith & love & unity, that is the cure for all. From next Saturday on (when I arrive White Plains at about noon) we will have no more long terrible partings & everything will be easier & better for us both. I feel *sure* I can help you to get well *much much* quicker when I am with you. And everything hinges on that. All these problems will be smooth when you are stronger again, dearie. You will see. I played Pasadena last night.[1] Huge audience & great enthusiasm. Motored there with the Moodies.[2]

Today conduct the orchestra & tomorrow afternoon (Monday) wind up in Hollywood.

This is the last letter can reach you ere my return. Let us have deep faith & love, mumsie darling, pray from our hearts, & we will yet weather all things side by side.

Yr deeply adoring son

Percy

[1] Grainger had played before the Pasadena Music and Art Association in the Pasadena High School Auditorium.

[2] Earl and Elsie Moody, son-in-law and daughter of Grainger's agent in Los Angeles, L. E. Behymer.

15   *To Balfour Gardiner*

In train, California to New York, May 3, 1922

Darling Balfour,

My poor darling mother died last Sunday, fell, or threw herself, from an 18 story window in New York City. I heard of her death just after conducting, last Sunday, but not the details. The details I read, *accidentally*, in a local newspaper here on my journey.[1] She had long been worried about losing her mind, as a result of her long nervous illness.[2] The day of my New York Recital (Feb 11) her mind was wandering for a time, but soon got better. Her last letters were so hopeful, tho weak, but her last wire to me distressed about nervous condition. When I meet Mrs Sawyer, my manager, from whose office she fell, I shall know more.[3] In the meantime, I find it hard to bear the strain. My heart & head alarm me & I wonder if I can live thru it all. I *want* to come thru *so badly*, for I am all in life that remains of my beloved mother, & I wish to live so as to make her as sweetly remembered as possible

1 because of her unusual intensity of mother-love (I shall write her life)

2 how, thru her love of art & innate critical sense, she made me the first great composer of Australia

3 to show how terribly she struggled & suffered all her life (as none but I know), the intensity of the fight for my goodness she put up.[4]

But to be able to do all that I must live many years longer & *prove myself* (as well as hint towards) the great artist & generous man she planned me, from the 1st, to be. But should my body break under this strain, then I must rely on you *doing all you can* to have my unpublished works published in the right way.

---

[1] The news was prominently featured in many of the nation's papers. The *New York Times* ran the story on its front page under the title 'Grainger's mother is killed by fall'. Following subtitles read 'Director of noted pianist's career plunges from 18th-story window of Aeolian Hall; CRUMPLES ON ROOF BELOW; skull crushed, she dies soon—suffered from old injury—son hurrying here'.

[2] In another unsent letter to her son, of 29 Apr., Rose Grainger had written: 'Every day gets worse—I am sorry—I have loved you and so many others so dearly. Your poor insane mother.'

[3] For Sawyer's account of Rose Grainger's death see her *Songs at Twilight* (New York: Devin-Adair, n.d.), 136–42.

[4] In 1923 Grainger privately published his volume of homage, *Photos of Rose Grainger and of 3 short accounts of her life by herself, in her own hand-writing*. The title-page acknowledged the volume as being 'reproduced for her kin and friends by her adoring son Percy Grainger'. It also contained statements of her 'strongest esthetic impressions' and 'cultural tastes'.

I forget whether our last wills make any provisions for my money to go to you in order that you may publish my works. So all I can do, before reaching home, is to give you a blank check on the bank where I think most of my money is. Draw *all* that is in that bank & use it on my compositions (publishing). The Bank Manager's name is Mr Paul Cooley & the Bank is

The Mechanics & Metals National Bank
Corner 60th Street & Madison Ave
New York City.

Of course I would like *all* my moneys, belongings, royalties, bonds, interests, life insurances, etc turned over to you (for publication expenses) but do not see how I can do that legally while in this train— & I am writing this in case of a breakdown of my forces en route. If thru this letter you could induce my monies, belongings, etc, to be turned over to you, that is what I would wish.[1]

The manuscripts (music, etc) to be published will be found

1   In a bankbox in *the County Trust Co* at White Plains, New York
2   In mother's (smaller) bankbox at home in 7 Cromwell Place, White Plains
3   In a strongbox in our White Plains home
4   Strewn around in the music room on pianos, in drawers & in the loft (attic) at White Plains home.

I would like all that is decipherable in my sketchbooks published & all that is mentioned in a manuscript I wrote on entering the army, which will be found with my music M.M.S. entitled '*What to do with them*'. Some 15 to 20 Duo art rolls (played on entering army) of mostly unwritten-down things should be noted down & published.[2] These include 'Tjindundi Biðil' & other Færösk songs, Seven men from all the world, Room-Music 'Warriors' slow movement (a work partly based on 'Warriors' ideas—perhaps called 'Lullaby'),[3] Foster's 'Old Black Joe', Dorset tune (played by *mother* & *me*), accompaniments to British Folksongs, etc. An index, covering these works, will be found elsewhere & is very important. By the way, in 'What to do with them' the description of 'Death Song for Hjalmar Thuren' is the most poetic

---

[1] On 21 June 1922 Grainger did make a new will. In it he left $5,000 to his aunt Clara Aldridge and the residue of the estate to Gardiner. In the event of Gardiner's predeceasing him, the estate passed to Cyril Scott; in the event of Scott's prior death, it passed to Willy Strecker of Schott (now Mainz).

[2] These rolls are held in the Grainger Museum, Melbourne. They were made between 22 and 28 Feb. 1918, at a time when Grainger was expecting to be sent with the band to France.

[3] This *Warriors* version used some materials taken from Grainger's *Bridal Lullaby* (1916–17).

literature I have written. (Is it in Index to large Green sketchbook?) You understand the general need of bringing out everything, all kinds of sketches, unfinished works, etc, that, together, could place me a[s] Australia's 1st great composer & make Australia & *my mother's name shine bright*. Apart from that, however, I want to give you a list of the works to be concentrated upon *first*, because of their importance or ready condition. They are as follows:

1 All the works you have photocopies of.

2 Danny Deever (get special permission from Dr Walter Damrosch[1] for copyright, if need be)

3 Kiplings settings: 'Anchor Song', 'Widows Party', 'Running of Shindand', 'Hunting Song of the Seeonee Pack', all sent recently to Volkert, Schott & Co.[2]

4 2 piano arrang. of Delius 'Dance Rhapsody' (ask Mr Fred. Morse,[3] C/O Antonia Sawyer, Aeolian Hall, New York City, for M.S. & photocopies of this) to be sent to Dr Hertzka, Universal Edition, Vienna[4]

5 'The Warriors' Score & parts (including 3rd piano to replace or support the unusual percussion insts)

6 'The Warriors', dished up for 2 pianos, 6 hands.

7 Hillsong I, latest score for 22 insts, finished Dec 1921.

8 Hillsong II, Percy Hall—Percy St version,[5] in Green binding.

9 English Dance (done at yr concerts) dished up for 2 pianos, 6 hands

10 "   " for orchestra (same as above) full score

11 Green Bushes for 21 insts (finished early 1921) *compressed* score & parts, all together in black 'Mappe'[6] (folder?) in Music room. The alterations *in the parts* are correct. The compressed score should be altered accordingly.

12 Full score & parts of 'Bride's Tragedy' (ask Mr Fred. Morse for these)

---

[1] (1862–1950), conductor associated with the New York Symphony Society for some five decades from the 1880s. He and his brother Frank (1859–1937) were among Grainger's earliest supporters in New York.

[2] Charles G. J. Volkert (1854–1929), managing director of Grainger's London publisher, Schott & Co., from 1887 until his death.

[3] Grainger's secretary, and husband of Grainger's concert agent from 1925, Antonia Morse.

[4] Emil Hertzka (1869–1932), Universal Edition's managing director from 1907 until his death. Grainger had made this transcription (for two pianos, four hands) early in the spring of 1922.

[5] The 1907 version of the shorter Hill-Song No. 2 was tried out at this Tottenham Court Road venue in London on 4 May 1911. Grainger considered it better than his latter version of 1911–12.

[6] = portfolio, file (Danish).

13 Full score & parts of 'March. Song of Democracy'. G. Schirmer, Inc. has them.

14 Full score & parts of 'Merry Wedding'. Oliver Ditson Co, Boston, has them.

15 My corrected *score & parts* of 'Colonial Song', for orchestra & 2 voices (or orch. alone) is better than printed version. These alterations should come into published version.

16 '*The Power of Rome & the Christian Heart*' sketches. Expressing feelings about the tragedy of the war, conscientious objectors, the iron heel of the State ('The State is the chilliest of all cold monsters' Niet[z]sche), the poor trodden on individual heart— feelings felt by *both mother & me.*

17 'Tribute to Foster' sketch, chorus, solo voices, orchestra, glasses, etc. Important record of memory of mother, love for her.[1]

18 Death Song for Hjalmar Thuren sketches & abovementioned Erläuterung[2] of same—perhaps in 'Index to (big green?) sketchbook'.

19 Decipherings of (5?) Rarotongan partsongs. These should be compared with my phonograph records of same

20 200 English folksongs & shanties in M.S. In Tyndale cabinet upstairs, White Pl. home. Should be published complete as they are. In some cases the versions in Folksong Journal 12 are the more later corrected, I believe(?).[3]

21 As many Kipling settings as possible including 'Rhyme of the 3 sealers' sketches, 'Merchantmen', & particularly chamber scorings of 'Mowglis song against people', & 'the fall of the stone'.

22 'Bold William Taylor' for voice, concertina (or reed organ) strings, 2 clars.

23 'Shallow Brown' using pencil indications in score for entries of guitars & ukeleles, piano, strings, etc. String parts also, & ask Mrs Williston Hough (517 West 113 St, NYC) & Mr Ralph Leopold[4] (NYC) re same.

24 'The twa corbies' voice & 7 strings. Publish voice & piano version also.

[1] In programme notes for this work Grainger commented: 'One of my earliest musical recollections is that of my mother singing me to sleep with Stephen Foster's song *Camptown Races (Doodah).*'

[2] = explanation (German).

[3] 'Collecting with the Phonograph—The Old Singers and the New Method', *Journal of the Folk-Song Society*, 3/12 (1908–9), 147–242.

[4] (1883–1955), New York pianist, with whom Grainger collaborated in several recitals and recordings.

25 Sketch for 'Sea Songs' style or 'Grettir the Strong' Overture (only a few bars) which I hope to send you tomorrow. This is indication of 'beatless music' or material to be used for experimenting towards same. Very important.[1]

26 'Random Round'[2] ask Roger Quilter to help explain these parts (no score) *also study quotation* of 'R. R.' in my article 'The Impress of Personality in unwritten Music' (Schirmers 'Musical Quarterly', 1914 or 1915)

27 Publish together my article[s] on:
Cyril Scott (The Music Student?)[3]
The Impress of Personality etc.
The Value of Natalie Curtis's transcriptions of Negro folk-music[4]
Richard Strauss: seer & idealist.[5]
Glimpses of Genius (The Etude, Philadelphia)[6]
Sketches on 'Nordic Characteristics in Music'[7] (Mrs Williston Hough has these & others) etc
The Value of Icelandic to an Anglosaxon (here my racial & political attitude is clearest summed up)[8] etc.
Diary (1907) while at Griegs home[9]

28 All artistic & other letters to you, Cyril, R. Quilter, Herman Sandby,[10] etc

29 All very intimate letters or notes should be deposited in an Australian Grainger Museum, preferably in birth-town Melbourne

30 Mother's ashes & mine (both cremated) to be placed beside her mother's in cemetery (which?) in Adelaide South Australia. Apply to my mother's sister
Miss Clara Aldridge[11]
'Claremont'
East Parade
North Kensington, Adelaide, S. Australia

---

[1] Three weeks later, on 26 May 1922, Grainger did work on a new version of this 'beatless' music, originally formulated in 1907.

[2] Composed in *c.*1912–14, with flexible scoring, this work was 'an experiment in concerted partial improvisation' based on the practice of Rarotongan part-songs.

[3] *Music Student*, 5/2 (Oct. 1912), 31–3.   [4] *New York Times Book Review*, 14 Apr. 1918.

[5] In Henry T. Finck, *Richard Strauss: The Man and his Works* (Boston: Little, Brown & Co., 1917), pp. xvii–xxv.

[6] *Etude*, 39/10 (Oct. 1921), 631–2 and 39/11 (Nov. 1921), 707–8.

[7] Sketches for a lecture given at Yale University on 6 Mar. 1921.

[8] Published, in Icelandic, in the Winnipeg journal *Timarit*, 2 (1920), 60–8.

[9] Held in Grainger Museum, Melbourne.

[10] See Biographical Register.   [11] See Biographical Register.

31 Could plot of ground (owned by me) next to White Plains home be used for building small *fireproof* Grainger Museum?[1]

  If so, place there Grieg's watch, Grieg mementos, mother's collection of Scand. & Tartar Embroideries, scarfs, some of her most characteristic clothes, my collection of beadwork & native art, my toweldresses & army uniforms.

32 In concert performances, try to establish me *first* by
  Hillsongs I & II
  The Warriors
  Bush Music sketch
  March. Song of Democracy
  Green Bushes
  by 2 piano dish-ups of my works

33 sketches for 'Room music Warriors work' or 'Slow movement Warriors work.' Mrs Williston Hough has very valuable sketches for this (one of my lov[e]liest works), others at Wh. Pls home.

I hate to burden you with all this. Know you would hate it. But you are the only reliable one I can turn to *for so many different things involved* & I must think of Australia's fame & the brightness of my adored mother's memory before all else.

All this is only a precaution.

Dont reply until you hear from me again, which will be very soon, if I pull thru, which I expect to & intend to.

Love from yr heartbroken, distracted
  Percy.

Was playing yr 'Joyful homecoming'[2] in California.

Mother & I were just expecting to begin the happiest part of our lives. I delayed too long, worked too long, did not bring leisure to her early enough. I have used shocking judgement in all things.

Yr letters, kindliness, made mother so happy, lately.

[1] Eventually Frederick and Antonia Morse built their home on this land, with Grainger's assistance.

[2] For piano, composed and published in 1919, dedicated to Grainger.

1922–1939

'An Untamed Buffalo'

16   *To Cyril Scott*

[In August 1922 Grainger returned to Europe, for the first time since 1914, in an attempt to regain something of places and times once shared with his mother. He resuscitated the plans of 1914 to collect Danish folk music in Jutland and gave concerts in Scandinavia and Holland.]

American Hotel, Amsterdam, Oct 21, 1922

Cyril dear,

In a day or two I will be sending you the photo of my beloved mother that I like best & (if I can find a copy) one of her & me together playing the English Dance that is dedicated to you, last summer.[1] You say you have a small postcard of us both. Will you tell me its number on the charts I am sending you, & which I wish back afterwards? Do you like the look of 13 or do you prefer 24, the latter looks much better in the real photo than on the chart.[2] The above Hotel (American Hotel, Leidsche Plein, Amsterdam) will find me until about Nov 26. I expect to go to Germany in December, but my movements are still quite undecided. Will let you know later on.[3] I hope all will go well with yr wife & the expected baby & that all things will be happiness for you in every way.[4] I can easily understand your wish to be home all you can under the circumstances. I have thought & thought about the question re 'the water's edge' but cannot remember a single occasion on which mother & I sat by the water's edge. I do not think she can have been fond of sitting near water. But we were always so terribly busy & it was the greatest rarity that we sat down out of doors. If, however, I should come to remember such an occasion (by the water's edge) I shall let you know at once.

It has made me very wretched that you have tried to deliver this 'message' to me in spite of what I wrote you of not wishing to receive

---

[1] Picture 46 in the 1923 volume *Photos of Rose Grainger*. See plate No. 8.

[2] See plate No. 11.

[3] Grainger stayed six months (Jan.–June 1923) in Frankfurt before returning to Denmark for further collection of folk music.

[4] Scott had married fellow occultist Rose Allatini in May 1922.

any such messages thru a 3rd person, because of my instinctive feelings about such things & my lack of belief in spirit messages.[1] It is not that I prize my disbelief higher than yr belief. On the contrary, I admire you deeply & yr religious nature & for the time you have devoted to these theories—yr beliefs being what they are. But I do not share yr beliefs & I *cannot* & *will not* have these things forced upon me. To receive a message that purports to come from my adored mother, of the genuineness of which you are convinced but of the genuineness of which I am not convinced, *is the greatest possible agony to me.* My feelings about these things are strong & instinctive & I cannot allow myself to be exposed to the display of the convictions of others if they seem to me (as regards matters between mother & me) unproven as far as I am concerned. This matter will break up our old & lovely friendship if you do not exercise tolerance with my disbelief just as I exercise tolerance with yr belief. If you will not promise me *to avoid all occult subjects where my mother is concerned* & *to refrain from all 'messages' from her, by letter or by word of mouth when we meet* I shall have to take the drastic step of not opening yr letters & of avoiding yr company wherever possible. That would be a terrible end to our dear old friendship & I think I am lonely & wretched enough as it is. But I cannot allow even you, whom I love so dearly, to force things upon me that I do not believe in & that are repugnant to me where my darling mother, & her memory, are concerned. At the same time I promise to let you know *at once* should my feelings alter on this point, or should I remember an occasion 'at the water's edge.' With all loving best wishes

Percy

17   *To Roger Quilter*

Address always Seven Cromwell Place | White Plains, New York
USA
In the train | Feb 14, 1924.

Roger darling,

I can now write you more definitely about my chamber concerts, which I certainly expect to give next season, unless I should get ill, &

---

[1] In his autobiographical volume *Bone of Contention* (London: The Aquarian Press, 1969), Scott describes one of his meetings with a lady of extraordinary psychic powers, at which Grainger's mother had appeared 'in spirit form' to them: 'In the hopes of it being a little comfort to her son, she asked us to convey a certain message to him, and this I was only too glad to do. But his reactions to my letter were so unfavourable that I wished I had refrained.' (p. 178.)

thus, or some other way, be stopped earning the money needful. My 2 chamber concerts will be given in March–April, 1925, dates not fixed yet. The 1st concert will be only my own works.[1] The 2nd concert, besides Quilter numbers, will most likely hold an American work or group (maybe Leo Sowerby),[2] Hindemiths larger 'Kammermusik' or Schreker's 'Kammersinfonie', & perhaps still more.[3]

I would not favor a small choir at this 2nd concert because I am having a small choir in the 1st concert.[4] Certainly there should be a group of your songs accomp'd by yourself. I would *strongly* favor Roland Hayes,[5] if he is available & not too costly. He seems to have quite worsted the color prejudice. His appearance with Boston Symphony was a real triumph, I gather, & he even goes *into the South*, singing to big *mixed race* audiences & packed New York's largest hall recently. Even so I would be chary of engaging him to appear with chamber-accomp. or orchestral accomp. in case some fool player might raise something & involve a 'Union' dispute, which it is better to avoid, both for my sake & for the weal of Negro musical progress. But I am certain *no one* would think of resenting R.H. singing to your or my accomp., & I doubt if any singer would be more advantageous for yr songs, as his vogue stands here at present. If you would favor R.H. please let me know, also please write him & ask him not to charge me more than he must, as my concerts will be in a small intimate hall (the 'Little Theater' maybe) where I cannot possibly take in much money. I will then write Hayes myself, but first I must know if you approve.

Then there should be an instrumental group of yr works. It might be your 'English Dances'[6] played by you & me (we could use the duet arrang. but play them on 2 pianos, & in places make them more brilliant or rich, as we easily could with the greater scope at our disposal at 2 keyboards. But they would appear on program 'for piano duet', perhaps with the added remark 'played at two keyboards for convenience sake' or the like).

Or it could be a chamber-combination group, consisting of

[1] Held on 26 Apr. 1925 in the Little Theater on West 44th Street, presenting numerous Grainger works, including *Hill-Song* No. 1, *English Dance*, and seven Kipling settings.

[2] (1895–1968), American composer; he studied in Italy in 1921–4 as first winner of the American Prix de Rome.

[3] Held on 3 May 1925 in the Little Theater of Carnegie Hall. Quilter did not come to America; none of his works were presented in the concert.

[4] The Kasschau Solo Choir.

[5] (1887–1976), American Negro tenor, at this time widely engaged in North America and Europe.

[6] *Three English Dances* (*c*.1909–10), for small orchestra; the piano duet version also dates from 1910. These dances were dedicated to Grainger.

'Gondolas', 'Lanterns', ('Moonlight on the Lake'?) & ending with one of the 'English Dances' maybe?[1]

Or it could be a combination-group, opening with 1 of the E. Dances for piano duet (you & me), with softer chamber instrumentation in the middle of the group, & ending the group with a sharper, larger instrumentation (chamber), with bright piano part, Celesta, etc? With regard to the chamber orchestration; you can choose your own combination of instrs, up to 12, or beyond if you like. The various pieces need not be scored for the same combination—variety of comb. might be much to be wished for. My own experience with chamber scorings has led me to consider the following as desirable points to keep in mind: Harp very delightful. Piano desirable for brittle bright effects, also to give 'snap' to chords played by other instrs much as brass gives 'snap' in the orchestra, also on account of its marvelous low bass. Harmonium as a gentle, vague harmonic background for solo winds or solo strings. Harmonium & celesta together supplement each other very nicely. It seems to me that in chamber combinations it is well to get well away from those conventional blends that have grown up in the orchestra & in older chamber music, & that it must be easy to build up fresh conventions & procedures (each man according to his own taste) with piano, harp, harmonium, celesta, etc in combination with the melody bearing instruments that will be fresh & telling. It would certainly be splendid to do what you suggest in yr last letter, to try yr chamber things in London before my concerts, so that what you present at yr instrumental debut in US would be as seasoned as possible & represent fully what you yourself approve of.

If in addition to taking part in my 2nd chamber concert you could give a composition concert of your own, or assist someone like Eva Gauthier,[2] or R. Hayes, or other good singer, in one of their recitals it would be a splendid thing for the vogue of yr compos over here. If you gave yr own concert & wished (for variety's sake) to do anything for piano duet or 2 pianos (like the 'English Dances') of course I would be glad to give my services, if you could need them.

In the chamber group of yr works at my chamber concert I could play the piano part while you conducted, or I could conduct while you played piano, whichever you preferred (provided the 'Union'[3] does not

---

[1] 'In a Gondola' and 'Lanterns' comprised the *Two Impressions* for piano (1919), which were dedicated to Grainger; *Moonlight on the Lake* (pub. 1912) was also for solo piano.

[2] (1885–1958), Canadian soprano.

[3] Probably the American Federation of Musicians, founded in 1896.

object—perhaps they would not object in chamber music). Should you need a small choir (10–20 voices) either for a composition concert of yr own or for part of my 2nd Chamber concert (in spite of my inclination, above expressed, to avoid a choir at my 2nd chamber concert) I could get you a very good one, the one that will sing at my 1st chamber concert, selected & trained by the excellent choirmaster (Mr Frank Kasschau)[1] who is training & conducting the 300 Bridgeport voices for my April 1924 concerts. Whether you could see your way to give a compo concert *of your own*, whether you could arrange to assist some fine singer in his or her recital, *at any rate* I hope you will *definitely decide* to come for my 2nd chamber concert *next* season (March or April, 1925). Interest in modern music is in full swing & the time is ripe for men like you, Delius, etc. If we wait too long, there may be a reaction, & the scene would be less well set for your advent.

In any case I feel sure we live in times in which *the composer himself must push his works by his own presence, personality,* 'durch den praktischen Einsatz seiner eigenen Persönlichkeit'.[2] Just think: Schirmers told me the other day that they have sold over 40000 copies of my 'Country Gardens'[3] over here since 1919. Yet in England I believe it sells hardly at all in comparison with 'Shepherds Hey',[4] which latter still enjoys the advantage of having been introduced by me long ago.

If you could devote part of a few seasons to USA I firmly believe you would reap royalties (& what is more important—performances) that would amaze you. As it is, with yr wonderful songs lying fallow here or nearly so, you are throwing something away for nothing.

I wish you could plan to stay with me (March–April, 1925) at White Plains for about 3 weeks or a month, so that you could hear the chamber concert of my own works as well as take part in my 2nd chamber concert. I could give you a nice bedroom at 7 Cromwell Place & the Morses who live there with me are a nice married couple, very practical, considerate, skilled in photography & concert management.

Let me know finally, as soon as you can, re next season, & give me an idea of what your choice of yr own works would be, & of yr

---

[1] Kasschau had become conductor of the Bridgeport Oratorio Society in 1923, and soon established a reputation for innovative programming of modern works by such composers as Rachmaninov, Bartók, Delius, Elgar, Grainger, and many of the earlier Americans.

[2] = through the practical application of his own personality (German).

[3] Undoubtedly Grainger's most popular work, for piano, published by Schirmer and Schott in 1919, and produced in many other versions over subsequent decades.

[4] Published in 1911 by Schott in chamber and solo piano settings. There were numerous later transcriptions.

orchestrations. I want to make all my plans for the 1925 concerts ere I sail for Australia, May 1924.[1]

Robin Legge & E. Thesiger[2] both wrote very nicely after getting mother's book. I replied (as I thought) very nicely to both of them, but have heard nothing from either since. Maybe there was no call for them to write again. If you *happen* to see them maybe you could see whether they got my letters. No hurry—just as it comes.

Love from *Percy*

18   *To Cecil Sharp*

April 14, 1924

Cecil J. Sharp, Esq. | 4 Maresfield Gardens
Hampstead, London, N.W. 3 | England

My dear Sharp:

Thanks so much for your very kind letter. I am distressed to hear that you have been suffering so much from asthma and bronchitis.[3] It must be a great torment, and I wish you could be, at least for the winter, in a climate where it would trouble you less.

How interesting your 'History of the Dance' sounds.[4] I shall look forward to its appearance greatly.

I was shocked to learn from your letter of the death of the three English musicians. Stanford[5] was awfully kind to me years ago and I always admired his genius.

At the risk of seeming impertinent, I take the liberty of again making a suggestion with regard to the royalty of 'Country Gardens'. It has proved even more of a success than I expected, and you will see from the enclosed photo copy that it has broken all Schirmer's sales records. I understand from them that it is now selling at the rate of over twenty-four thousand copies a year in America and Canada,[6] and I hope you will forgive me if I ask you once again if you will not con-

---

[1] Grainger was absent in Australia from May to Sept. 1924.

[2] (1879–1961), English actor.   [3] Sharp died two months later on 28 June.

[4] *The Dance: An Historical Survey of Dancing in Europe*, written with A. P. Oppé, published in London later in 1924.

[5] Sir Charles Villiers Stanford (1852–1924), Professor of Music at the University of Cambridge from 1887 until his death. From 1905 onwards Grainger had performed many times under his direction and also made a most popular arrangement of Stanford's *Irish Dances*.

[6] Grainger's royalty statements, however, showed only 16,875 copies of the solo piano version for 1923–4 and 22,632 copies for 1924–5.

sider sharing this royalty with me.[1] I feel it is quite undeserved that I should enjoy the whole of it myself. I would never have known of Morris dances and several other phases of English folk music if it had not been for your epoch-making discoveries and efforts, and I wish that you, the modern discoverer of the Morris dance in England, would share with me in the results accruing from the unexpected popularity of my setting of 'Country Gardens'. Whether you devoted such a share to your own health or to your art, in both cases it would seem to me most highly beneficial to the cause of music and I should be proud to think that I was contributing to such a cause in any way. In any case please forgive this suggestion and comply with it if you feel you can.[2]

You are right, I feel utterly lonely without my mother and find real solace only in my music.

You will see from the enclosed program that I am bringing Frederick Delius over and conducting two of his largest works very soon.[3] This is the beginning of what I hope to be a long and lasting campaign for the spread of Anglo Saxon music not only in America but also in Europe in later seasons. It was always my mother's idea and mine that I should some day earn enough money to be able to do for other composers somewhat what Liszt did in his day.

I shall be sending you the published copies of some of my works based on the melodies you collected.

In connection with 'Green Bushes'[4] I should like to tell you something that seems to me of interest. It was, I think, the first piece in which British folk song was treated in the Passacaglia manner, later much used by Delius, Cyril Scott and others. Delius told me last winter that it was this Passacaglia innovation as it appeared in 'Green Bushes' that led him to write his 'Brigg Fair'[5] and 'Dance Rhapsody' as he did; and Cyril Scott told me the same thing with regard to his two Orchestral Passacaglias based on Irish folk songs that were recently published by Schott in Mainz.

[1] Grainger had first proposed a payment to Sharp in 1920, soon after the initial success of the work, but Sharp had declined this offer.

[2] Sharp replied on 8 May accepting Grainger's offer and suggesting one-sixth of the royalties as his share; Grainger in a letter to Sharp, by then dead, of 8 July stated that Sharp would receive half the royalties. This payment to Sharp's estate continued until at least 1927. Among other projects, the publication of Sharp's two-volume *English Folk Songs from the Southern Appalachians* (1932) was assisted by Grainger's royalties.

[3] 28 Apr. 1924 (Bridgeport) and 30 Apr. (New York). Delius proved too ill to travel to America.

[4] Set for small orchestra in 1905–6, to a Somerset tune collected by Sharp.

[5] Composed for orchestra in 1907, based in part on a Lincolnshire tune collected by Grainger, to whom Delius's work was dedicated.

I wish I might have a word from you regarding the royalty proposal before I leave for Australia early in May, and I very much hope you will be able to tell me better news of your health. As regards the royalty, I get fifteen per cent from Schirmers of which the one half would be seven and one half per cent, and I believe 'Country Gardens' sells at seventy five cents the copy, but I am not quite sure.

With all best wishes and cordial thanks,

Ever very admiringly yours,

Percy Grainger

19   *Round Letter*

[Grainger wrote this form of occasional circular letter to his 'kin and friends' around the world through much of his American period. These letters were often more expansive and studied than his letters to individuals; sometimes they were openly pedagogic or accusatory, providing lectures on matters musical, cultural or linguistic.]

PERCY AT TAHITI, RAROTONGA & NEW ZEALAND, MAY–JUNE, 1924

My steamer (S.S. 'Tahiti', Union Steamship Co of New Zealand) stopped the whole day of Sat., May 31, at Papeete, Tahiti. The natural beauties of Tahiti & Moorea (the mountainous island a few miles off Tahiti) have not been exagerated & could not be exagerated. The depth & richness of the green, the pinky or magenta red of the rocks or rocky earth, with mountain tops wreathed in cloud do not disappoint. The scenes & the looks of the natives are almost absurdly Gauguinish—particularly the thick squat legs, the red & white aprons worn by the natives & the great winding trunks of the trees looking like huge eels & shining forth light from out the dark green of the great leaves. Gauguin[1] has not only woven a potent poetry round what he saw & rendered; he has also recorded very faithfully & accurately & the island seems to a Gauguinite like the imaginations of that great genius come to life & living on after his time. I saw little of the natives as I spent well nigh all my day climbing the exquisite hills. But what little I saw made me feel that both Pierre Loti's 'The marriage of

---

[1] Paul Gauguin (1848–1903), French post-impressionist painter, who lived for most of his last decade in the South Pacific.

Loti'[1] & Paul Gauguin's 'Noa Noa'[2] are true & reliable pictures of the national soul of the Tahitians & that the sweetness, the purity & above all the peaceableness that overflows from both those books is there today—in spite of all the corruptions & destructions of the whites. Australians, Americans, Britishers have much to say of the rottenness of French rule & of the degraded & dirty conditions of life in Papeete. I can only say that I found the French administrative buildings (Public works, hospitals, barracks, schools, etc) with their ruddy pink & white coloring excellently chosen to blend really beautifully with the foliage & trees around them, & that I saw nothing degraded or dirty looking about the native population, but only muscular grace & gentle mirth-fulness. Many of the halfbreeds were hardly less distinguished looking than the purer Tahitians & whether native-dressed or rather smartly dressed in European white clothes gave a never failing impression of extreme refinement, delicacy, peacefulness, superiority. They are said to be dying out, but I must confess I saw babies babies everywhere. No doubt venereal diseases are terribly prevalent there (so one is told) but I can only say that to my eyes the Tahitians looked mainly fresh, gay, pure, unsullied. Almost as many Chinese as Tahitians are to be seen, & in that climate the Chinese look utterly suitable, apparently on fine terms with the natives & the Chinese–Tahitian half-breed a pleas-ant & hopeful-looking product. I was told it was not a climate for a stranger, unused to it, to do hill-climbing in, but the many ridges of red rock, covered with exquisite green growths, all mounting towards the center of the island, with volcanic-looking hollows here & there, looked all too inviting. The highest peak of the island was too far off to try for in the time granted by the ship's stay, but I thought the sec-ond-highest peak a possibility. I tried to walk thru the bush but found it out of the question. All of it (except high up on the hills) is up to one's shoulders (whether fern or underbrush) the earth (its holes & unevennesses) are quite hidden from the eye & the dry grasses are slip-pery as ice. But after tramping thru banana plantations & up & down hillsides (where it took half an hour of the hardest effort to compass a hundred yards, because of the slippery grasses & tangled underbrush) I finally found a decent path that led right up to the very peak I had selected to climb. It went past a settlement that a white 'nature-man' & his followers had had there, a sort of summer-house without walls,

---

[1] Julien Viaud, pseud. Pierre Loti (1850–1923), French naval officer and novelist; his *The Marriage of Loti* appeared, in French, in 1880.

[2] Autobiographical novel of 1900.

very sad & empty now & the tin roof making strange noises in the breeze. Was his name not Darling? He and his following lived there without clothes, but passage from San Francisco was refused him & he went to Fiji (I think) & soon died. The Tahiti hills are very curiously formed, perhaps of lava. There is a ridge running along the center of most of them, from which the sides of the hill slope down very steeply. The ridge is often only 2 feet broad, & along this ridge runs the path, from which one, naturally, gets fine views all the time, being able to see both sides of the hill or mountain one is on—& deliciously wild the views are, tho always peaceable. At other times the hills are not ridged, & then the path is ever so hard to follow, for the grass & brush grow man-high (& higher) over the path & it shows merely as a faint thinness of the bush. What a blessed land—no snakes, wild animals. One could never venture into such thick underbrush if it were a snaky land (one cannot even see the ground, half the time, & keeps flopping full length into the brush every few minutes because of some unseen unevenness of the ground) & the nearest approach to anything uncomfortable are the spiders & their webs that cross the path at all heights—not dangerous looking spiders—still it is never pleasant to run ones face into a spider's web. About 2 or 3 miles away from the shoreman, & all signs of him save the faint path, vanish wholly. The hills are utterly deserted, tho they would be ideal places to build a hut, or to go moving about with a light tent. Occasionally white birds fly overhead, looking rather like big white pigeons & one had a long thin tail longer than its body. Everywhere flaming red flowers in the bush, rather like red wattle, & more rarely silvery colored trees with large leaves grew decoratively in plots or groups on the hill-sides, looking like some scroll-work in aluminium in the distance. The different kinds of scrubs or trees stand out very plasticly one from the other & one can guess how inspiring this must have been to Gauguin's decorative imagination. The decorative, massed impressions of the greenery & growths in his Tahitian pictures is close to the nature there & but little exagerated. It was good I was dressed in my US army clothes, leggings, etc; for ordinary clothes would have been torn to bits by the thorny plants & shrubs that abound. My hands were well scratched in all directions. It is true that it is a hard climate to climb in. Every few minutes I would lie down panting. But tho the sun can be very hot the breeze is always cool & even in the heat of the day under any tree one feels chilly if still for long. I had got to within 100 or 200 feet of the peak I was aiming at when I felt cramp or something in my right

leg—an involuntary contraction & loosening of one of the big muscles
of the upper leg; the result, I suppose, of some 4 or 5 hours unceasing
effort. Miles away from human habitation & with the steam[er] sailing
at 6 p.m. I did not like to risk trying the remaining few hundred feet
of climb, but turned back at once & got to the wharf with nearly an
hour to spare. My leg felt uncomfortable, but the contrast of the
downward path gave me full control of it after a few minutes.

To say that the Tahitians & Rarotongans are polite is to put it very
mildly. Their manners have a sensitive yet eager quality that is far
more than any politeness. They seem to envelop one in friendliness &
peaceableness & a complete & effortless unfolding of their own nature
seems to go with all they do. They are neither shy nor bold. Money &
all connected with it does not seem, even yet, to have a part in their
make-up. The islands are the first time I have seen mankind freed
from every sign of the struggle for existence. There is no struggle, calm
of demeanor is wedded to alertness of body & mental gentleness to
rugged muscularity.

Our boat had nearly 24 hours at Avarua (Rarotonga). It was from
these islands that the lovely music came of which the New Zealand
farmer A.J. Knocks (of Otaki) gave me the 5 phonograph records—
quick ant-like improvised polyphonic partsinging of great harmonic
charm.[1] You can imagine, therefore, how much it meant to me to see
the people & the place whose music I had studied & loved so keenly.
Rarotonga is only 32 miles around & inhabited only on the shore—a
mere handful of people, much purer in race (the good New Zealand
administration allows no Chinese or other non-Polynesians in—&
allows no white man to buy land from the natives, each of which latter
owns land & lives in plenty on the cocoanuts, etc) than the Tahitians,
more stalwart & undestroyed in every way. Here is an ideal island to
spend a few years, studying the lovely native music, the language, getting to know a race that is both peaceable & heroic & to whom money
seems to mean nothing.

There is no deep harbor & the steamer can not come ashore. One
goes ashore in native-run boats. The sight of these swaying boats in
the deep-blue water, a whole string of them slung behind a tug, bumping into each other, each boat filled with these splendid young
Rarotongans, wide in the shoulder & slim in the hip, the whole scene

---

[1] Grainger had received these recordings from Alfred Knocks (1849–1925) during his visit to
New Zealand of Jan. 1909. In a letter to his mother of 21 Jan. 1909 he described this music as 'a
treat no less than the best Wagner'.

dancing upon the background of the luxuriously beautiful island itself, is something never to forget, something mother would have relished as she used to relish Aden, Colombo & the like. The island itself is lov[e]lier than Tahiti, more romantic in its skyline (jagged & volcanic formation), more lusciously rich in its coloring, more primitive & unspoiled in every way. Hoping against hope that I might hear some of the native music I did not go hill-climbing, but motored round the island, took photos, etc. In the evening an Australian man & I went to a dance in which the natives danced with themselves & with the sailors & stewards from our boat. No native music but quite jolly playing of accordions, guitars & ukeleles by natives, very musical & rhythmic. I enquired for native music, of course, which, it seems one could hear at other times but hardly on a steamer-day, when all are attuned to the arrival from the outer world & when the younger people are at work loading & unloading in their boats, etc. I was told that many of the people who were at the Christchurch Exhibition in New Zealand around 1906 (& were then phonographed by my old friend Knocks) are still alive, so I live in hopes of later trips to Rarotonga & of completing my study of its unique music. A native who came on board wanted to show me pearls, but of course I was not interested. But we talked, & after a time he asked me if I could get him an apple. Apples do not grow on the islands. So I got him one. I thought it so typical. No asking for money, no forcing of his wares—just the simple wish to enjoy a certain taste that was a rarity to him. After having worked all night loading & unloading in the boats a tin of biscuits was passed to a boatload of workers. They could hardly be got to each take his share. They live communally. They know that each will get his share, they were not eager about details of distribution, & on the island is more than food enough for every man. As one passes great collections of oranges (on land) they call out: 'Take some oranges'.

I had thought my old New Zealand friend dead several years, getting no reply when I wrote him around 1919. While the steamer lay nearly 2 days in Wellington (New Zealand) I went up to Palmerston North to see a relative there. Coming back I got off the train at Otaki, just out of a sentimental wish to see again old Knocks' house where mother & I had spent such wonderful hours in 1909. Imagine my great joy on learning at the station that old Knocks was still alive. I spent one glorious hour with him before having to take the next train back to Wellington. I found him hale & wonderful, bearded & wild-eyed, a Walt-Whitmanish figure of a man, with his half-breed grand children round him. He had married a Maori, became a member of the Maori tribe at Otaki, & is, in his whole spiritual life, more Maori than white. He shares their beliefs, their second-sight, the power of a pure unspoiled human being to almost read the thoughts of other men. When I met him in 1909 he told me things about me, my life, my teeth, my problems—all of them true—that amazed me. This time he sat down in front of me, searching me with his honest, spiritual, deep-set eyes, & threw out amazing thoughts about me, my mother, the problems of my inner soul—all without one word from me. That countrified almost uneducated New Zealander can certainly read the human soul, its thoughts, its fears, & is not afraid to go right to the point. He is a poet, too, & to see him reciting his poems about the Maoris, swaying & gesturing, his eyes flashing, is unforgetable. I hope to see him on my way back to America next Sept.

Percy Grainger.

20   *To Nathaniel Dett*

7 Cromwell Place | White Plains, NY | March 6, 1925

Dear Nathaniel,

I am *deeply disappointed* to find in your letter of Feb 21 no *definite* answer to any of my questions. I do not know how many voices you want to bring, so cannot find out from the railroad what the transportation costs would be.

You have not sent your items for the 2 groups to be sung by your choir, so I cannot make up my program. You now mention the possibility of your choir assisting at a Carnegie Hall concert for the School.[1] Would that be before the concert at which I want you to sing for me, May 3 (my date has been definitely fixed for May 3 for some months)? Of course I realize that the school's needs must come first, but if you are to sing for me on May 3 I must stipulate that your choir does not appear anywhere in New York this season before that date. If you have to appear for the school in New York before May 3, then it will be better to put off singing for me until a season when you dont appear before my concert in New York.

---

[1] Hampton Institute, Virginia. By this time Dett's choir had toured in North America and Europe, to considerable acclaim.

I am sorry to have to send you an ultimatum—but, dear friend I cannot help myself. I approached you about this concert several months ago, and you do not give me the definite answers to my business questions that any manager engaging an artist would demand. So I must send you this ultimatum: *If you do not let me know definitely by Friday March 13 what your services & the choir's services will cost me for the concert of May 3, including transportation & any other expenses involved, & including fee to yourself & choir, also the exact titles of the choruses of yours, divided into 2 short groups, that the choir will sing, & your promise that your choir will not sing in New York City before they sing for me on Sunday evening May 3, I will have to call the matter off for this season, to my bitter regret.*[1]

I enclose a sheet with questions on it that you can fill out, if you wish, so as to save you time.

So much for the mere business facts & needs of the case. But I want to present to you my personal side fully & clearly. My beloved mother & I have always been warmly & affectionately fond of you & your art. I have certainly played JUBA all I could, in Europe as well as US & Canada & intend to make it as well known in Australia in 1926 & in Europe in 1927 as it is in America, if possible. The first public speech I ever made (I had a horror of public speaking) was made about you & your music, simply out of my passionate wish that Canadians should know you were born in Can.[2] I have never neglected to mention you & your art on any possible occasion, in any possible article. (By the way, I will be sending you an article in a Canadian music paper I wrote on my way to Australia. If you already have it please return it, kindly). I have also felt, and acted upon my feelings, that art should be one of the meeting-places of all races, without racial, national or local prejudices, jealousies, or smallnesses. I have always rejoiced in your successes as in my own. Therefore I thought it natural to want to present you in my first modern music programs (I could not present you orchestrally last year, because you have not written for orchestra). I thought also that it would open up new fields to you & your art— maybe not strikingly at once, but gradually, if persisted in. I know you have appeared with chorus in New York but always (as far as I know) as part of a purely Negro program & purpose—which is all as it should be, of course. Still, I thought it desirable to ALSO present you

[1] The choir did, in the end, appear at Grainger's second concert singing Dett's *Negro Folksong Derivatives*.
[2] During Grainger's Feb. 1916 concert tour of Ontario. See letter **3**.

as one of the modern international composers, important in the world of music today outside of all race movements & feelings, in a program together with men like Schreker, Grieg, Hindemith, N. Curtis, who are important creators in music just as you are.[1]

If my house at the Little Theater[2] is all sold out I cannot fail to lose much less than $5000 on the second concert (May 3) at which only other men's works are to be performed. It means that (after I have provided for the several people that are dependant upon me) my whole season's savings go in these concerts, or very nearly so. Do you know another composer who spends what I do on other composers' works, in time & work & money? I do not. I deserve & expect no CREDIT of this. I do it simply because I am an artist & art is my life, &, since my mother's death, my one sustaining joy. But I do crave & expect COOPERATION from my fellow-composers where the presentation of their own works is concerned. I do not ask you & your choir to come & sing for me for nothing. That would be absurd from my standpoint. I wish to pay decently for the performance if it is within my means—give up the cherished idea if it is beyond my means. That's why I suggested a SMALL choir, because I cannot believe that the transportation & fee for a larger body would be within my means. But I DO feel I am entitled to the same businesslike reply that any engaging manager would expect in a similar case. I do NOT feel that I ought to have to run to ticket offices to find out what the cost of your transportation would be. In any case I believe the boat trip would save money, & that we would have to save on the transportation end all we can.

Dear Nathaniel. If you are harassed with a few concerts, think of me with 100 concerts this season, trying to get ready big scores involving hundreds of hours of writing in the train, being jerked about all the while. After all, I AM A COMPOSER, & it would not be right for me to let too many other people's practical questions be saddled upon me. At any rate, whether I am right or wrong, there is a limit to human powers. And I know that I can only give these concerts of modern music (other composers' & my own) if the composers involved are willing & able to send me their programs in time & answer my business questions in a business way. Mrs Sawyer's office must have

---

[1] The remaining items on the programme were *Memories of New Mexico* by the American composer Natalie Curtis (1875–1921), Schreker's *Chamber Symphony*, Hindemith's *Chamber Music* No. 1 and Grieg's *Lost in the Hills*.

[2] 238 West 44th Street, New York City.

the programs out about March 20—a month & more before the first concert. So I MUST have my programs ready for her March 15 or 16. So March 13 is the last date until which I can wait for your information. And even that is MOST AWKWARD for me, as I have concerts almost daily thru then & I cannot easily play concerts & prepare programs & travel as well.

You can see that it would defeat my object if your choir appeared at Carnegie Hall just before. Here am I wishing to present your more INTIMATE side at a chamber concert with a small choir in a really small hall, in the most serious & esthetic way, as due to your achievements as a leading world composer. All that impression will be destroyed if you appear in a big hall, probably with much the same works, as part of a school propaganda not of an exclusively musical nature (the propaganda).

21 [In Danish]   *To Karen Kellermann*

RMMS AORANGI | Pacific Ocean | 8th May 1926

Dear Karen,

Some days ago, on 30th April (my mother's death-day) I held the most satisfying concert I have ever been engaged in, in Los Angeles Calif., together with the 'Los Angeles Oratorio Society'. The choir, orchestra, audience, newspapers—everything was exactly as one would have wished oneself.[1] I have asked my secretary in White Plains to send you a program and cutting about the concert. I do wish you could have heard the concert, particularly as I performed, among others, *Father and Daughter*[2] (which had to be sung twice just as that time in London)[3] which I haven't heard for 13 years and which reminded me so strongly of Svinkløv; because the piece was born in Svinkløv, either entirely or predominantly.

I would be glad if you could sometime get to hear well performed one or other of these pieces, which you knew from their beginning— possibly in the 1927–8 season, when I hope to be able to stay longer in Europe.

---

[1] Grainger conducted this concert.
[2] Setting of a Faeroese folksong, composed in 1908–9, for five male voices, double mixed chorus, and instrumental ensemble.
[3] Premièred at the first Balfour Gardiner concert, 13 Mar. 1912.

Now my American season is over, for I am now going down to Australia (where I don't expect anything particularly good in an artistic sense) to make a tour there. This season I have earned over $30,000, of which I have as good as nothing left over—it has all gone to poor people, relatives, publication of music and literature, etc. Next year I must really see to saving something.

I once said I would like to write you some things that in my opinion would throw some light on my mother's position towards you—etc.

Soon after I was born (I was perhaps 1½ years old) my father got syphilis and infected my mother with it, in an entirely unnecessary way. That is to say my mother was staying in the country, while father caught the disease in the town, travelled to her, infected her and told her the whole thing afterwards. People are hard to understand and we must not be hard on those we don't understand. My mother wasn't bitter towards him either, although she thought that to lose one's health was the worst thing that could happen to anyone. After that she never again lived with him as man and wife because she did not wish to give birth to sick children.

I have seen her drive him out of the room with a riding-whip when he was drunk and unwilling to follow her wishes in this matter. She kept house for him until I was about 8–9 years old, as she hoped to be able to get the better of his drunkenness. But when she realised that it was no good, then they separated (about 1891?)[1]—in all friendship.

Shortly after that the disease manifested itself in terrible neuralgic pains, and she was never really well again thereafter. If she wrote or read she got pains in her eyes or arms, when she walked, in her back (and at that time she had to walk a lot, in Melbourne, as she had to trot around to all her piano pupils; very few came to her) and her face drawn with pain was dreadful to see. I will never forget it.

When we travelled to Germany (1894)[2] she was somewhat better for a time. But she was always afraid that she would go mad or become paralysed or blind before I was musically trained and started on my artistic career.

When I was 12–14 years old she told me the whole thing and begged me to promise her that I would never knowingly do anything that could ruin my health in that way or occasion other similar calamities. I promised her and have kept my promise. In my own thoughts I promised her and myself that I would never leave her while we lived and that I would repay her everything she had suffered. This

[1] End of 1890.   [2] June–July 1895.

thought became my only religion, and although I was too weak a character to carry out the thought as I should, it never disappeared from me. My mother begged me never to tell anyone about her illness. She never told any of her own relatives about it either, not even her mother. She knew that her family was friendly to my father and she didn't wish to influence them against him, who was unhappy enough as he was.

Shortly after she became infected she went away from me to Adelaide, because she didn't want to infect me. She would never take me into bed with her, either, when I was very young for fear of infection, nor kiss me. Her relatives thought she was a 'strange mother' but she let them think what they liked, and had to.

About Christmas 1899 she asked a doctor in Frankfurt (who told me this in 1923) to give her poison which she could use if she felt she was going mad. All this tragedy (even if it was only felt unconsciously) naturally made a strong impression on me and made our relationship to each other something quite special. In 1899 and 1901 the first big breakdowns occurred, when she was unable to walk for long periods, cried nearly the whole day, and (in 1901) had to lie very long on ice cubes. At this time she also had daily rubbings with ointment.[1] The doctors said that she would never be able to live in large cities any more, forecast the worst and advised her to travel back to her relatives in Australia. I knew, however, that I could as good as cure her if I was loving towards her and if I satisfied her enough as artist and as human being. In that I was completely right. If I had always been able to satisfy her in the respects mentioned she would, despite all the syphilis, be alive today and stronger than many other people. Noble women with a strong emotional life can be saved and killed through their feelings.

Mother always told me that I should marry though she didn't want this to happen before my 'Career was made'. But this career was enormously delayed by my laziness as a pianist or because I really cultivated composition and piano simultaneously. I had secretly promised myself that I would never marry, because I instinctively understood that marriage would make impossible the plans I had made for my mother's future.

There have been moments in all the few fallings-in-love that I have had in my life, when I succumbed to my own weakness, or to my mother's earnestly expressed desire that I should marry. But these

[1] With the Swedish masseur Sigurd Fornander. See Biographical Register.

moments were short and I always came back to my original decision—
never to marry. But it wasn't so easy to get mother away from these
marriage ideas. (In reality she would never have been happy if I had
been married. This would have been quite unthinkable the way that
women are, and the way mother's and my relationship was, in particular. She did not understand all this herself. There were times when she
passionately wanted to see me married; other times when she wanted
just the reverse.) When she became too pressing about the marriage
idea there was always a weapon I could use successfully, and used to
use: to tell her that if I was married and had children I would live in
immorality with my own children and practise my sadistic lusts on
them. Then she was horrified and was happy to leave off thoughts of
marriage.

This weapon I used partly because I was afraid of marriage myself
but mostly because I wished to keep myself unmarried for her sake
and couldn't tell her the latter cause (as her happiness would be
destroyed by it).

When she met you and got to know you she was very happy with
you and said to me: 'Why can't you fall in love with a sweet girl like
Karen?'

But on account of the terrible things that I told her could happen if
I ever married, she became afraid, for everyone's sake. She had indeed
experienced unforgettable things with my father. She had wished and
wished that I would never show myself selfish, cruel and happiness-
destroying like him.

Therefore, she hated and feared everything (all people, all relationships) that threatened to call forth the bad sides in me. For this reason
she could become inexplicably furious about certain things which to
the uninitiated didn't seem, perhaps, to be of so much importance.
She feared above all to see me egoistic and heartless in my relationships with women. One moment she would wish to see me married,
because she thought that was the only way to arrange life properly for
me and the one I loved. The next moment she would wish anything
rather than see me married, when I told her the dreadful things I
would do if I were married.

Behind all this one must remember her illness and the shadow that
cast on her and me. Then one must remember that life (again on
account of her illness) had developed in such a way that it was impossible for her to want to get rid of me (to a quite different degree than
normal healthy mothers with their sons) and that I (through her illness

and altogether through our remarkable life, separated from our father-land and all relatives, etc) only knew this one religion—to make good her sufferings and never to marry. When I got to be fond of you she begged me to promise her that I wouldn't tell you about her illness, and I promised. If you had known it the whole thing would, perhaps, have been easier to understand. I always think that the truth—the whole truth—is always the easiest for all 'daran beteiligten'.[1]

That which came between her and you was first and foremost that I set myself so rigidly against marriage (with an eye to her happiness and illness) and the dreadful things I told her would possibly happen if I married. (I knew that I couldn't in the long run stand against the temptation of marriage if she kept on too long wanting to see me mar-ried. Therefore, I had to kill her thoughts of marriage with these terri-ble statements).

But she never ceased to be fond of you through the years; this was clear to me many times. After I had been engaged to Margot Harrison[2] and separated from her, Margot gave me a red jacket that I had been very fond of. One, or more, years later, when we unpacked we found the jacket and mother said to me: 'Which do you care most for, this red jersey or Karen's national costume?' and she was so happy when I answered 'How can you ask?'[3] and told her how I was bound up with the national costume more deeply. Not that she wasn't fond of Margot. She always loved Margot most highly. But she was deeply happy when she saw that I had loved you more. Fairly shortly before she died, she said to me: 'Karen would have made you the best wife of any woman you have loved. I think she is the only one who could have made you happy and would have understood the problems of your life as an artist.'[4] And she had always spoken in a similar vein. She could say many different things about everything and everybody because she spoke just as much without reserve to me as to herself. And I understood her as well as one can understand any person. And I know that she always liked you, remembered you with tenderness and love. It was natural for her not to want you to know about her ill-ness ('I don't want Karen to feel that I am unclean, to have a horror of me');[5] as she had never let her relatives know about it either. If you had known about this you would perhaps have understood better why I could never marry you as long as mother lived, and why it was so

---

[1] = the parties concerned (German).　　　　[2] See Biographical Register.
[3] This exchange given directly in English.　　[4] This quotation in English.
[5] In English.

hard for her to bear seeing me selfish in my relationship with people. I don't know whether it would have made any difference.

I know that I am not made for close association with people and that I have only brought unhappiness and suffering to all who have loved me and known me best—most of all to my mother, whom I loved most of all. Her life was destroyed by her sickness but much more destroyed by my ugly nature. To feel that one has given birth to a monster is the worst that can befall a loving mother. It is clear to me that it was this that killed her—directly or indirectly. I look back on everything (I have really nothing else to turn to, humanly speaking, as since her death I have kept away from close contact with everybody) and I see so clearly how I have ruined everything for all of you who came in contact with me. I see so clearly how I came between mother and you in my great need to avoid marriage. For this reason I want you to know everything there is to know. This is not to say that you will change your opinion of us. Most of all I want you to know how deeply I believe that my mother was fond of you.

Two things you wrote to me are true. The first, 'There is no bottom in you' and the other, 'Whatever you are or are not, you are a sincere artist'. I often think of these two utterances and realise how true they are. Therefore, I keep myself as exclusively to Art as I possibly can. It is a shame my mother can't see the great leaps forward I have made, as artist, in the last 3 years. It is a shame that she can't see how love-less and lonely I am now and be convinced that this is on account of my own empty nature and not out of consideration for her. It is a shame she can't see that her fear for my future was unnecessary—that I am one of these dry, hard characters for whom life doesn't contain many temptations and dangers (accidents excepted).

Only my bad conscience makes life difficult for me—extremely difficult and painful. But not worse than I deserve. When I think of the possibility of life perhaps being just (as some maintain) and that all guilt is revenged, then I am justified in dreading the future. (But I don't do so. I am just happy.)

If only you and your husband can have a lovely summer holiday. Where are you going to this year?

With all good wishes and greetings to you both from

Percy

Did you receive the gramophone records?

And *Warriors* score?[1]
Did you receive *Arrival Platform Humlet* in its original form, for viola?[2]
Address till August or September
C/O J. Nevin Tait
     His Majesty's Theatre
     Melbourne. Vic. Australia.

22   *To Ella Ström*

[Returning from Australia in November 1926 aboard the *Aorangi*, Grainger met the Swede Ella Ström. Their courtship lasted for nearly two years.]

Bloomington, Indiana
Jan. 12, 1927

My dear Ella

In yr letter from the Bigelows' place[3] (which reached me the day after you sailed)[4] you wrote that you would like me to keep on criticizing yr poems—that you would feel that I liked them if I did so. You may be quite sure that I like them very very much. How could one fail to like something so unseverably linked up with one who has brought one out of lifelessness into life? How, loving you, could I fail to love something that is as effortlessly yet powerfully evocative of you yourself as yr poetry is?—for the flow of yr verses is just like yr own self moving into life before one. But it is not to you as 'sweetheart in my imagination' that I want to write you of yr poetry, but as one artist to another. After thinking over yr verse & prose carefully & repeatedly & viewing it in the most ‚nyktern'[5] of critical moods I want to say this to you in artistic fellowship & honesty: I consider you have a *great natural literary gift*, a gift well worth making all kinds of sacrifices to cultivate loyally, a gift that might lead you to *all kinds of heights* in time. Your poetry 'flows'; it 'pours itself out like a glass of water' (as Wm. Lyon Phelps[6] said of a cat lying down); it creates the illusion of inevitability.

---

[1] Published by Schott (Mainz) that year in compressed full score.

[2] The first movement of the *In a Nutshell* orchestral suite, but earlier conceived for solo viola, for the British player Lionel Tertis. The viola version was published by Schott (London) in Mar. 1926.

[3] At Malden-on-the-Hudson, New York, owned by Poultney Bigelow (1855–1954), the author and adventurer. Ella Ström had probably come to know him during her years in London.

[4] Ella Ström had been returning to England, via America.   [5] = sober (Swedish).

[6] (1865–1945), Professor of English at Yale University from 1901 to 1933.

This is what enthrals us in all natural poets, such as Byron, Heine, J.P. Jacobsen, Burns, etc. This 'natural flow' is to poetry what melody is to music—the un-do-without-able gift. That you can do this in a foreign tongue as well as in yr own tongue is a further proof of wondrous natural facility. That yr poetry is so exactly yrself—light of limb yet deep of heart—hints to me that it is within yr powers to develop (naturally, unsought, of course) great personal artistic originality if you write *enough*; *often* enough, *steadily* enough. It seems to me a good sign for yr artistic future that you already have the power of reducing the motiv behind each poem into a concentrated essence, into a few pithy words: 'A lonely woman passing by'; ˌtanken är ens bästa skatt';[1] 'in the arms of my lover'—to—'mind'. The very thoughts behind yr motivs are economic, positively humble: Tanken är ens bästa skatt. Not love, not ecstacy, not genius is yr choice, but just simple, staid little 'tanken'. There is something truly touching in that—& it is truly *you*!

If you would care to send me more (or all) of yr poems I will be glad to write you my thoughts about them; tho my criticisms of poetry, of course, cannot have the same technical value as my criticisms of music might have. Naturally the poet is like the composer in this—one has to write *many many different things* & *very very often* before one's full-grown, authentic, personal voice hatches out. If I were you I should make every effort to *write daily*. I am *sure* it is worth while in yr case; you have the ease of utterance, the depth of thought & feeling, the instinctive sense of style.

Yr poems will always chiefly come to you (no doubt) unsought, in gushes of inspiration. But if I were you I would work daily at prose. Why not set yrself down daily to write out *all of interest that has ever happened to you*; yr imagination of an unmet father,[2] yr tussles (wrangles!) with yr mother,[3] yr kind foster parents,[4] the boy who would wash yr legs, yr love affairs, infatuations, strifes & trials, etc? When I recall how plasticly they all stood out as you told them (the young Swede who would have clawed himself breathing-room round his head had he been snow-covered & whom, I think, you remet haphazard at Eastbourne—the young officer who danced with you all night, his comrades shyly asking you 'will he be coming?'—yr description of the

[1] = our thought is our best treasure (Swedish).
[2] Ella's paternity had been contested in a Swedish court case in 1888. The claimed father's name was Brandelius.
[3] A hotel employee, with family name Anderson; she kept in reasonably close contact with Ella, despite the fostering arrangement.
[4] The Ströms, whom Ella called aunt (Tant) and uncle (Farbror).

chaste life of a sailor, 'with no place at all to make love in, on board'—the angry now-or-never Spaniard, who 'might have been true to me for one year, perhaps'—the heavier, sadder, bitterer revelations) I cannot doubt that you could pen a wondrous life-story of yrself, a story the outer world would relish to read as I relished hearing it from yr lips.

After all, to write one's own life-story is the healthiest root of all literature. Literature is just telling the truth, the whole truth. And that you could do as few, few others; for you have *thought* over yr truths; because tanken is yr best skatt. Is it not worth trying?

───────── " ─────────

Two short months ago, before I met you, I had only a past. I was not aware of a present or a future. Today, thanks to dear you, I am vividly aware of a present & a future, & I am no longer unhappy as I was. I sit in these trains, alone, day after day, or I sit at the piano, practising, always thinking of you, & I am *positively happy*. I think of you almost to the exclusion of all other thoughts. Tho I do not know when I shall see you again (for tho I can be sure to arrive in England early next August, how do I know you will not have to change, or want to change, yr plans ere then?), tho I have no reason to believe that you like me beyond a mere surface kindliness, yet I find unsayable, unmeasurable comfort in feeling love for you in my heart, in knowing that perfection *might* exist for me on earth.

Such a mere possibility, whether actually attainable or not, makes all the world seem lovable to me again, breathes purpose & worth-while-ness into all my tasks. (Not but that the *actual* realization of my longings would not be yet again a thousandfold more desirable than such imaginings.)

Very soon after my darling mother died, almost immediately, I began to realize that I was holy, in my own eyes, in the sense that I am *all that now remains of her*; that I must bend all my will & wits to bring to a bright & worthy end such talent & health as she had been able to make thrive in my soil. In one of her very last letters she wrote to a dear friend: 'Can no one help that dear creature?—a blessing he will yet be to so many people'. I swore to myself I would do my best to make those words of hers no idle boast. So I strove from the first, after the tragedy, to keep my health & increase my art & *to try to be happy*. ('No profit is, where pleasure is not taken.' Shakespe[a]re.) I despize those that hug their grief. But it was beyond me, till I met you, to rise above the ever-crushing mood of loss & doom. I could increase my artistic & commercial output & success (& I did), but I could not command my heart. As long as I was feverishly busy in my work I could half forget my feelings—only to find them grimly waiting for me the moment there was a lull in my tasks. Do you wonder that I bless you, since meeting whom a wholly new chapter in my life is opened?

Of course I shall never shed, or want to shed, constant thoughts of my little mother's tragic end & of my own guilt in contributing towards it; those we love best should never long leave our minds, & there is no profit in running away from one's own conscience. But my mother (tho she had a tragic keynote in her too) strove always so valiantly for happiness, & for my happiness in particular. Something of that, her longing, I feel I have fulfilled in meeting you, in loving you.

It seemed so natural to see yr dear, kind, clever, tender, strong, various, lovely face opposite me those unforgettable days in the train[1]—as if I had seen it always. It seems unnatural not to see it now. It is true that I feel the lack of it very bitterly. But what is that lack compared with the joy of knowing that such a face exists somewhere (shedding joy & goodness where it goes), with being able to see it in my imagination?

Forgive me writing about myself so much: But imagine what it was, after 39 years of closest communion with my mother as well as a rich life of love & friendship with other beloved ones, to suddenly, after the blow of greatest tragedy, to have no one to love, no one to confide in, no one to share one's thought with, & for that spiritual desert to extend for $4\frac{1}{2}$ years: And then to meet you, a creature of lov[e]liness, goodness & enticement, a fellow artist whose gifts I admire, a clever mind whose thoughts are delicious to follow, one who even knows the same lands & folks (Scandinavia, Germany, England, even Australia) that I do! No words can hope to tell what a boon it is.

And tho I do not know what yr feelings are towards me, tho we have never kissed each other even (for an affectionate farewell hug is not a kiss), yet to feel so closely bound to you!

'There is such a thing as being too proud to fight'. There is the fight between the sexes; there is the hunter & the prey, whether the prey be woman or man. Against such things (for those still able to partake of them) I say not a word. Only when one has been wretched enough, trampled on enough, when one has seen deeply enough into one's own selfishness & ignominy, the prayer comes that one may never again contribute to strife or deception or distrust where there is love.

[1] Grainger and Ström travelled together by train from Vancouver to Albany, New York.

And that is now my prayer. Honorable unfulfilment of one's desires, honorable separateness in place of closeness; such trials can be borne. But never again, I pray, selfishness in love, or lies, misunderstandings & strife. We artists are naturally enough, blended of keen contrasts; cruelty with kindness, selfishness with devotion, etc. It seems to me that I, amply provided with the 2 sides of my nature, took over many pains to do justice to the hard & inhuman elements of my make-up in the past. If I am to have a future, I must try to do justice to my kindlier, more human, sides. It is time they had their innings. I would be well content if my actions were such as to gradually lead you to feel that you had added to the steadfast security & harmoniousness of yr life in meeting me—that you had gained in comfort without losing in freedom. Deeds alone can show.

When, in the train, I read you Lindsay's poem 'Where is the real *non-resistant*[?]', ending

> 'To our White Cause of Peace
> Surrender—surrender—surrender'

& you asked me if I would ever surrender to woman I said 'no', but answered 'perhaps' when you asked me would I ever surrender to Christ.[1] I dont know what my final answers to those questions will be! But I know this; if I surrender to woman at all it will not be by halves, & it will be a surrender to a 'white cause of *peace*'.

In spite of the fact that I feel little else but long to see you again, yet I would rather do without seeing you than ever be a cause of grief, annoyance or disappointment to you, or that we should either of us ever lose our kindliness toward each other. Surely there can be such a thing as unbroken peace, unfailing helpfulness between 2 souls, whether their relationship be close or less close?

When I told you my tragedy in the train & you were so wonderful[ly] helpful to me, laying hold of me to kindly comfort me, & you said: 'You do not need a sweetheart; you need someone to mother you', you must have thought me boorish enough in my answer: 'It is not mothering I need. I never wish anyone to replace what I had in my mother.' It is true that I have a horror of trying to replace past relationships, particularly anything to do with my mother. But I also meant *something else* & did not make it clear to you, I know:

[1] Vachel Lindsay (1879–1931), American poet. This poem, subtitled 'Matthew V, 38–48', appeared in his *Collected Poems* (New York: Macmillan, 1925). Its final stanza reads: 'Who can surrender to Christ? Where is the man so transcendent, | So heated with love of his kind, so filled with the spirit resplendent | That all of the hours of his day his song is thrilling and tender, | And all of his thoughts to our white cause of peace | Surrender, surrender, surrender?' (p. 390).

To be as erotic as I am, yet to live for over 4 years with no sweet-heart, with never a kiss or a hand-touch passing between me & anyone other than my closest kin & oldest friends, & then to see before me 'my sweetheart in my imagination' who brought life to all things thought dead. But I knew you were grieved by bereavement[1] & I had promised myself before I left the boat to try & make yr trip across the continent as restful & unannoyed as I could. It was hard to be near you, feeling as I did, & to behave as I did, but I deeply felt it due to yr bereavement to give you whatever repose & security a stranger could. But it was too much to have you touch me in pity & to let the word 'mothering' pass unchallenged, when you were to me 'my sweet-heart in my imagination' & *never anything else at all*. Besides, it would have been an unworthy lie, the kind of lie I have sworn to myself never to live again.

To have you comfort me as you did, show yr compassionateness as you did, was heaven (since then I have known a new life, a new approach to happiness), but I could not accept even such heavenliness under false pretences. Will you forgive my seeming boorishness?

——————— " ———————

I think of you being now in London & of the sad comparisons with the past you cannot fail to make, now that yr friend is gone. I hope you will suffer as little as possible, will have no troubles or bothers, & that Elsie,[2] & others, will gladden you, & that you will not regret that you are there. After Australia, London may seem a little gloomy any way. I know that is the finding of many a returning Englishman. But then, you are not English.

——————— " ———————

I read today, in the Chapter ‚Samhällsmoderlighet'[3] of Ellen Key's wonderful ‚Kärleken och Äktenskapet',[4] lines that paint livingly the kind of enchantment you weave: ‚Ty vad mannen framför allt söker hos Kvinnan—och djupast älskar, när han finner det—är godhetens glädje. Det är denna, som i allt äkta behag blir synlig och vinner sin berättigade seger'.[5] Should you care to write me in Swedish, ever, you would confer special joy; as I naturally want to know yr dear tongue

---

[1] Just before reaching Vancouver on the ship Ström had learnt of the death of a former lover, the British politican Frederick Leverton Harris (1864–1926).

[2] Ella Ström's daughter. See Biographical Register (Elsie Bristow).

[3] = Social maternity (Swedish).   [4] = Love and Marriage (Swedish).

[5] = Since what man seeks, above all, in a woman—and most deeply loves when he finds it—is the joy of goodness. It is that which in all its true pleasure becomes visible and wins its justified victory. (Swedish.)

as soon as I may. All things Swedish are dearer to me now because of you; but you are also partly dear to me because of the noble race that is yours, & of which you are such a shining example. Should you be willing to write 'from Ella Ström' on the left topmost corner of any envelope you are addressing to me, then the Morses (they were so very glad to meet you that day) will take special care of such a letter & make sure I get it swiftly & safely.

Very fondly
Percy

23 *To Ella Ström*

[In 1927 Grainger started to experiment with his 'Nordic' ('Blue-eyed') English more systematically. In November of that year he began drafting his forty-two-page essay 'The Love-Life of Helen and Paris', an account of his meeting and growing friendship with Ella Ström. In his correspondence, too, he started to introduce an increasing number of words which were (or so he thought) devoid of Graeco-Latin roots.]

Home, Jan 31, 1928

My darling one,

Getting home today I got yr beloved letters of Jan 2 & Jan 6. (I believe there is some earlier letter that has not yet reached me, as you write of 'Helen & Paris' & the photos as if you had acknowledged them before, but I have no letter telling of their coming.)

First I must deal with your wonderful & weighty letter of Jan 2 (in which you write of yr New Year's cable to me, of 'result not knowable', of how all hinges on Ariki's[1] good-deeming,[2] in which you blame yrself for not being honest with me last summer, and so on): I suppose the whole tone of the letter must be called a greater blow to my hopes than any I have yet had from you, yet so great is my love of yr nature, so sincere my admiration for yr thots,[3] *that no letter seems to be more adorable than this one.*

Your love for Ariki is so *beautiful,* so lovable, to me. To read such words as 'T's beauty is a source of endless delight to me'; 'every turn

[1] Iyemasa Tokugawa (1884–1963), at this time Japanese Consul-General in Sydney; in 1940 he succeeded his father as Prince Tokugawa, and heir of the famous Shogun family. Ella Grainger had first become intimately involved with Tokugawa in 1922, in London, and reportedly bore him a child in the mid-1920s.
[2] = approval.　　[3] = thoughts.

of his mind is noble, diplomatic, practical & sensible'; 'my affection for T. is as true as it is undying,' fills me with upliftedness & pride in yr loyalty & love-rich nature. To be able to speak beautifully & openly of one lover to another is the height of human-ness & *the kind I have always hungered for*. Yr loyalty to Ariki, yr warm yet critical appraisement of his strong & gentle qualities, yr power of feeling exstacy afresh where you love, is all very dear to me. In all these ways you are so truly 'the princess'. Your willingness to own up to being 'in the wrong' is also so noble & princesslike. I, too, am always willing to admit how wrong I am in a thousand things, & I can understand & worship that activity of mind in you; for it is *lack of mind-energy* that makes folk consider themselves right always.

When I think back to a year ago I am enthralled to see how much deeper I love you now than then. Then I divined goodness, angelicness, giftedness in yr looks & art, etc.; but I knew too little of yr life & characteristics to say that my divinations had been proved.

Now that I know you so much more fully I find that my instinctive divination of yr wonderful nature is more than borne out by the truth, the proof of facts. You look the princess, & you *act* the princess. And in no whit does yr angelic bodily loveliness outstrip the loveliness of yr mind, & character & soul. Such a letter as yrs of Jan. 2 strengthens me in my limitless admiration for every side of you, deepens my adoration & makes me exult to be alive & to know that humanity can be so good & true & sweet as you are—in spite of the fact that it is not a letter to encorage my hopes of happiness. But I would rather lose my happiness with you than my admiration for you (tho in losing the second I would also, no doubt, lose the first), so very much am I yr loving brother & father. To see my dear little girl so utterly after my heart, to be able to so wholeheartedly applaud each new showing of her rich & manysided nature—how that *makes life worth living for me!* As for my own happiness—all happiness has been quickly snatched away from me in the past. Maybe there is something in me that destroys my happiness. Maybe my hunger for happiness is too greedy, too selfish. Maybe the spirit-powers (if there be such—I doubt it) wish me to learn to curb my hunger for happiness. I can bear to die of hunger for happiness. But I would hate to *find you less lovely than I guessed*. My life would be laid waste *to its inner roots* if I found you small, unloving, forgetful, disloyal, fickle. But no. I find you exquisite, flawless always & each new problem (what between other lovers might be termed strife or division—if we were not both of us so sensitive, so tender & so *selfcritical*) only serves to stiffen me in my surety that I can trust you, love you, admire you without the least fear of a 'let-down'.

As to yr New Year's cable: We all realised yr wishes were for the Morses as well as for myself & we all thank you for the gracious greeting. Nothing could have been better than yr wording of the cable (it takes a poetess to send a truly clear & revealing cable!).

'Result not knowable' was perfect, & the word 'knowable' could not be bettered, & is grammatical & wisely chosen in every way. In one of my cables I said 'result not unknowable if yr mind is made up as mine': That was because I did not realize that the unknowableness hinged upon yr need of such *utter* oneness & beauty between you & Ariki in the matter. I thot of you as being so eager for the wedding, & I did not allow for the very natural sweetening & tightening of the bond between you & Ariki when you are close to his sweet presence. I did not like to think of the result being 'not knowable' simply because you bowed blindly to his will or behest. But now that I see how happy you are with him, how truly devoted you are to him I can only applaud yr need for his full & well considered consent to such a weighty step as yr possible wedlock with me.

Yr lines about the way he took the news & yr request for wedlock with me paints a perfect picture. His 'you surprize me' is perfect—at once gentle yet awe-fraught.

You say 'he considers me as belonging to himself'. As a product of noble öländsk[1] samurai-thot that is maybe very natural & right. All races have the idea of *belongingness* except us Nordics. That is why other races are more loyal to king & country & kin & creed than we, & why they *breed* & *fight* better than we. Our gift to the world is the gift of *freedom*. And we Nordics, who fail in almost every other virtue of life as compared with other races, *dare not fail* in the matter of freedom. It is the one matter in which we have *gone further* than others. Forgive me therefore this one unsympatheticness; that I cannot (as a Nordic) right-deem anyone having the thot that another human being *belongs to him*—not in love, not in anything.

And I will be arrogant in one thing; in saying that *I am proving* my Nordic freedom cult in my love of you—for I *am* wishing you freedom, I *am* doing what I can to aid & abet yr freedom; & *nobody* could *need* you as much as I do, for I have *nothing else* in this world to live for but you! That you, as a woman (even a Nordic woman), may right-deem

---

[1] = from the island of Öland (Swedish), although Grainger may mean more generally just an islander.

his sense of ownership of you is something I cannot sit in judgement on. If you *love* him enough, no doubt all goes with it.

Certainly it is true that 'it is therefore only fair that he should have plenty of time to consider this question' & equally certain it is that the picture you have painted in yr letter of the way he took the news is a lovely one. Everything you say in yr letter—about his bodily beauty, about his lovely öländsk clothes, about his wisdom & gentleness, about his sweet seriousness & thoroness, about his manliness & energy—bears out my old love & homage to the noble Japanese race—reawakes something that was kindled when I read of Japanese history & the samurai code—so like our viking code, by the way!

You write 'I wish in a way that you two had met.' If Ariki should seem willing to give his consent to yr wedding on general grounds but would not like to give his final 'yes' without testing me with his eyes & nearness I could (if you wished) go out to Australia for the express purpose of letting him meet me—but only if *both you & he wished it* & if you would think that course begetful of good; I could sail after the Bowl concerts & be in Sydney in early September, 1928. But such a plan should not be lightly undertaken—only if you think it truly wise, & if you both wished it. But I am *yours to command*, & there is nothing good & sweet & true & humble I would not do to win you & to show my reverence of the nobility of Ariki's love for you. *But you have nothing whatsoever to upbraid yourself with anent me.* Please do not do so! You have been *perfection itself* to me in every way. I did not want you to treat me with the wariness of a lawyer. I have never (& never will) ask you not to lie to me, or ask you always to be open with me. I only ask you to be *natural with me* (as far as possible) so I may have the priceless boon of knowing yr enthralling nature just as it is.

I was not such a fool (from the start) as to think of you as other than deeply sought after & prized. If you were not run after by many (I argued) then you must be deeply tied to one, or a few. So the sudden news of Ariki being in yr life was no shock to me at Pevensey.[1] (If I had known it before, however, I might not have deemed it fair to you or to him for me to go to Pevensey. By the way, I do not think it fair that he should have the idea that I tried to take you from him, *knowing of your & his love for each other.* If you can, & care to—make it clear that I went to Pevensey unknowing of him. *But do as you like in all things.*) I did not go to P. awaiting anything from you. I told you

---

[1] Grainger had visited Ström at her holiday cottage, 'Lilla Vrån', in Pevensey Bay, Sussex, during Aug. 1927.

beforehand that I would not upbraid you if you refused to see me after I came, or if you kicked me out with or without rime or reason.

You must always remember that you have saved me from spiritual shipwreck. I was stricken when I met you. You have given me back life & hope, thankfulness to nature, the power to tonewright[1] again, joy in money earning (because it is for you, largely). There is nothing I can ever do to requite you for the deep good you have done me, & *are* doing me.

I cannot have you say to me that you are 'calculating & even crooked' & that you blame yourself that you were 'not as honest' with me last summer as you should have been. I *do not know what you mean: heart's dearest.* Did I not know that you were going to Australia to discuss matters with Ariki? Did I not gather that without his consent you 'could not marry happily'? If I did not know all that (whether actually said by yr lips or half guessed by me matters not) why did I urge you to go back to Australia? Why have I always used the (to me) cruel words '*if* you marry me' instead of '*when* you marry me.' Yes, it is true, we were a little carried away by our loverlike craving to touch heaven as soon as might be, & in our whirl of longings let our hopes somewhat outstrip our facts. But is that not a most natural & proper error? I do not like you to say 'I am a frivolous woman after all, because no doubt I drew you on to the intimacy between us.' I have seen nothing 'frivolous' in you. Your poem about Pevensey Bay, before I came, showed with how little frivolousness you viewed my coming. I yearned for you from the first & you did not have to 'draw me on' to anything. In my own typical way I *wooed you* just as hungrily & stick-to-it-ively[2] as any other true lover. Nothing but the knowledge that you did not care at all for me would have stopped me, & nothing less will stop me now. I revere yr love for Ariki, I respect his earlier claims, his longer helpfulness & sweetness, but I shall always remain 'yr lover in my imagination' whatever happens & I shall try to win you if I may *without causing misery to you or others.* I do not believe in love unions based on the misery of others. You write 'but I *blame* myself if the outcome of it all should hurt either of us three.' But how can it? If you *love me enough* you will come to me sooner or later & yr true & sweet love for Ariki will prevent your causing him pain or tragedy. You know that you can count on my tholesomeness[3] as well as my unbounded love. You have given me back to life. You have given joy & worthwhileness of life

---

[1] = compose.   [2] Grainger is here avoiding the Latin-derived word 'persistently'.
[3] = patience.

back to me. You have shown me that there is one human being that I can love with every part of my nature, that I can *admire limitlessly*. Shall I complain if that love I have for you causes me agony too? I am not a mean or a small nature, whatever else I am.

I wish you would not speak of yrself as 'guilty of deceit'. Do you mean towards me? Certainly you were *never* deceitful towards me. When you were with me I am sure you truly craved wedlock with me & since, too, in yr darling letters. Whether you still crave wedlock with me as keenly now that you are close to Ariki, united with him, is another question. Maybe you find, now that you are with him again & can judge, that his sweetness & grace & beauty & charm mean so much to you that you would rather carry on yr present life with him than be wed to me. I am a genius, & a genius is always wondrously attractive to me. I find it hard to explain how women can deny themselves to geniuses. But history shows that they mostly do. The soldiers & statesmen & men of action are able to awake more love in woman than we geniuses are able to, I think. No doubt we art-concentrated ones are very clumsy & lopsided in many ways. I know I am, for one. But it was precisely to *search yr heart* that you returned to Australia, was it not? I would not want you to wed me & *rue it after*. I would not wish you to marry me only to discover that you would liefer[1] have stayed with Ariki.

In my heart of hearts I feel so sure that you & I are perfect mates that I will not let my hopes be downed lightly by showings to the contrary. I will await yr & Ariki's decision with tholesomeness. In the meantime my heart is filled with love for you *& for all those you love*.

But make no mistake: Do not mistake my freedom-cult, my passiveness, my lack of jealousy for lukewarmness! You are the *only* hope of happiness I have in this life & I love you with the depths of my nature— overflowingly, helplessly, utterly. Do not forget my *need of you*, my *utter forlornness without you*, when making yr decision!

And thank you for your glorious, adorable letter of Jan 2, that has brought new beauty into my life. My worship of you grows & grows. Never upbraid yourself in connection with *me*. You are the perfect sun in my otherwise dark welkin. I give thanks merely to know you are in the same world as I. (O, but how much I want *more* than that!)

Lovingly & reveringly

Percy

[1] = more willingly.

24   *To Ella Ström*

[Ström and Grainger did marry, first in a registry office and then on 9 August 1928 before a crowd of thousands during one of Grainger's Hollywood Bowl concerts in Los Angeles. Despite many statements to the contrary, Ström did walk into wedlock fully aware of Grainger's lust for bizarre, even brutal, sex acts. Here he allows her to share some of his visions for their future together.]

Kansas City Station, Monday Ap. 23, 1928

Godgiven little playmate Ella-Viola,

Coming from Chicago (just now) there was a young fair mother with 2 young fair children near me in the train. The little boy (aged 4–6) was very self willed & playful, the mother very badtempered (tho not evilnatured) & bossy. She was smacking him all the time, & he taking it as a matter of course, mainly without tears or cries, but always with a wary eye on her when he disobeyed her, taking her blows as part of a well known game, trying to get his way & yet sidestep the smacks if he might. Mostly she was content to give him a single smack on his hands, legs or thighs, but once she got really riled &, laying him on his back, caught hold of one foot & thereby pulling the leg hard up (toward his face), she rained a sheaf of quick hand blows on his taut-pulled little bottom. Such delights are nearly the death of me. My heart leaps, kicks & cavorts in its bone-house like an untamed buffalo, I feel halfstrangled with rapture, my limbs faint with trembling weakness—as if melting away from me. Afterwards my inner guts suffer a gnawing tight neuralgialike pain—most likely because flooded with sex-mad blood. But such spasms are worth death, bedriddenness, disaster. I live only waiting for such life-oertopping moments, in which the all-world ((universe))[1] seems to suddenly do one's bidding so that one feels like god.

Can you not, will you not, be sometimes suddenly masterfully cruel to me as that mother was to her child? Not in *unhappy* anger on yr part, but just in quick, lighthearted avenging fury? If I yawn, if I bump into you when we walk (which I know I too often do), if I tread on yr feet, if I annoyingly repeat myself, if I rilingly talk to you when you

---

[1] Grainger himself frequently provided better-known synonyms for his 'Nordic' English terms. In this edn. these synonyms are regularly found within Grainger's double parentheses. Some other Graingeresque terms for sexual activities or parts he left unexplained, but their meaning is generally easily guessed.

94

are trying to mind-point ((concentrate)), if I say something that goes against yr grain—could you not (like that kindly cruel mother—who enjoyed herself thoroly) turn on me like a flash (as you would do to yr little boy if you had one) & smack my face, pull my hair, pinch my ears, kick my legs, hit my thighs or my bottom with a stick, or (when you are outoftheway-putout) make me strip & whip me thoroly? It would be quite understood between us that it was half a game, that you do not do it hatefully, that I should never withstand you. In public you should not do it, for folk would misunderstand it, & we dont want our love misunderstood. If I annoy you in public you could say 'come with me' (as a mother does to her boy), take me into another room, or upstairs, or behind a curtain & hurt me. (One of the most rapturous parts of being punished as a young child is the being whisked help-lessly & relentlessly away to one's doom, upstairs or somewhere, fore-boding the bitter-smart ere it falls!)

I would love my life to be filled with those quick storms—as they fall in weather out of doors—as long as I was sure that you were not *unloving* towards me, sure I had not *wounded* you (but only riled you, as even the sweetest child riles the sweetest mother). And I would like *your* days to know the befreeing relief that comes from *wielding power*, letting one's temper *run free*, the close-mood ((intimacy)) of treating a playmate like a dog, like oneself. I want you to till the wont ((cultivate the habit)) of stripping yrself of all reserve towards me, of all selfhiding manners towards me. I want to touch the *inner flesh* of yr soul moods, nerve-changes, yr see-saw of likes & dislikes—just as with my lips, my tongue, I want to caress the outward turned gateways of yr whangiti, (after 'eruption') to tickleentice yr bladderwaters to gush over my wor-shipping mouth. At times I want to be yr art-god, & at other times yr pitiless sadic god. But again, at other times, I want to be the dust under yr princess-feet ('how beautiful are thy steps in shoes, O prince's daughter'), want to be the helpless slave before yr chieftainess-ire, & *at all times* the mat you wipe yr moods on. I was so happy at Grez,[1] one morning on the white road between woods, when you let forth yr bel-lygasses as naturally as a child. It showed (O welcomed token) that you had no *respect* for me, that you were no longer *polite* in yr inner bearing towards me. I only wish my face had been close to your bodygates at the time. I want to taste as much of you as I can—in touch, in sight, in smell, in hearing. All natural types, I take it, like to smell themselves

---

[1] The two had called on Delius at Grez-sur-Loing during a short visit to France in Aug. 1927.

when sweaty, like to see their own parapara after momoe, like to see, sense, smell, study all the outputs, leavings of their own body. No healthy type feels vämjelse[1] towards any of these bodyhaps or body acts of his own body. How much less the vämjelse, how much more the drawness that one feels towards the body & bodyacts of the beloved! For here the slight strangeness of the beloved (as side-meted ((compared)) with one's life long wontedness to one's own body) heaps the fuel of know-hunger upon the fire of closeness-cravingness. I beg of fate that our wonts-of-oneness, our respectlessness, our unhidingness, our reservelessness, our nought-but-lovingness will outsoar anything ever done by lovers before; for our naturalnesses, our closenesses, our flinging away of conventional 'cleanly niceness' will not be the thrill-search of jaded sex-palates, but the overflow of our allembracing sense of loveliness, lovingness, atoneness. How I rejoiced when you licked my nostrils! Alas! That there are so few holes, way[s]-in, nests, hiding places in our bodies that may be explored by the inward-boring lover! The navel is a nice blind-alley. Truth bids me tell that there is one thing about you that I deplore in amazement: That you are not lustful to have yr uma, yr u licked, tickled, sucked, bitten. How can it be that heavenly lustful you are deaf, blind to the sweetest nerve-madness so many women draw from these hills of womanhood? Is it not, maybe, that I have failed to touch, to treat them the right way? Or may it be that your u, tho not answering the helm of lips, tongue or teeth, would answer blissfully to the tender pricks of gentle-used sharp needles, as my u answer to them? Whatever you feel or not, I fear I shall never long be able to withstand the temptation to love-treat in one way or another, those tenderly loved sweet umas of yours. You said that too much such treatment *annoyed*, *nerveteased* you. Then let me thus tease you while you punish me for the annoyance I give you: Let me lay my weight upon, momi-ing at yr heavenbringing uma, while you thrash my bottom, back & legs in rising annoyance.

Over a month ago I went to a movie for men only: '*Is your daughter Safe?*', which was followed by a sextalk by a (real or sham) doctor on sexduties & sexwonts. He said that 99 out of every 100 American men were shamelessly & unforgivably knowledgeless about the part they should play in the sex act—knowledgeless of where the seat of woman's joy lies, knowledgeless of how to call forth her highest bliss, uncaring for her sex delight. And as he talked I had to own up to

[1] = disgust (Swedish).

myself that I was as bad, or nearly as bad, as the rest. For instance I always thot that woman's bliss, her climax-bringing nerve-joys, lay normally inside the whanganui as well as just outside in the tara. I did not realise (until he told us) that the seat of all sexbliss, of all climaxswayingness lies normally *only* in the tara. I used to think it abnormal in you & others that the joyspot lay *only* in the tara. I did not know (until he told us) that it is the man's duty in momoe to keep the ureroa in friction with the tara all (or almost all) the time. Thus I came to know how knowledgeless I had been at Pevensey, how selfish I must have seemed to you. I bought a book on this lore at that same movie that I will not send thru the mail but would like to read thru with you when we meet. I am all eagerness to try & learn to be a more lovingly-knowing husband, lover. My hunger to try & coax forth in you the greatest muchness of swooning bliss is even keener than my also very great hunger for the delights of my own body at yr hands. Help me, teach me to be a tender, delicate yet madness-begetting tone-crafter ((musician)) upon the tone-tool ((musical instrument)) of yr goddess-body! (My body trembles, pants, is loveswollen at the mere thot of being allowed to try once more!)

And now I come to you with an *unwontedly selfish* beg-askment ((request))—which of course I beg you to turn down (without a moment's further thot) if my asking bores you, is distasteful to you, or if you merely lack the time. You see, I cannot come to you childlikely, freely, carelessly with begaskments if I am not *utterly sure* that you, in spite of yr all-too loving unselfishness, in yr all-too yielding kindliness & *Swedish hostlikeness* ((hospitality)), will be sure to guard against letting yrself be drawn into tasks & lines-of-thot that are too boring to you.

The beg-askment is this: You know how that Kansas City spanking case (curious that I should happen to be writing in Kansas City today—a mere chance) het me all up & that, about a month ago, I managed to fare thru Kansas City in order to pick up some newspaper reports of the law-trials.[1] I send you copies of these. Such a hap *in real life* forms a fine root for a whiplust story—the reading of which would carry me away to realms of purest delight. But the haps in real life do not go far enough, or are reported in the papers by fools lacking all sadic gifts. I could work up a fine whiplust story from these herewith-sent beginnings (I sent you others of the same case, before); but, alas!

[1] This was the case of a Mrs Christine Woodside, who was jailed for spanking her daughter. She was, however, freed the following day on a bond provided by her husband.

97

I got no thrill out of my own writings—partly because I always *remember* what I have so hardworkingly written, partly because my English is too self-some ((too special, too original)) to give me the needed illusion of reality, outside-myself-ness. Even the most stupidly written whiplust stories that I buy give me more thrill than comparatively wellwritten ones by myself. *What thrill would I not get out of such a story written cleverly by you*—blending the unforeknownness so needful with a skill of *normal writing* (in our giftednesses we must always balance each other—you by yr sweet normalness, I by my harddriving beyond-normalness—'male & female created he them') I could never equal. That is what I ask you to do—if you happen to have the time, happen to care to minister in that comradely way to my lust-wonts—to take these Kansas City roots & graft upon them a whiplust short tale of wild uphettingness.

I will sketch roughly how I would handle it myself. I would begin it as a newspaper report of the pending trial (quoting from the actual paper reports—giving a touch of reality) & then add in yr own story, telling it as if all revealed at the trial of March 9. Or maybe it would be still better to break away from the newspaper reports & the whole trial business, & tell yr whole story in the 3rd person (basicly), but basing it on the hints held in the paper reports. I would weave the following plot: Lorette takes the family car, seemingly to go to Lawrence, Kansas with 6 girls, & promising to be home at 5.30. But she does not. (Here weave in yr own story of yr first momoe.) She goes to afternoon party, takes drinks with man who takes her maidenhead in motorcar (or elsewhere) tears her drawers, etc (following strictly yr own splendid tale—to me one of the most thrilling of all the stories you ever told me—so that this part would be a sketch for that part of the story of yr own life).

She comes home late (8? 11.30?) & her mother is playing cards with friends. Guarded, selfcontrolled askings & answers back & forth between mother & daughter. When the cardplaying guests go mother shows her ire & asks daughter roughly where she's been, why she's late, etc—mother going towards daughter, daughter backing away. Daughter lies, mother senses lie & seizing coathanger (you know those light wooden ones)[1] starts to beat her to make her tell the truth, first on arms, sides, thighs, & then, wanting to beat her behind, finds the torn drawers. Mother, now furious & fearfilled, asks 'how-come' & begins to strip daughter, saying 'I'll get the truth out of you if I have to thrash you within an inch of yr life', or the like. Wordpaint

---

[1] Grainger drew such a coathanger here.

((describe)) the undressing, tell what she had on, tell the girl's efforts to withstand mother, the mother's not-to-be-nay-saidness. Wordpaint the girl's body when naked, whether thin or plump, how behaired, whether smallbreasted or how. State just where the marks of the coathanger show on the bare flesh. The mother now gets her riding whip (choose yr own drama anent this: The mother may seize the girls wrists & drag her, struggling against her, to the closet (or elsewhere) where she keeps her riding whip. Or the mother may tie her up to a bed or sofa or something while she goes to get the whip. Wordpaint the whip. A thin cutting lash is mostly more lust awakening than a thick heavy lash.) Now paint the drama of the mother striving to cut the truth out of the girl, the girl torn between wishing to give in (to escape the lashes) & fearing to own up to the truth of her lost maidenhead, unwilling to give her lover away. As far as possible wordpaint where each blow (or each group of blows) falls, & state how the girl looked, how she screamed, whether the mother gagged her or just kept on trying to force her to tell her the truth. As far as my taste goes, blows are most thrilling on breasts, bottom, inner thighs, sexparts. Next good are shoulders, upper arms, upper legs. Least good are neck, belly, back, lower arms, lower legs. But any parts may be drawn upon for contrast. End the drama any way you want—the girl may faint, or she may own up, or stranger or the police (hearing the screams & blows) may break in & end it. Into the very beginning of the tale I would drag in facts from the newspapers. 'She came back to live with her mother in her 6th year. Her mother always smacked her ("& you dont know how mother can hurt just with her hands" etc)—once because she failed to bring back a good diploma.['] Talks with school friends: 'Of course I love my mother, but she does whip me most unmercifully', etc. All that sort of thing gets the whiplustful reader simmering & by the time you embark on yr main story he is at the boiling point. That is my own idea of how to handle such a story. But you may have better ideas, or ideas that will seem better to me because less fore-known. But dont fail to draw in yr own story of maidenhood loss, delightful torn drawers, etc. (When the mother sees them, she can tear them off in fury, maybe?) You could build me a little heaven with such a whiplust story.[1] That you added the chapter 'Love & Sadism' &

[1] The obsession with flagellation would continue through Grainger's life. Writing his 'Notes on Whip-lust' on 24 Dec. 1948 Grainger would begin: 'But I cannot give a true picture of my tone-art & of my art-life if I do not tell of the cruel-joy ((sadism)) that is one of the main stirs of my being. How can a true man, I ask, feel anything but cruel-fain towards lovely women[?]'

wrote it *as you did*, filled me with the greatest thankfulness & bliss. I cannot read those pages without my heart thumping—almost as much as it thumped at **P.**

So here is another chance to spin me a web of most wondrous delight. But I shall thoroly thoroly understand if you cannot in any way see yr way to follow up this hot wish of mine. It may go against the grain, or you may just simply not have the time. *How you have found the time to do all the things for me, & to beget all the rimes you have is a mystery to me.* You have Ariki & Elsie to think of & be with. I dessa timmer är du icke *min* älskling (Käraste).[1] It is *not to be looked for* that yr mind could run much on me, my thots, my wishes. Yet you have managed to do a *real raft of work already*, better than ever before. It just shows what an allsided, many voiced nature you have—able to be lovingly loyal to sundry goals & ideals at one & the same time. You are my everwilling, everready, noblespirited little thane & artsister—kindly, givewilling, hostful, joybegetting. One always beats or overloads the willing horse (am I not myself a willing horse & am I not often over-loaded?). So I heap yet another beg-askment upon you, my deeply dearly beloved Ella, but begging you pay no heed to it if you would rather not.

Your evergreedy, but ever worshipful lover-playmate
    Percy

Is not the story of Velma West[2] pity awakening? The thot of sexlove between woman & woman is thrilling to me. Have you never tried, never thot of, sexlove with Gisken?[3]

25   *To Maurice Lowe*

In the train, Nov. 19, 1929
My dear Maurice Lowe:

Thanks for your splendid letter. That is just what I like—for musicians to *mean business* and to be 'provacable' [*sic*]. I delight to try to answer yr letter because the subject interests me especially, yr case

---

[1] = At such times you are not *my* beloved (my dearest) (mostly Swedish).

[2] On 6 Mar. 1928 West had been sentenced to life imprisonment for the murder of her husband. Her friend Mabel Young had also been named in the case.

[3] Gisken Wildenvey (1895–1985), Norwegian author and friend of Ella, wife of the Norwegian poet Herman Wildenvey (1886–1959).

being a particularly vital one, i.e., the case of the talented unconventional minded music lover who reaches music thru the piano and has the limitations of his approach. What is the great boon of the piano? That it opens the world of harmony and the possibility of florid arabesques as hardly any other instrument can. But it also tends to make our musical thought small (limited to 4 bar phrases, all phrases beginning and ending *together*). It gives us little insight into the very root of harmony and free musical form—different voices of different lengths and rhythms, beginning and ending at different moments, which interweave and together form harmony and formal impulses, such as

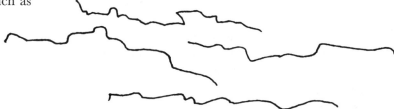

Should not the outlines of musical voices, in their normal condition, resemble the outlines of mountain ranges, each independent and individualistic in itself, but together forming block effects of majestic complexity?

The disgusting simplicity of modern life has laid itself like a disease over a great deal of music. What is the victory of modern civilization (over the Orient, for instance)? The victory of a deadening simplicity over a healthy complexity.

Of course not all our art is simple. Much of it forms *a corrective* to the weaknesses of our civilization, and it is these corrective examples we should study (among other things, of course), in my opinion.

Can you get a second piano (no matter how small and poor-toned) in your house? If so, all is very simple.

Take *Purcell's 'Three part, 4 part and 5 part Fantasias for Strings,'* recently edited by Peter Warlock, Curwen Edition. Order the score and 1 each of the string parts. Have these string parts played on your 2 pianos (violin I and viola on the 1st piano, and violin II and 'cello on 2nd piano), or, on four strings, if you have them. Or, yourself play 2 parts on 1 piano and have 2 other pianists play the other 2 parts on the other piano. Listen to the interplay of parts. Hear how they begin and end. Try experiments with them dynamically—see which expression marks are the most effective. See how these parts *breathe independently*, how each has a separate life, and thus is able to weave into a complex whole. I know of no lovelier examples of *real* many-voiced music (nor of British-mooded music) than these Purcells.

Then try the Bach Fugues (well-tempered Clavier) in the same way—soprano and tenor on 1 piano, alto and bass on the 2nd piano. Get really familiar with what freely moving, independently moving, voices mean, and what musical form is when freed from the slavery of the 4 bar phrases. I will try and send you a vocal and piano score of my '*Father & Daughter*' setting, as an example of a 7 bar *tune*. There is another good 7 bar tune at the end of my 'Jutish Medley' piano solo. (G. Schirmer).[1]

Then consult the moderns that have many voiced expression, irregular rhythms, etc. Such as:

Richard Strauss: Sinfonia Domestica, 2 pianos

Grainger: Hill Songs I and II, 2 pianos (G. Schirmer)

Cyril Scott: Piano Sonata, Op. 66 (Elkin)

Stravinsky: The Rite of Spring, piano duet

Above all, *compose at a harmonium or organ*, not a piano. The legato, sustained, continuous tone of the harmonium is closer to the continuous tone of the orchestra than is the piano.

In order to learn orchestration it is not needful to write for the orchestra at once, or even to read score at once. Begin by writing for a few instruments, such as violin (or flute or clarinet) and cello and harmonium. Or, write for a voice (or 2 voices) and a few instruments. I will send you an example by Vaughan Williams if I can find it. Please send it back to me later.

Get to know the range and color of the various registers of the various instruments by writing for them singly (as my 'Arrival Platform Humlet' for unaccompanied viola) or in small combinations with harmonium—the harmonium supplying the harmonic background, the other instruments giving the standing-forth, soloistic melodic voices. Then gradually get to know the various woodwind instruments, saxophone and brass the same way. Go and listen to individual instruments as they play in theatres (better still if you can play in a theatre orchestra yourself), in bands, in records. Test their tone, usefulness, range, strength—memorizing their qualities. That is the basis of orchestration—knowing *many* instruments *individually*. Then begin to listen to orchestral records, score in hand.

---

[1] No. 8 of Grainger's *Danish Folk-Music Settings* (1928), eventually the final movement of Grainger's *Danish Folk-Music Suite*.

To sharpen your ear: Note down music from pianola rolls, testing your accuracy by looking at the holes in the rolls afterwards.

Good scores to study, afterwards:

Debussy: 'L'après midi d'un faune'

Wagner: Good Friday Spell Music[1]

Finest work to study for all around varied musicianship:

Bach's Matthew Passion

Other modern works that I approve of are:

V. Williams: Pastoral Symphony

" " : Variation[2] for strings on a theme by Tallis.

Grainger: English Dance, 2 pianos, 6 hands (Schott & Co. Ltd. London.)

Schönberg: 5 Orchesterstücke (Peters).

Delius: The Song of the High Hills (Universal).

Please try the harmonium, and try many-voiced music (1 player to each part) such as Bach and Purcell, on 2 pianos. Get to hear parts moving separately and together weaving harmonies (parts played individualistically by separate players) and you are close to the root of the world's best music, old or new—I admit no real difference between old and new music.

Let me know if these suggestions mean anything to you—later on.

Best wishes and greetings

Can't you form a choir of 8 or more voices (need not be good voices) to try thru (at home) old and new part songs? I know no training as good as this.

26　　　　　　　　　*To Robert Atkinson*

[Train], New York to Kansas, April 16, 1931

Dear friend Robert

I rejoiced getting thy March 1st letter[3] & to know that thou and thine are well. When I hear nothing for a long while I begin to worry; for thy well-being means unsayably much to me—partly for the whole-

---

[1] From *Parsifal*, Act III scene i.　　　　　　　　[2] Correctly, Fantasia.
[3] Not extant. For a detailed exposition of Grainger's relationship with Atkinson see Michael Roe, 'Robert Atkinson, Percy Grainger's "dear over-soul friend"', *Papers and Proceedings of the Tasmanian Historical Research Association*, 28/1 (Mar. 1981), 8–16.

somely selfish reason that I want to work with thee & learn from thee later on. So please send me a sign of life every few months, if only a postcard saying 'we are well', or the like. I, like thee, am overworked & I understand thy overworkedness & grieve over it—as I do over mine, too.

I wish thou might see thy way to foreready a book opening the door to thy whole thot-world, setting forth thy thots about nations (the goods & bads, the steadytypenesses & the othersomenesses of the sundry nations thou has known & what thou thinks about them & their input—already done & what might be—to the world's weal), about tonecraft, about bookcraft, and, as well, thy oversetting of the old German poem, & any other rime-craft (selfborn or overset) of thine. There are few men like thee, that have seen so much & can think so well. The world should be able to get at thy thots & I again-say my offer to pay for the forthprintment of such a book.

I am thankful indeed that thou is not jobless in these trying times. The business let-down over here is almost unbelievably dire & harassing. It is very hard to make things pay. On some concerts that in other years *always* paid well I have this year had heavy losses & the whole how-state ((conditions)) tries one to the utmost. Other branches (such as 'performing right' fees) have gone up, however, & I guess I can keep going.

But all things, in such a time, take *double work* & I am really rather worn out, after over 1½ year's unbroken touring. In spite of all my piano concerts & many blend-band ((orchestral)) concerts I have managed to tone-wright a lot & have forthprinted an unwonted lot of works. The scores are ordered (or will be ordered) to be sent thee. Thou will see that some of the forewords are in 'Nordic English' while others are unashamedly in the wonted 'bastard English'. I am not taking my Nordic English seriously in my tonecraft foreprintments yet— not until I bring out my book on N.E.

Thanks for all the Jankó-keyboard[1] enlightenment. As far as I can judge, without trying it in realness, I samedeem with thee as to its thoro betterness. I shall see if I cannot find a Jankó tonetool to try somewhere. But it seems clear to me that all keyboards should be thusly built & likewise all tonetools (such as hammer-wood, glocken-

---

[1] Invented in 1882 by the Hungarian Paul von Jankó (1856–1919), but finding little favour amongst pianists. It consisted of six manuals, allowing a typewriter-like movement of the fingers and, thus, a wider range of note combinations.

spiel, marimba) that follow the keyboard-layout. Does thou want me to send back to thee these Jankó prints?

The 'Basic English' quotement is very mindstirring—tho I same-deem with thee in not rating the news item oversetting very highly. I deal with it on the page marked speech-craft.[1]

I have been urged to do an Australian tour beginning about June 1932. If I do, I shall give my time free of charge to blend-bands, choruses & the like in all the main towns as forthspeaker ((lecturer)), tone-leader, & the like. I will give no common-or-garden 'piano recitals', but only 'lecture recitals' at the piano. The whole undertaking would be [to] help group music-making & to showforth Nordic Music. If I do it (& I dont know yet if my purse will allow) I will plan for sundry quiet months in Hobart.

I have been playing gardener to the group music idea more than ever before just lately[2]—giving my time free to all kinds of groups & greatly helped by darling Ella's fine playing on unwonted bells, & other hammer-played tone-tools. I will send you bills-of-tone-fare & clippings. The heartiness of the artistic comeback was never so good before as it is this year of business downheartedness.

I will try & get thy fine Reed organ writ-piece ((article))[3] into some good music paper. It is good indeed. Yet I lean towards believing that what holds the reed organ back is not the flaw in its buildplan as much as folk's unableness to see its mightbeness as a groupmusic tone-tool. To my mind no keyboard tonetool (whether it be piano, pipe organ or reed organ) should ever be anything but a tone-background-tonetool upon which the tune-bearing tone-tools (those that voice but one note at a time) can spread themselves with their greater depth & life of tunefulness. As a group music tonetool both the piano & reed organ must thole the drawback of being hard to move around. Therefore (from a do-some viewpoint) there is a lot to be said for light, small reed organs with a strong tone, no stop-contrasts & a small key-

---

[1] Found at the conclusion of this letter.

[2] On 2 Dec. 1929 Grainger had written an essay 'To Conductors and to Those Forming, or in Charge of, Amateur Orchestras, High School, College and Music School Orchestras and Chamber-music Bodies', which appeared as a preface to a number of his scores published in 1930. Grainger stated there that his 'elastic' approach to scoring was intended to help 'in weaning music students away from too much useless, goalless, soulless, selfish, inartistic soloistic technical study, intended to coax them into happier, richer musical fields—for music should be essentially an art of self-forgetful, soul-expanding communistic co-operation in harmony and many-voiced-ness.'

[3] This was, perhaps, Atkinson's 'The Modern Reed-Organ', which appeared in the *Illustrated Tasmanian Mail* on 27 Jan. 1926.

board range. And in fact the carryable foldup reed organ *does* sell very well.

But there is also no reason why there should not be some extra fine bigger, more subtle reed organs. But we must always keep this in mind: music, to be healthy, must be tuneful (single-voicedly or, still better, many voicedly tuneful). Music should not be mainly made up of chords & their offspring (arpeggios, passage work begotten of chord-feeling). In my deeming all tonecraft & all tonetools will (& ought to) fail that do not clear-see this root-fact.

The same sickness that blights tonecraft with single-display ((soloistic)) nonsense such as piano solo & organ solos is also blighting the dosome world with this business slump. I do not believe it is only that the machines have taken the place of workers. It is (in the main, I feel) because all the changes have been made without being swayed by forward-looking minds & hearts filled with goodness. Farms have been run, not to feed the farmers themselves, but in the hopes of making farmers rich. The gain-greed that has undone the silly business folk has also poisoned the farmers, who now are no longer a woodcarving, homespinning, folksinging, folkdancing class but merely wouldbe business men working on the land & struggling for 'worldmarkets'. Greatness (as well as kindliness) begin[s] at home. The root of greatness is *selfhood*. We must feed ourselves (at first hand), sing for ourselves, think for ourselves, rely on ourselves.

Stretching the sealine of our hopes to all men, all lands, all branches of dosomeness is, to my mind, a sort of endless 'passing of the buck', a sort of glorified 'Let George do it.' We must not leave the writing out of tonecraft parts to copyists, we must not leave the choice of forth-printment to business forthprinters. In a world where fools rule & most things are so badly done we must (I feel) make up our minds to do & choose & sway all things (bearing on ourselves & the things we like) ourselves, as far as maybe.

Lots of fond love to you all from us both.

Percy

SPEECH-CRAFT

Anent 'Spoken English', wordstock of 850 words, & the oversetting of news item 'The R101'[1] into 'Basic English':

Undoubtedly the working together of 'doers' such as 'put', 'come',

---

[1] The British airship R101 had crashed near Beauvais, north of Paris, on 7 Oct. 1930, while on a flight to India. Forty-eight lives were lost.

'go' & the like with 'out', 'at', & the like is what we need. Such words as *input, inputter,* are stunning. But I feel we must be on our guard against following the lead of German & Latin too slavishly. Thus I ill-deem 'foredeal' (Vorteil) because 'fore' as a living root in now-time English seems to me to mean 'before' & 'in front of' rather than 'better' or 'gain'. Thus without a knowlege of German I guess that 'fore-deal' would merely hint at some such meaning as 'a deal (a business deal) done in advance'. I feel that 'advantage' (Vorteil) should be over-set by some such blend as 'gain-deal', 'gain-act', 'gain-deed'. I would sidestep 'fore' & 'for' both, whenever doable, on the ground that 'fore' as in 'forethot' & 'for' as in 'forswear', 'forgo' naysay each other & tend to make nonsense of this fore-word—or rather, I would use it, as far as may be, only in the sense of 'in front of'.

I would overset the weak spots in the news item as follows:

Basic English news item	Rightsettings
Under the direction of Sir J. Simon. *Important facts.* the *record* kept by Lieut-Col. V.C. Richmond. This *account* of the test flights	Under the *steer-sway* of—. *Much-meaning* facts, & so on the *fact-keep-list*, & so on This *fact-forthtellment* (fact-tale?)
Weather *conditions* near Beauvais	Weather *how-nesses* (or 'the howness of the weather').

Good 'Nordic' Americanisms noted lately:
'That great gittin'-up morning' (Judgement day). (Am. Negro).
'Uncorking the most dazzling play of the season.'
Railroad 'Safety first' warning: 'The chance-taker loses.'
'Steerer' (one who pilots out-of-towners to speakeasies).

I feel we must be careful not to lose the othersomeness that comes from fore or aft placing in such words as *outwork* & *work-out, outtry* & *try-out,* & the like.

Of-late-some (recent) Speechcraft thots:
Intermediate = betweensome.
Compare, comparison = match-side-by-side, side-by-side-matchment
study psycology [*sic*] = soul-delve, psycology = {soul-delfth / delvement}
scenery, scenic = land-looks, landlooks-some.

criticise = wordflay, wordflaysome (ment).
phonetics = word-sound-craft.
factory = make-house (on lines of 'cookhouse') or makery (like brewery)
subject = thot-field.

I cannot feel that 'name-word' really gives the true meaning of 'noun'. This, I feel, is better given by 'thingword'.

27   *To Hubert J. Foss*

'Lilla Vrån' | Pevensey Bay. | Sussex.
August 15th, 1931.

Dear Mr. Foss,

Mr. Willy Strecker[1] writes me that he spoke to you about a matter that he and I had been discussing, viz. the publication for the British Empire (excluding Canada—the works in question having been published in America for USA and Canada for several years) of certain larger choruses of mine that have been widely performed in America, Australia etc. but have (to my knowledge) not yet been given in Gt. Britain.

I am more a choral composer than anything else. Not only have I composed much more for chorus than for any other medium (I enclose a recent list of published choral works), but it was with choral works such as 'Irish Tune from Co. Derry', 'Brigg Fair', 'I'm seventeen come Sunday' (1906–1909) and 'Father and Daughter' (1911)[2] that I made my reputation as a composer. Therefore it is a regret to me that my larger and most typical choral works (such as 'Marching Song of Democracy' and 'The Merry Wedding') have never (to my knowledge) been heard in Great Britain—the country where the world's finest choral bodies are found and where the interest in choral music is more vital than elsewhere. As the technical innovations I introduced into choral writing about 30 years ago (such as the extended use of chorus singing without text) have been adopted by Delius and other

---

[1] (1884–1958), of the publisher Schott (Mainz), who had originally contracted to publish Grainger's works in London in 1911. He was largely responsible for the firm's growing interest in contemporary music, especially in Britain, in the years preceding the First World War.

[2] Schott had published all these works in 1911–13, although some had previously been published with Forsyth Bros.

British composers I would like to know that the original forms of these choral innovations had also been heard in Britain.

Discussing these matters with Mr. Strecker, I told him that it seemed to me that some of these more important works of mine should be handled in Britain by a firm that is in touch with the festival and large choral societies. Mr. Strecker agreed and mentioned the Oxford University Press as the leading English house for modern choral music.[1]

Do you think your house would be interested in considering the British Empire (excluding Canada) rights in one or more of these more important works? The question is, do you think your house would be likely to be able to *promote performances*? If not, the matter would hardly be advantageous to you or to me. The matter is a purely esthetic one with me. Therefore I would be pleased to *waive all royalty*, up to 1938, on any work published by you during any year in which 1000 or more copies were sold (royalties to be paid me, however, after 1938 and for any year in which less than 1000 copies were sold). 'The Marching Song of Democracy' is the most representative and effective of my larger choral works, (I value it as an expression of a typically Australian democratic athletic sentiment otherwise perhaps not voiced in music). When brought out at the Worcester, Mass., Festival of 1917 by Dr. Arthur Mees, the 'Marching Song of Democracy' had a better reception than any work of mine up to that date. But after that I was in the American Army for 1½ years and for several years after my discharge was unable to push the work because of poverty and lack of time. From 1924 on I have been able to push the work and have had many performances in Australia, New York (twice), Bridgeport, Conn., Los Angeles (twice), White Plains, NY, Chicago, Lawrence Kansas, Ann Arbor, Mich., etc.

I enclose you programs and notices of this year's performances in New York,[2] Los Angeles, and Lawrence, Kansas,[3] and also reprints of some earlier notices. A few years ago it seemed a stiff work to the average American choir, but that is so no longer—and to English choirs (so far ahead of those elsewhere) it would offer no difficulties.

The full compressed orchestral score and the orchestral parts are published for all countries by Universal-Edition, Vienna. I have also made a chamber orchestration for 12 instruments (including 2 pianos

---

[1] From its inception in 1923, with the Oxford Choral Songs and Oxford Church Music series, Foss's department had been renowned for its interest in choral music.

[2] 22 Apr. 1931, at Columbia University.   [3] 6 May 1931, at the University of Kansas.

and organ or harmonium), so that the work can be done by small choirs of 20 (or less) voices. One of the best performances was one in Los Angeles by Smallman's *a capella choir* of 30 voices accompanied by 12 instruments.[1] I could supply photostat copies of this chamber orchestration.

Thus all that would need to be printed for a British Empire (excluding Canada) edition would be the vocal score, similar to the Universal-Edition vocal score of which I am sending you a copy separately, together with copies of 'The Merry Wedding' and 'Love Verses from the Song of Solomon'.

'The Merry Wedding' is very popular, being quite easy to perform. It is representative of my *choral dance* style. The 'Love Verses from the Song of Solomon' were much liked at the first performance at Bridgeport, Conn., a few months ago[2] and are interesting to me because of the sonorous blend of voices with the chamber orchestra (but the work can be accompanied by almost any chamber music combination, or merely by piano duet) and because they were (when composed in 1899–1900) the first fruits of some studies I made of the irregular rhythms of prose speech. I can only send you a photostat copy of the 'Love Verses from the Song of Solomon' at present because the USA and Canadian edition is at present in the press.[3]

If you would be interested in considering any of these proposals please let me know to this address up to August 28th.[4]

It was so nice seeing you again in Oxford.

With cordial greetings,

Yours sincerely,

Percy Grainger

---

[1] John Smallman (d. 1943), English-born choral conductor of several choirs in the Los Angeles region. Grainger refers here to a concert of 30 Apr. 1926. See letter **21**.

[2] On 28 Apr. 1931. Grainger had conducted the Bridgeport Oratorio Society in this première.

[3] Scores, both for voices and piano duet, and for voices and harmonium, appeared from G. Schirmer in Nov. 1931.

[4] Foss replied on 31 Aug. expressing his interest, and followed up the matter with a letter of 23 Dec. in which he offered to publish for the Empire (excluding Canada) *The Merry Wedding, Love Verses from the Song of Solomon* and *Tribute to Foster*. These scores were published by OUP, probably in 1934.

28   *To Clara Aldridge*

Seven Cromwell Place | White Plains, New York | Sept 6, 1932

Darling Aunty Clara

We arrived here (after a splendid voyage on the 'Kungsholm'—we came 2nd class, & found it very enjoyable) only to find the concert in Hollywood cancelled (bad business out there on their earlier concerts of the same series). So we cut our holiday[1] short by 3 weeks all for nothing, & got here just in time for me to get my hay fever—which I dont get in Europe or Australia.

It just shows how uncertain the concert business is at present & makes us feel thankful that I accepted the university post for this year.[2] My university duties start today, & I cant say I relish the thought of them very much. I do not like dealing continually with groups of people & being in a responsible position. What I like best is to do some studious work quietly—either composing, or noting down folk-songs, or writing.

In connection with my university lectures I have had to study some phases of music I had not thought of much before, & examine a lot of gramophone music, etc. All that has been very pleasant, & I shall probably learn more from my lectures than my audience will![3]

There are some lovely gramophone records of native music from Java, Bali, Madagascar, India, China, Japan, etc, that have fascinated me greatly. I wish you could hear them. Perhaps you may, as it is not unlikely I will bring them with me to Australia, for my lectures there.[4]

This summer it is 10 years ago since my beloved mother died & it hardly seems so long. It is only like yesterday that we were struggling together with the problems that seemed so heavy to her.

I am longing to have a letter from you, darling Aunty Clara. We are so far away from each other & one longs to know how one's best beloved ones are. So please let me have a line when you can.

My darling Ella is in good health, I am thankful to say. All the work last season wore her out & she had a lot of headaches. But I took care

[1] The Graingers had visited England and Scandinavia.

[2] Grainger had taken a post as associate professor and head of the music department at New York University for the 1932–3 academic year. He would not seek renewal in the position.

[3] Grainger soon found he was not well suited to this formal role of university lecturer. Martin Bernstein, a junior colleague of Grainger in the department, described his lectures as 'free thought, somewhat analogous to his free music' in an interview of 1984.

[4] These, and later acquired, materials did form the basis of Grainger's series of talks broadcast by the Australian Broadcasting Commission during his 1934–5 visit. See letter **31**.

she got a lot of rest this summer & as a result she feels fine now. We both send our fondest love.

Percy.

29   *To Arnold Dolmetsch*

[In the 1930s and early 1940s Grainger was especially interested in music pre-Bach, his enthusiasm having been kindled by attending Dolmetsch's Haslemere Festival of 1931. During these years he produced many performing editions, in collaboration with Dolmetsch and also Anselm Hughes.]

Jan. 23, 1933

Dear Arnold Dolmetsch,

I regret that it has taken me so long to write my article on you (partly because I was ill for a time, and partly because my work at New York University and my concert work has been unusually heavy—so that I often spend 7 nights on end in the train)—but it is done at last and I took it in today to Mr Carl Engel[1] (editor of 'The Musical Quarterly') who assures me that it will appear in the April issue.[2] I am very anxious that it should be read *before* your next festival.

I enclose a carbon copy herewith. Please tell me if there is anything you particularly would like altered, and I will try to do so—if I get your reply in time.

For illustrations to the article Mr Engel tentatively selected the following from those pictures, etc., I showed him:

Q. 1. The last two pages of the Wm. Lawes Fantasy and Air in G minor (in your handwriting). It seemed to us that these pages were very typical and lovely.[3]

2. 'Arnold Dolmetsch playing the Archlute' on postcard announcement of 1928 festival.

3. Photo of you, by Alwyn L. Coburn, on outside of announcement of 1932 festival.

---

[1] (1883–1944), chief of the music division at the Library of Congress (1922–34) and president of Grainger's American publisher, G. Schirmer Inc. (1929–44).

[2] 'Arnold Dolmetsch: Musical Confucius', 19/2 (Apr. 1933), 186–98.

[3] William Lawes (1602–45), English composer. At the end of this manuscript is written: 'Scored for Percy Grainger Aug. 9 1931 by Arnold Dolmetsch'.

4. Photo of Dolmetsch family (6) playing a consort of viols, outside a door at the top of steps, on page 7 of 'Dolmetsch and
his Instruments'.

I have, of course, the manuscript of No 1 (Lawes Fant. and Air). In
order that the illustrations may be as clear (sharp) as possible, would
you be willing (if convenient) to send me 'gloss' prints of 2, 3, 4?[1]

When the article has already appeared in 'The Musical Quarterly' I
will see if I can get it printed also in musical magazines or newspapers
in Canada and Australia.[2] I will probably have reprints made by the
'Quarterly' of the article. If so, would you, or the Dolmetsch foundation, care to use some of these reprints? If so, please tell me how many
and I will have them sent to you.

In June we shall most likely have to go to Australia, where we may
spend a whole year—concertising, lecturing, conducting, etc. The
Melbourne University is considering building a 'Grainger Museum' in
their grounds and if so I will want to start it going with a Sargent picture,[3] Grieg manuscripts and lots of other letters, manuscripts, etc. that
I have been collecting for such a purpose. I feel greatly tempted to
donate to the Melbourne University a complete chest of viols, suitable
for performing any of the 6-part works for consorts of viols. If my
Australian tour succeeds, so that I make enough money to do so, I
would like to do this while I am out there this time. Could you find
time to let me know exactly what instruments would be needful (2 trebles, 1 alto, 1 tenor, 2 bass? Or 2 trebles, 2 tenors, 2 bass?) and what
they would cost me in Dolmetsch viols with bows. If I had this information before leaving for Australia I could wire you from there if the
outcome of my tour enables me to realize this intention.[4] I would
dearly love to give my birth-town (Melbourne) a complete chest of
these incomparable instruments and to start them off on 'the
Dolmetsch road'—especially if I myself, later on (when I am able to
retire from my present concert work), could learn at Haslemere something of the right viol-playing traditions and carry them to Melbourne
on a later visit. But maybe you already have a student or desiple [*sic*]

---

[1] The published article contains five illustrations, including two of the Dolmetsch family playing together.

[2] The article appeared in an abbreviated form in the *Australian Musical News*, 24/10 (May 1934),
8–9.

[3] By John Singer Sargent (1856–1925), London-resident American portrait painter, who made a
drawing of Grainger around 1907.

[4] Dolmetsch later in the 1930s made a gift to Grainger of one of his 'German antique' alto
viols. It is now on display in the Grainger Museum.

in Melbourne who has learnt these things from you? So much the better, if so.

I have had great pleasure in reading Robert Donington's delightful book 'The Work and Ideas of Arnold Dolmetsch'.[1] It is most engagingly written and highly instructive.

Hoping you and your wonderful family are all well and with hearty greetings to you all from my wife and me,

Yours deeply admiringly

I am keenly looking forward to the gramophone records of your Bach clavichord playing. It is a boon to us all that you are recording these! Would it not be possible to someday record the Lawes and Jenkins viol works?[2]

30   *To D. C. Parker*

[By 1933 Grainger's New York publisher, G. Schirmer, was wanting to issue a revision of Parker's 1918 study of Grainger's life and music; Parker's drafts drew forth such adverse comment from the composer, however, that the revision eventually had to be abandoned. Parker expostulated: 'If other journalists care to have their stuff changed about by other people—that is their affair. But this sort of thing is not going to be done to my stuff by anyone.' Their correspondence during 1933 was, none the less, fruitful in eliciting from Grainger some of the most illuminating, as well as self-promotional, statements of his musical and social views. His anti-Christian and anti-Semitic stances, in particular, emerge more clearly than hitherto in this early letter of their exchange.]

April 26th, 1933

My dear Charlie,

Now in this bus (New York to Brantford, Canada) I at last get a chance to write to you about your splendid 'Personalia' section, which I admire keenly for its clear, pithy and entertaining presentation of ideas, tho I also must criticise portions of it as giving a misleading picture of some of my views, tastes, aims. While I naturally wish you to be entirely *personal* (wholly yourself) in your estimate and criticism of

[1] Published in 1932 by The Dolmetsch Foundation, Haslemere. Robert Donington (b. 1907) was secretary of this foundation during 1934–8.
[2] John Jenkins (1592–1678), English composer.

my music and work I feel it important that you should be passive & transmitive where you are unfolding my ideas. If we could read a passive account of Tchaikovsky's ideas & feelings (why he killed himself, for instance—if he did) it would be very valuable today. Tchaikovsky could easily have explained himself completely to a friend, but no friend, it seems, wanted to be the passive mouth of this great man's aims, ideas, tastes. I hope it will be different in our case. My own views, and aims are well known to some people in America and Australia thru the articles I have written, the lectures I have given, etc. Soon, when I write my books about music, they will be somewhat known in Europe also. When these views of mine thus become known I do not want them to contradict the views standing in your book. I want your book to stand as a standard & reliable account of my views & tendencies for all time. And when the revised edition appears I want it to be somewhat *ahead* of folk's present knowledge of my views. That is why I ask you to let me criticise this 'Personalia' section very sharply, because it seems absurd to me that two friends cannot co-operate to produce an absolutely accurate & 'normal' record in such a case as ours. If you will forgive my saying so, you seem to have the same difficulty in understanding my temperament & tendencies that most Britishers experience with me. It is obvious to me that to Britishers such as yourself, Cyril Scott, Basil Cameron[1] & others I appear 'thrawn', perverse, inconsistent, queer & often highly original, whereas to Germans & Scandinavians I appear quite normal, human and elastic—tho much less original. This is probably because my mind (musically & humanly) is influenced thru and thru by German, Scandinavian & Oriental thoughts, but has never understood British thot. Unless you are familiar with German & Scandinavian daily life & feelings, unless you know those languages thoroly, I fear I will always remain somewhat of a closed book—unless I explain myself, which I will here do. The matter of 'inconsistence'. I do not *resent* being that 'inconsistent', for it seems to me a quite forgivable weakness in an artist. But as I am sure I am painfully consistent (being weak in spontaneity rather than in consistency), and owe all my commercial well-being to this fact, I feel I must put my arguments before you—to be finally judged by you, of course.

If I were inconsistent I would be hard to handle by publishers and managers, whereas the facts are: Never changed my German, English

---

[1] (1884–1975), English conductor.

& American publishers, nor my Dutch, Scandinavian, American or Australian managers; got interested in the Anglosaxons & Scandinavians when about 10 years old & have married a Swede; have never altered my views on Bach, Kipling, Walt Whitman, etc.; have kept up a steady propaganda for British, Scandinavian & American music for over 30 years; have never lessened my enthusiasm for Brahms, as most composers have, when he became (as they thot) 'old-fashioned'; never disagree with my views of 1898 or 1902 or any period when I read them now in old letters or articles. There is nothing inconsistent in an Australian turning to Scandinavia—since Australia is South of the Equator almost as Scandinavia is North of it and the climate in Melbourne is very similar to the climates of Scotland, Iceland, the West coast on Norway except that Australian summers are a little warmer. Furthermore, the agricultural *needs* of Australia tend to re-Scandinavianize us Australians, & many proofs of this are not lacking; Norman Lindsay's women look like typical Scandinavians; Australian women have grown 'man-fond' (yielding to their men & living with them without British women's female anti-male reactions) like Scandinavian women—& thus diametrically opposed to the main tendency of American & British women.

As to Scandinavians being 'individualists' or not: They may appear individualistic to Britishers because many of them have been engaged in lonely pursuits & therefore are silent & reserved & able to fend for themselves singly, without family & group support. But in their *inner* hearts I almost invariably find them more tribal, natural and *normal* than Britishers. The hero in Ibsen's 'An Enemy of the People'[1] *acts singly*, but his motive is *tribal*, & surely Jacobsen's 'Marie Grubbe'[2] is *normal* (& animal) rather than individualistic. I find Scandinavians *balanced* & *normal* above else, but what I prize most in them is their *truthfulness*. They are by far the most truthful people known to me & that (and their bodily beauty—which is simply the flesh-expression of their balancedness & normalness, as was also the very similar beauty of the old Greeks) is what draws me to them so irresistibly. On the other hand, life in Gt. Britain & America (but not equally in Australia) is so wholly woven out of lies and half-lies that I doubt whether you (or any other British-living person) can even guess what I mean when I say that I have found my mother and Ella utterly *truthful*. In Britain & America there are always *silent* lies (if not spoken lies) and *hidden moods*.

[1] (1882), by the Norwegian Henrik Ibsen (1828–1906).
[2] (1876), by the Dane Jens Peter Jacobsen.

As an active musician & as a critic of music I have tried hard to acquire a Scandinavian-like normalness & balancedness. I think you could safely say this of me:

'He is the only composer known to me who loves every kind of music (of whatever locality & period) that he has ever heard—be it the music of China, Japan, Java, Siam, Africa, Australia, Madagascar or the Red Indian; be it classical or jazz, art-music or folk-music, high-brow or lowbrow, medieval, polyphonic, romantic, atonal, futuristic or what-not. All styles and types of music find a positive response in his musical nature & there is not one that he would exclude from his world of music. The composers that he, as pianist & conductor, was the first to introduce for the first time into several countries—Debussy, Cyril Scott, certain unheard works of Grieg, Delius, Albeniz, William Lawes, J.A. Carpenter,[1] Sparre Olsen,[2] Nathaniel Dett, David Guion,[3] Arthur Fickénscher,[4] G. de Machaut, etc.—show the catholic[it]y of his tastes. But altho he *loves* all forms of music, he does not equally *admire* all: For instance, he sharply criticizes composers of the Haydn–Mozart–Beethoven–Schubert period for having submitted themselves too pronely to influences rooted in popular music, dance music & folk-music, thereby losing hold on the true traditions of art-music as they are seen in Palestrina, Byrd, John Jenkins, William Lawes, Purcell, Bach & other pre-Haydn composers and in 20th century composers such as Delius, Cyril Scott, Arthur Fickénscher & others—the art of melodious polyphony, the grand flow of "large form", the ability to sustain rapturous, ecstatic moods without "comic relief", sharp type-contrasts & display-passage work. Grainger criticizes the Viennese Classicist composers for their "appalling frivolousness, harmonic poverty, coarse orchestration & inability to write a genuine slow movement that does not become fast, energetic & distracted by reason of a change of tempo or the introduction of florid passage work of some kind or other." Even so, this critical attitude towards the technical equipment of the Viennese school in general does not preclude an admiration for certain works of the school. Beethoven is recognized as a "transcending personality", altho Grainger considers him greatly

---

[1] John Alden Carpenter (1876–1951), American composer.

[2] (b. 1903), Norwegian violinist and composer, with whose works Grainger had become acquainted in 1929. Later in the 1930s they would holiday together in both England and Norway.

[3] (1895–1981), Texan composer, best known for *Turkey in the Straw* (which Grainger recorded) and *Home on the Range*.

[4] (1871–1954), American composer, pianist and academic; inventor of the polytone instrument.

overvalued as a craftsman and perfectionist. Nevertheless Grainger prizes the Beethoven G major piano concerto above all other piano concertos and he concedes the first movement of the "Moonlight" Sonata to be a perfect slow movement (evincing a "sustained rapturous mood")—albeit the only example of a perfect slow movement to be found in all the Beethoven Piano Sonatas. Schubert is credited with "occasional flashes of rare harmonic inspirations" altho Grainger considers him wanting in "true melody" ("true melody" being defined as "emotional expression thru a single line of sound that is not enslaved by harmonic & rhythmic thought"). Grainger further admits that the scoring of several of his own folk-song settings (such as "Molly on the Shore", "Scotch Strathspey & Reel",[1] "Shepherd's Hey") were influenced by "the clarity, jollity & directness of Haydn's orchestrations".

Curious as it may seem to many, who know Grainger chiefly or wholly thru his "Folk-Music Settings", he is not specially fond of folk-music, resenting the strong rhythmic basis underlying this form of art. He became the ardent collector and arranger of folk-songs that he is simply thru a sense of esthetic duty. On the one hand he felt that Nordic folksong is a "record of the creative genius of thousands of unknown musically-illiterate men & women of our race" and as such should be preserved with pious fidelity; on the other hand he felt called upon to undertake his folkmusic settings as a means of making British inborn musicality more widely realised internationally.

Grainger's own personal musical nature is averse to all gaiety, humorousness, & strong rhythmic impulse. What he prizes most is painful, tragic & heroic expression as he finds it in William Lawes, Bach or Wagner, in the Icelandic Sagas or the "Hakas" of the South Seas, or serene, lofty, angelic or stoical expression as he finds it in Byrd, John Jenkins, Bach, Wagner, Brahms, Cyril Scott, Grieg, Delius, Skryabin, Sandby and Arthur Fickénscher.

Grainger is struck by the fact that the music of the Nordic (Scandinavian, British, Irish, American) races is generally more spiritual & deeply emotional than the more frivolous music of the more Southern European races. This general characteristic he finds equally borne out by the apparent origins of organum, faux-bourdon & gymel, by the pre-Bach English chamber music giants & by the 20th century British, American & Scandinavian composers. German music he sees

---

[1] Set 'for room-music 20-some (21-some at will)', published by Schott in 1924.

rising towards Nordic grandeur & loftiness while Austrian music leans towards Italian simplicity & frivolousness. In spite of these general views Grainger has a sincere admiration for Puccini (whom he praises for his spontaneousness & musicality and from whose lyrical pen he has never heard an unmusical bar) and a great fondness for a great variety of Belgian and French music, starting with the 13th century Guillaume de Machaut, including the 16th century Claude Le Jeune, and ending with C. Franck (whose "3 Chorales" for organ he considers the most beautiful & perfect art-works of the late 19th century),[1] Debussy, Ravel, Fauré, Albert Bruneau,[2] Eduard Moullé,[3] Henry Duparc[4] & their contemporaries.

Up to very recently Bach held the first place in his affections. It was as a boy of 10 in his native Melbourne, that he first learnt to play Bach, from Louis Pabst,[5] a German pianist and great Bach enthusiast and player. Nowadays Bach shares this first place with early Purcell (the Fantasies for strings), John Jenkins and William Lawes, the last 2 English "Fantasy" composers came into Grainger's ken at the Dolmetsch Festival at Haslemere, Surrey, England. Grainger feels that he is more indebted to Bach than to any other composer. (etc).[']

I am very anxious that there should be nothing *harsh* said about Schubert or Beethoven or any other great man, unless there is time to explain every angle of thot that led to such a verdict—& that would waste too much space in your book. After all, my childhood and youth were spent in loving worship of such geniuses as Schubert, Beethoven, etc.—lying on the floor, in Frankfurt, eating bread & butter & sugar by the hour while I read about them in Grove's Dictionary. Any irritation I feel at Schubert's early death is only because I love him. Any resentment I feel at the false position given to Beethoven (on account of ignorance of greater men of earlier & later periods) should be limited to purely cultural objections, to criticism of such composer's lack of technical & cultural resources & traditions—not a belittlement of their individual geniuses. I particularly want to avoid anything *harsh*, as it would not be true to my artistic nature, which has always striven to

---

[1] Dating from the year of César Franck's death, 1890. Grainger arranged the second chorale for band in 1942.

[2] Grainger probably meant Alfred Bruneau (1857–1934), French composer, mostly of dramatic works.

[3] Édouard Moullé, turn-of-the-cent. French arranger of songs, especially folksongs from Normandy. Grainger had been introduced to Moullé's work by Grieg in 1907.

[4] Henri Duparc (1848–1933), French composer, best known for his songs.

[5] (1846–1903), resident in Melbourne in 1884–94, where he taught Grainger piano and theory (1892–4). He later taught in Moscow.

keep a *balance* between all things, and *harmony* towards all geniuses & their endeavours. I feel I am alone in this, & should be given credit for it. I am the only composer I know who has not been affected by fashions & modes, who has retained his worship of Brahms after finding Debussy, & the like.

What we *should do*, in Personalia, is not to talk too much about the half-great German composers, but to talk more about the Nordic, Negro, French & other composers that I have spent my life championing. Let us learn from the Jews: The Jews have one great tactic— they talk only of Jews, & when they are not praising Jews they are attacking Jews—leaving the impression that none but Jews are worth talking about. In your Personalia you devote much space to the German, Italian & Polish composers, saying comparatively little about the Anglosaxon & Scandinavian & French composers that it has been my life's work to try to attract attention to. I think it might be said that I was the first to conduct any of the large works of Delius in America (I did, for the 1st time in America, 'The Song of the High Hills',[1] Piano Concerto,[2] Cello Concerto,[3] North Country Sketches), the first to play Debussy in 8 countries in 1902,[4] the first to bring forward Arthur Fickénscher's marvelous 'The Seventh Quintet',[5] the first to present Grieg's 'Norwegian Folksongs' Op. 66 & 'Peasant Dances' Op.72 in many lands, the first to popularize the Canadian Negro composer N. Dett's 'Juba' Dance, & the American folkpieces of David Guion, the first to play Carpenter's Concertino for piano & orchestra (1916, Chicago), the first to play Albeniz in several countries. I think you might tack your mention of Chopin (whom I like extremely) onto my love for the French composers, saying something like: 'Grainger's love for the French tendencies & subtlety in music extends to Chopin, for he opines it is the French side of the half-French half-Polish Chopin that particularly appeals to him.' It is a fact that no wholly Polish composer has so appealed to me yet.

Just as we should stress the less conventionally known composers & say as little as possible of the all too conventionally known ones, so also we should avoid all mention of Christ & Christianity, if possible.

[1] Performance of this work and the *Two North Country Sketches* at Grainger's concerts of 28/30 Apr. 1924 (Bridgeport/New York).
[2] Performance by Grainger with the New York Philharmonic Orchestra on 26 Nov. 1915.
[3] Performance by Herman Sandby (cello), conducted by Grainger, in an Aeolian Hall concert in New York on 29 Dec. 1925.
[4] Grainger's claim is not well justified.
[5] Grainger probably refers to Fickénscher's *The Seventh Realm*, an adaptation of part of his lost *Evolutionary Quintet*.

This is the old Jewish Trick of making a Jew the center of everyman's beliefs or disbelief. Christianity (pro or countr) has never played as large a part in my life as Buddhism or Norse or Greek Mythology, so why drag it in? By adversely mentioning Christianity we still advertize it. If one wants to kill Christianity (as I do) the thing to do is to kill it with silence (totschweigen). I think something like the following is all that need be said about my religious side (thereby giving us space for other additions): 'Grainger's religion—if any—is Walt Whitmanism, for, since about 1897 (when Cyril Scott presented him with "Leaves of Grass"), he has revered the personality and teachings of the great American seer much as Christians revere Christ or Buddhists revere Buddha. This predilection for an American Messiah, in place of a European or Asiatic religion, is typical of his Australian championship of the New World at the expense of the Old World, so strong in his teens and never since abandoned. Since his mid-teens he has always regarded the European Continent as hopelessly sunk in conventionality, sham intellectuality and parochialness. From such Europeanness he exempts Scandinavia, Holland, Great Britain & Ireland, taking the view that they are "colonizing races" and hence, with all their interests & hopes, leaning out of Europe into Asia, Australia, Africa, America, etc.

A knowledge of Walt Whitman is not the only lifegiving influence Grainger owes to Cyril Scott. Scott was the first composer to take Grainger seriously as a composer & to urge him earnestly to develop his creative powers. These two composers owe more to each other than meets the casual eye: Many elements in Grainger's early style (such compositions as "Love Verses from the Song of Solomon" & "The Inuit")[1] were strongly influenced by Scott's then style, while it was from Grainger's experiments with irregular rhythms & barrings around 1899 that Scott adopted similar methods in his Piano Sonata, Op. 66—getting written permission from Grainger to "adopt these Australian innovations in his English art." These innovations proved history-making, for the irregular rhythms of the Scott Sonata, played by the composer widely in European countries around 1904, preceded by several years the use of such rhythms by Continental composers such as Stravinsky & others.'

I think you exaggerate my worship of Strauss. I thought him very cheap when I first heard him in 1896, but after the war, when he was

---

[1] The fifth of Grainger's Kipling settings, completed around 1902, for unaccompanied mixed chorus.

too much belittled, I tried (with my usual effort at *balance*) to emphasize my admiration, which is only partial.[1] So too much space should not be given to Strauss, whom I think *much less important* than Cyril Scott, Delius, Herman Sandby & Arthur Fickénscher.

It is not true that 'Little in German music between Bach & Wagner appeal[s]' to me. I was brought up on it & feel its beauties deeply. All I do is to point out its *cultural defects*; that it is technically & culturally lower & more frivolous than the best Nordic music. It is also not true that I have 'an instinctive loathing for academic & scientific music, etc.' or that I 'believe in the folk'. I much prefer academic music (such as Brahms) to folkmusic. Folkmusic I am inclined to view as *old artmusic* merely kept alive by the folk, but not necessarily created by them. I strongly take the view that music (modern music) should *not* be learnt from wandering fiddlers & savages, but *evolved out of musical progress* without any backsliding to the music of the past (folkmusic or otherwise).

Folkmusic I approach *scientifically* rather than purely artistically. I am myself so much of a 'hot house' musician that I hardly enjoy folksong collecting from the folk. I would prefer to sit in a laboratory merely *investigating* what others collect in the field. I have done field collecting [of] music myself because I distrust the average collector as being lazy, sentimental & unscientific, just as I distrust the average selfstyled classicist or highbrow as being too frivolous & low-brow. My quarrel with everybody (including myself) is that none of us are hardworking enough, scientific enough, hot-house-like enough.

It is true that I get my inspiration from 'nature', from mountain & sea, as well as from books & cultural influences. But we must not forget that all my early influences were Bach, Schumann, Wagner, Brahms—that I had a solid non-frivolous basis to build on. I must be understood to be strictly 'arty' & *in my own way* academic & scientific. Why I don't join with existing academic & scientific musicians is because I find them too ignorant, too sentimental, not truly academic *enough*. In this respect men like Dolmetsch & Fickénscher are *really* academic after my own heart. I think something should be said about my strong (& long held) views on *balance of tone* (see my Dolmetsch article when it arrives).

---

[1] Grainger had described Strauss as 'a great cosmic soul of the Goethe, Milton, Nietzsche, Walt Whitman, Edgar Lee Masters caliber: full of dross, but equally full of godhead; lacking refinement, but not the supremer attributes; and uniquely able to roll forth some great uplifting message after gigantic preliminaries of boredom and inconsequentialness.' ('Richard Strauss: Seer and Idealist', in Henry T. Finck, *Richard Strauss: The Man and his Works* (Boston, Mass.: Little, Brown, and Co., 1917), pp. xxiv–xxv.)

I like what you say about Chopin & about the piano as a 'bumping' instrument, & about my love for interweaving themes, etc. I would say 'polyphonic nature' rather than 'contrapuntal'. Instead of 'he has not enough sympathy' etc. I would say: What he calls his 'Australian democraticness' makes him unwilling to see a hundred orchestral musicians accompany subserviently a single soloist. Grainger is one of the many who believes that soloism ruins music.

If possible leave out all mention of Carmen—which I consider an overpraised work (let us ignore what I don't specially admire).

I like very much what you say about Brahms. If you want to test my Brahms derivativeness, look at:

(1) Colonial Song[1] opening (middle melody just as in Brahms).

(2) The pretty Maid milking her cow[2] (song) the opening arpeggios, the sixths & syncopations towards the end are surely Brahms-derived.

(3) The beginning of 'English Dance'. Surely the phrases are typically of the beginning of the 4th Brahms Symphony & other works.

Please ask Schott (London) for free copies of these if you lack them.

I like all of your pages 5 & 6.[3]

Page 7 should contain: Grainger sees in the polymelodic music of Java and in the improvised polyphony of Rarotongan natives the same subtle complex texture that he worships in John Jenkins, William Lawes & Bach.

Page 7. I wish we could leave out all mention of Scandinavian superstitions, or else say something like this: 'The Sagas are full of accounts of trolls & spirits; but they always show the heroes *indifferent* to these superstitions, showing what seems like an early scientistic or rationalistic slant'. I would also sooner leave out all mention of Strindberg (whom I don't admire) & Brandes (whose writings I don't know). But put Sigrid Undset[4] down with those I most worship.

On page 7 I think you should add the Anglosaxon 'Beowulf' & 'The Battle of Brunnanburh' (both the Anglosaxon original & Tennyson's glorious translation) & Evald Tang Kristensen's Danish Folksong publications & 'Minder og Erindringer'[5] to the things I 'love to linger over'. We must remember that such a book as yours will be read in all kinds

[1] Originally composed for soprano, tenor, harp, and full orchestra in 1911–12 (many subsequent revisions and adaptations).
[2] Lincolnshire tune set for voice and piano by Grainger in 1920.
[3] Parker's draft appears not to have survived.
[4] (1882–1949), Norwegian novelist, Nobel prizewinner for literature in 1928.
[5] Grainger probably means Kristensen's four-volume *Minder og Oplevelser* (Memories and Experiences), which appeared between 1923 and 1928; in 1956 he described these memoirs as 'the most entertaining book I have ever read, in any language'.

of countries & should be reasonably in touch with my Danish as well as my British and American activities.

Page 8: The mention of slang words is inclined (it seems to me) to suggest again my love for the 'popular' & the 'folkish', which is actually abnormally weak. No man uses less slang in his speech than I, and my only interest in American slang lies in the fact that it generally substitutes a Nordic-rooted word for a Latin-rooted word and thus is part of my preparations for my 'Nordic English'. I think this 40-year-old plan of mine should be mentioned in your book, in some such way as: 'since a boy of 9 or 10 Grainger has wished to sweep the words of French, Latin & Greek origin out of English and substitute for them words of Anglosaxon & Scandinavian origin. He is preparing a book on the subject of this "Nordic English" of his, in which "see-thru-able", "hope-thwart", "soul-tilth" & "tone-tool" will replace "transparent", "disappoint", "culture", "musical instrument (or voice)" and the like. Grainger's contention is that no composite words should be formed out of roots that are not "alive" in English. It is this interest in his 'Nordic English' that has given rise to some of the rather queer musical terms in his printed music. Thus he was unwilling to use "quintet", "increase" for "crescendo" (as MacDowell[1] did) or "prominently" for "hervortretend" on the grounds that "quintet", "increase" & "prominent" were Latin-derived words, preferring to use "five-some", "louden" (in line with "soften") & "to the fore" instead, in view of their English roots. The reason for some of these queer "Graingerisms" has, naturally, not been clear to those ignorant of "Grainger's linguistic passions".[']

I like what you say about Schönberg & Fauré—in fact, all of page 6.

Page 7: He views the inspired use of intervals closer than the half-tone in Arthur Fickénscher's 'the Seventh Quintet' as prophetic of the music of the future and is not afraid of the threatened introduction of microtones in any form. He looks forward to the day etc.

Page 11: I like what you say about Tolstoy & non-resistance.

Re page 8: You can say 'he cultivates many hobbies & takes a serious interest in some subjects unrelated to his art' if you like. But my own view is that I have no special art, but simply express my Australian & Nordic viewpoint in several all-equally-important activities: Long-distance walking (do you want to mention my walks? 65 miles in S. Africa, Pietermaritzburg to Durban, between a Friday eve & Sat. eve

---

[1] Edward MacDowell (1860–1908), American composer.

concert in 1904. 36 miles Masterton to Ekutahuma,[1] New Zealand, in 7 hours, in 1909. 80 miles across the South Australian desert[2] in 1924) music, beadwork, designing of clothes (we did some beauties last summer—I regard a lovely & lordly appearance as part of Nordic man's & women's racial duties), sexual fury, language-reform, book-writing (to begin seriously very soon), racial propaganda by means of concert-activities, folksong collecting.

As to the racial & international inspirations in my music I should rate them about as follow:

Australian nationalism, about 20%

Nordic racialism, about 30%

Cosmopolitan culture, about 30%

Affinity with Negro, South Sea, Arab, Mongolian & other fierce & primitive races, about 20%

I like what you say about 'Industrialism in England' & 'were the topic the Anglo-Saxons', but as I know nothing of the Battle of the Swold, & next to nothing about Olaf Tryggvason,[3] I wish you would say: 'he would quickly respond were the topic the Anglo-Saxons, the origin of the Polynesian race, life in the old Stone-Age or the characteristics of Mongolians'. (All these have very special interest for me & I would not like your readers to think I am more interested in the North of Europe than in the South Seas or the Stone Age.)

I like all you say about your & my different views about the solidarity of mankind, about the onward-march of democratic humanity.

I like what you say about the relative values of the heritage left by Rome & Scandinavia. Greece I except—seeing little difference between what the Greeks & the Scandinavians stand for.

I do not recognise the 'temper' incident on page 10, but there are 3 happenings it might refer to:

(1) when about 7 my little dog followed my father to the station when I wanted him to stay home with me. I felt angry & threw a chair at a chest of drawers. That is the last time I remember showing or feeling anger in my life.

(2) A manager, in Australia, in 1903, was rude to me, calling me a liar. But I showed & felt no anger—he was merely angry with me.

(3) In Holland, around 1912, in a 3rd class carriage, a railway guard ordered me to put a suitcase, placed in the rack above my head, under

---

[1] = Eketahuna.   [2] From Tailem Bend to Keith.

[3] (*c.*964–1000), Viking king of Norway who attempted to Christianize large tracts of Scandinavia. He died at the Battle of Svolder. Grieg attempted an opera about his life.

my seat. I thot his request & manner unneedful & pretended not to understand Dutch, altho I understood him perfectly. Then also, I felt & showed no anger, but I involved myself in conflict and as a result my heart beat very hard & I felt miserable & ashamed. Afterwards I vowed never again to fan the fires of another man's anger or to excite myself in any avoidable conflict.

I don't know whether we will gain by the inclusion of any such 'moral' indications. You must judge of this.

I know that you are very individualistic as a writer & do not like to be interfered with. (There I do not agree with you—as I do not agree with extreme individualism ever. When I wrote my Dolmetsch article I tried to make myself the servant of his ideas, quoting his actual words or expressed opinions where I could, & only introducing facts & arguments of my own where I felt sure they tended to prove Dolmetsch's points. For instance: I was tempted to say that the 17th century English Fantasies sound as well on Saxophones as on strings, which I feel to be a fact. But I suppressed that statement because it seemed to me out of harmony with one of D's main tenets: that compositions should be played on the instruments for which they were intended by the composer.) I feel that you have a right to follow this individualism in all parts of your book on me except the parts dealing with my views, tendencies, etc. Here I feel that guess-work or approximate fact-fulness is not enough & that I should supply you with absolute correct facts & definite statements and that you should use them or else give up this Personalia section altogether. I repeat that I feel this section (if included) should show you closely in touch with my views & that there should be no feeling that you have to guess because you cannot get the information from me or that you prefer to guess. In this portion of the book you don't appear as critic (it seems to me) but as interpreter and as such need not take a stand of aloofness or uninfluencedness. I repeat, I think it absurd that any statements in your Personalia section should be negated by my own writings, so shortly to appear. It is true that our meetings, and therefore our talks, have been short, but any gaps in our discussions can be filled up by letters, it would seem to me. In any case, I hope my drastic criticisms of this Personalia section will not offend you. I criticise it only because I consider this section can only be what it ought to be if we cooperate impersonally in it. I do not want us to bungle it (for want of patience & painstakingness) as such sections usually are bungled. I want the facts & accuracy of it to be up to the splendid style & attractiveness you display in it.

Anxious to hear your views re all this,
Ever yours

31   To Walter Conder

[The Graingers spent most of 1934 and 1935 in Australia. The country was still in the grip of depression and many of Grainger's concert plans were initially thwarted. He persevered, however, soon capturing better audiences and fees through his promotion by the broadcasting authorities in Australia and, in late 1935, New Zealand. Most of Grainger's earnings from his over two hundred engagements went towards building the first stage of his museum, on the grounds of The University of Melbourne. He raised further funds for building through a short American concert tour during the winter of 1934–5 and a generous donation from Balfour Gardiner.]

81 Palmer Place | North Adelaide, SA[1] | June 27th, 1934.

Dear Major Conder,

You may remember that I sent you a rough sketch of 11 illustrated radio talks (to be entitled 'A commonsense view of all music' or 'Music as a universal language', or some similar title)[2] and that when we met at Mr Herbert Brookes's[3] you suggested that I should some time give 12 such talks. I suggested that these radio lecture-programs had better take place after the conclusion of my piano recital tour with J. & N. Tait,[4] as the radio-talks would entail much preparation, and some rehearsal, on my part, which would be difficult to sandwich in between piano recitals.

But the scope of my tour with Taits has now been much extended and will now also embrace choral, orchestral and chamber-concerts in many cities in Australia and New Zealand, so that it will continue well into the new year, and probably until our departure for Europe. So Taits (who are always awfully good in their willingness to further my

[1] Home of Marion (May) Aldridge (née MacFie), Grainger's aunt.
[2] Eventually, 'Music: a commonsense view of all types'. Synopses of Grainger's twelve lectures are reproduced in John Blacking, *A Commonsense View of All Music': Reflections on Percy Grainger's Contribution to Ethnomusicology and Music Education* (Cambridge: Cambridge University Press, 1987), 151–80. The topics were vintage Grainger, ranging from 'The Mongolian and Mohammedan influences upon European Music' (Lecture 3), and 'The Superiority of Nordic Music' (Lecture 6) to 'Tuneful Percussion' (Lecture 11).
[3] (1867–1963), then Vice-Chairman of the Australian Broadcasting Commission. He had known the Graingers since the late 1920s, when he was Australian Commissioner-General in the United States. The Graingers had stayed at Brookes's Melbourne home during Apr. 1934.
[4] Firm of concert directors, which Grainger had dealt with also on his 1908–9 and 1926 tours.

esthetic plans) very kindly suggest that they will deal with your Broadcasting Commission, in the matter of my fee and dates (so that there may be no cross-purposes or confusion with regard to my possible dates with you and the dates that Taits are arranging for me), but that they will take no percentage on any fee your commission may pay me. I think that Mr Claude Kingston will be writing you about these matters.

The 12 illustrated radio-talks that you and I discussed are, of course, of an educational nature rather than of a concert nature. The enclosed sketch for 4 chamber music lecture-programs in Perth gives a rough idea of what I would propose for 6 to 8 radio lecture-programs of a more concert-like nature, if you would prefer such a scheme to the 12 educational talks originally proposed.

My own view of the matter is that the more educational 12 talks would be the preferable scheme, as enabling me to deal thoroughly with the vast mass of musical material I have with me (which, in its variety and scope, has probably never been got together before anywhere in the world, partly because much of the music, and information concerning it, has only been published in the last few years).

However, either type of series would interest me keenly, as I would like to do something of this sort while in Australia that is more comprehensive and exhaustive than anything of the kind that has been done in Europe or America. Either type of series would call for the same numbers of performers (in addition to myself); about the following: 4 women's voices, 4 men's voices, 6 strings (2 violins, 2 violas, 2 cellos) which occasionally might be increased to 8 or 9 strings (2 violins, 1 bass in addition to those mentioned), 1 harmonium or reed organ, 4 pianists on 2 pianos, and several percussion players for 1 or 2 programs.

If you are still interested in the idea, I wish you would arrange the matter of dates and fee with Mr Kingston, and that you would let me know the exact duration desired for each talk, so I can begin to work out the time, etc., of the programs accurately.

The above address will always find me.

        With cordial greetings
          Percy Grainger

32   *To E. C. Hands*[1]

C/O Australian Broadcasting Commission
264 Pitt St, Sydney, NSW | May 4, 1935

Dear Mr Hands

Ever so many thanks for your splendid letter of April 16.

You have, indeed, done wonders with my NZ tour plans since I last heard from you. I am delighted with the whole lay-out as you have conceived it.

First, as to programs: I entirely agree with your choice of the studio piano broadcasts.

Are all of these to be national broadcasts? If so, it occurs to me that we ought to begin with the most *popular* & *effective* program first (will the first piano broadcast be from Wellington?) & that I consider your Auckland No. 1 (containing the Chopin B flat minor Sonata Op. 35) to be. Would it, therefore, be wise to use this program (Auckland 1) for my first studio piano recital, wherever it is? Another point. The Cyril Scott Piano Sonata (on the Dunedin 3 program) is a very *heavy* work, though a very delicious one. Might it be too stiff for Dunedin or does that make no difference? I also very much indeed like your scheme of studio performances with small orchestra, but (with yr permission) I would like to arrange these *studio programs with small orchestra* so that they contain a goodly showing of the many examples of exquisite old music that I have with me. It may be years before New Zealand has a chance to hear the masterworks of these periods (13th to 17th centuries) so I am anxious to present them while with you. When making up these small orchestra programs for Major Conder I had already presented over the air all or most of my old music in the 12 lecture recitals ('A Commonsense view of All Music') I gave in Melbourne around December, & that is why I did not include the old pieces in these sketch programs for small orchestra.

How would it be if I made the first of each small orchestra program (in each centre) *a historic program* (beginning with Early European harmony, passing on to 17th century English Fantasies & folk harmonisations & ending up with some daring examples of modern music—much along the lines of my 2 Sydney chamber music

---

[1] This text is taken from Grainger's rough draft of the letter.

programs of March 13 & 16)[1] & made the 2nd small orchestral program (in each centre) more usual or modern in character—along the lines of Wellington No. 2? In that case I would like, for the historic programs, 6 mixed voices (2 sopranos, 1 alto, 2 tenors, 1 bass) & 6 strings (2 violins, 2 violas, 2 cellos) if that were convenient, *instead of the small orchestra.* The 6 voices should be just choir voices, not soloists. But if there were difficulties (or undue expense) in procuring such 6 voices, then I could present all the old music (even some of the vocal numbers) on strings (without voices).

If you would prefer me not to give any definitely historical programs, but to mix my old & new music to some extent on all (or most) of the studio small orchestral programs, please let me know, & I can plan my programs that way. But in that case, also, I would like to use 6 voices in some of these programs, if agreeable to you.

On programs using the 6 voices I would cut down on the number of instruments used.

Will you allow me to postpone the final makeup of these studio small orchestra programs until I know a little more about the items chosen for the *public concerts,* so that I can avoid needless repetitions of pieces in the same city? Or does that not matter? Will the Public Concerts be broadcast (national broadcasts?)? Thus, if 'Blithe Bells'[2] is to be played by orchestra in the Christchurch Public Concert (Christchurch 5), perhaps it had better be omitted from the 'Tuneful Percussion' Studio program in Christchurch (Christchurch 4)? So may I wait with the final choice of the studio small orchestra programs till I have your replies to several questions?

Wellington Public Concert:[3]

I would be delighted to play the Tchaikovsky Concerto & Carpenter Concertino. I could bring the orchestration of the Carpenter with me, but there is a fee of about 20 dollars to Schirmers for the hire of this orchestral material, each performance.

---

[1] These concerts were presented at the State Conservatorium. As stated in their publicity material, they included 'examples of the earliest known European Music, dating from the 13th to the 17th Century, Folk Music of Various Nations, Vocal Ensemble Music, Instrumental Chamber Music, Songs and some of Mr Grainger's recent compositions'.

[2] Free Ramble on Bach's 'Sheep may safely graze' (from BWV 208), elastically scored by Grainger in about 1931.

[3] This New Zealand Broadcasting Board concert eventuated on 21 Nov. 1935, with Leon de Mauny conducting the Wellington Symphony Orchestra in Grainger's performances of the stated Tchaikovsky (No. 1) and Carpenter works. The programme also included shorter items by Grainger, Sandby, and Katherine Parker.

Is this concert *in addition* to the choral & orchestral program planned between Mr Temple White[1] & me (for Wellington) long ago, & to which you kindly gave your sanction (time permitting) in your letter of Dec. 11 last? I am particularly anxious to carry out my program with Mr Temple White, & hope nothing may interfere with this.

Dunedin Public Concert:[2]
I enclose a copy of my letter to Mr Vernon Griffiths,[3] which I think explains itself. I am most delighted that you have been able to arrange this with him. I am sending sample copies of choruses to Mr V. Griffiths.

Christchurch Public Concert:[4]
I should be delighted if this took shape. I enclose you 2 copies of a sketch of 3 different program-suggestions for this (Christchurch) concert. So you can send one copy to Mr Peters, if you wish. I am also sending him (as far as I can) sample copies of the choruses under discussion.

Auckland Public Concert:[5]
I would be happy to play the Grieg Concerto. Is this to be a purely orchestral concert, or mixed choral & orchestral? If the latter, perhaps my sketches for the Christchurch Public Concert will be some guide.

Answers to your Questions:
I will always take part as a pianist (or on harmonium) in any number where I do not need to conduct. Am I to conduct any numbers in the concerts with Mr Peters & Mr V. Griffiths? As regards the Public Concerts I have indicated where I myself play the piano. I will also

[1] A second Wellington concert was held on 23 Nov. 1935, when Grainger appeared with the Wellington Harmonic Society and the Apollo Singers, conducted by H. Temple White.

[2] This concert, with the Dunedin Orchestral Society and Dunedin Choral Society's Madrigal Club, took place on 23 Oct. 1935. It concluded with Grainger playing the first movement of Grieg's Piano Concerto. The concert was conducted by Vernon Griffiths and Alfred Walmsley.

[3] (1894–1985), Cambridge-educated teacher and composer, at this time director of music at the King Edward Technical College in Dunedin. Grainger was interested in his experiments to involve all 800 of the school's pupils in group music-making. In 1942 Griffiths was appointed professor of music in Christchurch. He was particularly interested in the music of Cyril Scott and organized a four-concert Cyril Scott Festival in 1958.

[4] Held on 31 Oct. 1935, this was an all-Grainger programme mounted by the Christchurch Harmonic Society and a chamber orchestra, conducted by Victor Peters (1890–1973).

[5] On 5 Dec. 1935 this concert was presented by the Auckland Choral Society, the Commercial Travellers' and Warehousemen's Choir, and the Bohemian Orchestra. The programme did end with Grieg's Piano Concerto.

make this quite clear when I send you my final suggestions for the studio small orchestra programs. Have you a studio conductor in each centre who would conduct the voices or instruments while I play the piano?

My wife will be with me in NZ & will play her special percussion instruments when needed.[1] After the NZ tour, you can send some of these instruments back to the Grainger Museum in Melbourne, as you suggested in a former letter. I am delighted that yr studio orchestras will be playing low pitch. What pitch will the orchestras be using in the Public Concerts in the 4 cities? Our percussion instruments are about A440, which, I believe, corresponds to about C522. We have no wooden marimba. Have you none (at the correct low pitch) available? If not, we would need to hire a low pitch wooden marimba in Sydney, for the NZ tour, or omit this instrument. The compass should be

 (actual pitch).

Orchestrations (orchestral parts):
I am glad you have the parts of the Tchaikovsky & Grieg Concertos. I will supply all the other orchestrations needed for the studio performances & public concerts. That is, I will bring *one orchestration* of each work needed. If the different orchestras each need copies simult. a long while in advance we must plan something else for them. I can tell when the program[s] for Public Concerts are decided.

Choral Copies:
I will supply all stencilled copies (see program sketches) free to the choruses to any extent needed. But I cannot (as a rule) supply *printed* choral parts, as it is not fair to the publishers.

The works published by Oxford University Press (Tribute to Foster, Love Verses from the Song of Solomon, The Merry Wedding) should be ordered from Mr E.E. Bartholomew, Oxford University Press, Cathedral Bdgs, 205 Flinders Lane, Melbourne. I understand that he has plenty of copies on hand there.

I'm Seventeen,[2] Irish Tune from C° Derry (Chorus) & Australian Up-Country Song[3] should be ordered from Allan's, 276 Collins St, Melbourne. The other choral numbers have the publisher mentioned

---

[1] These instruments included the aluminium marimba, which Ella Grainger played in the Bach–Grainger *Blithe Bells*.

[2] *I'm seventeen come Sunday*, setting of Lincolnshire folksong (1905).

[3] Composed in 1928, for unaccompanied five-part mixed chorus.

Plate 1. Grainger's painting of
the Eschersheimer Turm,
Frankfurt, 1895. (Grainger
Museum)

Plate 2. Grainger's painting of
the Taunus, Frankfurt, 26 July
1896. (Grainger Museum)

Plate 3. Grainger's watercolour of his mother, Frankfurt, 1896–7. (Grainger Museum)

Plate 4. Grainger's painting of his wooden-framed Hartford bicycle, Frankfurt, 1897. (Grainger Museum)

Plate 5. Grainger's
embryonic sketch for the
cover of his suite *In A
Nutshell*. (Grainger Museum)

Plate 6. G. Schirmer's cover
of the orchestral piano solo
part of *In A Nutshell*, 1916.
(Grainger Museum)

THE 15TH C.A.C. BAND. CONDUCTOR, ROCCO RESTA
MR. A. A. CLAPPE IN Centre

OFFICIAL INSTRUMENTATION OF THE 15TH BAND, C.A.C.
FORT HAMILTON, N. Y., APRIL, 1918

ROCCO RESTA . . . . . . CONDUCTOR
PERCY GRAINGER . . . . . SOLOIST
ROBERT E. SHADDOCK . . . 1ST SERGEANT

Flute and Piccolo
Harry Kravetz

Oboe
Owen W. Hoffman

Clarinets
Francis Resta
Ejnar E. Frigga
Magnus V. Lund
Robert E. Shaddock
Samuel Berlin
Joseph D'Amico

Bass Clarinet
Mark Sandfort

Bassoon
Richard Savolini

Saxophones
Percy Grainger
Anton Vlcek
William W. Leonard
Willard Y. Cain

Trumpets
William F. Bruederly
John Soczko
Nathan Rosen
William Hammond

French Horns
Robert H. Brown
Stephen Laton
Harry H. Green
William Miller

Baritone
Ralph Stearns

Trombones
Harold Brown
Edward L. Rives
Frank Pechacek

Basses
Harry D. Walters
Humberto Ciauri

Drums
Howard H. May
Charles J. Meisner

Tympany
Barney Holub

Plate 7. The 15th Band, Coast Artillery Corps of the US Army,
1918 (Grainger, front row, fifth from right). (Grainger Museum)

Plate 8. Grainger and his mother, Rose, playing his *English Dance* at their home in White Plains, New York, 17 July 1921. (Grainger Museum)

Plate 9. A publicity shot from about 1922. (Grainger Museum)

PERCY GRAINGER wrestling with his
    secretary,Frederick Morse, they
are both devoted to wrestling and
enjoy this experience almost every day
that Grainger is at his White Plains
home----which is not often.

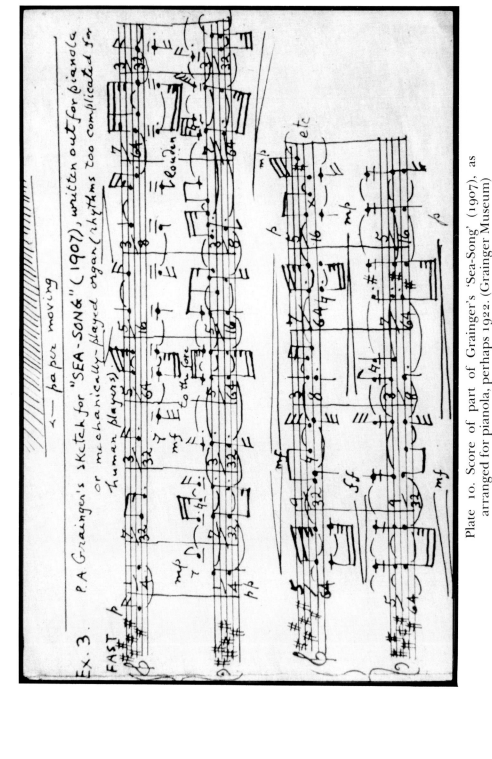

Plate 10. Score of part of Grainger's 'Sea-Song' (1907), as arranged for pianola, perhaps 1922. (Grainger Museum)

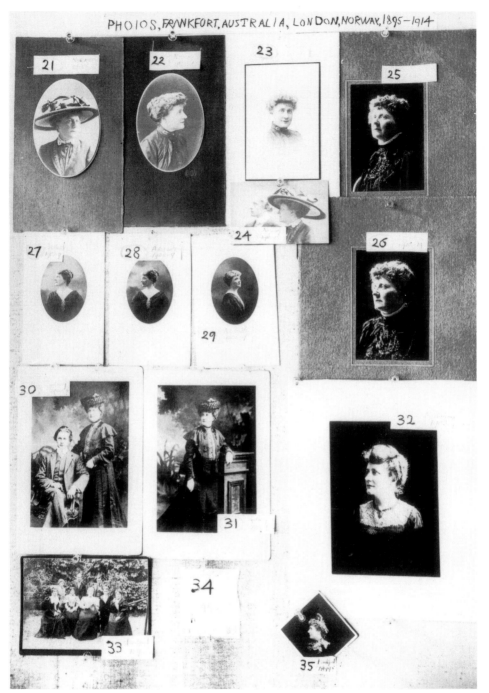

Plate 11. A collage of photographs of Rose Grainger, used by her
son in compiling his memorial volume to her published in 1923.
(Grainger Museum)

Plate 12. Cyril Scott (left),
Roger Quilter and Grainger
at the Harrogate Festival,
Yorkshire, 25 July 1929.
(Grainger Museum)

Plate 13. Ella Grainger
teaches her husband how to
ski, Segeltorp, Sweden, 1929.
(Grainger Museum)

Plate 14. Henry Cowell, in the year of his imprisonment, 1936. (Grainger Museum)

Plate 15. Grainger on tour with musicians of Gustavus Adolphus College, St Peter, Minnesota, February 1942. (Wendell Holmquist)

Plate 16. Building of the second stage of the Grainger Museum, Melbourne, 1938. (Grainger Museum)

Plate 17. Grainger lectures, 1941. (Grainger Museum)

UNIVERSITY OF MICHIGAN
OFFICIAL PUBLICATION

SUMMER SESSION COURSES

July 3 to August 26, 1944

SCHOOL OF MUSIC

DEPARTMENT OF PHYSICAL EDUCATION (FOR WOMEN)

DEPARTMENT OF SPEECH

NATIONAL MUSIC CAMP ★ INTERLOCHEN, MICHIGAN

Plate 18. Cover of the 1944 National Music Camp booklet of courses. Grainger plays Delius's Piano Concerto under the direction of Thor Johnson. (Grainger Museum)

TOWN HALL
Presents

THE FIRST OF THE

SEVEN
UPLIFTERS
SERIES

PERCY GRAINGER

OLIN DOWNES

Curran Theatre - Sunday, Sept. 27, 2:30 P.M.

OLIN DOWNES, N. Y. Times Music Critic (Moderator)
PERCY GRAINGER, Pianist - Composer, Conductor

PROGRAM

"Folk-Tune," opus 38, No. 1..Eugéne Goossens (English, born 1893)
    The folksong here harmonized is the "Sheep Shearing Song,"
    collected by Cecil J. Sharp in Somerset, England, in 1904
"Shepherd's Hey," English Morris Dance Tune, set by....Percy Grainger (born Australia, 1882)
"The Carman's Whistle," Air and Variations.........................William Byrd (English, 1538-1623)
Ballade, opus 24, in the form of variations on a Norwegian folksong....................................
....Edvard Grieg (Norwegian, 1842-1907)
Polonaise, in A flat, opus 53..Chopin (Polish, 1810-1849)

INTERMISSION

Aria (from "Prelude, Aria and Finale")....................................Cesar Franck (Belgian, 1822-1890)
Fugue, from Piano Sonata, opus 66..Cyril Scott (English, born 1879)
"Beautiful Fresh Flower"..Chinese Melody
    with "pentatonic" harmonies by Joseph Yasser (Russian, born................)
"Islamey," Oriental Phantasy..Balakirev (Russian, 1837-1910)
"Little Sparrow," American Folksong from Kentucky (from "Lonesome Tunes"), set by....
....Howard Brockway (American, born....................)
"Turkey in the Straw," American folk dance, set by........David Guion (American, born............)

Reception and Refreshments following this program at the Roof Lounge, Clift Hotel

Hostesses: Mrs. Lenora Wood Armsby, Mrs. Marcus Koshland

60

Plate 19. A 'Seven Uplifters' lecture-recital programme, San
Francisco, 27 September 1942. (Grainger Museum)

CENTENARY SINGERS
with PERCY GRAINGER

PRESENT

Music of Contemporary Composers

W. NORMAN GRAYSON, *Pianist*

EDGAR H. SMITH, *Director*

1. English Gothic Music
   Transcribed and Edited by Dom Anselm Hughes, O.S.B., and Percy Aldridge Grainger
   Beata Viscera
   Puellare Gremium
   Sanctus   .   .   .   PERCY GRAINGER
   Fulget Coelestis Curia

   Agnus Dei   .   .   .   .   .   .   VIRGIL THOMSON
   The Centenary Singers

2. Scherzo, Op. 22 B .   .   .   .   DANIEL GREGORY MASON
   Rufford Park Poachers (From Lincolnshire Posy)   .   .   GRAINGER
   Symphonic Dance No. 1 .   .   .   .   SCOTT-GRAINGER
   Mr. Grainger and Mr. Grayson

3. The Chamber Blue (First New York performance) .   .   ARTHUR FICKENSCHER
   The Centenary Singers

4. Porgy and Bess (First performance) .   .   .   .   GERSHWIN-GRAINGER
   Mr. Grainger and Mr. Grayson

5. Lilting Fancy (Dedicated to Centenary Singers—First performance) .   HENRY COWELL
   Peregrine White and Virginia Dare   .   .   .   GAIL KUBIK
   I Like Men .   .   .   .   IRVING MOPPER
   Two Songs of Infinity (Dedicated to Centenary Singers—First performance)
      Chartless
      Astronomy   .   .   .   .   IRVING MOPPER
   Rewritten   .   .   .   .   .   DOROTHY EMERY
   Alma Mater   .   .   .   .   arr. GRAYSON
   The Centenary Singers

STEINWAY PIANOS

Tickets: $2.40, $1.80, $1.20, 90¢; Loges, seating 6, $18.00; Per seat, $3.00

Kindly make checks or money orders for tickets and contributions to the Organ Fund payable to Centenary
Junior College and mail to:

CENTENARY JUNIOR COLLEGE
HACKETTSTOWN, NEW JERSEY

Plate 20. Programme to a mixed choral–piano concert, New
York, 21 April 1951. (Grainger Museum)

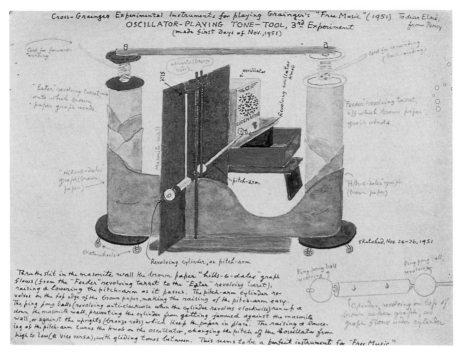

Plate 21. Grainger's diagram for a 'Free Music' oscillator-playing tone-tool, November 1951. (Burnett Cross)

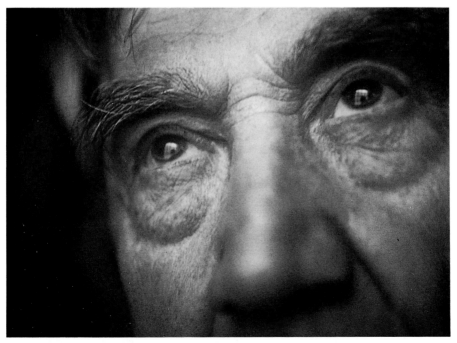

Plate 22. Ralph Vaughan Williams's eyes, 1954. (Burnett Cross)

Plate 23. Grainger working on a 'Free Music' machine, early 1950s. (Burnett Cross)

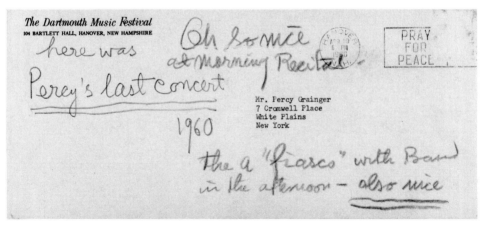

Plate 24. Grainger's recollection of his last concert, in Hanover, New Hampshire, on 29 April 1960. (Grainger Museum)

on the sketch programs—most are published by Schott & C⁰, 48 Gt Marlborough St, London W1.

I believe the following of my choral numbers (choral parts) can be hired from The Lady Northcote Library, Conservatorium of Music, University of Melbourne, Melbourne, N3, Vic., for a nominal sum:
Father & Daughter (for each performance by a 100-voice choir about these proportions: 5 vocal & piano scores,

20   1st chorus, women
15   1st chorus, men
40   2nd chorus, women
25   2nd chorus, men)

Recessional, There was a Pig, The Fall of the Stone, Nightsong in the Jungle, Morning Song in the Jungle, Tiger-Tiger, Mowgli's Song against People, Anchor Song, Dollar & a half, We have fed our Sea[s], Marching Song of Democracy, Shallow Brown.[1]

This, I think, covers the choral material (choral parts) pretty thoroughly. But, as a further precaution I will try to loan choral copies (about 100 copies of mixed chorus numbers, about 50 copies of items for male chorus or women's chorus) from choral societies in Australia (or, failing that, order them from the publisher at my own expense) & have them sent to you as soon as possible. You can then use yr discretion about these copies. I do not like to lend *printed copies* of choruses, as a rule.

But in the case of NZ (this being my first appearance there as a composer), I would rather that you lend 50 or 100 copies of a chorus to a society than that they should omit an important item from a program because they cannot afford to buy it. In particular, I do not want *Father & Daughter* or *Marching Song of Democracy* omitted, if possible, as they are especially effective & representative. (But 'The Hunter in his Career'[2] may be substituted for 'Father & Daughter' if *absolutely necessary* (therefore I shall try to have 100 copies of 'The Hunter' sent to you).)

The above remarks about loaned copies of my choruses do not, however, apply to the choruses printed by Oxford University Press (Love Verses from the Song of Solomon, The Merry Wedding, Tribute to F.) or by Allan & C⁰ L^td (Irish Tune from C⁰ Derry, I'm

---

[1] The majority of these are Kipling settings. *There was a pig went out to dig* is a setting of a Lancashire song; *Dollar and a half a day* and *Shallow Brown* are 'Sea-chanty [*sic*] settings'. *Marching Song of Democracy* involves vocal parts of nonsense syllables.

[2] Grainger's 1904 setting of a tune from William Chappell's *Old English Popular Music* (1858).

Seventeen, Australian Up-Country Song). These must be ordered from the addresses given earlier in this letter. But any choral parts that reach you in bulk (100 or 50 copies of each) you may deal with at yr discretion. Perhaps, in some cases, such copies might be lent to choral societies for use until their own copies (ordered from the publisher) arrive.

———————————————— " ————————————————

I think this is all for the present. Again thanking you for your fine letter & with admiration for the generous & well-balanced scope of yr plans,

Yrs cordially
  Percy Grainger

P.S. On second thoughts I am asking my London & NY publishers to send you (at my expense) complete orchestrations of the following:
  Spoon River
  Lord Peter's Stableboy
  The Nightingale & the 2 Sisters
  Jutish Medley
  Shallow Brown (also 50 vocal parts)
  Irish Tune from C° Derry N° 29[1] (also vocal parts)
This Irish tune (N° 29) is quite a new setting of the 'Londonderry Air' (has nothing in common with my earlier settings). Perhaps it could be used in the Auckland Public Concert, if choir is used.
  Lord Peter's Stable-Boy, *The Nightingale & the 2 Sisters*, & *Jutish Medley* form, together, a *Danish Folkmusic Suite*.[2] This might be used in the Auckland Public Concert, if desired.

33   *To Storm Bull*

[One of the most idiosyncratic and effective qualities of Grainger's music is his scoring. In this letter, written as Grainger was completing one of his masterpieces for band, *Lincolnshire Posy*, he outlines various quick ways for gaining a good grasp of the sound resources available in the band.]

---

[1] = *British Folk-Music Setting* No. 29. (Earlier settings of the tune were Nos. 5, 6, and 15.)
[2] Only in 1941 did Grainger add 'The Power of Love', as the first movement of the suite.

'An Untamed Buffalo'

Train to Duluth[1] | March 25, 1937

Dear Storm,

Agnes & Eyvind[2] were right about you, & about the methods they pursued in developing your pianism, & I was wrong. And I am *overdelighted* it is so. I have never thot a Scandinavian or other Nordic capable of reaching first class virtuosity, & in your case I doubted it specially—I say 'specially' because it was obvious that you were very gifted, but it seemed to me in other directions. You were wordy or argumentative (which pointed, I shallowly thot, to a writer, a lecturer, a musical *thinker*, rather than a player) while your playing halted and stammered. You seemed more willing to *explain* than to *play*, & as I have always felt that way myself I viewed the symptom as darkly as possible. Above all I doubted your hardworkingness in the *technical* pianistic field. To understand my doubts, you must remember my own difficulties and laziness in the technical field.

It all goes to show the old story: that the all-round genius is the hard one for outsiders to understand (it is a blessing that Agnes & Eyvind did not have this difficulty)—partly because there are two all-round methods: the man who nibbles shallowly at many things, & the man (like Goethe) who struggles thoroly with many things, *one at a time* (at least concentrating on one at a time, tho possibly keeping the others going at the back of his brain—like a juggler keeping 5 balls in the air). It seems clear now, that you belong to the 2nd type, & I congratulate you & yours with a whole heart. You have certainly made the most of your teachers, your talents & have developed a *hair-raising* virtuosity (in the Bartok[3] & in my Flower Waltz[4] I noted it equally) that I marvel at more than any pianistic virtuosity I have witnessed since Busoni's.[5] When we think of your arresting, provocative, & lovable personality (for all those *many* who have been specially interested in you have always *stayed* interested), your memorable name, your bodily strength & health & the unique support & help you have in your wonderful parents—not to mention your great & varied talents—one can only be sure you will go *very far indeed*. Why should you not become the greatest American musician of your generation? I see nothing to hinder it. You are a composer, a natural conductor, already a first class

[1] Minnesota.   [2] Bull's parents. See Biographical Register.

[3] Bartók's Piano Concerto No. 2 (1930–1).

[4] Grainger's Paraphrase on Tchaikovsky's 'Flower-Waltz', much performed by him in his earlier London years and first published in 1905.

[5] Ferruccio Busoni (1866–1924), Italian pianist and composer. Grainger had studied with him briefly in Berlin during the summer of 1903.

virtuoso & are a born writer and lecturer. That was, I suppose, the sort of combination such men as Lyonel Power (1400?), Guillaume de Machaut (1300–1377), Bach & Wagner must have had (perhaps Balakirew a bit also?), & we see that such manysidedness (of the *thoro* kind) leads to the greatest greatness.

I will do what I can about the pianistic side, with conductors, etc. I was very impressed about your remarks about 'those that have the most to give—those that make the most of what they have' in composition. It is a most *original theme*, a very critical & discerning viewpoint & gives (thank goodness) no comfort to those that link Mozart with Beethoven (because of period) & Grieg with Moszkowski[1] (because both were published by Peters, the *popularising* publisher?). Your insight into this theme explains Grieg's adoration of Mozart—something I have hitherto never fathomed. If you are going to think along these very original & penetrating lines, you ought to become a much read & sway-ful writer on music—for just the penetration & discrimination you show is what music lovers of your generation are looking for. So if you sell, or give (for publicity purposes), articles to musical magazines, be sure you retain the full book rights. If you cared to work up that thot (about having the most & making the most) into an article, with a clever & revealing title (something that always floors me), why should I not try it on the 'Musical Quarterly.' Carl Engel (editor) likes statements well substantiated, verse & chapter. If not successful there (or in addition to the Quarterly) I might place it in England. I think I could easily do so in the 'Australian Music News' & 'Music in New Zealand,' tho I have never heard of these two latter paying for articles. But as publicity & perhaps as forerunning radio engagements in Australia & New Zealand (which I might be able to bring about—at least I could try) it might be worth considering. If you have *real thots* about music, as you have, surely it is the right thing to have one's voice heard, in all quarters, is it not?

Now about the Band: the fragments from your own that you played yesterday all seemed to me *highly suited* for band. But why not test them out when we go to Bainum's.[2] Take some fragments from your own (giving each a title such as 'Lament' or 'Chord Study' or merely an alphabetical letter—so they are easy to rehearse), and repeat & go back to [them] in rehearsal—the shorter the better—and orchestrate

[1] Moritz Moszkowski (1854–1925), Polish-German composer.
[2] Glenn Cliffe Bainum (1888–1974), director of bands at Northwestern University, and organizer of the Evanston Festival, which both Grainger and Bull attended in Apr. 1937.

them in different ways: (a) the melody on combined clarinets, accompanied by saxophones, alto & bass clarinets, bassoons; (b) the melody low on reeds (flute, oboe, clarinets, alto & bass clarinets, saxophones in unison) accompanied by brass (cornets, horns, trombones, baritone,[1] euphonium, tubas); (c) melody on saxophones, (unison) accompanied by clarinets, alto & bass clarinets, bassoons; (d) melody on horns & baritone & euphonium (unison) accompanied by reeds (clarinet family, bassoons, saxophones); (3) melody 2 or 3 octaves apart on massed reeds, accompanied by spread (or close) brass; and so on.

Or take a mere passage of chords, and score them in different ways: (a) for brass alone; (b) for reeds alone, spread and close; (c) for saxophones alone (close); (d) for brass muted. In rehearsal you can combine (c) with (a), (d) with (b), and combine all together. Such experiments take only a few hours to write out (parts) and only a few minutes to rehearse, yet it seems to me they will tell one almost all one needs to know *before* composing for band. One needs a *clear, normal* picture of the chief sound-color types (in the band) before proceeding to blend them. Then, if I were you, I would take some of the shorter items in Grieg's Opus 66 and score them preferably in different ways—each way marked with a special letter (A or X) so it is easy to handle in rehearsal. 'Ranveig'[2] (transposed down a whole tone) for example: (a) for clarinet family only, top voice for 1st B♭ clarinet, next top voice for 2nd clarinet, 3rd voice for 3rd clarinet, lowest voice for alto & bass clarinet in unison. Also write (under same alphabetical letter) the lowest voice for bassoons and baritone saxophone, the next lowest voice on tenor saxophone, in case the lower voices are weak, on bass clarinets; (b) for saxophones only, top voice for soprano and 1st alto, 2nd voice for 2nd alto, 3rd voice for tenor, bass part for baritone; (c) brass only, top for 1st cornet, 2nd voice for horn, 3rd voice for baritone (treble), bass for euphonium (bass); (d) militaristic brass only, 2 cornets, 2 trombones; (e) bagpipe reeds, 2 oboes, 2 bassoons; (f) reed octave treatment, like (a) but with the flutes octave above 1st clarinet, 1st oboe octave above 2nd clarinet, 2nd oboe octave above 3rd clarinet, E♭ clarinet (ending on his lowest G) octave above bass clarinet; (g) reed 2 octave apart treatment like (a), but with piccolo 2 octaves above 1st clarinet, flutes 2 octaves above 2nd clarinets, E♭ clarinet 2 octaves above 3rd clarinet, oboes [2] octaves above bass clarinet.

---

[1] Instrument closely related to a euphonium.   [2] Op. 66 No. 12.

For (f) and (g) you don't need to write out (a) again each time, just write out new parts. In rehearsal you merely say, 'I want (a) and (f) together.'

Then you can combine the best of these various versions in rehearsal, seeing how your fuller combinations are built up out of these various simpler elements. Really, a very full grasp of the band's resources could be learnt in about 30 minutes rehearsal if one had one's examples prepared in advance. For such an experiment there is no need to have a complete score; just the first measure of each letter (1st measure of (a), 1st measure of (b), etc.) is enough. So, in rehearsing, one can see at a glance what one is listening to. For the staccato side, the mere first phrase of 'En liten graa man'[1] would be useful: (a) staccato bass melody on baritone saxophone, accompanied by the other saxophones, (b) staccato melody on unison saxophones accompanied by clarinets, etc.; (c) staccato melody on saxophones accompanied by horns (in this case the saxophone parts can be marked *B and C*); (d) melody on baritone (treble) and euphonium (bass), accompanied by horns, or reeds, or saxophones. Of course *the whole* of 'En liten graa man' would shed bright light on the *whole staccato resources* of the band, working up from the tonally small (but explosively expressed) sound of 1 or 2 saxophones on the opening staccato melody to the full brass (or full band) staccato on the climax section. Another good Grieg fragment to experiment with is the *4th Norwegian* (not Symphonic) Dance[2]—the opening phrases, etc. Good ones to experiment with are 'Det er den største Daarlighed'[3] (to get the middle voice *prominent enough*, perhaps horns, alto and tenor saxophones, baritone (treble) and euphonium (bass) on the middle melody (reeds accompanying)). 'Det var i min ungdom'[4] (massed reeds for expressive parts—adding one clarinet *onto another* in crescendi—horns and other brass thrown in to impassion middle voices). 'Gjendines Baadnlaat'[5] (4 *solo* clarinet family voices contrasted, sectionally, with massed clarinet family). 'Der stander to Piger'[6] (sections of mellow [*sic*] on reeds and saxophones—or muted cornet, accompanied by saxophones—contrasted with crashing on full brass— or with blended brass and reeds. A good thing is reeds for the main parts, with an expressive middle voice reinforced by horn, cornets, baritone, or euphonium. In writing out parts for such experiments:

[1] = A little grey man (Op. 66 No. 13).
[2] Op. 35 (1881), for piano duet.
[3] = It is the greatest folly (Op. 66 No. 2).
[4] = It was in my youth (Op. 66 No. 5).
[5] = Gjendine's lullaby (Op. 66 No. 19).
[6] = There stood two girls (Op. 66 No. 11).

write out the complete part (flute 1 complete, baritone (treble) complete) for all the numbers (if taking more than 4 sides of paper, sew them together) so they are easy to rehearse. Never write on both sides of the paper (so you can cut out and use again—paste in—any part you approve of). Perhaps better to write continuous letters (a)–(x) or numbers (1)–(100) rather than 'Gjendines Baadnlaat (a)' etc.—easier in rehearsal. Or you can use titles ('Ranveig') as well as continuous numbers or letters.

Why the method I have above sketched is better for learning the tone color of the band than writing out a *whole composition* is the same if writing parts. To test the reed sound in 'Ranveig' for instance, you don't need to write any brass parts you don't want to hear. (In that case write in your brass parts: 'Ranveig' tacet—or (12) tacet, (40) tacet. Then for brass passages you *do* want to hear, you need write no reed parts you don't want to hear.

I don't want to lead you into a will-o-the-wisp with this band business. Naturally I want to make an esthetic success of my summer with Maddy (organizer of the National High School Camp).[1] He is paying me ***[2] to take charge of the band because he wants (1) the band to play more delicately than it has (2) because he wants them to know a wider range of music (3) because he wants American composers to be induced to compose more for band (4) because he wants the more talented members of the band to learn band orchestration in a go-ahead manner (far beyond the ordinary march scoring). Naturally you are the type I want—fine personality, a Nordic American, an electrifying player, a real modern go-ahead composer. My interest in having you is obvious. I would like to propose that you come to Interlochen for a whole week (as the guest of the camp, or as my guest), so you have plenty of time to rehearse your things and *absorb band experience* in the daily rehearsals for a week. What I would like you to do while there is:

(1) conduct a composition of your own in concert or broadcast
(2) conduct an arrangement of your own in concert or broadcast
(3) play 'Totentanz'[3] with orchestra in concert or broadcast
(4) give us a lecture on some musical subject.[4]

[1] See Biographical Register. This annual camp was held at Interlochen, Michigan.
[2] The sums mentioned here and later in this letter, as well as certain names, were omitted by a copyist. In a letter to the editors of 29 July 1992 Storm Bull could throw no light on these omissions.
[3] Liszt's work for piano and orchestra, R. 457.
[4] Bull did attend the Interlochen camp, where *Totentanz*, one of his own compositions and his arrangements of several Grieg Op. 66 pieces were performed.

I do not like to ask Maddy to pay for your piano performance, because the camp is a non-profit concern (Sousa,[1] Goldman,[2] Damrosch, Howard Hanson,[3] myself, etc. have always performed for nixie) because I know they are struggling to pay off a heavy debt. But if you cared to play 'Totentanz' or other piece with the orchestra, I would certainly ask Maddy (at once, now, when I hear from you) if he would pay all of your expenses. I would have to do the Bartok with you myself, but I would not ask Maddy to pay $30.00 for the performance, and I would not ask the publishers to waive the performing fee (which they wouldn't do either, most likely). Should you wish to do any or all of those things, I would like to ask you (if you have the time) to prepare a set of experimental parts which we could try out at Evanston around April 20–24, consisting of short snatches of your own compositions and ditto of Grieg's Opus 66, or *any other work you prefer*. After such trials at such a rehearsal (in which you would hear Bainum's wonderful arrangements and probably my 'Lincolnshire Posy'[4]—the best example of my own band scoring) you ought to be equipped to do justice to yourself as composer and arranger at Interlochen, if you wished to.

I repeat: I don't want you to do anything that will waste your time or take you away from more profitable jobs, just because I am keen on the band and want to do my summer job well. You, Agnes, and Eyvind must be the judges of what is best for you, not I. But as against the thot that your band activities might be a waste of time (or not as essential as other things you could do) I put forward the following facts, from my own recent experience:

(a) I earn about ******* yearly on the royalties I get on the compositions and arrangements I have done for band (Children's March, Molly, Colonial Song, Shepherd's Hey, Irish Tune).

(b) In the last year, I have earned ******* in two engagements (1936, 1937) to play the piano part in my Children's March with band and conduct my band numbers in Miami, Florida.

(c) I am to get ******* for the band work at the Camp (as aforesaid).

(d) My manager has had a proposal to pay me to conduct in a

[1] John Philip Sousa (1854–1932), American composer best known for his band marches.
[2] Edwin Franko Goldman (1878–1956), American bandmaster, founder in 1911 of the Goldman Band.
[3] (1896–1981), American composer and conductor, director of the Eastman School of Music (1924–64).
[4] Collection of six folktunes scored by Grainger for wind band early in 1937. He used the word 'posy' because he considered the collection a 'bunch of "musical wildflowers"'.

band concert on Long Island in May (not settled yet)—this is the result of my recent activities in Brooklyn.

The High School, School, and University bands are more numerous than the orchestras. The publishers regard band publishing as much more lucrative than orchestral publishing, but they are looking for *symphonic* band music—away from the militaristic, circus-like, march-like, old type of band music. Such men as you are the ones they want. You (and your type) are the ones to own the band public of the future. Not to the exclusion of orchestral, choral and chamber writing, not to the exclusion of pianism and concertizing, but as a very natural, interesting *extra string to your bow* (esthetically and commercially worthwhile).

Let me know what you, Agnes, and Eyvind feel, and *decide*, about this band proposal, about writing an article (that I would try to place in the Quarterly or elsewhere), about spending a week there, about experimenting at Evanston. And whatever you decide *will be right with me*. In the meantime I will write to *** and *** about you as soloist, as soon as I get home to my address books, and will try to think up other places, such as ***. I congratulate you on the *wonderful* pianistic work you have been doing, and I am *so glad* your mother and father were right and I wrong.

Love from Percy.

34   *To Herman Sandby*

Indianapolis, Ind. | Dec. 9, 1937

Darling Herman,

As you will see from the enclosed, I have been doing a Scandinavian program (with an awful fool of an American woman[1]— she engaged me) with 2 of yours. This program is to be repeated at Washington, DC,[2] maybe elsewhere also.

Working at yr old things awoke all the old glamor they had for me from the first. It is lovely to fall in love with a woman, but it is almost a bigger loveliness to fall in love with a land. And few men have ever fallen so deeply in love with a (to them) foreign land as I did with

---

[1] Marion Frank Leslie, a 'dramalogist-commentator'. They had presented a joint recital of Scandinavian music, poetry and drama in Detroit on 1 Dec. 1937, and in Saint-Mary-of-the-Woods, Indiana, on 6 Dec.

[2] On 3 Mar. 1938.

Denmark—& all thru you. Is there any joy purer & greater than that we feel in the first poems we learn in a beloved strange tongue? Each new word (as we get to know its meaning) carries a depth of imagined feeling with it. I remember how you taught me the words of Elverhøj[1] gave them to me. The thrill of ‚jomfruer'[2] & ‚gangendes fram'[3]—I will never forget them.

Og alle smaa fisken i floden var
De lagte med deres hale.
Og alle smaa fugler i skoven var
begyndte at kvidre i Dale[4]

‚floden', ‚haler', ‚kvidre'[5] were magic words for me. And then yr harmonies to the lovely tune; not ‚haardt imod haardt'[6] but ‚blødt imod blødt'[7]—like the laying on of a tender hand! Yes, you & yr genius were the magic key to a magic land. And, for me, a key that never loses its magic & a land that never loses its magic. Later, the hardness of life (or my own individual hardness of heart) put us asunder—just as I was sundered from Cyril & my English composer friends by the hardness of life or the hardness of my own heart. An Australian is not 'a good loser' & I have always had plenty of political spaadom[8] in me. I felt the big war coming many years ahead—just as now I feel great struggles ahead. I could not sit down as you & Cyril could—supported by the love of nearby friends and kinsmen & even by some money. I needed a smashing victory for myself & Australia. I could not 'possess my soul', follow my Gemüth,[9] as you Europeans were able to. My mother had had a hard fate (it is hard to have one's healthy body spoiled by syphilis) & it cast its dark shadow over me. My father's fate was hard. And my fate hard—to have to be a 'society' pianist when at heart one is a composer, a yeoman, a sailor. You even had yr sweet land to fall back upon, which, small as it is, could give yr compositional life a background (stipendium) that none of our big Anglosaxon lands could, or would, ever give me.

So you must forgive me if I grew hard, amidst so much hardness. (Even now, my life is terribly hard. Here I am on tour; I rise at 7.00 & work till midnight, day after day. What do I work at? The allround

---

[1] = *Elfhill*, the five-act tragedy (1828) by the Danish writer Johan Ludvig Heiberg (1791–1860). Sandby's own *Elverhøj*, a folksong setting, originally for string orchestra, was published in 1931.

[2] = virgins (Danish).   [3] Perhaps meaning 'going forward'.

[4] And all the little fish in the river | They lay there with their tail. | And all the little birds in the forest were | Twittering in the dale. (Danish).

[5] = river, tails, twittering (respectively) (Danish).

[6] = hard against hard (Danish).   [7] = soft against soft (Danish).

[8] = foresightedness (Danish).   [9] = feeling (German).

cause of Nordic music, whether in Scand, England, America, Australia.) But my heart was never hard to you. I just could not afford to follow my heart, those days. That was all. But in my heart the magic of yr harmonies, the magic of yr Danish tunes, the magic of yr Danish land dwelt enshrined. I could not handle Alfhild,[1] her Anglosaxon worldliness, so I had to give you both up, for the time being. It was hard to go touring in Denmark without you. But there were many hard things. It was hard for me to give up several sweet-hearts that I adored (for life without woman is just nonsense & to have to live so much without woman's love was harder for me than for many men. Some men seem to fear woman, & for them it is not hard to live without woman's love). It was hard for me to see Mimi give me up to stay with Pfitzner.[2] I was never the same since, quite. And I had other hardships in giving up sweethearts that I have never spoken to you about (perhaps I shall, someday). It was hard for me to lose my mother in such a cruel way. But it was hard for her to feel so ill that she found it needful to leave life in such a hard way (or she found me so hard. Some terrible hardness there was in it for her). Australian fates are hard. I have seen it again & again. It is something in the weather, or the big size of the land, maybe. I dont know. But I know that all we Australians are wrapped round with hard fates. But some Australians have hearts hard enough to match their fates. I have not. My heart has never been a hard one, as I think you will agree my har-monies show. But I live in a hard age, & belong to a hard race. The English have drawn their empire together thru hardness, greed, crime, & other sins. I rue such wickedness & would be glad to see our Empire (& all empires) fall apart & leave all races free & safe. Yet there is studiousness, gentleness, wit, spiritualness in the English that I love. They have some kinds of softness, yieldingness that belong to them alone. My old folksingers, for instance, & the soft, free, gentle songs they sang. But the English are a blent (blandet)[3] race, with different racial qualities inharmoniously crossed & at feud with each other. I could willingly see the English lose to the Scandinavians, or to any *gentler* race. But not to the swinish Germans. And my life was early dedicated to a war in music, in which I was in the van—tho nobody noticed it then, or today. For me the war (my war against Germany in

[1] Sandby's wife. See Biographical Register.
[2] Hans Pfitzner (1869–1949), German composer and conductor, who had been Grainger's rival in affection for Mimi Kwast (1879–1926), the daughter of Grainger's piano teacher in Frankfurt. She became Pfitzner's wife.
[3] = mixed (Danish).

music) began 14 years before 1914. And any war is hard. You did not have such troubles, nor did my English friends. Even the war did not strike you (any of you) as it struck me. You were hardly aware of it, *in yr inner souls*. It did not dishonor you; it did not cut yr connections with the lands you were representing in art. It did not tear you in two—yr art-duties & yr duty as a man. I had a hard time. And a still harder time when I lost my mother. I had done many hard things in the hopes *of not failing her.* Yet it seems I failed her so much that she had to leave this life. Hard for her & hard for me. That is already 15 years ago & in 5 years time I will be as old as was my mother when she killed herself!

Since I married Ella I have had a sweet, happy life—as far as a sinful, hard-fated man can be happy. Ella is always sweet & kind to me & she always *holds my mind away* from my own life & fate. It is like having a sweet daughter—a new life, a fresh life, not weighted down by sin & hardness. But my duties (my war) still keep me in these hard lands, where (for me) life is but a nightmare, & no real life at all. There is much that I admire in the English speaking life, but next to nothing I *enjoy*. All the sweetness is so mixed with sin, wickedness, stupidity—just what you would expect in a blent race! Perhaps I shall soon be able to get away from this treadmill, when my museum duties are fulfilled. (We go out to Australia in June with things for the museum, & after that I shall feel much freer). If Ella & I could live in Scandinavia, in the Faeroes, in Iceland, or in the South Seas (for a time) I think I could be happy. But that is *the future*. I am talking of *the past*. In the past I knew full happiness only in Denmark. I was utterly happy the very first visits I paid to Denmark, to you. When I slept in a furnished room (had 'wet dreams', being chilly at night) & had meals with yr family. I loved yr family, was truly happy with them all. I adored one or 2 days at Sønderjærnløse with Frederik,[1] Alfhild & you. I adored that falling in love with Miss Ahren in Göteborg that day, & I adored yr kindness, making faces at me all the way home, on the platform of the train, to cheer me up. I adored when you came up to me (at the West End Platz, Frankfurt) after I had played my compositions to you, Cyril (Roger?), when you said that *you* saw nothing to laugh at in my Kipling songs. I adored our stay at Kandestederne, & the whole walk from Fred[e]rikshavn to Skagen. The wind & rain on the roof, on the windows, at Kandestederne is with me always. I loved when you made

---

[1] Sandby's brother, a doctor in this village. The visit took place in mid-Oct. 1904.

Grieg's Op. 66 known to me, & when I first heard yr matchless ‚Elskov'[1] & ‚Pagen højt paa Taarnet sad'[2] on the 4 or more cellos. I loved many things with you in London. But yr & my samvær in London[3] was marred as my life with Ella is marred in America or Australia, by the roundringment of perfectionspoiling English speaking-ness, Englishthinkingness. I had flawless happiness with you in Denmark. There are those that say that a man gets more perfect happiness with a man friend than with a woman sweetheart. George Moore says that there are few women a man would wish to meet in Paradise. I know nought of such sex differentiation. With me *it is the race*, not the sex, that matters. I was happy with you, as a friend. I was happy with E.T. Kristensen, an old man. I was happy with Karen, a sweetheart. I am happy with Ella, a wife. If *the race* is right, & *the land* is right, I am in heaven. In Denmark I was freed from the torture of hardness, sin, stupidity. The terrible hardness, & the cruel fate, that weighed on me elsewhere *was lifted* in Denmark—by the sweetness of the land, the *cleverness* of the Danes, the *normalness* of Danish life, the kindliness of you & other Danes. The other night in Detroit, after the concert, that silly (American) Miss Leslie had a reception, to which wellnigh only Danes & Danish-Detroiters came. I saw it all again: the sweet looks, the sweet ways, the clever heads. And it rounded out the memories aroused by working at yr 2 beloved pieces: Pagen & Elverhøj. When you came to NY in 1926[4] I think you heard in my harmonisations of Danish melodies that I was true to my Danish memories, friendships, loves. I am still true to them, always will be. Those old days (yr gift of *Denmark to me*) are with me always, & the bloom is just as thick on yr harmonies & melodies as of yore. The text of Elverhøj is just as magical to me as ever, the words still mean *more than they mean*. And my thankfulness to you, my love for you, is alive & awake.

And now, what remains? Have we 5 years of life before us, or 10 or 15 years more? Shall we sink into our graves with our tasks half

[1] = Love (Danish). Grainger probably refers to Sandby's *Love Song* for four cellos, composed in Dec. 1899, of which Grainger made various arrangements, including one of 1939 for his *Chosen Gems for Strings* collection.
[2] = The page sat up high on the tower (Danish). In 1900 Grainger arranged this song under the title (Solemn) Chant for an eight-piece chamber ensemble.
[3] = being together (Danish). Sandby had stayed with Percy and Rose Grainger several times during their earliest years in London. His London début, in a joint recital with Grainger, took place in Apr. 1902.
[4] Grainger and Sandby performed together many times during the winter of 1925–6, including the American première of Delius's Cello Concerto.

finished, or shall we have done our jobs, fought our wars, well? Shall we ever know holidays, or shall we go on grinding at our careers to the end? Shall you & I ever have a holiday together, & will it be longer than the Skagen walk? Or will we die first? I feel the same as when I was 16. I know no awareness of age (except that I work easier, & *can work much longer*). I feel just as sexual, just as lustful, just as egoistic. From the way I *feel*, I do not see why one should ever grow old or die. But history teaches otherwise. So I wonder if I shall live long enough to carry out my artistic plans & duties & yet have time to enjoy myself in Paris, Iceland, Java, Bali, etc? And what about you? What would you like to do?

By the way, would you like me to take up my pianistic setting of yr Elverhøj (my pianistic free treatment of yr harmonies, as I have with Brahms, Bach, etc.) into my 'Free Settings of Favorite Melodies',[1] with the royalty to you, of course? I dont know that you would like my treatment of it. But it expresses (to me) the charm I feel in yr harmonies, the heartbreak I feel in these memories. It is my *memory* (not very accurate) of yr Elverhøj setting in a pianistic form. I would have to play it to you for you to see. Even if you approved, would Wilhelm Hansen[2] let my setting appear as part of the above mentioned series, published by Schirmer for USA and Canada, published by Schott for all other lands? It is not important. It might not sell well. The Brahms cradlesong[3] sells wonderfully well of course. But my transcription of Fauré's entrancing 'Nell'[4] (in the same series) sells not at all. Mad world! Only *enemy music* sclls!

Hoping you & Alfhild are well (Ella would send her love if she were here. She's very well, has lost her headaches since getting new eyeglasses!) & with old love

Ever yrs
    Percy

---

[1] Grainger sketched an arrangement of this song in 1937; it remains unpublished.

[2] Sandby's publisher in Copenhagen.

[3] Grainger's arrangement, the first in his *Free Settings of Favorite Melodies* series, was published by Schirmer in 1923.

[4] Grainger's arrangement of Fauré's song (Op. 18 No. 1), was published in 1925 as the third in the series.

35   *To James Barrett*

[In the second half of 1938 the Graingers lived in Melbourne, where they supervised the building of the second stage of the Museum and arranged its initial exhibitions. The Grainger Museum, and associated Music Museum, was officially opened on 10 December 1938.]

Victoria Hotel, | 123 Beaconsfield Parade,
Albert Park, S.C., August 24, 1938

The Chancellor,
University of Melbourne, Carlton N3.

Dear Sir James,

The object of my present visit to Australia is, as you know, to carry further the museum project started three years ago.

I am anxious to complete the whole outer corridor of the ground floor of the building and to increase the Grainger Museum Fund so that the interest on its capital will yield a yearly sum to provide for repair and upkeep of the museum building and for the salaries of a curator-caretaker and cleaner. As the museum should not be opened for indiscriminate public inspection during its first few years (though available to special students and special visitors, at the discrimination of the Conservatorium) the duties of the initial curator-caretaker[1] should be quite light—to periodically go through the exhibits and contents of the museum, see that they are sprayed or treated against silverfish, etc., and to see that the museum is kept clean and in repair. A few hours work every few weeks ought to be ample for this task and in my opinion the salary of this initial curator-caretaker could be rather small. But in a few years time (when I have collected many more exhibits, have sent out many exhibits already collected in White Plains, and can devote a whole year to arranging all these into effective order, and when the museum can be opened to the public) a full curator, able to further the aest[h]etic aims of the museum, will be needed, and it is my intention to then so increase the Grainger Museum Fund as to provide a fitting salary for the full curator.

Mr Gawler's rough estimate for the extension of the ground floor (to

---

[1] As part-time curators Grainger appointed Richard Fowler (b. 1910), an employee of the Science and Technology Museum of Victoria, and his wife Dorothy (1911–75). They remained curators until the early 1960s, when Fowler became director of the Science Museum.

include a circular section and one store-room) is £2450.[1] Allowing for this, and reserving £500. for equipment (safe, fireproof filing cabinets, cases, frames, etc.), I would be able to add £2736. to the Grainger Museum Fund (which at present amounts to £2264., I am told) bringing the total of this fund up to £5000. I would be glad to make this addition to the Grainger Museum Fund as soon as desired.

I propose that the title of the building be 'Music Museum and Grainger Museum', the contents of the 'Music Museum' to be chosen and arranged by the University, and the contents of the 'Grainger Museum' to be collected and arranged by me, but the displaying of all exhibits in the Grainger Museum to be subject to the approval of the University. One museum could start to the left of the entrance hall, the other museum to the right of the entrance hall. The two museums need be distinguished from each other only by the titles 'Music Museum' & 'Grainger Museum' where they meet or begin. These boundaries could be quite elastic. The upkeep, cleaning and curating of both museums could be paid for out of the Grainger Museum Fund—unless the University, at any time, should prefer to have a separate curator and cleaner for the Music Museum.

As I see it, the purpose of the Music Museum would be to preserve and exhibit things of *general* musical interest and things connected with the *general* musical life of Australia. For instance, the Mss and printed compositions of Professor Marshall-Hall[2] would seem to me most fitting for this museum, not only because of their value as music but also because of the immense part played by Professor Marshall-Hall in Australian musical progress. Records of outstanding musical undertakings in Australia (for instance, the programs of the 1888 Exhibition concerts, which I believe Mr Sutton Crow[3] has secured) might be housed here, as should musical instruments that are of educational value and publications and Mss of *general* interest (for instance a Ms of Mozart's, if available).

The Grainger Museum would preserve and display exhibits collected by me during the last 40 years for the purpose of:
1. stressing the creative side of music, as distinct from the merely executive side. Australia has, in the last 60 years, seen and heard many outstanding *servants of music* (singers, instrumental virtuosi and

[1] £1,960 sterling (US$9,564) at prevailing exchange rates. See plate No. 16.
[2] G. W. L. Marshall-Hall (1862–1915), English-born composer and first professor of music at The University of Melbourne. He had supported Grainger's musical development as a youth in Melbourne. Grainger purchased Marshall-Hall's musical and other MSS from his widow in 1935.
[3] J. Sutton-Crow, Secretary of the University Conservatorium in Melbourne.

conductors) but to my knowledge none of the *masters of music* of that period (creators such as Grieg, Elgar, Delius, Richard Strauss, Debussy, Ravel, Cyril Scott, Vaughan Williams, Arnold Bax, Skryabin, Roger Quilter, Stravinsky, Schoenberg, Gershwin) have visited Australia. I hope that the display of photographs, relics, letters, MSS, typical of such men may prove stimulating to creatively-minded Australian music-lovers.

2. preserving the MSS of Australian composers—such as the 'L'Allegro' of Alexander Burnard.[1] All first editions of my own music and practically all my musical MSS are, or will be, deposited in this museum.

3. showing the great part played by Great Britain in the development of what we call 'classical music'. From about 1200 to about 1680 Britain continually led musical Europe not only in the beauty of its music but also in the originality and daring of its musical innovations. 'Worcester Mediaeval Harmony', the Reading Rota, John Dunstable, William Byrd, William Lawes and Henry Purcell are examples. From about 1680 to about 1890 British compositional life suffered an eclipse, to re-arise into its former radiance around the turn of the last century. Continental Europe today has few composers that can be compared with such British geniuses as Elgar, Delius, Scott, Vaughan William[s], Roger Quilter, Arnold Bax, Holst, Balfour Gardiner and many others. I happened to be the close associate of these men just at the time when English music was resuming its old supremacy and I have preserved their letters, MSS, programs, relics, etc. since 1899 because I thought that they might one day be of special interest to Australia.

4. creating a centre for the preservation and study of the early music of Europe and of the 20th century music. (At present the only music well known to the musical world is that written between 1700 and 1900).

5. creating a centre for the preservation and study of folksong, by means of gramophone records of the singing of genuine folk-singers. I have about 500 records of English Folksinging, about 200 of *Danish*.

[1] (b. 1900), senior lecturer from 1935 at the Conservatorium in Sydney; he gained a doctorate in music from The University of Adelaide in 1932. Grainger had been impressed by his compositions, writing in this year: 'He is, beyond all doubt, Australia's greatest composer, combining in his compositions a beautiful balance between the best bequeathments of the past and modern experimentalism.'

6. creating a centre for the preservation and study of native music in, or adjacent to, Australia, such as aboriginal Australian music, the art-musics of Java, Siam, Bali and the Hybrid music of the South Sea. In the opinion of some students the music of Java is the world's most beautiful music. To my own ears the hybrid music of Polynesia (Samoa, Tahiti, Rarotonga, etc) surpasses in subtle complexity all other music known to me. The very least that can be said is that Australian-Pacific portion of the globe is richer in many-fold types of lovely music than is Europe today. It would seem to me a proud Australian task to adequately study these exquisite native musics adjacent to Australia and present them to the world. I have already a considerable body of gramophone records of Maori music I took in 1909. By exchange of copies of these with museums such as the Bishop Museum in Honolulu it would be possible to acquire copies of gramophone records of representative Polynesian and other Island musics.

7. facilitating a study of the nature (personality, racial characteristics, working habits, etc.) of composers and of the family traits and environmental influences that appear to make for greatness in composers; to examine the indebtedness of composers to early influences coming from music-loving parents, guardians, teachers, friends; to examine the indebtedness of composers one to the other and the extent to which composers give practical help to one another—how Schumann helped Brahms; how Brahms helped Dvorak; how Liszt helped Grieg; how Grieg helped Delius; how Delius helped me. I feel that a great deal of nonsense has been talked and written about the composers of the past, and I would be glad if the lives of English-speaking composers could be examined in a more exact and scientific way. To collect evidence bearing upon the question: are composers specialists or 'all-round-men'?—the museum to display examples of paintings, drawings, literature by composers and accounts of their extra-artistic enterprizes. Do composers marry fellow artists, or do they cho[o]se non-artistic wives?—The museum will house many examples of books, pictures, drawings, and other artistic work by the wives of the following composers: Grieg, Delius, Cyril Scott, Herman Sandby, John Alden Carpenter, Hans Pfitzner, Grainger, etc.

8. to cor[r]elate, in the museum exhibits, many different aspects of composers and their works. Suppose that a composer has asked permission to use the theme of a fellow composer: I would like to

display the letter asking permission, the reply granting (or refusing) permission, the two musical MSS involved, first edition of the published versions of the two compositions, wax figures of the two composers as they appeared at the time of the correspondence clad in the clothes they wore at the time. In other words, to supply facts to questions too often answered by fiction.

9. showing the connection between the various branches of Nordic music—Scandinavian, British, Irish, American, Australian. Here Grieg's influence, as encouraging musical expression in English-speaking lands, is of paramount importance. The influence of Australian music on other Nordic music, and vice versa, will be shown.

The above intentions may be grouped under present and future plans, as follows:

Present Plans

During the next three months to prepare as many as I can of the following exhibits:

a. Grieg's watch and chain, his letters to me, one of his musical manuscripts, some signed photos and other relics.

b. Many manuscripts by leading British composers of our era.

c. Letters, signed music and other relics of Frederick Delius, and paintings by his wife, Jelka Delius.

d. The complete volumes of the English Folksong Society.

e. Gramophone records of the singing of Joseph Taylor,[1] genuine English folksinger.

f. The complete works of Evald Tang Kristensen, Denmark's greatest folksong and folklore collector, and photos and relics of him.

g. Complete programs of the 'Balfour Gardiner Concerts', where 20th century British music got its start with the public; also several MSS and the complete published compositions of this inspired composer.

h. Old English viol (the forerunner of the violin), gift of Arnold Dolmetsch, one of the greatest students of ancient music; MSS and portraits of Arnold Dolmetsch and his programs of the last 30 years.

---

[1] (1833–1910), bailiff in Saxby-all-Saints in Lincolnshire, who had in 1905–6 sung to Grainger a number of the folksongs he later set. In 1939 Grainger wrote of him: 'He was a past master of graceful, birdlike ornament and relied more on purely vocal effects than any folksinger known to me. His versions of tunes were generally distinguished by the beauty of their melodic curves and the symmetry of their construction.'

i. Many relics of my own musical life and work, including the piano I practised on from my 6th to my 12th year, first editions of all my published compositions, many MSS, portraits of me by John Singer Sargent and Rupert Bunny,[1] exhibits showing my mother's taste in music and other arts and her devotion to great music and to gifted composers. (My contacts with great composers in many lands were the direct result of my mother's life-long passion for musical greatness—as distinct from mere technical skill or professional success or popularity,—and I hope to show in the museum how her unswerving worship of deeply emotional musical expression led me to seek creatively great musicians and to keep records of their work and life as they came under my hand.)

Future Plans

j. To collect further MSS, letters and relics of great composers and to procure wax figures and other representations of their personalities and characteristics.

k. To procure rare gramophone records of primitive music, folkmusic, oriental music, early European music and 20th century music.

l. To co[r]relate the various exhibits in the Grainger Museum so that a musically-untrained layman, passing through the museum, may feel the natural connection between life and music in our era, may realise the true importance of English-speaking music, past and present, and sense the vast vistas of music in the Australian-Pacific area.

m. As soon as I can afford it, to increase the Grainger Museum Fund so it will be able to provide a composing stipendium (say £300 to £500 yearly) to an Australian-born composer of genius—the post of curator of the Music Museum and Grainger Museum to be filled by this composer without further remuneration than this yearly stipendium. Such a post might be a godsend to a gifted Australian composer like Dr Alexander Burnard, enabling him to devote almost his whole time to composing—instead of wasting it (compositionally speaking) teaching harmony as he does at present. Such a stipendium would be comparable to the composing stipendiums paid by the governments of the Scandinavian countries and Finland to such composers as Grieg, Herman Sandby and Sibelius, and might tend to make music-loving Australians more composition-minded.

[1] (1864–1947), mainly French-resident Australian artist; he had known Grainger in London just after the turn of the cent.

n. The giving of 'Grainger Concerts' (chamber, choral, orchestral) in the programs of which will be reflected the universalist taste (interest in the music of all times and places) of the composers of our era—these concerts to be financed out of the Grainger Museum Fund at the discretion of the University. I have made irrevocable life-time settlements on composers, other artist and my dependents to the extent of about £10000. (English), which capital will revert to me or my heirs on the death of the beneficiaries. My present will provides that the bulk of this capital (after my wife's and my deaths) be paid into a Grainger Museum Fund in America, partly for the giving of Grainger Concerts on the above-mentioned lines. When the Grainger Museum is firmly established in the University of Melbourne I propose to make a new will directing that the bulk of these moneys, and also income arising out of my composition royalties and performing rights (which at present amounts to about £2500. English, yearly), be paid into the Grainger Museum Fund in the University of Melbourne, partly for the purpose of giving the above-mentioned Grainger Concerts.

Thanking you most heartily for your most kind and greatly appreciated interest in my plans and proposals.

> I remain,
> Yours sincerely

36   *To Henry Cowell*

Melbourne, Oct 6, 1938

Dear Henry,

Your splendid letter of Sept 7, about Samoa, etc, just arrived and has delighted both Ella & me very much indeed. I am terribly glad you feel the vitality of the South Sea music & also the human charm of their joyeous, cooperative, friendly lives. Another friend, to whom I wrote at the same time as to you, about South Sea music & the exquisite normality of life in Samoa, etc, accused me of being an 'escapist' because of my interest in such things & places. But I do not think he is quite right. The Samoans have to face the problem of economic life, as it is TODAY, just like Germans or Americans & all the rest of us do; and if they make a happy & successful job of it they are worth studying, I contend. As for their music: They are not content just to wallow in their past—to cling on to their old traditions, regardless—but they accept our (European) gift of harmony & manyvoicedness & THEY GO BEYOND US in the freedom & resourcefulness of their use of it. There is surely nothing back-water-ish about that, I should think. From your wonderful knowledge of primitive music, as revealed in yr glorious lectures, & from your unique assortment of records of that type (that you let me hear 4 or 5 years ago)[1] I hoped that you would have a warm spot for the Polynesian music. I am delighted to have this hope confirmed.

I agree with you that it would be an ideal goal to aim at—to live in Samoa (Tutuila is American Samoa—that was the sweet island we saw. Upolu—where R.L. Stevenson lived & wrote his 'A Footnote to History', to my mind the finest of all accounts of the Polynesian life— is British Samoa) cheaply, simply & wholesomely (as one can there) & collect its glorious music. It might be possible to get the Guggenheimer [sic] Foundation[2] to give you a fellowship for such a purpose. I know nothing of how the Guggenheimer works, except that it seems to have a Norwegian secretary, & Norwegians are usually liberal-minded & clear-thinking. It would be certainly the GREATEST POSSIBLE BOON TO MUSIC if you could be induced to enter the field of research of Polynesian music. When I get back to America I will be glad to try & have an interview with the Guggenheimers, if you like—after seeing you first (when I am in San Francisco), of course. But in my opinion you would waste some time if you went to Samoa without some working knowledge of Samoan speech, & a birdseye view of the other Polynesian languages—the texts being so kindred in the various South Sea song-poetry & one being so helpful to the other. I would suggest that, if you could get parole,[3] that you come first to us at White Plains (where I have plenty of Samoan bibles & other Polynesian bibles, dictionaries, collections of South Sea folklore) where you & I can study Polynesian together (I made a beginning on the Maori, etc, languages in 1910) & where you could note down for me my Rarotongan &

---

[1] In 1931–2 Cowell had studied ethnomusicology in Berlin with Erich von Hornbostel and teachers from India and Java. He had communicated many of his new experiences to Grainger in 1932–3, while Grainger was teaching at New York University.

[2] Cowell had already been supported by the John Simon Guggenheim Memorial Foundation for his studies in Berlin.

[3] Cowell had been arrested in May 1936 and charged with a sexual offence involving a 17-year-old male. He had been convicted and sentenced to imprisonment of up to fifteen years. For details of Grainger's support for Cowell at this time, see Michael Hicks, 'The Imprisonment of Henry Cowell', *Journal of the American Musicological Society*, 44 (1991), 92–119.

Maori gramophone records, thus preparing yourself for the Samoan enterprize? Then, when you feel you are quite ready, we could apply for a fellowship for you to study folkmusic in Samoa, etc. In the mean time, you could live rent free with us at our White Plains house, & I could give you a small salary (if agreeable to you) for you to act as my musical secretary, the duties of which could be as elastic as you like[1]— ranging from the noting down of Polynesian & other folkmusic or primitive music to the organisation of my music library (now very dis- ordered) which you & I could undertake together. I have lots of real jobs to give you, if you would care to become my musical secretary— jobs that would be REALLY HELPFUL TO ME, if you did them. But I would only offer you the job if it was strictly understood & agreed upon between us that you never take on any job (even if I suggest it) unless it APPEALS to you personally, from YOUR OWN esthetic angle. But I have heaps of jobs to offer, & you could take your choice. I believe in the communal life. I believe in composers living together, working together in music, criticising each other, influencing each other, yet each KEEPING HIS OWN ARTISTIC INTEGRITY. I will not say that our White Plains house is very delightful—it isnt. But you would be VERY VERY WELCOME there, to both Ella & me, & I believe you could make a good start there, after the San Quentin life. Our life at W.P. is a rather dull one, from a 'social' view point. We see few people, we are not effected by public opinion, & we work con- stantly at our arts (Ella at drawing, painting, poetry). You could do your American music propaganda from White Plains, if you chose, or you could throw all your weight into preparations for the South Sea study. Perhaps you & I could collect together in the South Seas—you more steadily, I more intermittently. This is all in the air. The one thing that is certain is that I want to discuss the possibility of a Guggenheimer or other fellowship for you when we next meet, & that I want to offer you the job of musical secretary to me in White Plains, if you can be paroled. HOW GLORIOUS IT WOULD BE, IF THERE IS SUCH A POSSIBILITY. Would it be a good thing if I wrote to Mr Daniel F. Bush, stating how much I would like to have you as my musical secretary at our White Plains home, with a view to our mutual preparation for South Sea music collecting, if there were a possibility of a parole for you. I would LOVE to do this, but only if you think it wise. I would not want to seem unduly interfering to Mr Bush. But the

[1] Cowell was paroled in 1940, with Grainger as guarantor of his good conduct, and did work as his 'musical secretary' into 1941. His unconditional pardon followed in 1942.

fact is that both Ella & I would be so overjoyed if you could come to us at White Plains. I know nothing of your life-plans, should you be paroled. But should you wish to marry, at any time, that would not upset the White Plains suggestion.[1] There is room in our funny old White Plains house for several couples.

The enclosed letter to the Chancellor of the Melbourne University[2] sets forth my museum aims, which you so kindly asked about. The wish to create a home for records of my mother's personality, art-love & life-struggles is stronger in my mind than it appears in the enclosed letter. The museum is something I want done, something about which my personal & artistic conscience feels most strongly. Yet it is an awful strain & grind (financially & in work) to have to do it at present. I would so much rather devote myself to composing & folkmusic study. But I felt I HAD to get my museum exhibits out to Melbourne before there is a long & upsetting war (somewhat unlikely, I am glad to say I think) in the Pacific.

We shall be here till mid-Dec. So please reply to me here.

All best thoughts, wishes & greetings from us both,

Yours ever

37   *To Roger Quilter*

In the train, Feb. 25, 1939

Darling Roger,

It was very nice of you to write me so fully yr resentment at my letter to you about helping Jews,[3] & I am very thankful to have it—and also very sorry to have annoyed you with my views. It stands to reason that such a very loving, tender & warm nature as yrs (so fully forth-shown in yr music as to leave no doubt of it in any music lover) would answer as you do to Jewish suffering & act as you do. And of course that kindliness & helpfulness is not hard for me to understand, as I

---

[1] Cowell did marry the ethnomusicologist Sidney Robertson in Sept. 1941.

[2] See letter **35**.

[3] Quilter's letter of 14 Jan. 1939 stated, in part: 'when I see a fly caught in a spider's web, struggling in despair to get free, & knowing that the spider is coming to eat him alive my heart is wrung with pity & horror—and I feel terribly for the fly & rescue him if I can—but I am not interested in flies! . . . The Jew is a perfect scapegoat—the world *must* approve of this splendidly-organised marvellously carried-out persecution. Every great nation has to have its great purges! . . . You see I am pretty sore! But I wont inflict any more on you—what's the good, anyhow?'

have a good deal of something not unlike it in my own make-up. Thus I am this season playing 2 pieces by a young, rather unlucky, Jewish composer.[1] I have, in the past, rather avoided Jewish composers, because I have disliked the lack of inner liveliness in most of their music (but not in all Jewish music, by any means); but this year I felt it almost a duty to play something Jewish, in view of the bad treatment they are getting in the world at present—& not only from Nazis. (I can see that an awful day of reckoning is piling up against the Jews in America). My own secretary is a Siberian Jew & I have been as kind to him as he has been to me, which is saying a great deal. After my mother's death, when I was continually threatened with hiccupping (which however I staved off with long hard walks) & when my sleeping wasnt so good, Mr Morse gave up all other business & devoted himself to me, walking with me nearly all day long, & being very fatherly & kindly in every way. And he has been kind ever since: when I quickly need photographic work done for the museum, or for my musical needs, he will always do it for me, however tired he is & however much work of his own he has. And I, too, have been kind to him: in 1923, when I thought a photographic partnership he had in Brooklyn was no good, I bought him out of the partnership & set him up in White Plains, where he has done so well. I have joined him in sending money to his unlucky kin in Manchukuo,[2] Palestine, etc. Ella & I advanced money to help him build his house (next door to ours) & then wiped out the debt, when times were bad. I mention this as typi-cal of my gettings-on with many Jews. Like Italians, & many other darker races, I find them much more honest, more truthful, more *remembering* & therefore more just & grateful than our fair folk. And often when I am in a roomful of 'Christians' (it is no laugh!) & a Jew enters, I find him the only man in the room with whom I can talk *freely* & agree. But that is generally because he has some sort of ger-manized background, as I have.

Nor have I any wish to pass any of the fault findings I may have against them. Their bad points do not seem to me worse than those of other groups & races. In fact, I cannot for the life of me see what the world has against the Jews! The Germans, of all folk, should not dislike them, for *no race* in America (certainly not the German-Americans) was

---

[1] Lewis Slavit (b. 1913), who was at this time psychologically dependent on Grainger, writing some 400 letters to him during 1938–41. The two pieces were *Spirit of 1939* (an American national dance) and *Mississippi Flood-tide* (an American nocturne), both published by G. Schirmer in 1939.

[2] The Japanese puppet state set up in Manchuria in 1932.

so pro-German as the Jews, during the last war. Whether they were 'English' like Harold Bauer,[1] Russian like Gabrilovich,[2] French like ***[3]—all seemed rabidly pro-German. And for a very simple reason: Yiddish is, after all, only a dialect of German & German culture has always been the ideal goal of Jews *everywhere*. Under me at New York University was a German American Jew (Martin Bernstein, the secretary of our music department)[4] who was so pro-German (still is, I guess) that not even the Nazis could alter it. He would ask me for music to play on the string orchestra he conducted. I would name British, French, Italian, Spanish, German, Jewish etc work, & he would play only the German. He has, in an exaggerated form, that *conservative* belief in the infallibility of German aims & methods that seems present in all Jews I know.

No, my horror at the helping hand held out to the Jews has nothing to do with *dislike* of Jews or due to any feeling on my part that Jews behave badly. My horror arises out of a wish to see nature realise her dreams—horror at needless destruction of nature's dreams. I do not pretend to understand nature, or even to sympathize with her aims. I do not know why nature should give birth to dreams like *peace, kindliness, impersonality*. I will not say that I am sure I really share these dreams myself. I think I would always prefer to see some cruelty practised (provided it had a sexual color: for instance to see a child or a woman whipped or otherwise ill treated) than any kindness I can imagine. But I am passive in the hands of nature. I bow to her aims & dreams, as far as I understand them. And I can see that nature has given birth to peace, kindliness, impersonality, tenderness, wistfulness, etc, *in one race*: the Nordic. I see this scheme of nature's at work, equally, in Britain, Holland, America, Scandinavia & the colonies peopled by these countries. I see faint traces of this same *impersonality* (or rather more-than-personality) showing in countries where there is some Nordic strain—in France, Germany, Italy, Russia, Poland, etc—tho not strongly. In other lands (free of Nordic strains) no sign of it at all—I mean China, Japan, Polynesia, Negroes, etc, etc.

I will not say that I consider our Nordic impersonality very important—it is so unimportant that most people cannot see it at all. I am

[1] (1873–1951), Anglo-American pianist.

[2] Ossip Gabrilovich (1878–1936), Russian-born pianist and conductor, who settled in the United States in 1918.

[3] The space was left vacant.

[4] (b. 1904), teacher at New York University between 1926 and 1972, being head of its music department in 1955–72.

sure the Germans, the Japanese, etc, are not aware of any impersonal, pity-rich, wistful qualities in the English, for instance. But since nature has started this experiment (Nordic impersonality) I think we shld give it a chance. The problem is that the Nordic impersonality makes us un-eager to breed, to work & to get on with each other.

The selffondness of all the other races makes them eager to breed, work & get on with each other *& WITH US*, which is the worst of it! For they are deadly to us, while we are not deadly to them.

If my Siberian Jew tells me the troubles of his family he not only gets my help, but he upsets my (too easily kindled) Nordic mind. But if I tell him my troubles he (while helping me, in some cases) is not upset by my troubles, as his duller mind cannot see them. He always explains to me that I have no troubles at all. I really *worry* about Hitler,[1] about Japan overriding China, etc. He only enjoys it. He tells me that China is making a very good stand against Japan, & that the Nazis *will be punished* for their bad behaviour to the Jews! Yes, *WE* will punish them as usual, & in the end there will be more of our lovely angel-boys (no longer stirred by the *will to fight*) killed & more Nibelungs overliving us.

After all: why do the Jews, the Germans, the Italians, the Japanese seek our lands? Because they like *the fruits* (prosperity) of our Nordic impersonality (peacableness, wistfulness, dreaminess), altho they do not understand *its roots*. Of course the Jews will get nothing out of Palestine; because they will waste their strength in quarrelling. In America, Germany, Australia, etc, the Jews (& also the Germans, the Japanese, the Italians, etc) also quarrel (as usual), but the large mass of Nordic folk keep things impersonal (peaceable) & therefore prosperity arises & our lands are sought by the quarrelsome races (Jews, Germans, etc) whose quarrelsomeness has ruined their chances at home. In 1923 I came back to America & told Fred Morse 'the Jews are going to have a terrible time in Germany very soon, & elsewhere too.' He only laughed, replying 'No country can do without its Jews'. He is still wondering how I foresaw the present situation *in 1923*! And when I now tell him: 'In a few years all Jews & Italians will be deported from America, & a dark man like my father will be hindered by law from mating with a fair woman like my mother,' he still laughs.

---

[1] Grainger's views about Hitler appear to have soured since 4 Sept. 1938, when he wrote to Lewis Slavit, 'The thing that all the gifted men of our age (you, I, Roosevelt, the Soviet, Cyril Scott, Hitler) have in common is PURE GOODNESS. The catch-as-catch-can opportunism of the 19th cent. is over.'

Is it any use having the sane & the insane mix freely together, pretending that both are equally sane? From a Nordic standpoint we Nordics are sane & all the rest (in that they are greedy & fightfinded) are insane. And all the rest (of the insane breeds) agree with us *up to the point* that they want to inhabit our countries & want to hold the jobs created by our sanity. I hold no brief for the Nazi purge—neither for its aims (for I consider mere Arianism, without Nordicness, no aim at all) nor its methods (the brutality of which partly shows their utter un-Nordicness). In fact, my own strong wish is to see the Nordic world (Britain, USA, Holland, Scandinavia) at war with Germany as soon as possible.

In the meantime, I view all planting of Jews (whether as individuals or as groups) in our midst as just one more of the countless & endless set-backs nature sets in trying to launch Nordic impersonalness (tenderness, peacableness, etc). In the end they (the poor Jews) will hate their life with us as much as we will hate having them amongst us.

My mother had all-Jew as well as all-Christian & all-mixed classes (learning English) in F'furt & she sometimes said to her Jewish classes: 'Why is it that you Jews hate us English so much? My German classes don't hate the English in the same way. Have not we English behaved better to the Jews than other Europeans have?' And they would say: 'Yes, you have. But it is true, we *do* hate the English more than all other races.'[1] Mother found that the Jewish classes liked to read of only 2 personalities. Napoleon & Nero. Of course, the Jews are always individualistic in a sense. I mean, they understand the individual (like N. & N.) who is not *at one* with his mob.

But all that is nothing, as between you & me.

What about this? Peace is the outward form of the Nordic deed-world. Beauty (beauty of face, of body, of melody, of voice-sound, of the laying on of paint as in Turner) is the outward form of the Nordic eye & ear world.

Do these things mean nothing? When a Jew paints, he paints as if with bird-shit. They have so little singing voice that even their love of ease & wellbeing cannot turn them into successful opera & concert singers, despite the easy earnings of a singer. They are so short-winded in their spirits of progress that even their best men (whom I worship,

---

[1] At the time of Grainger's writing, too, tensions between the British and Jews were high because of Jewish resistance to the British plans to partition Palestine.

up to a point), often being progressives, have to backslide into neoclas-sicism.[1] What a badly equipped race! How pity-deserving! How really poor & unlucky. All of which (you say) is why we shld help them. I say No, we are still worse off, because the world treats us Nordics a thou-sand times worse than it treats the Jews. The Jews are allowed to marry early. You & I were not allowed to marry early—yet marriage is the only fun in life. The Jews are allowed to hear their (mainly ugly) music. You and I are never allowed to hear our music. You hear yr opera under conditions too hard to be called passively hearing it.[2] I have never heard my Hillsong I at all.[3] The Jews have to earn for their families, but *we* have to save for the families of our foes! We have to give up sex (life's only joy) for ideas & thots & feelings, only (in the end) to find that no one (if they can help it) will let us voice our feel-ings—in any case will not listen to our feelings.

You & I are so popular (so attractive, so young-in-old-age, so melody-birthing, so loving, so kindly, so helpful—so *angelic*) that no one will do our music unless we pay for it. So every penny given by you (or by me) is money taken away from our music—from our beauty world. You must forgive me if I prefer yr music to that of most Jews. You must forgive me if I prefer the lovely children you will never father to the ugly brats the Jews father. And in particular you must forgive if I resent the fact that some of your (& my) precious Jews (or Germans, or Russians, or Italians, or Greeks, or other riffraff) will marry into the melodious broods you & I could (but never will) breed & bemuddy the clear Nordic stream. Do not think, darling Roger, that I misunderstand the nature of yr Jew-help, or that I fail to see its lov-ingness, Christianness, Nordicness on yr part. It is only the *degree* of the thing I resent. The *degree* to which we are bothered, the degree to which we are barren, the degree to which we are tortured all thru life, the degree to which we are slighted & shamed. Because I am a Nordic, I dislike feeling overheated & like washable clean clothes (therefore wear cotton trousers I can wash myself every few days) I am taken to the police station. (See enclosed.[4] On same page as America's Nazi-mildness!)

[1] Grainger is undoubtedly thinking of the Russian Igor Stravinsky (1882–1971), whom he con-sidered Jewish (perhaps because of Polish ancestry on his father's side).
[2] Quilter's *Julia* had been produced at Covent Garden in London in Dec. 1936, and was well received.
[3] See letter **52** for an expression of Grainger's joy at finally hearing this work in 1947.
[4] The enclosure is lost. When arriving for a concert in Wausau, Wisconsin, on 21 Feb. 1939 Grainger had been held by the police as a vagrant, partly because of his 'inappropriate' clothing.

I love yr music. I love yr sweet nature & fatherly heart. But best of all I love yr bodily beauty—your vision of pure Englishness (*East-Englishness* on both sides? Or not?) You look like the Anglosaxons who *did not* mix with their British (non-Saxon) slaves, enemies! And I have to imagine you welcoming ugly, fat, self-indulgent, family-loving, art-loving, *food*-loving, reasonable, cultured, *normal* Jews to the shores of Britain. Or welcoming equally normal, family-loving, *natural*, civilised, *plausible* Germans or Greeks. You, who have no civilisation in you, but only the call-of-the-wild & bodily beauty like that of the sunrise, a taste like gooseberries or raspberries! It is hard when the princes of the world are set to street clean the muck of slaves. But our realm is falling to pieces (or already fallen) & it is only natural things are upside down. Or our realm *has not come yet*, & I am pregnant of hopes to come? I want to see our princes (you, etc) on thrones not yet built.

All my life I have lived only for patriotism—patriotism for the Anglosaxon & Norse races, patriotism for the nowtime Nordic world of Britain, USA, Scandinavia, etc. 'Individuals' (love of individuals) never existed for me, because I lived only for patriotism (of my own, futurebent, kind). Even my mother I did not quite appraise as an individual, being so soaked in patriotism. And when the war came, I had to act (out of patriotism) as a turncoat. A nasty knapsack for a patriot to shoulder! But what could I do? Every Jew has Jewish doctors who keep him out of the army, or out of its worst phases (so they say. I hardly believe it.)

Most Englishmen have family connections or class privileges that somewhat temper the wind to them. When Balfour Gardiner was a private it was not his genius (or his fatherliness to British culture) that saved his life, but the fact that the colonel *knew his father!* Who would have bothered about me? My longing for Australian selfhood, & Nordic selfawareness meant nothing to nobody. There was not even a regiment, a band, a niche in which I could have found friends or kept friends—for all were alien to my patriotism. So I had to *love myself* very much & be my own Jewish doctor, my own class privilege, my own colonel-friend-of-my-father's. Well, I survived—with loss of honor & security, of course. But it was worth it—worth it to me & to Australia, as I see it. *But all this has made me a bit mean about how I waste my time, my life, my money on my enemies.* The time I waste on Jews is the life I stole, as a turncoat, from other Nordic lives. Other Nordics died, in order that I lived—in order that the Germans did not have the fun of killing an Australian composer (me) before his time! We are all somewhat in the same boat. And now what is left of our wasted, dishonoured, bachelor lives is (partly) to be squandered on Jews—or if not on Jews on Greeks, Germans, or other riffraff *WHO LOVE THEMSELVES!!*

Love from *Percy*.

1940–1949
'The All-Round Man'

38   *To Agnes, Eyvind, and Storm Bull*

[The Graingers visited England and Scandinavia during the summer of 1939, returning home in August, just before war broke out in Europe. Although the United States had not yet entered the war Grainger feared invasion. He hurriedly set about copying and dispatching to several different locations the more important musical and personal items in his possession at White Plains.]

Auditorium Hotel | Michigan Boulevard and Congress Street
Chicago | Saturday, Oct 26, 1940

Dear Agnes, Eyvind, Storm,

When my mother arrived in Germany, the first time, in 1895, she said to me: 'I feel so happy here. I am so glad to be away from all the chaffing (ragging?) that goes on in Australia'. I did not agree with her then, but I do now. What is this wonderful humor that you 3 see in everything? (How dare any Norwegian—after the exhibition of cowardice, or silliness, or treachery, or perhaps just sissifiedness that Norway has shown to the world[1]—make fun at all? I, for my part, feel thoroly ashamed, as an Anglosaxon, for the silliness & childishness of my own group. The last thing I want to do is to make fun, or see others make fun. Is one not capable of realising when there is a time, or not a time, for this display of middleclass good humor?) You make fun of my Wausau misfortune,[2] without waiting to ask whether *I* think it funny or not (what rotten manners! Do you think Storm, or anyone else, will get far in the musical life without good manners?) You seem to think it so funny (queer, original) that I wear white pants. I will tell you why. I have suffered from vericosale[3] all my life & doctors have told me to wear cool trousers. I wear my white pants as a cripple carries crutches—because they are helpful, not in order to be funny. (In a

---

[1] Norway had expected to remain neutral in the war; Germany had, however, attacked Norway on 9 Apr. 1940, completing its occupation by June. A government under the Nazi collaborator Vidkum Quisling was then established.

[2] See letter **37**.   [3] = varicocele (dilatation of the spermatic veins).

few years time I shall hope to be able to show you the *sequel* to the Wausau episode—not in the least funny.)

You, Agnes, are very glib in remembering (all wrong) the circumstances leading up to my diphtheria attack.[1] I think it very mistaken to talk as if I were careless of my health & did cranky, crack-brain things that impair my health. The facts are that I was somewhat delicate as a young man & have gradually strengthened myself by reading 'cranky' books about diet, & the like, & following what I read. In the last 48 years I have played about 70-100 concerts yearly (on an average), & have only missed 2 concerts thru being ill. You Agnes, criticise me for carrying baggage too much. But I think carrying baggage, & getting hot, is good for the hair. (I do not share this middleclass notion that one must never *carry* anything!)

Ever since we first met you (Eyvind & Agnes) have been on to me to 'do things' for Storm (if you come to a concert where I am playing you ask me to 'do something' for Storm before you mention my composition or my playing). Why not? You know that I have always sincerely admired Storm's gifts. But you also know that I am a fanatic (for the Nordic race & its art. I do not ask special favors for my race & its art. I only ask that music be universal & that Nordic art be given its just place in that universality). Yet you (all 3 of you) steadily ignore my fanaticism. How can one be so stony-hearted? (The old aristocratic code enabled its followers to win success, for it was a Christian & Knightly code that was *aware of many claims*. Your middleclass code, with its emphasis on *self assertion at all costs* & *greed* makes failures of quite gifted middleclass folk—for the world does not respond to bad manners. The Jews get on, for they have good manners—*of their own kind*. But you middleclass folk have plunged the world into out-of-workness & slump.) You pretend to be my friend, which means that you pretend to be able to look into my heart. If you are able to look into my heart you must know that I am a fanatic—a fanatic working (if I can) for the recognition of my (our) race. Yet you boldly ignore my wishes on all points. You ask me to do for you the things you want done, but you *never* try to do for me any of the things you must *know* (if you are my friend) I want done. What use is it (from *my* standpoint) to recommend Storm to an orchestra? He only goes & plays enemy music—the music of countries that were against us in the last war or in this war. What gain is it (to my cause) that Storm is engaged rather

---

[1] Suffered while in Chicago in late Feb. 1930.

than a Jew-pianist, if Storm goes & plays just the same old muck that a Jew plays. In fact, it is worse. It seems natural that a Jew should play round-sculled music. But that a Norwegian-American should play round-sculled music & ignore Nordic music seems to me a gr[i]evous setback for the Nordic cause. Storm could play the Gershwin F major Concerto,[1] or Stanford's 'Down among the Dead Men' variations,[2] or Sparre Olsen's Theme & Variations.[3] But no. As far as I know he confines himself to enemy music. Storm could play Fauré's exquisite 'Ballade' for piano & orchestra,[4] or Ravel's sparkling piano concerto.[5] Instead he plays that ½-Jewish Rachm[an]inoff[6] (not that I am against Rachmaninoff; I worship his genius. Not that I am against Jews. But I believe in keeping a fair balance between Nordic & round-sculls) & that tune-less Bartok. How can you (Storm) be so heartless? You have sat in my classes & heard me inveigh against rhythm. Yet you (or yr father) urges me to bring you to Stock's[7] notice *in order that you may play the most rhythmic possible piece*[8]—the kind of thing you know (from my classes) I hate. This is (may be) Norwegian independence? Where has Norwegian independence (I ask you) brought Norway today? A few months before the outbreak of the present war, in a meeting of the combined representatives of Scandinavian university students, the Norwegian & Swedish representatives told the Danish ones 'at vi ikke længere betrakte Dein som Nordboer'[9] (because of the Danish Ikke-Angrabs-Pakt with her neighbor.)[10] I have always hated every form of independance. In friendship & in love, I believe in utter slavishness. Last year (altho I had little time to learn it) I put Fauré's 'Ballade' on my orchestral programs, not only because I love & admire it, but chiefly because I remembered Sargent's love for Fauré & I remember Sargent's kindliness & helpfulness to me.[11] I often build my programs more out of deference to the taste of my dead friends & beloved ones

[1] (1925). Grainger's interest in the music of George Gershwin (1898–1937) was at its height in the 1940s. He first performed this concerto in concert in 1944.

[2] = Concert Variations on an English Theme, Op. 71 (1898), for piano and orchestra. In his 'Anecdotes' Grainger described this work as a 'patchwork quilt of good and bad'.

[3] Probably the Variations on a Norwegian Folk Tune, Op. 5 (1932).   [4] Op. 19 (1881).

[5] In G major (1931). Grainger appears not to have publicly performed this work.

[6] The Piano Concerto No. 2, Op. 18.

[7] Frederick (Friedrich) Stock (1872–1942), German-born conductor of the Chicago Symphony Orchestra (1905–42).

[8] Bartók's Piano Concerto No. 2, given its American première, with Stock, in 1939.

[9] = that we no longer regard Nordics (Danish).

[10] During the spring of 1939 Hitler had offered all the Scandinavian countries non-aggression pacts. Denmark was the only one to accept, signing on 31 May 1939.

[11] Grainger had been introduced to the French composer Gabriel Fauré (1845–1924) by their mutual friend John Singer Sargent during Mar. 1908.

than out of consideration for their effect on a living audience. I often put on a piece because I think Grieg, or Rathbone,[1] or Sargent would like it, or because my mother would like it. This year I am beginning my programs with Paradisi's[2] A major Toccata, because I remember my mother playing it. What is the use of pretending to be friends if one doesnt do anything to please one's friends? If you were really friendly to me you would program American, or British or Scandinavian pieces, to please me. Or leave the friendship out. If you had *a good business sense* you would sometimes do things to please me, since you so often want me to do things for you. Then there is a Norwegian comic song called 'Sirre, sirre' (Sei du, sei du), in which the singer says 'And when they drive me to jail I'm riding in my carriage, just like you in yr carriage—saa er jeg lig'saa god som dig, sirre, sirre'. And so on. I had to think of that song, Eyvind, when you told me, the other day, that Storm was about to write orchestral pieces based on folksongs (or a 'synthetic' folksong. A middleclass man does not go *to the folk*. He does everything syntheticly. It saves so much time!) 'just like you' & use them as a popularising factor with orchestras. There is just this difference. By 1897 I was already arranging folksongs in great numbers. And it was not till 1914 that my first orchestral setting of a folksong ('Shepherd's Hey') came before the public. If Storm thinks he will 'popularise' himself with his 1st, or 5th, or 20th, or 30th setting of a folksong, he is probably mistaken. (I hope *not*.) If you want to know how I popularised myself as a young man, I can tell you: by playing *new music* (Poldini,[3] d'Erlanger,[4] new Griegs, the first Debussy & Ravel, Albeniz, Röntgen, Cyril Scott, Balfour Gardiner, etc.) &, of course, by cultivating good manners.

When you (Storm), were going to Europe I begged you (first) not to go & 2ndly not to study with a Jew. It was obvious you would not please me by studying with a Hungarian (an *enemy*!). I would (of course) have liked to see you study with a Britisher, or Frenchman (not a Hungarian Jew living in France)[5] or Scandinavian. But, of course,

---

[1] William Rathbone (1849–1919), English businessman and enthusiastic patron of Grainger during his London years.

[2] Domenico Paradisi (Paradies) (1707–91), Italian composer.

[3] Ede Poldini (1869–1957), Hungarian-born composer.

[4] Frédéric d'Erlanger (1868–1943), Paris-born British composer, whose concert studies Grainger had performed at his first major London recital in 1901.

[5] Bull had studied in Paris with the Belgian-born French pianist, Lazare Lévy (1882–1964). In a letter to Grainger of 30 Oct. 1940 he admitted that studying with Lévy had been a mistake, but not studying with Bartók.

you never considered my wishes for a moment (Norwegian independance). When you came back from Europe you (Storm) were eloquent
in pleading Hungary's cause. Did you think I wished to hear that? All
I could think of (or ever will) is that Hungary helped Austria to crush
the Serbs.[1] Thru Hungary, & her gang, my mother's kinsmen (serving
in the Australian forces) might have been killed. Do you think I can
think of anything but that when Hungary is mentioned? (You did not
come back enthusing about France, or England, or even Norway, if I
remember rightly. Only about Hungary!)

And now that Hungary has got her claims recognised,[2] her wrongs
righted (& I dont say they are not good claims. I have no wish to be
unfair), & now that Norway has handed over her airfields for attacks
on England (when I was last in Australia one of the workmen on my
museum said to me 'I believe that old man (Chamberlain) would
rather sell out the British Empire to Germany than have something
good happen to us working men'.[3] Likewise I suspect yr middleclass
Norwegian university folk, yr embedsmænd[4]—Riksmaal folk[5]—of preferring foreigners to Norwegian peasants. One of the objections of the
Riksmaal folk to the Maalmænd[6] was the latter's unpatrioticness. What
price Riksmaal patriotism?) & now that my mother's kinsmen again
stand a good chance to be butchered by Hungary & her allies you
three come & 'chaff' me about my clothes, my weight, my diet, my
Wausau episode, etc. You must think I have a very soft, good
humored nature. Well, I havent. I have no sense of humor & understand no chaffing whatsoever. And I understand no useless friendships.
I am not interested in myself as a person—only as a composer born in
Australia. I am not interested in you (Storm) as a person—only as a
gifted Norwegian-American. But if you do not further the Nordic
cause (to a reasonable extent. I dont expect hyperboles) why should I
be interested? As a gifted Norwegian American playing Rachmaninoff
& Bartok (playing the Grieg Concerto I do not count. It is not a nov-
elty. And not a very good example of Nordic music, it seems to me)
you merely are an enemy of my hopes & intentions.

I do not ask you to share my hopes & intentions. But I do ask you

[1] During the First World War; Serbia lost 23% of its population during that war.

[2] Under the Vienna Awards of 1938–40 Hungary regained some Hungarian ethnic parts of
neighbouring states which it had lost through the Treaty of Trianon in 1920.

[3] Neville Chamberlain (1869–1940), British Prime Minister in 1937–40, who had participated in
the Munich Agreement of Sept. 1938.

[4] = civil servant (Dano-Norwegian).

[5] Speakers of official Dano-Norwegian (Bokmål, earlier known as Riksmål).

[6] Speakers of New Norwegian (Landsmål, now Nynorsk).

not to be so 'independant' as to ignore all my clearly-expressed ideals & still expect me to be interested in yr career. What are these careers for? To show how *abject* we Nordics have to be before every Hungarian & ½-Jew that appears on the horizon?

I dare say my fanaticism seems rather far-fetched to you. But yr 'rut-slavery' (as my friend Robert Atkinson translates 'convention' with Nordic-English) seems equally strange to me. And in any case: is not art the domain of the personal, the unique, the intense—rather than the domain of the general, the common, the slack?

Yours in ever-growing despair at our Nordic urge-to-destroy-ourselves.

Percy

39   *To Cyril Scott*

[Fear of invasion—by the Germans on the East coast and Japanese on the West—drove Grainger to desert White Plains in November 1940 for Springfield, Missouri, in the centre of the continent. Once the United States did enter the war, it proved a most convenient base for his myriad concert activities in aid of the war effort across the central and western states.]

Springfield, Missouri. | June 17, 1941.

Darling Cyril,

Ella has arranged with Scribners to send you Boericke's Pock. Man. of Homop. Materia Medica,[1] but as the air mail sending of it would cost 3 dollars, & as I find that books & music move quickly between here & England by ordinary post, I have taken the liberty of asking Scribners to send it to you by ordinary mail—NOT air mail.

We are so glad to hear of the pending broadcasts of your Trio & 5tet, & wish we could hear them. I am so glad you are having Mirabelle[2] sent to me (that was the one I meant). I shall try to get it done. I am hoping to conduct your Festival Overture at a concert at the University of Kansas, about July 27.

You bucked me up hugely by your letter of May 11, written after hearing my 'Storecloset-Music Delicacies' on the air. I wonder whether it has ever happened to me before that a musician has told me of

[1] *Pocket manual of materia medica, comprising the characteristic guiding symptoms of all remedies* (1901) by William Boericke (1849–1929).
[2] Scott's cantata, for chorus and orchestra, composed about 1903.

hearing anything of mine on the air! Certainly none has gone into any details, such as 'that surprising jump of an octave', 'the cooing accomp. of Died for Love', or the like. (During the 26 years I have lived in USA I cannot recall any of my English composer-friends telling me of having heard either a concert or radio performance of any of my works. It is as if I were never performed.) It cheers me unspeakably that my stuff still is 'alive' to you, & that you still feel my 'genius'.

I am AWFULLY glad you have taken to typewriting, for it is so convenient to me, from a Museum standpoint. WILL YOU DO ME A BIG FAVOR? When you send me typed letters, will you kindly follow the following habits?:

1. Date all letters. (At present you give the day & month, BUT NO YEAR. (It means, I have to add in the year myself.)
2. Make a carbon copy, or copies (it is a good plan to keep at least one carbon copy for yourself. But that is your affair.) Please always send me 2 *copies* (or 3 copies, if you want to be really helpful): one for me & one for the museum. Otherwise I have to go to the bother of having COPIES made—as it is too risky (from a museum standpoint) to have only one copy (in a museum one copy must be available for examination, reference, etc. But a second copy must always be salted away, in reserve, in case the 1st copy gets lost—while being examined, worked over, etc.)

I am enclosing copies of recent letters of mine to Mrs de Glehn[1] & to Balfour, because there are things in them that you might like to read or know, & it will save me writing it again to you. When you have read these letter-copies, please kindly return them to me—always to the White Plains address: 7 Cromwell Place. Separately, I am sending you prints of the 2 little choruses that complete the Kipling 'Jungle Book' cycle.[2] Please keep those.

As I think over the course of the war (over the fact that our side is always TOO SMALL & TOO MEAN WITH EVERYTHING—that there are never ENOUGH troops, ENOUGH equipment, at any point; that, therefore, the initiative always goes to the enemy because he has ENOUGH of everything—having thought BIG) I see clearly the root of my unhappiness & anxiety as a composer, & as a friend of composer-geniuses, all my life. (Incidentally, this drift towards meanness &

[1] Jane de Glehn, wife of the English painter Wilfred de Glehn (1870–1951).
[2] 'The Beaches of Lukannon' and 'Red Dog', both of which where published by Schott (London) in 1958. Grainger later added a further piece, bringing the cycle finally to eleven settings.

smallness is the race-disease of the whole Nordic race. Grieg said to me: 'Always hold to big issues where you can. Do not do as I did: always clinging on to everything that is small—letting the big things escape'.) When you 1st started to publish in England, & I begged & implored you not to publish 'Potboilers' (small piano pieces & songs), I was warning you against THE SMALL. When we were students in Frankfurt you had A NATURAL FLAIR for THE BIG. Your Magnificat was big, & so was your 1st Symphony.[1] And even later on, the 'Symphony' that now survives only in the 3 Symphonic Dances[2] was big in size. But none of these have ever been published—so the music-public has no notion of what you are, & always NATURALLY have been, in the realms of large form. Not that I am hipped on symphonic form. As you know, I have always been against them. Of course, your operas are Large form. But they are not published,[3] & opera is not a living art in English-speaking lands. I have made the same mistake—in not having works of my own that are the size of the Bach MAT[T]HEW PASSION, a Wagner opera, a Brahms symphony. In my case there is this excuse: All my works, prior to my FREE MUSIC, are only orchestration studies for the FREE MUSIC. None of my published works, none of the things of mine you know, are really my mature muse—are only studies. They are to me what your Magnificat, early Symphonies, etc, are to you. But how ill-advised I would have been if I suppressed them on that account! You can feel, yourself, that that would have been wrong. That is how the suppression of your BIG FORM works seems to me. It is not that I exalt your early works above your later. It is merely that I see the value of having available works in really large form, as well as in smaller forms. Not that I undervalue small forms. My love of the older musics of Europe, & the musics of Asia (all small), give the lie to that thought. But I realise that SIZE is part of the fate of European man. The size that we see in Bach, Wagner, Strauss, Sibelius, Delius, Skryabin are part of the European destiny. Why do the gifted English-speaking composers (I am not talking of the dull, less-gifted, Continent-copying ones such as Vaughan Williams & Bax) content & disgrace themselves with the role of being clowns (J.A. CARPENTER, Gershwin, etc), entertainers, crowd-pleasers? That was what I warned you against, when you began your compositional career. The

---

[1] Scott's symphony had been first performed in Darmstadt in 1900. He later withdrew it.

[2] This original Symphony No. 2 dates from 1903.

[3] Scott wrote three operas, *The Alchemist*, *The Saint of the Mountain* and *The Shrine*. Only the first was performed, in Essen, in May 1925.

average American composer, however gifted, always debases himself with writing jigs, dances, capers. He feels he has to be so god-damned FUNNY! Why on earth? This is a big country, a big population. When they build skyscrapers, bridges, they build seriously. And Walt was big, uncompromising, crowd-indifferent, difficult. Why have you all (British, Americans) got to be so filthily EASY, LIKABLE all the time? Why cant YOU BE A NUISANCE, GIVE TROUBLE? Is there nothing in you that demands, occasionally, that you STAND ON YOUR DIGNITY & demand your artistic rights? Dont you like, now & then, to write something before which conductors stand like beaten silly sheep?

You told me, a few years ago, that your biggest & finest compositions were to be written after 60. I yearn for that to be so. I wish you would write something THE SIZE of the Mat[t]hew Passion, the size of The Hero's Life.[1] If so, I WILL SEE THAT IT IS PERFORMED. I am sick to death of unreadiness, smallness, meanness, after-you-Alfonse-ness, selfeffacingness in music & in the war. I want to see our English-speaking people show themselves TO THEIR FULL HEIGHT. They were not always small, in art. The Anglosaxon Chronicle is a mighty book, and so is Beowulf. It is only after the Norman Conquest that smallness, pessimism, South-worship, self-belittlement start to mar English art. Even so the English Gothic cathedrals are big enough, proud enough. (Have you got my 'Lincolnshire Posy' & have you read the foreword?)[2] Only Delius in England, Fickenscher in America have dignity, size, artistic pride. And, alas, it must be owned-up to, that they are both of German blood. Cannot we others, of purely British origins, write music that is big, proud, exacting, crowd-indifferent, uncompromising? Please weigh my words, darling Cyril. Let us try, before we die, to live up to the largest, best, wildest of our youthful plans. Let others defeat us, criticise us, belittle us, if they will. But let us not commit ARTISTIC SUICIDE by being modest, considerate, obliging.

All races, peoples have bad habits. The Germans have their silly beer-gardens, their silly confabulations, their silly jealousies & quarrels, their silly classicism or neo-classicism in music, their silly worship of Italian-derived musical forms, their pedantic respect for fugue, imitation & other out-worn Smart-Alecries. And we Anglosaxons have our own silly habits, such as answering letters (I suspect you of spending a

---

[1] Strauss's tone poem, for large orchestra, of approximately forty-five minutes' duration.
[2] There Grainger had written a charming essay on the folksongs found in the work and their original singers.

certain part of the day, regularly, in answering letters. No doubt your reasons for doing so are excellent ones. But it helps nothing. All habits are art-destroying), being woman-led ('and miles of shopping women served by men'), being fashion-swayed (it was non-artistic respect for artistic fashions that caused you to turn your back on your early works), being afraid of seeming conceited. The only way to live, for an artist, is to es[c]hew all duties, all habits, all loyalties. Just fly from sweetheart to sweetheart, inspiration to inspiration, from arrogance to arrogance. PLEASE, dear Cyril, ARISE in your artistic might, now, in your sixties, and write BIG, BOLD, TROUBLESOME, INCONSIDERATE WORKS. I will perform them.

Love from us both, Percy

40   *To Balfour Gardiner*

Vinita, Oklahoma. | Sept 27, 1941

My dear Balfour,

As I wrote you the other day that I was feeling so feeble & groggy (as an outcome of old age as well as of motoring about in the heat & dust at the height of my hay fever) I now want to tell you that I already feel much brighter & stronger—now that the days are a little cooler & the fall winds have blown the hay-fever-bestowing pollen away a bit.

But that is not the main thing I want to say. We are both growing old & may not have so long a span to say things in. So while I still may, I want to tell you what your friendship & oversoulship ((genius)) have meant to me & also to state the ruths as well as the hopefulfilments I have felt in our friendship.

Your tone-art ((music)) has *always* been hopefulfilling ((satisfying)) to me; but I will go into that later. On the other hand, I have always rued ((regretted)) that you & I have not been closer, as friends. I love a closeknit bond, a close-living wont, between men who are drawn together in the same life's-work & whose outlook upon that life's-work is same-deemy enough to make dove-tailed living fruitful.

I prized most highly those times, in Frankfurt, when you & I walked together in the Taunus. Maybe it was only once we did it, but it was call-to-mind-worthy. We were walking or half-running down the slope of a hill & you said to me 'I find this such a splendid way to run down-hill' & you showed me a way of running, with a hoppity-skip in it.

After mother died, I would have loved to have lived some of my life with you. I do not care much for 'un-sunderable friends', it is not that. But I also do not like the thought that fond & like-minded friends never live together. Sailors at sea, & soldiers in the army, see plenty of each other. The bond is loose, yet they get to know each other in their daily life, doing their daily jobs. And I think that is a fine, rich way to live. As a boy I was much struck by the way King Olaf the Holy & his Marshall (Kolbjörn?) formed a 2-some. They dressed alike, wore the same mantel, & men never knew which was which. In the end—some battle in which Olaf was fight-beaten—both leapt overboard & sank beneath their shields in the sea.[1] Such a trick is at once the 2-folding of a being-type and the de-one-bodying ((depersonalising)) of the lone-hander ((individual)). It puts the job above the man, the type above the one-body ((person)). Not that you & I could have been mistaken for each other, or that the same cloak would have fitted us both. Yet, tone-somely speaking, we stand for the same things: Englishness, sturdiness, manliness, boundingness. We are both more or less English Schumanns. And we are the only two tone-wrights of our age who have nothing 'arty', or womanish, or schoolmasterish, or Chelsea-ish, or stylish, or Smart-Alecky, or vanguard-minded, or ism-y about our tone-art. Yr & my tone-arts, whatever their flaws, are as English as cricket, football, horseracing. Most English (& other) tone-wrights have the bodies, the looks, the bodily wonts of clerks, or of clergymen, or of counter-jumpers, or of loungelizards. But you & I look like yeomen, & the sounds of our tone-arts are bounding, lusty yeoman sounds. Some tonewrights are misguided enough to lean towards 'Bohemianism'— the last thing that mixes well with tone art, seeing that tone art makes for taughtness[2] & drill-dom ((discipline)). Others mix yogi-dom or Jewish she-pianists or the Royal College of Music with their art-life. You & I have never been tempted to be so ill-bred. Nor are you & I unduly churchy, as many British tend to be—forgetting that Englishness is older than Canterbury, Iona or St Augustin[e].

When I hear the Walton Viola Concerto[3] I hear something that

---

[1] Although Grainger mentions Olaf the Holy (i.e. Saint Olaf (c.995–1030), he seems to mean Olaf Tryggvason (c.964–1000), who leapt into the sea following his defeat by the Danes at the Battle of Svolder.

[2] = tautness.   [3] Composed in 1928–9 by William Walton (1902–83).

sounds lik[e]able & is somewhat tinted with Englishness—but (for me) it is not England itself. When I hear Vaughan Williams's 'Job'[1] I see an Englishman setting out 'for foreign parts'. Yr tone art is, like Thomas Hardy, very England—a bit of England. *The Stranger's Song*[2] is a stark snatch of raw, doomfraught, cruel yet soul-ful English life as first-hand, as merciless, as shudderingly racy as a page out of the 'sizes.[3] It is one of the world's few life-changing songs. (One of my jobs, when I am an old man in Australia, must be to find the right voice-types for songs like this. Such a song is misheard if carried by a barking, low-colored voice. There must be something he-high-voice-like ((tenor-like)), aloft-held in the voice to kindle pity-wrenches in the hearer). Your *English Dance*[4] is another world-changing tone-work. You do not rate it flawless. But if one hasn't heard this work there is something (bounding, lilting, highhearted) in life that one has missed; when one has heard it there is something in English life that is one's for keeps. The opening of the *English Dance* is one of the loveliest, smoothest, balmiest stretches in all tone-art. Another life-changer, life-bericher is yr setting of 'The Golden Vanity'.[5] Yr gift is such that it has become THE 'Golden Vanity'. I think the here-quoted phrase one of the most unforgettable I have ever laid my ears on:

'News from Whydah'[6] no less fills its own world—a world it shares with nothing else. Until we have heard N. fr. Wh. we have never stepped into that world. The chords, the tone-lines may have much in common with other Gardiner writings. Some of the phrases (as so often in yr & my works) may even be commonplace. But the tone-art has a magic howth ((quality)). It opens a door that has never been

---

[1] 'Masque for dancing', composed in 1927–30.
[2] Gardiner's song of 1902–3 was to a text by Thomas Hardy (1840–1928).
[3] = assizes.
[4] For orchestra, first performed in 1904, dedicated to Grainger, who arranged it for two pianos in 1925.
[5] Setting of a Hampshire folksong (1907–8), for bass and piano.
[6] Ballad for chorus and orchestra (1911).

opened before, & we pass thru that door, not into the realm of art, but *into part of England's world.* Michaelchurch,[1] Clun,[2] Shenadoah,[3] Mere,[4] Noel,[5] Jesmond[6] & sundry others, all have this witchery—that they usher in *new worlds*—not worlds of tone art, but chunks of real life, real England. I know that the tone-crowd ((public)) thrills to most, or all, of these works when they hear them. But I doubt whether the by-&-largely tone crafter ((musician)) is manly, un-arty, soil-rooted enough to guess the full meaningfulness of these lightning flashes of race-lay-barement. But I know that they bring the tears to my eyes if I only think of them.

You (Hardy-in-tones), I (Kipling-in-tones), you for rural England & I for the yeoman Colonies, we *should* have meant something to our race on the threshold of its doom-fraught trial, in the hour before its threatenedness. No one has hinted that you & I were poor or unseaworthy tone crafters. No one has said that our tone-works are unplayable or unsingable. All they fail to do is to harken to the race-message that is intwined in every bar we write. It is as if one listened to a song but balked at listening to the rime-piece ((poem)), it is spun on. At least your muse has not sung unheard to me, dear Balfour. (I am not hinting that others have deaf-heard it. I am only saying that yr tone works have given me some of the greatest thrills of my life, as man & art-man; & that they will never thrill me less, while I live.)

The very first Con. tone-feast ((concert)) mother & I went to in Frankfurt (1895) she singled you out as the best of all the piano-players. It was a lovely time when you came to the midday meals at the Emerson's Pension.[7] (What a boon it was, seeing you every day! I did not then guess that I would grow to be an old man without ever again seeing you with such daily oftenness!) Mother said, then, that she liked you the best of my tone-wright-friends—dear & noble tho they all were to her. She said you would be the only one she would have cared to have been married to, had she been a young woman of your breed-link ((generation)). The whole Frankfurt timestretch as between you & me, awakes no rue that I can recall. For I was not yet earning my own living & my time was my own—in the main. I had plenty of

---

[1] Composed during 1920–3 for piano, dedicated to Grainger.

[2] For piano, the name of the second of the *Five Pieces* (pub. 1911), when published separately in America (1923).

[3] For piano, composed in 1921–2, as part of the collection *Shenadoah (and other pieces)*.

[4] For piano (pub. 1905), dedicated to Grainger.   [5] For piano (pub. 1908).

[6] The name of the first of the *Shenadoah (and Other Pieces)* collection, when published separately in America (1924).

[7] Where the Graingers stayed in Frankfurt in 1900–1.

time to give to friendship & art. But from the time of our coming to London on, I feel rue aplenty. I call-to-mind how you would come to King's Road & say 'I'm up for the day. Now what have you got to show me?' And I would have to say 'I have pupils all day. And I cannot afford to put them off'. I rue that bitterly—all the lovely hours of tone art sampling we might have had together, had I not been so hounded by earning-duties, as I thought. You must have thought me a very poor tone-fellow. And I have had ample time to think of those lost chances to share tone-thoughts—I who have lived 27 years in USA without forming a single close friendship, without ever opening my lips or ears in tone-talk.

And I rue, too, that I could not, or would not, join thoughts & plans with you when you came, after the 1st season of Balfour Gardiner concerts[1] & you said: 'You & my pieces have had much too much success. Next season I am going to put your & my things at the beginnings & ends of programs, where they can't make such a success.' Such a jolly plan, & so paltry of me to talk as if I couldn't welcome it—I, who was doomed to be overlooked, deaf-heard, in any case, whatever I did.

I loved our meetings at Grez. I loved & worthprized all that you did for Fred.[2] (You may have thought I seemed impish & small-minded towards you & Fred at times at Grez, maybe I was. But I never failed to *love* yr greathearted & truly tone-serving behaviour to Fred.) It was sweet to me to dove-tail with another oversoul in bringing sounding tones (our 2-piano bouts) to that mute oversoul of tone.

I have loved (as I have written before) Ella's & my holidays with you in Argeles,[3] Norway, Sweden, Fontmell.[4] I relished, outstandingly, when you took us to afternoon tea one Sunday in Salisbury. I have loved all my hours with you. But they have been too few, & I too often came to them in a wornout state (& therefore was unmannerly & unfellowly—all of which I rue keenly), & they were but snippets of togetherness—not the life-sharing war-paths of tone-tilth I always longed to live with you. There were you, a tonewright strangely close to myself—in mood, in type, in race-fate. You had money & were born to shake it like a flag in the world's eye. I, too, had things to shake like a flag. I had my piano-fain following, in Holland, Scan-

---

[1] In 1912.

[2] Gardiner had materially supported Frederick Delius during the 1920s and 1930s, and even bought Delius's house at Grez-sur-Loing so that he did not have to move.

[3] The Graingers, Scott and Gardiner had holidayed together during Sept.–Oct. 1936 at Lourdes and Argelès in the French Pyrenees.

[4] Gardiner's home, in Dorset.

dinavia, Australia, New Zealand, America. Both you & I delighted hearer-hosts with our own tone writs. Neither of us was luck-begrudgesome to others. We both had friendships for other tonewrights, rooted in our worthprizements of their gifts. We both chose our men well. You & I—two manly men without priggishness or isms, without 'arty'ness or Smart-Aleckry, neither of us drawing room minded, both of us with means or able to earn, both able to time-beat riddle-rich new works in a seaworthy way, both with enough showmanship to run tone-feasts tellingly (but neither of us giving a damn for showmanship), both abreast of our era (neither vanguardminded nor stick-in-the-mud), both good foreign speech learners—one would think that you & I were cut out to pool our resources & art-hopes in an art-war-path (so lissome, so careless, so friendly to the tone-crowd, yet so little in awe of it, as we are) for Britishness, Nordicness, Colonialness, beside which the brotherhood of Russian tonewrights,[1] 'les six', & the like, would seem like small stuff.

Well, it was not to be. But I want you to know that I rue every lost chance (whatever its whenceness) of team-work with you, just as I gem-hoard every call-to-mindment of all our meetings, tonefellowship & of all the good redes you gave me about my English Dance & other things.

You added greatly to the glow & sparkle of life when you came to Frankfurt: a *big* Englishman, fresh from the Oxford oarsman's bench— big in body, big in mind, big in means, big in heart, big in tone-skills. And you had then (as you have now & always have had) a wilful & truthful straightforwardness which is the root of what I call well-bredness—an unfaltering instir for how rightly & justly to deal with all things as they come up. (As I sat in the bus this morning we passed a calf in a field that made me think of Walt Whitman's line: 'and the look of the bay mare shames silliness out of me'.)[2]

You can mind-picture what it meant to me in Frankfurt when you, Cyril & Roger turned up—the first tone-oversouls I had ever met. All my boyhood I had read in Grove's Dictionary of Music the lives of the great tonewrights whose toneart I worshipped—Schubert, Handel, Bach & the like. But I had never met such men in the flesh. But when you 3 came, I did. It was upheartening, around 1897, when an English

[1] The Russian 'Five' group of composers.
[2] From section 13 of 'Song of Myself', *Leaves of Grass* (1891–2 version): 'And do not call the tortoise unworthy because she is not something else, | And the jay in the wood never studied the gamut, yet trills pretty well to me, | And the look of the pretty bay mare shames silliness out of me.'

Rugby team (such hot-hearted, selfunsparing young Samurai) came to F'furt & wiped the floor with the German team. So, too, it was hope-raising & pride-raising when you 3 great English tonewrights turned up & utterly dwarfed the un-noble groping tone-thralls that filled our classes with dullness. For the shining sparkle of all-giftedness, lordliness, helpfulness & understandingness that you brought into my life I can never thank you enough. All I have seen of you, all I have known of you, has been a golden soul-gain in my life; but there has been too little of it; I have seen too little of you. I do not doubt that I have often been riling & boring to you—I talk too much & I am cursed with samishness. So it may well be that you saw enough of me, & have not gone hungry for me as I have gone hungry for you. But I have never seen enough of you, never could see enough of you. I liked you when you were a young man; I love you as an old man; I look up worthprizingly to all yr noble deeds; I take pride & joy in yr tree-planting; I am gladened by your kin—yr brother & Rolf;[1] I love your homes; I worship you for yr greathearted helpfulness to fellow-tonewrights—Fred, Austins,[2] Holst, & all of us that gain-drew from your matchless Balfour Gardiner tonefeasts;[3] I love yr taste in book-art (Hardy, Chaucer, Masefield, & that rimster in Dorset or Somerset stead-speech) & I gem-hoard yr bookgifts (Baermann's Klarinett-Schule,[4] Chaucer, the Swedish word-root word-book); I gloat over your big bear-like body. But best of all I love yr tone-works; for I know them best & I can get closer to them than to any other showing of you.

Do you recall one evening (was it at yr father's house?), when you & I (& I think Cyril, & may be Austin) dined together, & I afterwards played Ravel's then new 'Le Gibet' & 'Ondine'?[5] It must have been around 1908–1910. You said '"Ondine" is very exquisite, but there *have* been things in modern French music somewhat like it—such as Ravel's own Jeux d'eau for instance. But "Le Gibet" stands absolutely alone & I consider it the most outstanding of all modern French piano pieces.' (or words of that meaning).

The time Cyril & I stayed with you at Moody's Down, Barton

[1] Gardiner's nephew, Henry Rolf Gardiner.

[2] Frederic Austin (1872–1952), English baritone and composer; his son, the conductor Richard Austin (b. 1903); and brother, the composer Ernest Austin (1874–1947).

[3] Gardiner's eight concerts of 1912–13 had presented works by nearly twenty contemporary British composers.

[4] *Vollständige Clarinett-Schule* by Carl Baermann (1810–85).

[5] From Ravel's *Gaspard de la nuit* (1908).

Stacey,[1] was a winner. Then, & when you & I were together, at Frome (when we stayed with the doctor at Frome who had the let-happensome-mooded daughter; when we bicycled round to the village bands & heard the saxophone; when we heard a nightingale on the way home that night, was, I guess, my best time-stretch with you. At that time it seemed that you liked me for what I was; I was very untrammeled with you & my other English friends just then & I did not feel as if I were 'under a cloud' in any of your minds; I was over-weaning & heedless—sure of myself. Later on (long before yr B.G. tonefeasts) I seemed to lose my carefree 'place in the sun' with you all. From fun-feeding ((amusing)) you all I seemed to pass into riling or boring you all. I recall how Fred Austin (at Robinson-Smith's near Aylesbury—was it around 1911?) spoke of my having lost my purity as a tonewright—that the first works he met of mine were 'pure', but that by 1911 I had grown knowing & soiled. To some length it seemed to me that I 'lost caste' with you all about that time, between 1904 & 1911. I dont know how it came about—how I sank in yr eyes, I mean (if that is what happened). I am not thinking of hows & whens. I only want to say that I *rue greatly* anything I did that made me seem less pure as an artman, less jolly & wishworthy as a fellow, to you & my other English friends. It may be that my great in-love-ness with Scandinavia (which had been brewing since I read the sagas at the age of 9, or 10, or 11, but which came to a head when I first fared steadily in those lands, 1907–1914) made me less well tuned to England & Englishness & therefore a duller dish to my English friends. The fact is that since about 1910, or thereabouts, I have felt just the least bit held-at-arm's-length, nothing to make a fuss about—just a shadow of an otherness, as side-matched with 1897–1908. If this was so (& not just a thought-ghost of my own raising) I want to say that I rue wholeheart-edly whatever I did to cause it. I touch on this point, not to grumble, but merely to stress anew how much I rue all things that held us apart, how thankful I am for all things that drew us together. When you stood on the boat's deck at Arendal,[2] in 1922—as it drew away from the wharf—you said, with tears in yr eyes, 'I am sorry to leave you, Percy.' That is what I feel, always. I am always so grieved to leave you & I rue deeply every sway, duty, task that holds you & me so far apart—apart in miles, apart in life-paths, apart in the tone-world.

[1] The Hampshire home of Gardiner's family, until 1920.   [2] Norway.

I wish it could have been given to me to see much much more of
you, to have shared much more of life with you.

> Percy

41   *To Ellen Bull*

[Grainger's racial views reached their most fervent expression in the early
1940s. His outspokenness led to a cooling in relations with his friends the
Bulls, over the issue of Storm Bull's marriage to one supposedly non-Nordic.
A heated correspondence with Storm Bull's new wife Ellen ensued. In this,
Grainger's second letter to her about 'Nordicness', he retreated from his initial condemnation of racial intermarriage but exposed a thoroughly confused
understanding of both racial types and individual lineages.]

> Springfield, Mo. | Oct 23, 1941

Dear Ellen,

On getting home, here in Springfield, I find your letter of Oct 8. It
was good of you to write me again.

My interest in 'Nordics' did not start with my partly non-Nordic
father, but in my mother telling me that her mother said to her (when
my grandmother heard my mother wanted to marry my father): 'I
cant think how you can like a dark-eyed man. All my troubles in life
came from dark-eyed people'. Hearing about that, when I was 6, or 7,
or 8, made me think about race-types very early, &, maybe with somewhat of my grandmother's slant. My associations with my father were
never 'revolting' or 'terrible'. He was always pleasant & kindly. That
he drank himself into disaster & gave syphilis to my mother we always
regarded as bad luck on his part & never held it against him. Neither
my mother nor I had any dislike for my father. I simply regret that I
have picked up so many of my father's feebler qualities & lack so
much of the bravery & steadiness of my mother's breed.

I am not against race-blends. I do not disapprove of matings or
marriages between Whites & Negroes, Whites & Japanese or Chinese,
Nordics & Mediterraneans, Nordics & Alpines, Jews & Nordics, etc,
etc.[1] I think it MOST valuable to try ALL KINDS of race-blends, & see

[1] Grainger's understanding of European racial types was largely based on the work of Madison
Grant (of which he had become aware in 1919) and Lothrop Stoddard, whose article 'Racial
Realities in Europe' (*Saturday Evening Post*, 22 Mar. 1924, pp. 14–15, 156–8) Grainger carried about
with him as a kind of racial ready-reckoner. Grant had divided Europeans into three basic types:
Nordics, Alpines, and Mediterraneans. About Jews, gypsies, and other 'Asiatic races'

what comes out of them. Without wholesale experimentation, I am wholly unable to guess whether so-called 'mixed' or 'pure' races are best. I believe in everything being put to the test of experimentation. As for the blond Jews (who must have a lot of Nordic in them, since there is no other source of fairness, other than Nordicness), one must admit that they hold some of the most outstanding Jews, certainly in music: Mischa Elman, Rachmaninoff, Siloti,[1] Tchaikovsky, Joseph Hoffman,[2] Frederick Delius, Menuhin.[3] You ask me 'do these fit into your Nordic pattern?' Yes, up to a point—depending upon the amount of Nordicness in them. Delius I always FELT to be a Nordic. He looked like a Nordic, he acted & spoke like a Nordic. He thought he was a Nordic—he always told me he hadnt a drop of Jewish blood, & his wife (while admitting SHE was partly Jewish) told me the same. Yet the family evidence convinces me he was partly Jewish.[4] No doubt the Nordic strain was overwhelmingly strong in Delius, so I always think of him as mainly Nordic. Yet it would be most unfair to Jewry to deny his Jewish roots. Is he more Nordic than a dark Norwegian such as Johan Svendsen?[5] Of course he is! Is a fair Italian (such as Martinelli),[6] more Nordic than a darkish Norwegian such as Arne Garborg?[7] Of course he is! The Nordic blood in Northern Italy is enormous (look at Botticelli's types). Houston Stewart Chamberlain (have you read his fascinating 'The Foundations of the 19th Century'?)[8] claims Botticelli, Dante, Michel Angelo as Nordics or

Stoddard, following Grant, concluded that whether they married into the surrounding races or not their effect had been to 'confuse and complicate the situation', creating unstable racial conditions. Grainger's own identification of Jews was often based on nothing more than a hunch arising from such features as hair- or eye-colour, facial features, shape of skull, family, or national origin. Writing during Aug. 1954 in his long essay 'The Things I Dislike', Grainger recognized categories of definite Jews (Mendelssohn, Bizet, Gershwin) and 'supposed-to-be-Jews' (Delius, Rachmaninov, Tchaikovsky, Wagner). For a short, sympathetic study of the development of Grainger's racial views, see Bruce Clunies Ross, 'Percy Grainger's "Nordic Revolt against Civilization"', *Musicology Australia*, 9 (1986), 61–2.

[1] Alexander Siloti (1863–1945), Ukrainian-born pianist and conductor, cousin of Rachmaninov.

[2] = Josef Hofmann (1876–1957), Polish-born pianist and composer.

[3] Yehudi Menuhin (b. 1916), American-born violinist.

[4] In a letter to Eric Fenby of 6 Dec. 1936 Grainger explained that he had come to know a niece of Delius, Miss Krönig, in 1933 and 'she said there was no doubt at all that D's mother was ¼-Jewish. . . . I think that also explains (in part) his dislike of markedly Christian composers such as Palestrina, Sibelius & Bach (at times, not always) & his *marked* liking for so many Jewish composers: Mendelssohn, Albeniz, Ravel, Bizet, etc., as your book shows'.

[5] (1840–1911), violinist and composer.

[6] Giovanni Martinelli (1885–1969), Italian-born tenor.

[7] (1851–1924), pioneering author in Landsmål dialect.

[8] (1855–1927), Anglo-German precursor of Nazism, husband of Richard Wagner's daughter Eva. Chamberlain's volume, expounding theories of Teutonic superiority, first appeared in 1899. Grainger had come to admire his work in 1926, Hitler somewhat earlier.

part-Nordics, which may be good or poor guessing—I dont know. Naturally, NATIONALITY has nothing to do with it. There have been Nordic settlements all over Europe, etc—in Sicily, Nth Africa (the blue-eyed Berbers), Spain, etc; just as, in the old days, there was a vast Negroid population in Scandinavia. The half-fairness of the Jews goes back to the Ammonites,[1] say some.

So we come to the question; apart from part-Nordicness (which a Jew, a Negro, can show) what is Full Nordicness? I dont know if there is any agreed opinion on this, among race-students (you must remember that the study of races is very new—is still in the vague stage, like a sketch for a composition. But it is not needfully worthless because it is unfinished). My own word for Nordic is 'blue-gold-rosy-race'. If the eyes are not blue or grey, the hair not golden, the skin not rosy, I do not count the man fully Nordic. If the hair is fair but not golden, the skin fair or fairish but not rosy, the eyes hazel or purple but not blue or grey, I count the man a part-Nordic. Mischa Elman, with colorless greyish eyes, SALLOW fair skin, colorless fairish hair is, obviously, a part-Nordic—& must be counted as such. But he lacks the sparkle, the lustre, of a full Nordic. We need not be partisan or sentimental about these matters. Treat the Jew & Nordic in Mischa Elman as you would a glass of mixed milk & water. If it is 9 tenths milk you would say it is almost milk. If 9 tenths water you would say it is almost water. If it is 50/50 you would say it is a half-breed. I am very ignorant about races. But that doesnt prove the SUBJECT to be uninteresting. But there is one thing I am not—I am not partisan in racial matters. I am not for or against Nordics, or Mediterraneans, or Jews, or Negroes. I merely say: let us aim at ALL racial experiments, including (comparatively) 'pure' races (this experiment has never been consciously tried)[2] & blended races. In the case of our Nordic race I merely say this: We are the only race that is not race-conscious; we are the only race that betrays its kin on a wholesale scale (British betraying Norwegians & Dutch, Americans betraying British); we are the only race that hates itself & prefers foreigners (do the Jews hate themselves? Do the Japanese hate themselves—as Americans hate English, as English hate Irish, as Norwegians hate Danes?); & we are one of the smallest of the 'great' races (even in Scandinavia the REALLY NORDIC elements are small). So I feel some care should be taken to prevent our being out-

---

[1] A Semitic people of biblical times living east of the Jordan.

[2] Grainger did not know of the 'conscious experiments' at racial purification already being set in motion by Nazi Germany.

bred. That doesnt mean that Nordics should not marry non-Nordics. That is a most wish-worthy experiment. But we must, I feel, ENCOR-AGE SOME NORDICS TO MARRY NORDICS, sometimes. (At present, the only cases where Nordics willingly marry Nordics is where no other choice presents itself. Almost.) In this appeal I have no thought of the Nordic being superior or inferior to any other race. I merely warn against his extinction as I would warn against the extinction of the buffalo, the duckbilled-platypus, or any other rare phenomenon.

There is something in your letter I really do dislike: Your words 'your desire to have Storm & me separate'. I have no 'desire' in the matter, because I regard it as wholly outside my sphere. (If I were a world-dictator I might 'desire' & do many things I now dont & cant.) In listing for Eyvind the many things that had saddened me in my relations with the Bulls I mentioned Storm's marrying a non-Nordic (or partly non-Nordic, shall we say? Probably both you & I are on the border line of Nordicness) wife—together with his ignoring Nordic music, his expressed dislike of England & Norway (as it seemed to me), his championing of Hungary, his studying with non-Nordic piano teachers. Having written these things to Eyvind, I was not going to hide them from you.

But I was not expressing a 'desire' or even an opinion. I am not a soldier, fighting the FIGHT of life. I am merely an artist, trying to RECORD MY FEELINGS & trying (to some small extent) to keep a record of my age. So I expressed my griefs to Eyvind. I had no desires to express—I do not deal in such things. If I should have any desire in the matter it would be (of course) that both you & Storm should always be happy in each other.

Yours ever,
Percy

42 *To Ella Grainger*

Kansas City → Springfield, Mo.
Wed midday, Sept 30, 1942

Beloved Help-art,

You may have heard me say that I never did myself justice in playing before a hearer-host till I was over 30.

And now I come to say another queer thing: I never felt *deeply hopeful* about my piano playing till I got 60—until last Sunday in San Francisco. For it was a hard task—to get up that Downes[1] tone bill-of-fare in so short a while, with him teetering back & forth about the choice of tone-bill-of-fare, & it inholding things like the Franck 'Aria' that I've always been out-of-the-way scared of. I had said to myself: 'I will see if it cant be hurdled by hard work, mindpointing.' And it was. On the way West, in the train, I crowded out every other thought, but of the toneworks I was to play & in San Francisco I was merciless with the Rappaports & myself in forcing upon each day the muchness of keyboard-swink I felt I needed. The 1st day (Friday) I keyboard-swinked from about 2.30 to 11.30, with hour off for meal—as I wrote you. Saturday I rehearsed with Downes most of the morning & then stuck to the keyboard 2.30 to 6.00 & again (after an evening party at Rappaports), 6.00–11.00, 11.30–1.30. Sunday morning I did all I could. I must say, the togetherness with Downes be-braved me greatly. First of all, he & Rappaport strongly urged me to talk-out the Foe & Friend Tone-art askment freely, both at Friday morning's interview (Downes & me) & at the tonefeast. At the interview Downes started off by saying to the interviewers (fact-fully not interviewers, but the best San Francisco tone-judges ((critics))—that's what one gets from the Downes angle of it!) 'What unique powers Grainger has of expressing himself in words'. So I opened-up to the press—as much as I thot wise.[2] I had already said to Downes & Rappaport: 'All right. Let me say my stuff to the press. But not at Sunday's tone-feast. What quarrel can I have with Sunday's tone-bill-of-fare, seeing it is a "banded Theeds" ((Allied Nations)) tonebill of fare?' I bore upon Downes (1) my willingness to play a mixed bill of fare, from the start; (2) his will-waive-ment in saying [*sic*] to an allied bill of fare; (3) my hope that we forthshow an utterly at-one-full front at the tonefeast. Our rehearsal on Sat. morning was a spark-striking unfoldment.[3] After the very first piece (Goossens)

---

[1] Olin Downes (1886–1955), music critic of the *New York Times* from 1924 until his death.

[2] The *San Francisco Chronicle*, 26 Sept. 1942 (p. 9), reported: 'Grainger did practically all of the talking yesterday. The subject of their performance is "The Allied Cause in Music". Grainger interprets this to imply the desirability of performing much English, Scandinavian, French and Russian music which has been neglected in the past. He cited a long list of neglected composers and works which, he felt, are of equal significance with the established masterpieces, among them the compositions of Arthur Fickenscher of Fairfax.'

[3] Grainger's programme consisted of folksong arrangements by Goossens, Yasser, Brockway, Guion and himself, Byrd's *The Carman's Whistle*, a Grieg ballade, a Chopin polonaise, the fugue from Scott's Piano Sonata, the aria from Franck's *Prelude, Aria and Finale* and Balakirev's *Islamey*. The main theme of Downes's talk was the need for art music constantly to return to folk music for its revitalization. The concert, the first in an 'Uplifters' series, was held on the afternoon of 27 Sept. in the Curran Theatre. See plate 19 in this volume.

he asked me 'However did you get that sensitiveness of touch from study in Germany? I never knew a German-trained pianist yet who could modulate his tones as you just have', and so on. He fell in love with the Byrd, which he didnt seem to know well. He was all afire for the Fugue of the Scott Sonata, talking of its 'immense drive' & same-deeming with me in what a feat of aheadness it was for Cyril to have penned such an idol-breaker ((iconoclasm)) in 1904. Then, after hearing the Franck Aria, he wholly underwrote my deemth that it stood well alone, without its other 2 movements. He said 'I was very skeptical of this choice, but you are right. The way you play it—with that singing sustained quality in every voice—it is a perfect picture of Franck's tenderly devout muse. I am extremely glad you insisted on this number', and so on. Of Balakirev he said 'Your virtuosity utterly amazes me. I have only once before heard a performance of Islamey that I could place beside yours, & that was one by Busoni, way back in (Berlin? New York?).' About the whole tone-bill-of-fare he said 'I am completely won over to it' & Rappaport told me that he (Downes) had never before heard me 'in such magnificent form'. On this Sunday Downes was kindliness itself to work with. He unfolded my ideas (as voiced in my send-writs to him) as well as his own & he worked in almost every gossip-bit ((anecdote)) about the tonewrights & their toneart that I had written him or told him in the rehearsal. (I worked hard in that rehearsal—nervously. I strove with might & main to catch my man, & afterwards I was wringing wet & my bladder was on fire—as nerve-strain always makes it.) It suits my yielding, in a sense somewhat wo-manish, make-up (this is what makes me a good setter of folksongs—'ich gehe in dem Volkslied auf')[1] to tone-outfill another man's Talk-feast. I easily melt myself into another's mould. I think D. felt this, for at the end he said: 'I hope we can do many more of these joint shows. I find I can collaborate with you perfectly. But there are many with whom I cannot collaborate at all.' I'll tell you what it is: All men with a lively thot-life can work together—no matter how other-whithered ((divergent)) the thots themselves may be. And Downes is quite a fury-feelthy ((passionate)) one-body ((person)). I had breakfast with him Sunday & he said: 'I believe in just 2 things: suffering & corage'.

I troth-gave D. to look him up in N. York, & I, too, truly hope there may be other blent-shows between him & me. I will tell Tonie[2] so, & think out further tonebill of fares with D.

[1] = I become absorbed into the folksong (German).
[2] Antonia Morse, Grainger's concert organizer.

So much for the tween play between Downes & me, which (as I said) was most upheartening for me. But it was something else that sprouted my 'piano hopes at 60'. It is the proof of what I can do with hard work, at the keyboard. There is no doubt I have 'stepped up' my keyboard swinkment of late years. Mother had always urged me to 'work hard & be done with it' at the piano. But I had always thought 'no'. Such hard work as I had put in (in my earlier years) at the keyboard had not raised my hope of 'fightwin thru work'. All hopes of reaching *high* keyboard skill—thru however much work—seemed to me vain. And so it has seemed to me until just lately—the last few years. And this new hope-birth all goes back to the hopefulfillment of my life with you. To do his best a man (at least my kind of a man) must be plugged full of win-stir. I am the greedy type. Hunger & nay-sayment ((denial)) do not stir the fightlust in me. I must be given my reward *first*; then I will earn it *afterwards*. It is a sulky kind of a makeup—that needs thawing-out by the sun of gift-heapingness before it will unlimber. But that's the way I seem to be. A woman of my own—a beauty queen & princess-of-art—who roundrings me with richness & choiceness beyond what I have earned: that is the key to feats-readiness in me, all right. But the right-code ((moral)) in all this is a very sad one: you & I have got to work *much harder than ever before*. We are just beginning. All the way from San Francisco I have had to share a seat with someone (until here in Missouri—KC → home). From San Francisco to Cheyenne (2 nights) it was a drunken Minnesota soldier; from Denver to Kansas City a nice Sardinian (Italian-raced island belonging to England, between Malta & Turkey—so the man said),[1] 43-years old, blue eyed, a former railroad foreman on the Union Pacific RR, now a deputy-sheriff in Santa Clara county (San Jose), Calif. I *always* find Italians nice. *No* nonsense, *no* run-with-the-crowd-madness, *no* swell-craze ((megalomania)).

But about the drunken Minnesota soldier, by name Carl (or Carlo) Johnson. He said he was Irish; but he didnt look Irish, & Carl Johnson is not Irish, tho his unbelievable wittiness might be Irish. He looked Swedish or German American & his knowledge of Swedish Revivalist Meetings bespoke some early closeness to Swedish-American life. And at that—to naysay one's Swedishness (like the big strong square-shaped Swede in the Jewish Army & Navy Store in Chicago, around 1928), & to sham Irishness (as a cloak over one's Rosy Racey thinskinnedness)

---

[1] This description is simply wrong.

might be a very Swedish trick. Upheartened by beers (at last he fell asleep with his head in my lap with 3 unemptied beer cups of paper alongside him) he heldforth to the whole train, apeing the Revivalist stuff in a louder voice, but interlarding small lewdnesses in an under-tone that kept his fellow soldiers in a steady uproar of laughter. This is the true army wit (as I saw it daily at Governor's Island): herd-wit; wit un-one-body-somely ((impersonally)) outsweated, thoughtlessly, for the happiness of a group with which the wit-man is at-one. He had the most over-matching wealth of wordchoices—not only using real words clearly sounded & cleverly picked, but also using words & word-hints that lived in a twilight of sense—that stir that lies at the root of Joyce-ness. It may be that what he did was not quite so clever & gifted as it seemed to me; it may be that I only half-heard much of his word-froth & pinned a dream-guessed overworth to much of it. But to me it seemed the freest & most as-is-y show of word-giftedness (talk-life) I have ever witnessed in my life. Just what speech-twist ((accent)) Carl Johnson had in his wontsome speech I could not make out, but there seemed nothing Irish to it. And when he be-aped the preaching at the Revivalist Meeting his speech-twist became screamingly-funnily Swedish-American, or just Swedish. In apeing the Swedish sermon he did not (as far as I could hear) use real Swedish words, but just Swedish-like nonsense-sounds, mainly of the type of hände, with my broad ä. And he got into this something slow, dull, stiff, sulky & threatening that was funnier than anything of this kind I've ever heard. Just what C.J. did 2 nights ago is not what makes me laugh inwardly. What makes me laugh is the mind-sight of a little boy, sitting hateingly & becrittleingly & stupidity-searching at a big meeting that his silly elders took earnestly & solemnly. The thought of small clever-ness sitting root-piercingly & bubble-burstingly in the midst of big stu-pidness is always relishable to me. This drunken outpouring is the proper doom-deal befitting the rottenness, silliness & falseness of Christ-beliefsome warpaths.

Percy

43   *To Ella Grainger*

Nearing Chicago, Sat morn, Feb 6, 1943

As long as I am with my darling I feel buoyed up, but the moment I am alone I am stricken with dire-fear. A man in the dock (on trial) has a right to be afraid—he is unlikely to clear himself. A man about to play to a hearer host is also unlikely to clear himself—he is unlikely to prove his call-to-mindment flawless.

Last evening, in my dire-fear, I tried *thinking thru* my pieces (for tonight) as I did the Fauré with you that time, in White Plains. But of course I dont know my pieces that well—not even the Bach, which I have played unbrokenly since 1904 or 1905.[1] But maybe it helps (to try & think them thru) all the same. One clutches at a straw. So I thought them thru as much as I could to St Louis, but kept falling asleep.

Then I thought I would try thinking them thru all night. It started well, for there was no seat. But even so, I fell asleep crouching on my thighs. But the guard opened up a new car & there I fell for the temptment to sleep.

My life has been too full of wretchedness & direfear. The greatest part of my life has been spent in fear—& well-grounded fear. One really is tempted to pray 'let it come to an end'. Still, I never do that.

The Flynn case[2] scares me stiff, & worries me to death. So do the losses of our foes.[3] I know it is what the world calls for—needs. But it sears me, nevertheless.

Only thru my darling do I know balm,

    Percy

There is snow here (Chicago) everywhere. How horrid! The fruit & Swedish bread are fine. But to feel as *sick* as I do is also a rack-pain ((torment)).

P.S. Everywhere I go I hear folk laugh & see that they are hungry & thirsty & full of life's stirs. All I can feel is puke-stir & fearstrickenness.

---

[1] Grainger probably refers to Busoni's arrangement of the Prelude and Fugue in D, BWV 532, which he had first performed in public in Oct. 1905.

[2] The film star Errol Flynn (1909–59) was facing two charges of rape. He was not convicted.

[3] On 3 Feb. 1943 the Germans had declared three days of national mourning for their forces lost in the futile six-month battle for Stalingrad. They had suffered nearly three hundred thousand casualties.

44   *To Clara Aldridge*

National Music Camp, Interlochen, Michigan | July 6, 1944
Darling Aunty Clara,

This is a letter about my business affairs, as I think it might interest you to know the main outline of my earning channels in these exceptionally prosperous times.

We are here at this camp for 8 weeks & I am giving piano lessons every day from 8.30 in the morning to about 5.00 or 6.00 pm, tho sometimes I begin earlier & end later. For this I have a guarantee of one thousand dollars (over 200 pounds), but my summer's earnings will be much above that—maybe something [like] this, 300 to 500 pounds.

From the ASCAP (American Society of Composers, Authors, Publishers) I get something like five thousand dollars (over 1000 pounds) yearly. These are performance fees from my compositions—in moving pictures, broadcasts, etc.

From my American publishers I get something over a thousand dollars (over 200 pounds) a year from the sales of my compositions (sheet music).

From my English publishers I get between 100 and 200 pounds yearly, for the sales of my compositions (sheet music), but at present these English payments are being paid out to an English friend of mine[1] who is badly off. These English royalties would be much higher if it were not for the stiff income tax, due to the war. They would be almost double as big in normal times. But I do not dislike high taxes. I am proud to think that my music is (to a small degree) helping to finance the war in dear old England, who stood the brunt of this war alone for so long!

My Australian royalties (sales of sheet music in Australia & New Zealand) are very high at present—the last yearly payment was about 94 pounds, I think. This is very high, considering the small population of Australia (as compared with England & America) & I am very grateful that my music does as well as it does in my native land.

I do not know exactly how much I earn with my concerts, these days. Of course there are very heavy expenses in connection with the concert work—travelling outlays, hotels & expensive advertising in musical papers, etc. But my concert work more than covers all these expenses, so that all my earnings on my compositions are clear profit.

[1] Cyril Scott.

The last 2 seasons have been regarded as difficult ones by concert managers, as the universities, colleges, etc, were uncertain of their enrollment of students, owing to the war—in particular, the drafting of young men for the army & navy. Nevertheless, I have been personally quite satisfied with the last few seasons; and as for next year, everybody has to admit that it looks UNUSUALLY PROMISING.

I have never thought much about money, & have seldom striven DIRECTLY to earn money. But I have seldom refused a chance to earn, if it came my way, however unsympathetic the work might seem to me.

Of late I have been playing my own arrangement of a song by GERSHWIN (called 'THE MAN I LOVE')[1] adapted to the piano by the composer—a very lovely treatment of an exquisite song. The publishers of this song have long been wanting to publish this arrangement of mine,[2] but it was difficult for me to get permission for this from my main publishers—who have first right to my writings. But by a lot of palavering I got them to agree, & it MAY BE that this arrangement will prove a new source of income that will be worth while—as the song, in itself, is such a favorite. We shall see!

Somehow I have always made money without any special effort or difficulty, tho I have often disliked the KIND of work I have had to do (such as concert playing) in order to earn. The gift of making money is clearly in the Aldridge family, & it always seems to me that the main part of it is (1) being able to read character (as Uncle Jim[3] said he did), (2) trusting those that are worthy of trust, (3) being willing to share profits with those who help to create them.

This is a lovely spot, & it is a nice change to be here (by lakes & amidst pine trees & sandy ground) after the rest of the year in towns, etc.[4]

Both Ella & I are unusually well—feeling much better than other summers at the same time. We send our fondest love—will write soon.

Your affectionate nephew, Percy

---

[1] From Gershwin's *Lady, Be Good!* (1924).
[2] Harms Inc. (New York) did publish Grainger's arrangement for piano later in 1944.
[3] James Henry Aldridge (1849–1925), who lived in Adelaide.
[4] The camp was situated on the eastern shore of Lake Michigan.

45 *To Joseph E. Maddy*

[Despite his enthusiasm at the start of the Interlochen camp by its end, on 26 August, Grainger was beginning to feel giddy and depressed. He worried whether there was any worth in his teaching, feeling that after forty years of exertions neither he nor his students had made any real progress. The same problems were presented for the same correction from one decade to the next. From this time, when Grainger was aged 62, can be dated his withdrawal, first from such sustained teaching activity—he would not return to Interlochen in 1945—and then, gradually in the early post-war years, from regular professional concertizing. In this polite farewell letter to the Interlochen camp's director he tried to communicate his visions for the piano department's future.]

August 30, 1944

Dear Dr Maddy,

I received safely the last 2 checks from Interlochen ($1564.88 from the Camp, $240.00 from the University),[1] for which many thanks.

It seems to me that a wonderful piano department has grown up at Interlochen, both from the financial standpoint & from the artistic viewpoint. The students, as a whole, were not only much more gifted this year, but also more earnest in their work & better behaved.

As regard the piano department, I should like to make the following suggestions:

1. That the chief piano teacher should be able to hear all students before they are definitely booked with him.
2. That the Classes of Four be turned into Classes of Three, each pupil thus getting 20 minutes tuition out of the hour class. (You mentioned the possibility of charging the student more for the Class of 3.)
3. I feel that the Free Class for Advanced Piano Students, taking place 3.30 to 4.30 on Saturdays, was a good innovation, & should be continued.
4. It seemed to me that 3 classes a week of Free Piano Ensemble was too much & that the 2 such classes a week (3.30 to 4.30 on Tuesdays & Thursdays), to which the schedule was reduced, was sufficient & worked out as well as could be expected. I say 'as well as could be expected', because the piano ensemble work suffered from lack of PERFORMING POSSIBILITIES. The number of musical attractions at Interlochen are so great & many that it is (naturally) difficult to get the students to concentrate hard on anything short of

---

[1] The University of Michigan, which during the war started to sponsor the camp.

PERFORMANCES. So I suggest that piano ensemble students should be treated as harp and trumpet students are treated: that is, AS MANY OF THEM USED IN PERFORMANCES AS IS POSSIBLE. I understand that the Interlochen attitude (very wisely) is that all musical practising should be mixed with actual playing. I think it entirely wise that all available harps, all available trumpets, all available clarinets are welcomed into band & orchestra at Interlochen. Not only is the experience golden for the student, but the SOUND in orchestra & band (as a result of this massing of instruments) is the most beautiful sound in the world! Where does one hear a band, an orchestra, sound as luscious, as rich, as expressive as at Interlochen? In the summers when I was in charge of the orchestra at the Chicago Musical College we used 16 small upright Miessner pianos[1] in the orchestra & encoraged all piano-ensembleists to take part. I propose that this method, on a smaller scale, be tried at Interlochen—of course, only with regard to compositions containing a bona fide piano part, or pieces for piano & orchestra, or concertos. There are plenty of compositions or arrangements for 2, 3, or 4 pianos that members of the Piano Ensemble Class could have performed at concerts (I am not thinking of works with orchestra, or with string orchestra, or with band), but I did not suggest them because of the difficulty of placing 2 or more pianos on the stage under present conditions.

But could not these conditions be changed? You have plenty of nice-sounding uprights at the camp, &, could not 5 of these uprights be placed in the pit (where the orchestra plays for the opera) for the whole summer, with their backs to the platform & the players facing the conductor of orchestra or band (on the stage)? A tarpaulin, attached to poles at the backs of the pianos, or attached to the edge of the platform, could cover the pianos when they are not in use. The pianos should stay in the same positions for the whole summer, with their backs right along the front wall of the platform (the wall I jumped up onto in the movie).

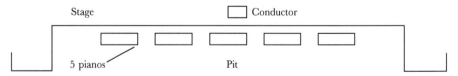

<hr />

[1] Made by a piano company specializing in school instruments, once headed by W. Otto Miessner (1880–1967).

194

Together with the grand piano on the stage, this would give 6 pianos for ensemble purposes. In works for 2 pianos, each piano part could be trebled. In works for 3 pianos, each piano part could be doubled. (When concerto is to be rehearsed with the orchestra, one of these pianos in the pit could be used, obviating the need to bring out the grand piano each time.) Apart from the many attractive works for piano ensemble without orchestra or band, that could be given, there is a large body of works with orchestra, or string orchestra, or band, in which the piano ensemble could profitably & effectively take part.

(a) Concertos for Piano & Orchestra. A concerto such as the Haydn Piano Concerto in D is very suitable for massed playing & would be a good means of using the talented YOUNGER pianists. Let all the 6 pianos play most of the work massed, while the more delicate solo passages might use one player at a time. Concertos such as the Mozart ones, the Grieg Concerto, the Gershwin Rhapsody in Blue, the Liszt Hungarian Fantasia, the Tchaikovsky No 1 would sound magnificent with massed pianos, with certain expressive passages played solo (first one student, then another, getting the solo).

(b) Compositions such as REPARTEE (by Bennet?) for piano & band.[1] In such compositions as my CHILDRENS MARCH for piano & band[2] the piano part was, of course, ALWAYS INTENDED to be played massed.

(c) Works for Piano & String Orchestra (If the String Orchestra meets at 3.30 & the Piano Ensemble Class also meets at 3.30 this would be convenient). There is the magnificent Bach Concerto in C major for 2 pianos & strings. There are several Bach Concertos for 3 pianos & strings, and at least 2 for 4 pianos & strings. There is Ernst Bloch's splendid CONCERTO GROSSO for piano & strings.[3] There are several works of mine for the same combination (Handel in the Strand, Lord Peters Stable-Boy, etc). All these works (Bach, Bloch, etc) would gain from the pianos being MASSED—just as the harps & trumpets gain from being massed.

I feel that if we could give the piano-ensembleists at Interlochen actual ENSEMBLE PLAYING EXPERIENCE like this we would be creating for the Interlochen piano students something comparable to what others get in band & orchestra.

[1] A composition originally written for piano solo by David D. Bennett (b. 1892), band composer and arranger.
[2] 'Over the hills and far away', composed in 1918–19.
[3] Composed in 1924–5 by the Swiss-born American composer Ernst Bloch (1880–1959).

46   *To Ella Grainger*

Macomb, Ill., Sunday eve, Nov. 12, 1944

It is very thoughtful of my darling wife to send a white day shirt to Grand Rapids, for there is no doubt it will come in very handy—the un-ironed self-washed white shirts are not such winners as the blue ones!

It is not only with money that I must be thriftier as old age sets in (I mean, in not taking on too many houses,[1] too many kept-folk, not being too wild about the museum), but also anent the jobs I take on.[2] Now there is this Grieg Sonata that I am playing now & which I am so sorely tempted to score as a Grieg–Grainger Symphony.[3] I have been led on by the thought ever since I first was in Amarillo[4] (Jan, 1943). It will score like butter & my Grieg-fame cuts me out to do such a feat. Whenever I get a hire-job ((engagement)) to bandboss a blent-band ((orchestra)), as somewhere this winter, & maybe at Lawrence, Kansas, when the boys get home,[5] it is dashed handy to have a Symphony *of one's own* that others know less about than oneself, & yet which fills out the Symphony-craving. So I fear I will have to set to & score this—shelving my own pieces in order to do so. This is the kind of job (however handy it comes in to have it) that I must do less & less of, as I get older. It is twaid-class work, & it makes my heart bleed to shelve really birth-some jobs in order to do hack-work. Yet I fear I *must* do it, just this one time!

There is one thing I love & joy-quaff almost as much as my beloved wife, & that is the Maori tongue. I love its words (so many of them sounding like puns on each other: ratou, kotou, tana, rana, Kotahi, Otaki) & no less do I love its grammar, or rather, its lack of grammar. Grammar, in the White men's tongues, is just a bad wont stepping in between a man.

I inlay a cutting about bed-wetting—an art I plied until I was 13 or

[1] Grainger's Aunt Clara had died the previous month. Grainger did, eventually, decide to sell the house she had left to him rather than to turn it into an Aldridge–Grainger Museum, as planned.

[2] In an earlier letter to his wife of this day Grainger listed two 'duties' for the coming years: to reduce concert touring to three or four months per year; to curb his spending on dependants and the Melbourne museum.

[3] Only the sketch of the opening of Grainger's orchestration of Grieg's Piano Sonata in E minor, Op. 7, is extant.

[4] Grainger had performed the Grieg Concerto with the Amarillo (Texas) Philharmonic Orchestra on 26 Jan. 1943.

[5] In summers of the early 1940s Grainger had participated in the Mid-Western Music Camp, held in Lawrence.

14—for I recall still doing it when we were in Germany. And that brings home the why-ground why I had so many whippings—because of the bed-wetting (years afterwards one is very apt to recall goings-on, but forget why they happened). It was hard for mother to know whether I was part-guilty in this riling wont (a great bother when one fared in trains or boats!) or not. And it is hard for me to make up my mind, even now, whether or no I could have given it up long ere I did. For I used to dream I was doing it & then wake up & find I had done it. One might take the view that if I had had a right-wise grown-up *hatred* of bed wetting I would have swayed my dream-self against it too! But there is no doubt that some inner part of me thought it great fun. It is an outward sign of the inward sinfulness & funfullness & lust-fulness of my soul-type. I am not one of those that can easily be weaned away from my 'younger (more baby-ish) self' or from my 'lower self' or from my self-pampering self. Artmen are not swayed so much by fear of wrong as they are by a hunger for grips—like Beowulf taking hold of Grendel until Grendel's arm is torn out.[1] And that is one main thing that ties me to you: you, too, are a thoro art-being in your fearless love of all the fun, sin, fairhood & power that is rooted deep within us. I dont think I could bear a timid, law-meek woman round me. Jag tycker om livets nödturft och förnödenheter.[2] I dont want everything to be too well trained, too house-broken. I like life to be full of slips & flaws. Life feeds on mishaps. Yr slip-master

     Percy

47   *To F. Cyril James*

April 24, 1945

F. Cyril James, Esq.,
Principal and Vice-Chancellor,
McGill University,
Montreal, Canada.

Dear Mr James,

   I am so touched by your gracious letter of April 20th in which you inform me of the great honor your illustrious university is willing to

---

[1] From the Old English epic poem *Beowulf*; Grendel was the troll who haunted King Hrothgar's hall.

[2] = I don't like the bare necessities and requirements of life. (Mostly Swedish.)

bestow upon me. I know that a degree from McGill University is known throughout the world as a very special distinction. Furthermore, that this honor is recommended by so noble a musician (& one so highly revered by me, personally) as Dean Douglas Clarke[1] makes your generous offer the more flattering.

Therefore it is with the deepest regret that I feel myself unable to accept a doctor's degree, for two reasons. (1) the democratic Australian viewpoint of my early years (for I have not lived there for over 50 years) makes me unable to accept any distinctions, and (2) the fact that I regard my Australian music as an activity hostile to education, and civilisation, leads me to regard myself as one to whom educational honors cannot apply. Also, as I have had only 3 months schooling in my life,[2] I feel that my music must be regarded as a product of non-education.

At the same time, I realise that there is always something inconsistent in any viewpoint such as the one put forth above; for although I have not been educated myself, I realise how much I owe to contact with beloved individuals who are highly educated. Nevertheless, the main facts and trends of my life as an Australian-born artist force me to take the stand I do.

I hope you will not think my reply to your deeply-prised proposal ungrateful. I assure you that I feel most deeply thankful to you and to Dean Clarke for the very great honor you wished to do me.

Yours sincerely,
Percy Grainger

48   *To Francis E. Resta*

7 Cromwell Place, White Plains, NY June 5, 1945

Dear Francis,

It was extremely kind of you to write me so generously & in such a warm note of tone-brotherhood—that same tone-fondness that shines thru all your performances!

It is MORE THAN KIND of you to say I may try out new works with

---

[1] (1893–1962), English-born Canadian composer, conductor and academic. He was dean of the music faculty at McGill University and conductor of the Montreal Symphony Orchestra from 1929.

[2] During 1894 in South Yarra, Melbourne.

your West Point artists—something that will be a great boon to me. I would like to take you up on that at once. I have just finished the sketch of the last-remaining movement[1] of a 5-movement YOUTHFUL SUITE for small orchestra, begun in 1899.[2] When the score & parts are written I would like AWFULLY to take advantage of your offer. I will not get the parts written (I expect) before I go to Chicago–Milwaukee–California, etc around June 27, as I have lots of concerts all the time (Canada, etc.) I expect to get back from the Western trip about August 6. Would some time after that suit you to have me come? Or would September suit you better, when we will be going up to Mr Bigelow's for his birthday party?

I have sent you the full score of my first HILLSONG. For the moment I am only lending it to you, as it was printed in Vienna & I dont know (yet) whether I can get further copies. If I can get further copies I will want to give you a copy. I want you to have this work (1) because it is BY FAR my best composition, so far, altho composed in 1902, (2) because I think you are the only conductor I know who could conduct it easily, gracefully, masterly. Some day I would be VERY GRATEFUL if I could hear you do a performance of HILLSONG I (private or public).[3] We can discuss the work, if you like, when we next meet.

It is (as I have said before) very generous of you to attach so much importance to my coming to West Point, & to say such kindly things about me & my music. But the boot is quite on the other foot, I can assure you! It means MUCH MORE to me to hear my most difficult works so exquisitely played, as you play them, than it can mean to you, or anyone to have me at West Point. For there are thousands of 'stars' that you can get. But where can I find another conductor with your combination of skill, friendliness, deep feeling for music & respect for art? There are heaps of skilful men; but they have such horrid natures, or they lack artistic feeling. On the other hand, I know several musicians with nice natures & a fine feeling for music & art; but such men are not usually very skilful. Your COMBINATION OF GOOD THINGS is unique.

So much for the less 'practical' side of music. But I have also something 'practical' to suggest. A few years ago[4] I made a band arr. of Cesar Franck's 2nd Organ Choral. I think the band arr. is good. As

---

[1] 'English Waltz'.   [2] The orchestral score appeared from Schott (London) in 1950.
[3] For Grainger's ecstatic response to Resta's performance of *Hill-Song* No. 1 see letter **52**.
[4] 1942.

for the composition: to my mind it is one of the SUPREME master-pieces of late-19th-century music—greater than the best of Brahms, because more perfect, better worked out, thought out. If you would be interested to play this thru, some time, I would keenly enjoy hearing you do so. I could send you the material, whenever you wished. If ever you are playing a concert for a hospital, or anywhere out of West Point (or anywhere at all), in which you would like me to play a concerto (or one movement of one), you can always count on me (giving my services of course). I am 'yours to command'. There is one fly in the Franck ointment. Due to war, I have not yet got in touch with the Franck copywrite owners, to get their permission. But I dont think they would be nasty about a band arr., or that [they] would even know about it. Love to you all from us both,

Percy

49   *To Sigurd Fornander*

[The conclusion of the war coincided with important changes in Grainger's life. Although he had moved back to White Plains and re-established most connections broken off by the war, he found it difficult to regain the energy and concentration of the 1930s. His playing was becoming more inaccurate, and he hankered after composing original works, publishing more of his existing works and restarting his experiments with free music. He increasingly sacrificed high fees and glamorous venues for opportunities to have his own and his friends' music performed by amateur musical groups. Lack of regular income, however, still kept him chained to the professional circuit for several months of the year.]

7 Cromwell Place, White Plains, NY, USA Sept. 4, 1945

Beloved Sigurd,

It was so kind of dear Mrs Schousboe[1] to write me, but Ella & I are deeply grieved to hear that you have been feeling so weak.[2] We hope keenly that you will quickly regain your strength. Conditions in all countries will gradually improve & that will make it easier for all of us to feel stronger, happier & more hopeful.

Fancy, that my beloved friend Sigurd (who was quite a young man when mother & I first met him in 1899) is now 80. Well, it will not be

[1] Hermie Schousboe (b. *c.*1860), a Norwegian friend of Fornander, living in Oslo.
[2] Fornander was living in Nice, where he died before the year was out.

long before I am 80 also (if I live that long, which I certainly hope to)—not so long as the time between our re-meeting in Frankfort in 1923 & now (1945)! And our meeting in Frankfort might never have happened if dear Mrs Schousboe had not come to one of my concerts in Oslo (1922) & said to me: 'I come to give you greetings from a dear friend of yours—Sigurd Fornander', to which I answered 'He is the man above all others that I long to meet'. And I was right; you were the man I most *needed* to meet, in that hard time after mother's death. That was the greatest comfort my soul could know—those sweet daily meetings & talks with the beloved friend who, in my teens (age between 19 & 20) had brought the romance of Sweden into my life, whistling Vermlandsvisan,[1] talking of Visby,[2] & looking & behaving like the 9th century Swedish viking described in the beginning of VATNSDAELA SAGA,[3] which I had bought (Reclam-edition) & was fascinated by.

I have met great musicians, poets, painters, such as Grieg, Richard Strauss, Gabriel Faure, Debussy,[4] Ravel, Sargent, Rodin, Stefan Georg[e], Edgar Lee Masters, Norman Lindsay, who touched me thru their art & creative greatness. But the individuals who have charmed me AS MEN (as representatives of the nobility & purity of their race or type) have been very few: you, Mortimer Menpes the Australian painter (London, 1902–1908),[5] & Evald Tang Kristensen the Danish folklorist (1914–1929). To love a man or woman I MUST LOVE THE RACE THEY SPRING FROM, REPRESENT AND TYPIFY. You & Ella represent for me the nobility, the calm, the gentleness, the cleverness, the heroism, the purity, the epicurean quality of Sweden, & I love you as individuals & also as ambassadors of your race to Australia (as embodied in me). It is a deep feeling, to love millions of a beloved race *thru one person*, & that is what I have done in your case, sweet friend. To know you has been a vast & unfailing comfort to me ever since 1899 & always will be. That is why I was so thankful to Mrs Schousboe for bring[ing] you & me together again in 1923, after our

---

[1] Swedish song. Grainger set it as the second movement of his suite for cello and piano *La Scandinavie* (1902), and in 1903–4 arranged it for five-part chorus.

[2] On Gotland in the Baltic Sea.

[3] Icelandic saga, probably from the 13th-cent., telling the story of a chieftain who helps his own killer to escape.

[4] Grainger had met Debussy in London in 1907. He was disappointed, finding Debussy 'a little spitting wild animal'.

[5] (As *Who's Who* of 1936 records:) 'painter, etcher, raconteur, and rifle-shot; inartistically born in Australia'. He published many books of etchings and essays in the earliest years of the century, during which time he frequently met Grainger in London. He died in 1938.

long separation. What a misery these long separations are! In your & my case, 1902–1912, 1912–23, 1930–36, 1936–46.

Ella & I feel more rested, just now, than we have for some years. I have a heavy concert season ahead (beginning in 2 days from now). But it helps to think that next summer we may be able to go to Europe—when we hope to see you & Mrs Schousboe.

With a thousand loving wishes for your recovery from Ella & me,
Ever devotedly Yours

Percy.

P.S. Sept 25, 1945

Have just got Mrs Schousboe's second letter (Sept 14) telling us that you are feeling 'a little better'. How happy we are.   Percy.

50　　　　　　　　　*To Alfhild Sandby*

White Plains, NY, May 25, 1946

Dear Alfhild,

Ella & I have been away from home for months (concerts) & I then ask my secretary NOT to send on personal letters, as I dont have time to answer them when on tour. As soon as I got back (yesterday) I found your registered letter.

As you dont seem to understand my attitude to you (my lack of friendliness) it would seem better that I explain it. When I met you, around 1905, I was crazy about America, loving Stephen Foster's songs, Mark Twain's LIFE ON THE MISSISSIPPI, &, above all, Walt Whitman. I was crazy to know more about America & your Americanisms were then golden to me. I knew too little about USA myself to realize how ignorant were some of your remarks about America—as when I said I would like to have a Negro sweetheart & you warned me against it (as you al-warn against everything jolly) say-ing that the fate of the Poor White Trash in the South showed how dangerous it was to take up with Negroes—as if the P.W.T. (the purest of things white) had taken up with Negroes. I did not realise then, as I do now, that America was in the sway of a matria[r]chate civilisation—with the men poor prunes & the women school-marming & nurse-maiding them around. I say nothing against such tactics—if folk like it. But I DONT like it & will have nothing to do with it. I myself dont want to boss women round &, also, dont want to be bossed round myself by women. It is the American woman's tactics to salvation-army the men—to make them admit their weaknesses & then REFORM them. Thats what you pulled on me in 1905. I told you I had some sex-sickness & that gave you a good chance for you to urge negativeness on me—NOT doing something always being better than DOING something, according to the Anglosaxon. I myself had read a lot against self-help,[1] & many individuals had spoken against it very strongly to me. I am a very trusting person, willing to give ANYTHING a trial. So your negative sex advice seemed quite good to me at the time, & I thought it kindly meant—which no doubt it was. What I didnt know then (as I do now) is that it was just the ordinary school-marmy, nurse-girly advice that any American would give any man, at any time, in my plight—instead of saying, which is much more helpful: Fall in love, have a love affair; that will probably cure you (as it did, in my case). That you cold-shouldered me (because you preferred Herman) on the Jutland tour, I didnt take badly.[2] And you can see by my letters to you at that time (which you have quoted to me) how thankful I was to you. But when you came to London, annoying mother with idiotic statements (such as that YOU knew the REAL Percy—as if mother didnt!) & interfering between me & what I thought my duty to Grieg (not to tire him out by Herman & me playing the Cello Sonata to him)[3] I began to think differently & when you tried to upset & make unhappy my love affair[4] I reached the end of my friendship with you, tho not the end of my admiration for you as a swashbucklering type. But I am not one to forget or forgive anyone who interferes with me in my love affairs, nor am I one to want to sit in the same room with one who had ever said rude & silly things to my mother & dared to upset my worshipful attitude to a genius like Grieg. I do not blame you for any of these things. You have a right to be as you are. You have a perfect right to behave in a matriarchal manner (making little whipped dogs of your men, if they will let you do it) & to be as Sunday-Schooly & moralistic as you like. But I was not brought up to tolerate such

---

[1] = masturbation.

[2] The interpretation of this trip of 1905 had been a point of debate between Alfhild Sandby and Grainger since 1936.

[3] This issue over the playing of Grieg's Cello Sonata, Op. 36, in London in May 1906, had caused the first major rift between Grainger and Alfhild Sandby. In his following letter to Alfhild Sandby, of 13 June 1946, Grainger clarified the cause of his bitterness: 'I nevertheless resented *being forced* into playing a long work to a tired (practically dying) old man, *who had just played it himself* (with Becker).'

[4] With Karen Kellermann (née Holten).

things—my mother being a FREE SOUL who didnt boss anybody round (being wilful in an inspired way is not the same as being matriarchal & bossy) & who was ALWAYS on the side of sex, the sinner, & who never joined the man-hunting, witch-burning gang under any circumstances.

I do not agree with you about anything. As when you said, in 1939: 'I hope the English are not going to plunge the world into war on behalf of English capitalism'. I do not agree with you about bombed civilians. I like soldiers & I dislike most civilians & I am jolly glad that comparatively few soldiers were killed & that comparatively many middle class civilians 'got theirs'. In a former letter you spoke of translating into Danish the texts of my Kipling settings. Do you really think I would ever allow anyone who had been hostile to a sweetheart of mine figure on a program as a translator of the texts of my songs? Do you not realise that I am a LOYAL MAN, even if a sinful & selfish man? Years ago, you took hostile stands towards two of those I loved. You had a perfect right to do so, & I may have been in the wrong in many ways. But I am not one that can forget or forgive. You waste your time on me. Percy

51   *To Daniel Gregory Mason*

7 Cromwell Place, White Plains, NY Jan 24, 1947,

Dear Dan,

Back from San Francisco, I find your wonderful letter of Jan 17. I am most touched by what you quote from your Journals about the last vars in Fauré's Vars in C♯ minor,[1] as they have always been high favorites of mine.

Your proposal to let me have the original score of your SUITE AFTER ENGLISH FOLKSONGS[2] (with all the added value of priceless alterations!) made by the WPA[3] is bewilderingly glorious. OF COURSE, I WOULD ADORE TO HAVE IT, for the museum; but is it fair of me to allow you to make such a great sacrifice?

---

[1] For piano (1895).
[2] Op. 32, for orchestra (1933–4). Grainger appears not to have acquired this score.
[3] The Federal Music Project, set up and monitored between 1935 and 1941 by the Work Projects (Progress) Administration, was designed to offer support to composers and performers affected by the Depression.

Mr Joseph Fischer[1] wrote me about the PRELUDE & FUGUE,[2] making the very generous proposal you mention in your letter also: to let me have the material for $55.00, which is a price I would be *most willing* indeed to pay for that exquisite work.

All the same (if you will forgive my saying so) neither your unbelievable kind offer (to let me have the folksong suite MS score) nor Mr Joseph Fischer's offer (altho both offers present a perfect solution to my museum needs) go to the root of the matter, which is the question: HOW ARE WE TO KEEP OUR LARGER, GRANDER & MORE DIFFICULT-TO-PERFORM ENGLISH-SPEAKING MUSIC IN CIRCULATION, & AVAILABLE FOR THE FUTURE? What is the international spectacle that has unfolded before our eyes in the last 50 years: That Europe (with the exception of England, Switzerland, Scandinavia, Holland, & maybe a few other 'go-ahead' countries) have despaired of civilisation, progress & everything we have thought we were building on for 2000 years. In the publishing field, the undermining, decivilising despairing contribution of German & Austrian publishers around 1910, was the idea that modern works could not be sold & therefore should be rented. The effect of rental I tried out conclusively around 1912. Schott London wanted to try renting a piece of mine so I (heartily disbelieving in rental) let him put on rental my COLONIAL SONG for 2 voices & full orchestra (just engraved & published). In that year there were in Brighton over 60 orchestral performances of my MOCK MORRIS, &, during the same period, ONE REQUEST to see the score of my on-rental COLONIAL SONG (which perusal did not however lead to renting it!). From an ASCAP standpoint it is easy to see which is the right method. I have always (since that day) induced my London publishers to avoid renting my music (& to have every piece always FOR SALE) & what is the result? This year (after 50 per cent British income tax was deducted) I got about 350 pounds British Performing Right payment.

These days, in USA, Austria (Universal Edition), etc I am confronted with unwillingness on the part of publishers to print a second edition of orchestral works that have exhausted their first edition, but have SOLD SLOWLY. In such cases I realise that I, as a composer, have failed doubly: in the first place, I failed to write a work that 'caught on', secondly, have failed to push it properly. Nevertheless, I am unwilling to have the works sink into the oblivion of the rental

---

[1] Secretary of the music publisher Joseph Fischer. [2] Op. 37, for strings (1939).

library—especially as I now want to deposit free copies of the scores of such works in the leading music libraries & orchestral libraries of the world (Chicago Symphony Orchestra, Australian Broadcasting Commission, BBC in London, etc). So I asked Schirmers what it would cost me to finance the print of a new edition (the plates are there, of course), with myself taking (free) 100 or 150 complete sets (score & full parts) to distribute. And I find that it would only cost me about $1000 (thousand) dollars to reprint 'To a Nordic Princess' & Suite 'In a Nutshell'. So that is what I am intending to do.

I feel that we composers have emerged from the 'servants hall' status of Mozart to the capitalist status of Delius or Paderewski. We have been paid more or less well, all our lives, for the musical jobs we have done, & I feel very strongly that composers, as a class, should no longer go around wondering how they can earn a little more with their compositions, but should go round wondering how they can SPEND A LITTLE more of their capitalist-sized moneys ON MUSIC, especially on & for THEIR OWN MUSIC. In this connection I want to point out the difference between raw-material Anglosaxon composers & factory-life-typed composers, such as those of Germany, Austria, Italy, France, etc. In those latter countries the composers are not only incapable of writing melodies of their own, but they also have no folktunes of THEIR own to turn to. When 'Schwanda' Wienberger[1] came to America & wanted to ingratiate himself by writing an 'American' piece, he not only took the theme of Delius's 'Appalachia'[2] but also Delius's harmonies (when asked about it he said he thought that Delius's obviously modern harmonies were NEGRO FOLK-HARMONISATIONS!) to the same. When Ravel wants to write a real 'tune' (Bolero)[3] he has to borrow a Spanish tune, or at least to imitate a Spanish type of tune. On the other hand it is equally obvious that if a Jew like Gershwin is BORN in America (or in Britain, as in the case of Sullivan)[4] that he is able to WRITE TUNES OF HIS OWN.

In other words, we English-speaking composers have the advantage of owning MUSICAL RAW-MATERIALS, just as our countries own other sorts of raw-materials. As compared with our rich resources the non-Nordic composers (for it is obvious that Grieg & Sibelius are in the same raw-material state as ourselves) are more or less bankrupt.

---

[1] Jaromír Weinberger (1896–1967), Czech-American composer, best known for his opera *Shvanda the Bagpiper* (1927). He emigrated in the late 1930s.

[2] Variations on a plantation song, for orchestra and chorus (1896–1903).

[3] Ballet (1928).   [4] Arthur Sullivan (1842–1900), British composer of Irish–Italian ancestry.

One has only to hear recent works by Stravinsky, Shostakovitch, Schoenberg, etc, to see that this is so.

One has only to hear YOUR WORKS, on the other hand, to find oneself in the presence of pristine power, inventivity, human purity & high-heartedness, as well as THE CONTINUATION AT FULL POWER OF EUROPEAN MUSICAL CIVILISATION (in the sense that Gabriel Fauré represented the full continuation of symphonic culture, whereas Richard Strauss—writing at the same period, more or less—did not.)

What you are doing stands on a par (in my mind) with what Purcell was doing when he wrote his heavenly Fantasies for strings, & what John Jenkins was doing, as compared with the operatic nonsense generated in Italy & imitated in Germany & elsewhere at the same period.

Just as it always was clear-to-see that the exquisite Polyphonic composers (G. de Machaut, Claude le Jeune, Dunstable, Bedyngham, des Prez, A. de Cabezon, Adrian Willaert, Heinrich Finck, etc)[1] would 'come back', so it is equally clear-to-see that your rich, many-sided, full & cumulative (I mean: full of the accumulations of centuries of musical high culture) music will 'come back'—10 or 50 or 100 or 500 years from now! That is what I am wanting to build for, NOW. That is why I am not terribly keen on photostat—I am not sure that photostats will last 50 or 500 years! That is why I am keen on black-&-white prints made by a blue-printer from MSS written in India ink on transparent 'tracing' paper—because I think it will last (at any rate the 'negatives'—master copies—will) & because the copies can be made cheaply enough to be used for 'sales'.

I (as I said) am more than willing to pay $65. for the parts of your PRELUDE & FUGUE; but the orchestras & the 'trade' will not.

What is the use of your Folksong Suite being published at all IF NOT A SINGLE COPY OF THE SCORE is to be deposited anywhere in Australia (Australia is going to be a very important country, musically. They already pay more for music, per capita, than any country in the world)? A hundred years from now, what will have happened to those 8 copies of the score now at Schirmers? If such a work is not going to be put 'on sale' (I would have bought it at once, had it been on sale), then, at least, free (or otherwise donated) copies should be fed into all the leading music libraries in EVERY QUARTER OF THE GLOBE. If works like your Symphony, Folksong Suite, Prelude & Fugue cannot be bought, & are not planted in all important libraries, then they

---

[1] Grainger had made arrangements of works by all these composers.

cannot be said to be PUBLISHED at all. All that happens is that there has been some FLIRTATION with the idea of publishing.

In the case of the PRELUDE & FUGUE, for instance, the score IS on sale. Now what should happen (in my opinion) is that the composer (you) should pay to have the parts well written out by a copyist onto the transparent paper, then print (at your expense) several hundred complete sets of parts, donate them to libraries & orchestras & broadcasting libraries & feel secure against the future.

It is no use expecting the publisher to incur this expense. FOR WE COMPOSERS HAVE ALREADY FAILED OUR PUBLISHERS—by not devising means to perform & popularise our own works. We have earnt good money performing the music of foreign countries & writing books & lecturing about the music of foreign countries. Now let us apply our money to propaganda on behalf of our own music & the music of our own racial group. I wish we could have a talk on this!

Percy

52 *Round Letter*

May 21, 1947

To Aunty Margaret,[1] Cyril Scott, Roger Quilter, Balfour Gardiner, Elsa Bristow,[2] Karen [Kellermann], Herman Sandby, Victoria & Geo. Greenwood,[3] a.s.o. (in Blue-eyed-English).

Dear Ones,

The PG who writes to you today is a wholly other man than the one who wrote to you about tone-art matters some months ago—& for many years. For I have just passed a mile-stone in my tone-life: Francis Resta's forth-playment of my Hillsong I at West Point on April 20. Rocco Resta (Francis Resta's brother) was my band-leader in the army, at Fort Hamilton, 1917–1918—& I was VERY happy there with Rocco. Francis Resta (younger brother) came to Fort Hamilton before I left there to go & teach tone-art in the ARMY MUSIC TRAINING

---

[1] Née Hislop, second wife of Charles Edwin Aldridge, an elder brother of Rose Grainger.

[2] See Biographical Register.

[3] George Greenwood (1884–1952) was a banker and amateur pianist in Spokane, and later Seattle, Washington. Grainger came to know him and his wife in the early 1920s and kept up a regular contact for several decades. In Aug. 1928 they joined the Graingers on their honeymoon hiking trip to the Glacier National Park.

SCHOOL at Governors Island, & he soon came on to Gov. Isl. himself, having won an army scholarship. So we were at Gov. Island together for nearly a year.

Since then he became bandleader at United States Military Academy in West Point & has become one of the world's most graceful, skilful & polished band-bosses. He has that feeling of strict duty to the rights of the MUSIC ITSELF, & that sense that every sign & word on a page of tonery ((music)) means one-&-no-other thing, that stamps Italian tone-men as a race apart. He also has that bodily ease in time-beating that makes it so much easier for Italians to win at out-singledly hard tone-tasks. (If a Blue-eyed-race-y man wants to give the signs for the start of a loudening, 10-to-one his left hand will be somewhere high up, near his head, whence it is hard for him to raise it much further. An Italian time-beater, about to start a loudening-sign, will most likely find his left hand quite low somewhere—just where it should be for the job ahead.)

A year or so ago Francis Resta did my LINCOLNSHIRE POSY most wonderfully, steering his way thru the hard-to-beat 'Rufford Park Poachers'[1] with lazy ease. So I said to him: 'I guess you are about the only man who could time-beat Hillsong I'. But I said it more out of a sense of judgement of his powers than out of any hope that I would ever hear him do it. Then & there, he let me know that he would like to tackle it. (So I gave him the score & parts—printed by Universal-Edition, in Vienna, 1924.)

Why do some people, who owe one nothing (Francis Resta owes me nothing) want to do so much for one; while others (who may owe one a lot) want to do nothing at all for one? For it is the greatest gift in the world—to hand a tone-wright a flawless forth-play-ment of an almost un-forth-play-able work. Think what it means: Dragging a bunch of unwilling, unbelieving players day by day, for many days, thru a gruelling task they hate! Yet Francis Resta's kindliness to me, & his bow-the-knee mood to art, is so great that he can shoulder this burden without any loss of bide-willingness ((patience)), grace, ease or smoothness to his men.

Hillsong I was scored for Small flute, 6 oboes, 6 English horns, 6 bassoons & Double-bassoon in 1902 (some day I must try out that scoring, tho I fear it would prove much too sameish). Without ever hearing the as-first-was ((original)) scoring, I re-scored it in Frankfurt,

---

[1] The work's third movement, which involves changing metres, following the flexible rhythm of the original folksong.

1923 & tried it thru, there, in sundry rehearsals, sometimes time-beating it myself, sometimes getting Alexander Lippay[1] to time-beat it for me. I used the work in a tone-show ((concert)) only once, at my room-music tone-shows in New York in 1925. I got the mind-dent ((impression)) that neither Lippay (skilful time-beater tho he was!) nor I were ever able to carry thru the quickest-changing odd-lengthed ((irregular)) bar-changes (when they happened at high speeds) up to time, but that we let the tonery ((music)) drag because we lacked some boldness in forcing the pace & sticking iron-willed to the letter of the score. But Resta was not only able to carry his 24 single players (one player to each part) along at full speed (even in the hardest spots) but also to spell-bind them into playing with what seemed like utter free-dom, singingfulness & rich feeling-show-th ((expressiveness)).

It was a grief to me that none of my tone-wright friends (out-count-ing Delius) were able to be with me in Frankfurt in 1923, when I re-scored Hillsong I in its be-ended state & tried out freely it, 'The Warriors' & the tone-tool-some ((instrumental)) background of 'Marching Song of Democracy'. And I was sorry that those same dear friends (to whom I am bound by close ties of same-race-ness & time-mate-ery ((contemporaneousness))) could not be with me to hear Hillsong I done so wonderfully by Francis Resta at West Point. One's art—and one's happiness in one's art—is made much the poorer by never having the friends of one's youth on hand to pass judgement on the art-works of one's youth when they are forth-played. And I have such a bunch of stick-in-the-mud friends, as far as faring ((travelling)) goes. In an age when everybody else rushes around the world madly (which I think witless enough) my friends, alone, are not to be budged; not to hear MY tonery, at any rate.

What did I get out of this flawless forth-playment of Hillsong I, 45 years after it was mind-birthed? The most awful swell-headedness ((conceit)). It has left me with the feeling that I alone am right about everything & that it would be a waste of time (from now on) for me to doubt myself in any line any more. I feel that all the judgements that have been passed on me & my tone-works by great tone-wrights such as Delius & Balfour Gardiner are wholy misleading. For sample, about my use of harmonium in such works as Hillsong I, Delius said 'If you go on using that old harmonium as you are doing you will spoil all your beautiful music. It will end up sounding like that noise from the

---

[1] A conductor at the Frankfurt Opera House.

old Dom over there'. (Delius was living over-against the Frankfurt
Cathedral at the time & hated the sounds from its organ that were
wafted over to him all day long). And Balfour said, on the same
thought-theme: 'The harmonium is such an intermittent instrument'. It
is the least gap-typed tone-tool in the world, if it is played half-wise
well—as it was at West Point. The frail sounds in Hillsong I, got by a
very few single tone-tools being thinly back-grounded by the harmonium (so altogether othery than the sound of a single tone-strand being
backgrounded by 7-part harmony on 7 other tone-tools!), are among
the most winning strokes of the score. Viewing the piece as a whole, I
feel that the new tone-wain ((sound-vehicle)) that I birthed in scoring
such works as Hillsong I for 23 single tone-tools (instead of scoring it
for smaller room-music, or for the full wind-&-string-band ((orchestra)))
was a deed of meaningfulness as great as Wagner's in birthing his own
great wind-&-string-band. Nowhere is the self-hood of scoring more
felt than in the whole-band ((tutti)) stretches, which always sound like
real room-music, & never for a moment like a wind-&-string-band or a
wind-band! By 'real room-music sound' I mean something much
harsher & keener than the wontsome wind-&-string-band sounds. It is
such a boon to get away from the everlasting sound of fiddles soaring
high, & low strings groaning low, while horns fill up the gap with a
he-high-typed ((tenor-like)) heroicness—a lovely enough sound-wont,
but long since worked to death. And it is a boon to get away from the
'arm-louts-geruch' ((proletarian odour)) of string 4-somes & other poor-
hood-stricken ((poverty-stricken)) sound-wains ((tonal vehicles)). In the
wont-some wind-&-string-band ((orchestra)) the weight of the brass
lends a somewhat bursting or pomp-fain ((pompous)) how-th ((quality))
to almost anything one writes for it. And the reeds sound far-of[f] &
frail because they are so cruelly out-weighted by the strings & brass.
Thank goodness, all these tiresome flaws of wantsome scoring (tiresome in themselves & doubly tiresome because they have been worked
to death for far too long) are unheard in the Hillsong scoring. The
reeds always sound big & starred. And the big time-spots ((moments))
of strength & up-pile-ment sound fierce rather than rough, snarling
rather than blaring. And the drop from the full-group sounds to the
few-tone-tool sounds (backgrounded by harmonium) covers a far
greater range of change-shock ((contrast)) than that heard in wont-
some scoring.

But of course I care far more for the tone-thoughts themselves (in
such a work) than for the tone-dress they clothe themselves in. My

greatest joy lay in seeing how MOURNFUL the moods of the work are. It is shrouded in a large-size mournfulness—not mere wistfulness; it is sturdier than that. But never for a time-spot does the tonery seem to voice the mood 'Gods in his heaven; alls right with the world'. Never (one feels) can the tone-wright be stopped in his wailing! And I deem this to be timely & seemly; in an age that has murdered so many young men & betrayed so many old folk there is no place for mirth, coyness, sprightliness, pomp-fain-th—or even dreaminess. I am glad to find that in 1901–2 I was fore-boding the worst. I do not have to guilt-judge myself for having been hopeful or life-fond. For me, all tone-art might well begin and end with mourning for the dead—not merely dead men, but dead (wasted in wood-pulp-trees, dead folk-wonts, dead stead-speeches ((dialects)), dead (forgotten) feelings).

As I listened to this 18-minutes long Hillsong I, I understood what I had meant when I said to Jacques Blanche,[1] when he showed me Debussy's Pelleas & Melisande (the first Debussy I had heard): 'That is very lovely. But its only one of the trees in my wood'. Side-matched with this Hillsong the tone-works of that time-stretch were either smart-alec-y like R. Strauss, or back-water-mooded like Debussy, or stick-in-the-mud like Sibelius,[2] or 'dated' in some way or other. But Hillsong I is grand, group-wholesome ((normal)), time-less, long-breathed & fury-filled (is not the lack of fury one of the sorriest show-ings of our age—that is, our age when forth-shown without over-soul-ship?) as the hills themselves (or any other branch of the all-th ((nature))) are.

I look upon the whole business very selflessly (as I have had little but beshamement & wretchedness out of my art-life I am not tempted to view any of it with pride or back-self-pat-ment) & I cannot help ask-ing myself: What is wrong with me & my friends that we have allowed half a hundred years to slip by without forth-playments of this work of first class over-soul-ship ((genius))? What ailed me to be so meek about myself, when I had such a masterpiece up my sleeve? And what ailed my friends to be so meek, or speechless on my behalf? Here (if I am not utterly self-drunk & swelled-headed in my now-y judgement upon this piece) is one of the tone-world's greatest masterpieces—the match of the Mat[t]hew Passion, Delius's Mass of Life, Wagner's Ring. And

---

[1] (1861–1942), French artist and amateur musician who had introduced Grainger to Debussy's music in 1902.

[2] In a letter to Victoria Greenwood of 24 Mar. 1938 Grainger had accused Sibelius of 'daring along safe lines' through his sticking to the symphonic form: 'He has what all true middleclass folk have: an inborn, positively atavistic, instinct for what leads to success.'

during the 45 years since its mind-birth no word (as far as I know) has been raised for or against it by friend or foe. It has been drowned in utter speechlessness. All I can say is: That a mother-country who could not cough up pride in such a Colonial as I, a young country like Australia who could not rejoice in its first great tone-wright, a main-land ((continent)) of tone-skill that could not welcome such a great on-add-ment to its soul-stock-in-trade—all have guilt-earned ((deserved)) all the bad luck that has hit them. Are my friends (also, the world's time-beaters) UNABLE TO READ SCORE to such lengths that they, face to face with the score of such a work, did not real-see what they were up against—or real-seeing it, felt no stir of manhood to do any-thing about it? It seems funny nowadays, that there were heaps of tone-men in France who had seen the score of Franck's Symphony,[1] during F's life-time, & THOUGHT IT SEEMLY to do nothing about it? In the years-to-come its going to seem still funnier that none of my tone friends felt stirred to put thought, or money, or ANGER into the task of getting this masterpiece heard & judged. And it will seem funny, too, that I have put so much time, money & keenness into the task of getting my friends' works played & heard AND HAVE NEVER ONCE BESTIRRED MYSELF TO GET HILLSONG I PLAYED? I was scared of it (as all mean Nordics are scared to do anything but hide & un-speak)! And it took gentle, graceful Resta, with his art-drenched Italian art-fondness & at-home-in-art-ness to un-scare the cowardly Blue-eyed-race-man in me. Shame on us all.

But Hillsong I was not the only up-heartenment that came my way in April–May. At West Point I tried thru my new Kipling setting 'The Only Son'[2] & it seemed all right. On the other hand my old (1905) 'Bold William Taylor' setting (the tone-thoughts of which I am so far of[f]), which I also tried again in West Point, proved, as of yore, hope-thwarting in its scoring. In Detroit, on May 1, a few voices got together & sang thru my 'The Wraith of Odin' (1903), 'The 3 Ravens' (1904) & 'The Sea-wife' (1905), none of which I had heard before. All were all right. But the abacktaking one was 'The Wraith' (which Balfour liked so much in the old days that he himself copied out the full score) which I feared would prove unsingable—for the most part. But these young singers just read it at sight—almost flawlessly. And the sound of some of it (outsingledly the verse 'Then from his lips in music rolled the Havamal of Odin old') stirred me greatly. So the teachment

[1] In D minor (1886–8).   [2] The final Kipling setting, composed in 1945–7.

213

of all these rehearsals is the same: that the old stuff is all right & the older the better. So a great calm has come over me. I shall now give up testing things out so carefully—I shall give up being a kind of tea-taster, or wine-taster, in tones. I shall go back to the joy of my teen-years, which was: trusting to my mind-picture-ment of tones, trusting to my 'inner ear'—the only thing in tone-life I really care about.

Love to all, Percy

53   *To Bernard Heinze*

[As Grainger started to reduce his American concert commitments he pondered where he might best live in old age. He disliked many aspects of his White Plains home, which he found cold and draughty, and lashed out against the increasing commercialization of American society. He thought nostalgically of returning to Australia, living in one of his beloved Scandinavian countries or even searching for paradise in the South Pacific, but never did manage to sever his American connections. When the possibility of his occupying the chair in music in his mother's hometown of Adelaide was raised in 1947, he dismissed the idea as professionally, but also personally, impractical. Later letters reveal his growing bitterness against the country which, he felt, appreciated little of its son's talents or contribution to music.]

Dec 3, 1947

My dear Bernard,

It was so lovely to get your heart-warming letter—so characteristically well-wishing & enthusiastic—& to have the sweet greetings from yr dear ones.

Of course, we were awfully sorry not to see you, when you were in Canada. But we guessed that you had no free time. You made a TREMENDOUS impression in Canada. The other day Mr Wodson[1] (the clever North-English music critic of the Toronto 'Eve Telegram') said to me: 'We never knew what our Toronto Symphony Orchestra could do until your Australian genius Bernard Heinze came along. He certainly breathed the breath of life into them!'

In wanting me to consider the Elder Chair of Music in the University of Adelaide you certainly show a touching belief in my

---

[1] Henry Wodson (1874–1952), critic for over thirty years for the *Toronto Evening Telegram*.

powers—a belief for which I am deeply grateful.[1] If I were 40 years younger, & not so crushed by defeat in every branch of music I have essayed, I am sure that I would have welcomed such a chance to put my artistic aims to the test in such a noble frame-work as the University of Adelaide, & in my darling mother's birth-place. But alas! I am wholly worn out & good for nothing. I have pains all over me; my throat feels swollen, as if I had a cancer in it; my guts feel as if I had cancer in them too. And I will probably die very soon. I have been a fool & shown poor judgement in my life & career. I accumulated too many dependants, & as a result I have kept on with my pianistic career too long for my strength—which was extremely silly, in every way, as I have long earned much more on my compositions than on my concert work—tho I must confess that I have earned FAR MORE THAN I DESERVE at both.

But even if I were a giant of health & strength I could not bring myself to become the official music head of an educational institution, in the pres[ent] condition of music, & in my own present condition of disappointment, defeat & hopelessness. It may be that I am innately UNMUSICAL, & therefore cannot understand the current excitement about music, all the world over. To me it seems sheer nonsense—seeing that only the world's worst music is heard & liked, & that the only music that is respected is that which expresses the very qualities & beliefs they, our countries, go to extravagant expense to wage war against—the qualities of militarism, violence, arbitrariness, anti-individual-ism & demagogy. Even while the war is on, our publics divide their interest between the militaristic & pedantic music of Germany & the militaristic & pedantic music of Russia—the country they were fighting & the country they were getting ready to hate & oppose. As soon as a country is singled out for especial dislike & disapproval, in our countries, it is the signal for our musical publics & institutions to go crazy over the music of that country. Music, it would seem, is our approved method of 'communicating with the enemy'. That may be all right. It may be a healthy vent. But I'm too stupid to see the fun, or use, of it.

I'm not suggesting that all Russian & German music is pedantic & militaristic. Heinrich Finck[2] & Ludwig Senffl[3] seemed to me to write adorable Christian music, & Balakirev's 'Tamara'[4] seems to me more

[1] Eugene Goossens, recently appointed the director of the State Conservatorium of Music in Sydney, had also, in Oct. 1947, sounded Grainger out for this position, which had fallen vacant upon the death of E. Harold Davies (1867–1947), the professor since 1919.

[2] (1444/5–1527), German.   [3] (1486–1543), Swiss-German composer.

[4] Symphonic poem, completed in 1882, by the Russian Mily Balakirev (1837–1910).

than hear-worthy. But the spiritual (non-pedantic, non-selfassertive, non-authoritative, non-militaristic) music of Germany & Russia is just as little wanted as similar music in our (or 'friendly') countries.

My natural instinct is to consider music a not very important branch of human endeavor. But I could get enthusiastic about music if it were allowed to do any of the following 3 jobs:

(1) EXPOUND ADEQUATELY THE CHRISTIAN SPIRIT OF WEST-ERN-EUROPEAN CULTURE. I am not a Christian myself, & feel rather hostile to the whole gamut of Christian thought & feeling. I like the art & customs of almost all races & peoples until they come under Christian influence. From that moment on they are 'spoilt' for me. So when I say that the pre-reformation music of the Catholic Church seems to me the highest flight of music so far, I am speaking not from prejudice but out of criticalness—as far as I am capable of it. In spite of being a non-Christian, I am willing to admit that perhaps Christianity still has some message for mankind (perhaps more than ever before) &, if so, that there is no more perfect medium of Christian expression than music—with its demo-cratic equality & freedom of part-writing, its 'compassionate' part-writing (as in C. Franck) & its highly emotional & sympathetic harmonies. 700 years of the most exquisitely spiritual Catholic music exists, before the reformation—producing great creative giants in many countries (15th century in England, Dufay & des Prez in Burgundy, Dunstable, in England, Adrian Willaert in Holland, Antonio de Cabezon in Spain, Heinrich Finck in Germany, and so on) and everywhere music of the most flawless euphony, complexity & subtlety. Added to this is the glorious modern Christian music of France & Belgium—Gabriel Faure, Franck, etc. With the exception of Franck (to whom only a very GRUDGING recognition is granted, see article on him in last Grove!)[1] this vast world of Catholic Christian music (in volume, as in quality, vastly over-topping the meagre & spiritually low musical achievements of the Protestant countries & era) goes still unheard. And I am sure that nothing I can do will alter this. The purpose of protestantism (to be able to make war to their heart's content, WITHOUT TOO MUCH INTER-

[1] The article on Franck in the fourth (1940) edn. of *Grove's Dictionary*, by Harvey Grace, con-tained such statements as: 'One cannot avoid the conclusion that, lofty as his ideals were, Franck was subject to some strange lapses of taste. His high opinion of a good deal of public contempo-rary music; the odd mixture of triviality and devotion in his composition for the Church; the occasional touch of banality that disfigures even such a work as "Les Béatitudes"; these and other signs indicate a too-accommodating standard.' (ii. 297.)

FERENCE FROM THE CATHOLIC CHURCH) goes on apace, & no branch of art is a more willing slave to this protestant militarism & brutalisation of mankind than music AS IT IS PRACTISED TODAY.

(2) TO DEVELOP A WORLD-WIDE UNDERSTANDING BETWEEN ALL PEOPLES & CULTURES. This could easily be done thru music—if the 'White man' wished it so—since we are in possession of the most marvelous records of the most soul-satisfying music from the depths of Africa, from the South Seas, as well as from the great musical civilisations of Asia (Java, Siam, Bali, China, Corea, Japan, Persia, Turkey, India, etc). Being brought up on the conventional classics (as I have been), & being still very much in love with them—as I also am with all the developments of modernism & popular music—I am not one of those who has gone 'native' to the disadvantage of his Europeanism. And when I say that the musics of the South Seas, Africa & Asia are fully the equal of the best that Europe has produced it is no idle or thoughtless word. The worthwhileness of all races & all cultures is proved by all the world's music, & to delay needlessly a drenching of ourselves in all this glorious 'exotic' music is simply (in my opinion) to criminally postpone the dawn of inter-racial worldwide understanding & brotherhood. But what do you think would happen if I started making a knowledge of exotic musics obligatory in the Elder Con? Our people DO NOT WANT peace & world-wide understanding. And why should it be forced upon them by me, or anyone else?

(3) MUSIC AS A DEMONIACAL INFLUENCE, increasing the brutishness, violence, lustfulness & selfishness of mankind. I can see great potential value in such a sway, exerted by music. But I also understand that it would be foolish to propose such a program at present.

I do not think I am prejudiced against any of the forces of life, be they good or evil. I am (if I am anything) a nature-worshipper, & I am willing to follow nature into any depths of evil or heights of good. But I could not sit in the Elder Conservatorium, twiddling my thumbs while listening to MORE SOLOISM (when I am convinced the world is ill thru lack of more get-together-ness), more CONCERTOS (when I am convinced that music is dying of lack of large chamber-music), MORE TECHNIC (when I am convinced that what we need is more musicality). Nor would I like to sit in Adelaide, TRYING TO FORCE MY MUSICAL VIEWS ON AN UNWILLING COMMUNITY, & making all my colleagues distressed & unhappy. Unluckily, I do not have the gift of

217

PERSUASION, nor the ability to make others like what I myself like. Nor do I have the ability to get good performances of the music I believe in—whether it is my own music or that of other composers. In spite of my long career (55 years) before the public, I have never learnt the art of showmanship, or the technic of PLEASING. Curiously enough, I do have the gift of FAME: audiences want to go to hear or see me & all sorts of misguided conductors & musical societies are silly enough to let me try my hand on their forces. But always with the same result: mutual disappointment, ineffectuality, disgust. If I were misguided enough to take the Elder chair, or if I were foolish enough to try & put my music, musical opinions & feelings before the Australian musical public IN ANY FORM, it would simply leave a very bad taste in the Australian musical mouth & heighten my own distress & sense of artistic guilt. The fact has to be faced that I am merely (in spite of my long association with the public) an IMAGINATIVE & EXPERIMENTAL MUSICIAN, not a practical one. The strength of my imaginative side was proved to me about half a year ago, when Francis Resta (at West Point) performed my first HILLSONG (24 solo winds & strings) with a skill & perfection that I never would have deemed possible. I realised (to my own amazement) that all the most subtle gradations in my scoring (& scoring of such an untried & unpredictable kind) was utterly right (to MY ears, I mean) & that the reason why I am never able to achieve satisfaction if I meddle in any way in a performance is because of some human inability to adjust myself to the problems of practical performance. All this, of course, doesnt mean that I will always be sensible enough, in Australia or elsewhere, to keep my clumsy hands off practical musical tasks. But I hope I will never go so far, in my conceit, as to take on a major job (such as the Elder one you so very kindly ask me about), to my own & the public's mortification.

Have you thought of the possibility of asking such a man as H. BALFOUR GARDINER (Fontmell Hill, Iwerne Minster, Blandford, Dorset, England) for the Elder post? As you probably know, he is a superb practical musician & most punctilious organiser—punctual, precise, highly responsible. His knowledge of music is vast, his personality generous & constructive. In many ways he has been the good angel of British music—the comforter of Delius, the supporter of Holst, the financier of the London Philharmonic & the personal 'good fairy' of all good composers in need of a holiday or help. I have a feeling that he might possibly relish a change from England, where he has been cooped up during the war years. In spite of being a true composer (a man of imagination) he has a grasp on practical life, possesses fearless downrightness as well as a subtle ability to meet things & people half way. I am sure he would be a tower of musical strength in Adelaide.[1]

Thank goodness, I am retiring from concert life at the end of April, 1948. I have masses of finished MSS to publish, & masses of unfinished ones to complete. As soon as possible after my retirement Ella & I plan to come to Melbourne in order to arrange the exhibits of the museum, so it can be opened to the public. However, it may be needful to take one more trip to England (to collect MSS & acquire other exhibits) before we come to Melbourne. But we firmly intend to reach Melbourne within 1 or 2 years from now.[2] I feel deeply beholden to the University of Melbourne for having respected the privacy & unfinished state of my museum, all these years. So I am deeply anxious to put the Grainger Museum in open-able shape JUST AS SOON AS I CAN, with the hope of justifying that confidence generously placed in me by you & the University.

Ella & I are longing to see you & yr dear ones, & to hear yr glorious music-making, as soon as possible. In the mean time, we send you all our fond love & thank you most heartily for your truly friendly trust in my musicality.

Yours ever admiringly
Percy

54   *To Edgar Lee Masters*

7 Cromwell Place, White Plains, NY, March 28, 1948

Beloved and revered Edgar Lee Masters,

For several months (as I sat in trains, etc) I have been wanting to write to you & wondered what address to write to. And now Mrs Stanley R. Greene of Larchmont, NY got in touch with me, bearing the welcome message that you had been kind enough to want to know how Ella & I were faring. She also said that you had been in a nursing home (which grieves us very much, to know that you have been ill), but she thought you were returning to Ogantz, or already had done so.

---

[1] The Elder Chair was offered to the Melbourne musician John Bishop (1903–64), who remained in the position until his death.

[2] Grainger only managed to visit Australia once more, for nine months in 1955–6.

I am wondering whether it will not be possible for me to look in upon you in Ogantz, some time in the near future, if one of my still remaining concerts should take me near there, which it well might. There is nothing that would rejoice Ella & me more than to have a nice talk with you & your dear wife—something we have been longing for during all the war years. Please give our very warmest greetings to her.

We think & talk so often of you & yours—of your personal kindliness & charm, as well as of your transcending genius, about which latter I never cease to wonder, & at my good fortune at having been lucky enough to have come in contact with such a very great man as yourself & to be able to think of him as my friend.[1] The friendships we form thru art with men we never meet (Bach, Guillaume de Machaut, Wagner, Goethe, Walt Whitman, the writers of the Icelandic sagas) are good enough. But it is an added magic to have met, in you, one of these soul-giants of mankind, to have known him as a living man & to love him. As I passed thru Chicago 3 days ago I thought of what you had written about 'under bridges of iron' etc, & how you have made Chicago (as well as Missouri, Sangamon,[2] Spoon River[3] & so many other hallowed stretches of country) live for us. I think continually of such poems as the Desplain[e]s Forest.[4] These are the sounds out of the soul of Sorrow,[5] Starved Rock, many in The Great Valley,[6] the mind-shattering stories in Eleanor Murray,[7] & what they have meant to me in my life, & what comfort I got at a very desperate time of my life reading 'Children of the Market Place'[8]—& what such works as these (& also the better known ones such as Spoon River, To Silence,[9] etc) will mean to thoughtful beings down the ages, standing out like rocks of understanding from a vast sea of muddledness, forgottenness & meaninglessness; & it overwhelms me with the consciousness of the poverty-strickenness of all our lives that, knowing you, we still can have the luxury of seeing you so seldom, because the treadmill of

---

[1] The affection between the Graingers and Masters would appear to have been genuine. Writing in Feb. 1961 Masters's son Hardin Wallace Masters observed: 'it [Grainger's *Spoon River*] tickled my father mightily. First, because it was named after his immortal book, *Spoon River Anthology*, and, second, because Father was very fond of Grainger. They were good friends but saw little of each other until later years.' (*Edgar Lee Masters* (Rutherford: Fairleigh Dickinson University Press, 1978), 50.)

[2] 'The Sangamon River' was included in Masters's *Illinois Poems* (1941). He also wrote a vol. about the history of the river, published in 1942.

[3] Another river in Illinois, made famous in Masters's best-known volume *Spoon River Anthology* (1915).

[4] Included in Masters's first book of poems of 1898.

[5] 'Sounds out of Sorrow', from Masters's *Starved Rock* (1919).   [6] Pub. 1916.

[7] 'Elenor Murray', from Masters's *Domesday Book* (1920).   [8] Pub. 1922.

[9] From his *Songs and Satires* (1916).

earning one's living is so unremitting—because of all things one has of time the least.

I will not burden you with my grumbling, except to say this, that I have found earning my living (& that of several others, of course) almost insuperably hard, & particularly so during this last war. I played at about 170 camps, hospitals, etc, all on top of my usual concerts, & I must say the travelling in the trains & all the rest of it was a real nightmare. Luckily it is all over now, as I am retiring from 'commercial' concert life this May, when we will try to live on what savings we have & on the royalties from my music. In other words, at the age of 66 I will be starting in on my serious work as a composer. A little late, but I shall try to make the most of it. My darling Ella's health seems very good, I am thankful to say. My own health did not seem too good for the last year & a half, but a few weeks ago it suddenly got well & maybe it will stay so. (If I hadnt been feeling so feeble & overwhelmed with the last lap of my money-earning tasks I would have ferreted out your address somehow & written to you ere this some of the thoughts about you that I am so continually thinking.)

With the most affectionate greetings to you both from Ella & me & hoping, more than I can say, that we may have a glimpse of you both soon (please ask someone to let us know if you are back at Ogantz).

Yours ever in unspeakable admiration
Percy

55   *To Ralph Vaughan Williams*

[Grainger's interest in 'Blue-eyed' English had led him to hypothesize about the connection between eye-colour and genius. Although he never went as far as to suggest that one was a precondition for the other, he did observe that blue eyes predominated among his generation of British composers (although not conductors or performers). In the late 1940s he set about collecting colour photographs of British composers' eyes for permanent exhibition in his Museum.]

C/O Brigadier Robert C. Bristow,[1] 'Lilla Vrån',
Seaville Drive, | Pevensey Bay, Sussex | Oct 31, 1948
Dear Sir Ralph,

My wife and I have been in England for a month or so, hearing a great mass of beautiful and significant music—most of it for the first

---

[1] See Biographical Register.

time. I must say that I think the choice of music heard today in Britain—whether on the air or 'in the flesh'—is thoroly satisfying.

But the greatest of all our impressions has been in hearing a wider range of your music than ever before. The works heard, some in concert and some broadcast, include: The Wasps, 4th, 5th and 6th Symphonies, Job, Serenade to Music, Greensleeves, A Sea Symphony, An Acre of Land, Ca' the Yowes, On Wenlock Edge.

While all the works heard are perfections of one kind and another, and all witness to the transcendental scope of your genius and humanity, it has been the 4th, 5th and 6th symphonies that have thrilled me the most, and, I must say, OVERWHELMED ME. It is a long time since I was so overwhelmed. It seems to me I was very much overwhelmed when I heard Bach, as a boy of 10 in Australia. And again when I heard the larger works of Bach (Passions, etc), and Wagner and Brahms in Frankfort (around 1896). After that I heard many new geniuses who delighted me—Debussy, Ravel, Albeniz, Faure, Skryabin, Arthur Fickenscher, Arnold Schoenberg, Stravinsky, Elgar, Holst, etc—but I cannot say I felt overwhelmed by them; perhaps by the 3 last Chorals of Cesar Franck.

In my case, I think it is a combination of an impression of the forces of nature with the expression of the feelings of man that awakens that sense of overwhelming awe, rapture and immanence that I feel in Bach, Wagner, Brahms and in your music. The first time I felt it very strongly was in your Pastoral Symphony,[1] which did not seem to me (as so many nature-poems do) a mere looking-on (almost 'touristically') at nature, but as if the curving, twining, evoluting stirs and urges of nature itself were speaking thru the music. This quality of nature itself speaking (or being tallied) I feel again in your Sixth Symphony,[2] only much more so; for now (in the 6th) it sounds not only as if the forces and stirs of our own globe were speaking musically, but as if the stars of space, the voices of the spheres were singing to us. The 6th Symphony seemed to me a paragon of lyrical beauty and angelic moods. But it is to the 4th Symphony[3] that I most naturally give myself—no doubt because of my personal experiences in my teens in Germany, when I was not only terrified by the hostility of the German mind to our English-speaking peoples, but also unable to refute their claims to superiority over us and their belittleing of us as musically

[1] No. 3, composed in 1916–21.
[2] In E minor, composed in 1944–7, sometimes called his 'war symphony'.
[3] In F minor, composed in 1931–5.

[p]ale, small-sized and amateurish—for at that time I had never been to England, being in Germany from my 12th to my 18th year (1895–1901). When I did come to England I did sense a lack of grasp and drasticness in the methods of such English music as I met. If at that time I could have heard your 4th Symphony all my distress would have faded away, for what I hear in that work is the MASTERY OF EVIL BY THE BRITISH MIND. The British mind (itself so mild and dreamy) has been able to bring itself to UNDERSTAND, and therefore master, forces of evil (or shall we say, just urgency?) so foreign to its original self. This mastery is not only human, philosophical, imaginative; it is especially manifest in the MUSICAL MASTERY. I ask myself: Is there in Bach, Wagner, Brahms, C. Franck a musical mastery (in form, in characterisation, in orchestration) comparable to that in your 4th Symphony? And I can only answer that there is not. That work seems to me the 'farthest north'[1] in musical technic—the technic of expressiveness (not merely that of display). The joy of listening to your 4th Symphony—the joy of witnessing the SUPREMACY of the British soul and mind in music—is for me a transcending experience. I dare say I would get no less a thrill from the 6th Symphony if I could hear it in a hall, as I did the 4th under Sir Adrian Boult[2] (whereas the 6th I only heard over the air, from Edinburgh). As it is, had I not heard the 4th, I would have said of the 6th that it is the most lovely and super-human cosmic music I have ever heard. It is a marvel that you, who have written such a mass of gloriously-mooded and exquisite music all your life, have in your old age intensified and deepened your powers to such an extent that, to many of us, your latest works seem your very greatest and loveliest! It is an exhibition of what TRUE GREAT-NESS is like.

My wife and I are going to be in London from Nov 8th to Nov 22, staying at Hotel Regina, 110 Gloucester Road, London, SW7 (WESTERN 5151). We wonder if you will happen to be in London during that time and whether you would have time to take lunch or dinner with us some day—say at the Hyde Park Hotel Grill Room, or at Bailey's Hotel, opposite Gloucester Road Underground—or anywhere

[1] As explained in a letter of 10 Nov. 1910 to his mother (Dreyfus (ed.), *The Farthest North of Humanness*, 387–8), he looked upon Iceland as a place of 'whims, forlorn hopes, sudden impatiences, lightning reactions. Useless, purposeless, gainless, barren, nearly all. But tasting sweet to the future. Full of personal dialectic fragrance after a 1000 years.' By contrast, 'the rewards of English deeds lie always largely in the present, & the future finds their glory hopelessly mortgaged to passing gains that were not united in the everlasting currency.'
[2] (1889–1983), at this time conductor of the BBC Symphony Orchestra.

else more convenient to you? It would be such a joy to us if you could.

And there is another great favor I would like to ask of you, if you could grant it. For my museum in Melbourne I want to have color photographs of those composers of our era that I revere most. I have made arrangements with Tunbridge, Ltd., Photographers, Axtell House, Warwick Street, Regent Street, W1 (GERrard 7422) to take such color photographs for my museum. I feel that the luminousness (the absence of blackness) of the color photograph is a very valuable gain over the black-and-white photo and I am anxious to have the appearance of our greatest composers preserved in this better way, if I can.

Would you permit Tunbridges to take such a photo for me?[1] If you would, they will accommodate you at any time, if you will give them a day's notice. (I would be glad to take you there, so you have no bother finding the place.) Or if it should be inconvenient to you to be photographed in London, Tunbridges would send a man to Dorking, or anywhere else, if you would prefer that.

I shall be at the above Pevensey Bay address until Nov 7th.

Hoping very much that my wife and I may have the pleasure of seeing you before we leave England, and thanking you for all the joys your music has given us this time (the pinnacle of musical experiences).

Yours ever
        Percy Grainger

56   *To John Ireland*

Dec. 8, 1948.

My dear John Ireland,

It was a great disappointment to both Ella & me that we did not have the pleasure of seeing you again before leaving England. But the last few days were very hectic ones, & in addition, I was feeling rather ill—& still am. It was very kindly and friendly of you to write as you did about the colour-photograph question (that you would not utterly refuse my request, in spite of the fact that you have a violent antipathy to being photographed). Let me explain my purpose in trying to supply my museum with colour-photographs showing the colour of the eyes of the greatest British composers. Personally, I have no preference

---

[1] See plate No. 22.

for the music of blue-eyed composers. I *do* think that the music of blue-eyed composers (such as Elgar, Brahms, Wagner, R. Strauss) is larger & grander in conception than the music of any dark-eyed composer I know; thus: blue-eyed Tchaikovsky is grander than his fellow-Russian dark-eyed Balakirev & blue-eyed Vincent d'Indy[1] is grander & longer than dark-eyed Gabriel Faure. But it just happens that I, personally, like Balakirev better than Tchaikovsky & Faure better than V. d'Indy. Faure, Debussy & Mascagni (the Siciliano from Cavaleria)[2] seem *closer* to me than the music of most blue-eyed composers, just as Greek statues & vase-paintings feel closer to me than Rodin (blue-eyed) sculpture or blue-eyed Dutch painters, & dark-eyed Paul Gaug[u]in feels closer to me than blue-eyed van Gogh. But in spite of my seeming preference for dark-eyed art I consider *the truth* in these matters very interesting & important, & I think the baffling inconsistency of the existing facts *worthy of study*, consideration & comment.

Let us begin by accepting the fact that dark eyed & blue eyed are more or less equally balanced (50% dark, 50% light) in the 3 countries England, France & Germany. Isn't it strange, then, that practically all great German composers have been blue (or light) eyed, that practically ALL great British composers (living or recently living), such as Elgar, Parry,[3] Delius, yrself, C. Scott, Balfour Gardiner, Roger Quilter, Bax, Hezeltyne,[4] V. Williams, have blue or light eyes, while so many of great French composers (Debussy, Ravel, Faure, etc.) have had dark eyes. Isn't it strange that several leading British conductors (Beecham, Henry Wood, Malcolm Sargent, etc.)[5] have dark eyes, & that British orchestras are full of dark eyed players, *yet a dark-eyed British* composer is practically non-existent (or am I wrong here?)? Isn't it strange that there are so many darkeyed Jews, yet that most great Jewish composers (Delius, Bizet, Rachmaninoff, Tchaikovsky, Stravinsky, Arnold Schönberg)[6] are blue or light eyed? Does it mean (for instance) that there are just as many darkeyed composers in England as in France, to begin with, but that the national mood in

---

[1] (1851–1931), French composer.

[2] The opera *Cavalleria rusticana* (1888) by Pietro Mascagni (1863–1945), Italian composer.

[3] Hubert Parry (1848–1918), English composer and director of the Royal College of Music from 1894 to 1918.

[4] = Philip Heseltine (Peter Warlock) (1894–1930), English composer and critic. Grainger's main contact with him was through their mutual friend Delius.

[5] Grainger had performed with, or had his works performed by, all three. He found Wood the most supportive.

[6] As previously, Grainger's assertions of 'Jewishness' are, in some of these cases, poorly founded.

England is blue-eyed (thereby favouring the blue-eyed ones amongst the budding composers), while in France the mood is darkeyed, whereby the darkeyed young talents get encouraged? I do not pretend to know the answer to any of these questions, nor have I any wish to see the answer go in any particular direction (I am so out of mood, & out of touch, with the human tide in Nordic countries, or the world in general, that I don't care which way things go, or what the facts are proved to be—as long as they *are* proved.)

Yet there are some things I *do* set my face against, such as deliberate falsifications & false propaganda by the pro-darkeyed. You probably know that series of coloured pictures put out in Vienna, or somewhere, where all the blue or light eyed wellknown classical composers (Verdi, Schubert, Brahms, Wagner, etc.) are shown as having brown eyes. It is partly to counteract such nonsense that I am planning this section in my museum, entitling *What coloured eyes do British Composers have?* I do not wish to unfold any theory (for I have none) or support any preference. I simply want to show physical proof of the actual facts re the eyes of the greatest British composers. I do admit that I am anxious to do what I can (in spite of my devotion to Grecian art & my special fondness for French music) to counteract unreasoning South-worship. I think it queer, stupid & unjust that all my English friends seem crazy about Italy, Spain & the Tyrol & don't wish to see Holland, Iceland, the Faeroes, & Scandinavia. I think it queer that any ½-baked ignoramus will tell one that it is advisable to learn Latin & Greek in order to understand the classic roots in English words, & that no-one advocates a study of Anglosaxon & Icelandic in order to better understand the Germanic roots in English words.

One of the many things that bewitches me in your music is that the Northern stirs (Celtic, British, Germanic) are so powerful in your sturdy, heroic, yet mystic music—whether in *Island Spell, Forgotten Rite, These things shall be.*[1]

So you can imagine how frustrated & defrauded I would feel if the blue-eyes that have written your extraordinarily blue-eyed music should be missing from the collection in my museum! I do not ask you to go to Tunbridge's *against your own wish.* But I would be hilarious with delight & thankfulness if you could sometime (out of regard for

---

[1] Respectively: 'The Island Spell' in Ireland's *Decorations* (1913), for piano; *The Forgotten Rite*, prelude for orchestra (1913); *These things shall be*, for male voice soloist, chorus, and orchestra (1936–7).

my *special need*) find yourself able to face Tunbridge without dismay or dislike.[1]

With our warmest greetings & admiration,
Percy Grainger

57　　　　　　　　　　*To Arnold Bax*

Sweden, Jan 13, 1949

My dear Arnold,

Last night Ella & I went to see & hear 'Oliver Twist'[2] (now at another big movie house in Stockholm), Ella because she had not seen & heard it before (when I heard it here her boat from London was delayed by fog) & wanted to so much, & because I so very much wanted to hear your music again.

If anything, the music made an even greater impression on me this second time; in particular, it made a somewhat different impression, in that I noticed some things this time that I had missed before, & missed this time some points I had caught before. It is tremendously ORIGINAL as movie music; not only is the music original as music, but as a commentary on the action on the screen it strikes me as being quite unique. I would say it is the most PHILOSOPHICAL music I have ever heard to a movie; it is as if your music were offering a philosophical commentary on what happens. Nevertheless it is keenly dramatic & exciting, just from an action standpoint.

The sounds released by the piano alone, & by the piano together with other instruments (for instance, when Oliver is in bed with his first food & the nice old lady sits knitting in the sunlit room or something), are ENTRANCING. (By the way, have you heard that piece for piano, harpsichord, harp & strings by Martin, a Swiss composer? Delicious sonorities. I think it is called Concerto.)[3] There are many sounds in your Oliver Twist music that quite elude me—I have not the least idea what instruments produce them. And they are lovely. I think one place is as Sykes[4] & Oliver leave for the break-in & the girl is just rushing out to meet the benevolent old gentleman—there are

[1] Ireland did finally agree for his eyes to be photographed.
[2] Bax's film music and orchestral suite both date from 1948. He had first written film music during the Second World War.
[3] *Petite symphonie concertante* (1945) by Frank Martin (1890–1974).　　　[4] = Bill Sikes (a burglar).

some swirling, glissando-like, yet horn- or bell-like sounds there that make one's hair stand on end. I havent the faintest idea how you get them. The score is full of baffling (& therefore tail-twisting) sounds—something in the way you combine quite thin & transparent associations of instruments that sounds amazing. It seems to me you have shown great CRAFT & MASTERY in the technical use of sounds in this film, quite apart from the deeper & more creative side.

I was very happy to hear from you in December,[1] but amazed by what you had to say about being neglected by the BBC, etc. While I was in England I noted 11 performances of works of yours, of which 4 were long or important works (such as a symphony or other longer form). So I had the impression that you were being done a great deal.[2] But one thing I will say about the position of all English-speaking composers, whether we come from Britain, or USA or Australia: There is no wish, in any part of the English-speaking world, to treat our own music as a LASTING treasure, & as a thing over-riding momentary crazes & fashions. I heartily disagree with Bernard Shaw's saw: 'He who write[s] not for an age, but for all time, has his reward in being unreadable in all the ages'. This is just what the Anglosaxon wants—that everything in art shall be subjected to momentary gusts of taste, that works of art shall be rated like fashions in clothes; first novel & charming (or outrageous), then accepted & convention-hallowed for a short while, finally old-fashioned and scorned. It [is] in line with all the leading articles that every American paper wrote about Roosevelt: that no one is irreplaccable—which, however, did not prevent R. getting in each time, nor prevent Truman getting in as a continuer of R's policies.[3] Nor does the Walton-craze one year, nor the Britten-craze a few years later, prevent old Stanford from having many more performances than either Walton or Britten! When a music-loving Englishman is asked to name the world's greatest songs it seldom

---

[1] Replying to Grainger's request to photograph Bax's eyes, which Bax did eventually allow.

[2] In a letter to Herman Sandby of 24 Dec. 1948 Grainger provided his statistics about works which had come to his attention during his three months in England, either over the radio or in concerts. These included: Vaughan Williams 42 (9 important works), Bax 11 (4), Ireland 6 (3), Britten 20 (3), Walton 15 (4), Scott 8 (2), Gardiner 1, Quilter 21, Grainger 13, Delius 23 (9), Elgar 34 (4), Holst 19 (2), Stanford 33 (1), Parry 14, Moeran 16 (3), Rubbra 7 (2). By contrast, Hindemith's record was 8 (7) and Fauré's 43 (8). 'Important' works were, to Grainger, symphonies, sonatas, long chamber works and tone poems (not suites or overtures). Grainger wrote up the musical impressions of his visit to England in the four-page essay 'Music heard in England, late 1948', which he finished in late Feb. 1949.

[3] The Democrat Harry S. Truman (1884–1972) had succeeded Franklin D. Roosevelt as US president upon Roosevelt's death in 1945, after over twelve years in power. Contrary to expectations Truman had won the presidential election of Nov. 1948 against the Republican Thomas E. Dewey.

occurs to him to name some of Maude V. White's[1] mastersongs, or I'll sing thee songs of Araby,[2] or Hatton's To Anthea.[3] Why not? To my ears they are neither as old-fashioned (or as ANNOYING in a 1000 ways) as most of Schubert's songs—tho Schubert is a genius I greatly revere). A Norwegian is equally unlikely to mention Grieg's HAUG-TUSSA cycle,[4] Sigurd Lie's 'Snow'[5] among the world's greatest songs, while a German-speaker is quite capable of including 2nd rate German songs such as 'Still wie die Nacht'[6] (which I also like). We Nordics must learn that undue modesty about art is just as bad as undue conceit about art. Until we have learnt that, life for great composers in our countries will remain a slow torture.

Affectionate greetings from *Percy*.

58 *To Leopold Stokowski*

Jan 31, 1949

Dear friend,

My wife and I have just got off the boat from Sweden and the first letter handed to me was your very delightful one of Jan 17, in which you so generously express a wish to record 6 pieces of mine with special orchestrations.[7] I cannot tell you how much I rejoice that so great a genius as yourself, and a musician of such exquisite taste and such original thinking, should wish to record my pieces. And of course I will be overjoyed to make the special orchestrations for you as soon as I can, but I must warn that I am a slow worker, tho I work long—mostly 16 hours a day.

I utterly agree with everything you say: that when themes are repeated, there should be a change of instrument; that the lovely

---

[1] (1855–1937), writer of over two hundred songs.

[2] By Frederic Clay (1838–89), composer of light operas and songs.

[3] John Hatton (1808–86), composer of some five hundred songs.

[4] Cycle of eight songs, to words by Arne Garborg, composed in *c*.1895.

[5] (1871–1904), Norwegian composer; 'Snow' was based on a text by Helge Rode.

[6] = 'Calm as the night', by Carl Böhm (1844–1920), German composer of popular songs and piano music.

[7] Stokowski wanted to record six of Grainger's best-known works, but in new arrangements: 'My thought was that each time a theme is repeated, fresh instruments would play. . . . I notice that the orchestrations made by others are rather thick and "Symphonic". I feel that your music is *folk* music and should not be thickly orchestrated—but for a *few* instruments at a time. This would give clarity and at the same time have the atmosphere and impression of folk music played and danced on the village green.'

modern instruments (such as marimbas, vibraharps, celesta, saxophones) should be used freely; that settings of folkmusic should oftenest sound as if each part is played by a single instrument (or at least by FEW instruments) and that there should be a village green atmosphere about the whole thing.

I would LOVE to reorchestrate the 6 pieces you mention (IRISH TUNE FROM COUNTY DERRY, MOLLY ON THE SHORE, SHEPHERDS HEY, COUNTRY GARDENS, HANDEL IN THE STRAND, MOCK MORRIS) and it would help me greatly if we could talk over with you the details of the orchestration so that I can try to realise as faithfully as possible what you would like. I can come and see you any time you like to set (I have retired from 'commercial pianism', do not appear in public except where my compositions are played, and have no duties except compositional ones until lateish in March).[1]

I am sure that my publishers (Schirmers in New York; Schott and Co., London—Schotts are the holders of the original copyrights in 5 of the 6 pieces you mention) will be more than delighted to fall in with your exhilarating and generous proposal. But of course I ought to ask them, and I am today writing to Schott & Co, London.

However it is not true that my orchestral pieces are orchestrated by anybody but myself, with the exception of 'COUNTRY GARDENS', which I (stupidly) allowed Schirmer's arranger to orchestrate, from my sketches. All the others are entirely my own scoring, in the original Schott edition. In the Schirmer edition they are marked 'arranged by Langey, or Adolf Schmid' because a few instruments (such as Tenor Saxophone) were included in the American edition that I did not have in my original orchestration. The pieces were composed and scored by me as follows:

1. Irish Tune from Co. Derry, set for mixed chorus 1902, set for strings and horns 1913
2. Molly on the Shore, set for string quartet 1907, scored for orchestra 1914.
3. Shepherds Hey, set for 12 single instruments 1908–1909, set for orchestra 1913.
4. Country Gardens, sketched for 2 whistlers and chamber music 1908 (unfinished), set for piano 1918.

---

[1] Stokowski and Grainger did meet, but only on 3 Sept. 1949. Grainger then made the new arrangements between Sept. 1949 and May 1950. Finally, in 1951, with *Early One Morning* (first set by Grainger in 1899) and not *Country Gardens*, the recording of 'Grainger Favorites' was issued as RCA Victor LM 1238. Grainger played the piano part in these recordings. See David Tall and John Bird, 'The "Stokowski" and "1952" Settings', *Grainger Journal*, 3/2 (Mar. 1981), 10–17.

5. Handel in the Strand, composed for piano & 3 strings 1911–1912.
6. Mock Morris, composed for 7 single strings or string orchestra 1919 [*sic*; 1909–10], scored for small orchestra 1914.

With the exception of 'Country Gardens' none of these were arranged by me for piano until many years after the original scoring. In fact, I have never composed for piano solo (except Country Gardens) since I was about 15.

I dearly wish I could record with you one of my things for piano & orchestra, such as 'Spoon River', which I play such a lot with orchestras. Of course I would be more than happy to play in it without a fee. And I wish that one of my slow melodious things, such as 'COLONIAL SONG', could some day have the honor of being recorded by you and receiving that baptism of sensuous tone-beauty you confer on such things.[1]

Etc. Yrs gratefully, PG

59   *Round Letter*

June 7, 1949

Dear ones,

I do not take sides with the rut-bound leeches ((conventional doctors)) against the nature-healers or other 'faddists' or quacks, nor do I take sides with the nature-healers against the rut-bound leeches. I am sure that both have their usefulness. But when I go to a rut-bound leech (because of the sundry pains I have had in my guts & other insides for a year or two—as a matter of fact these pains have pretty well faded away!) he tells me that I have 2 or 3 growths that likely call for knife-curing ((operation)) & that I should be overhauled by a 'good guts-leech' once a month. Under such hands I would simply go from knife-cure to knife-cure until I was killed by one of them; & I am very keen on not dying until I have be-ended ((completed)) my sundry life-works. So I lean towards the nature-healers that Cyril redes ((advises)) me to go to, because they say that knife-cures do not touch the source of the health-flaw (which seems likely) & that one's ailments likely are rooted in ore-lack ((mineral deficiency)).

I write of all this merely to bring out something funny between my

[1] Grainger and Stokowski did in Sept. 1950 consider including *Colonial Song* on the recording, but agreed instead on *Early One Morning*.

dearest friends & me. When I write them about my ailments, & the cures reded against them, my dearest friends write back at once in most kindly vein, clearly worried & hating to think of me ill. But when I wail to them of the sorrows of my art-life & of my wrack-pains ((agony)) in having wasted 50 years 'earning my living' as a piano-player they answer nothing at all, or more or less don't-care-ing-ly. And yet, to me, the thought of illness & death (but for the fact that I dont like to leave my life-works un-be-ended ((uncompleted))) has no sting in it, whereas the wretchedness of my money-earning life as a piano-player was unspeakable. It was not only that I knew that my playing was not good enough to earn money by, that I winced when I saw my face or name on big hoardings, that I dreaded tone-judge-ments ((criticisms)) in newspapers, that I hated the foreign time-beaters ((conductors)) & tone-men ((musicians)) I had to work with, that I was hamstrung by the fear of breaking down on the platform; what I hated most of all was the fact of having to play tone-art ((music)) written by the foes of my race & full of the points of view that made those tone-wrights ((composers)) foes of my race. It was so awful, year after year, to know that one was playing into the hands of our foes.

But now all that hatefulness is behind me & I want my dear friends to know that I am UTTERLY HAPPY in my now-time-y ((present)) life (ailments or no ailments, leeches or no leeches). I like everything in my life to swing round ME & MINE. I like to hear MY wife learning MY tone-art ((music)) on MY bells; I like to hear MY tone-works ((composi-tions)) played or sung in the tone-shows ((concerts)) I take part in; I like ask-ments ((questions)) to be asked about MY wishes, MY deem-ths ((opinions)); I like time-beaters ((conductors)) to talk about the way my tone-works should be forth-sounded ((performed)). In other words, I like to be kow-towed to, & I like all the treatments that come to one with old age. (Of course, I mean the words 'MY' & 'MINE' somewhat stretch-lithe-ly ((elastically)). Under MY tone-art ((music)) comes all the tone-works of my dear friends & of a great many tone-wrights never met or not strictly my friends, such as Balakirev, Fauré, Albeniz, Debussy, Brahms, Bach; And under MY race come the South Sea Islanders, Africans, Mongolians—anybody but those swinish foreigners on the European main-land that are always so foe-ful ((hostile)) to us, our dreams, our hopes, our out-find-ments ((inventions)).)

I must say: now that time-beaters ((conductors)) & other tone-show planners ((concert organisers)) know that I set store only by my tone-works & not by my piano-playing (even if I still play a concerto for them—as a 'sop' to their listen-hosts ((public)) & to weigh up against the unpleasing task of having to play my tone-works) they try to be awfully nice to me about it—they really DO try to please me & give me hopefulfilment ((satisfaction)). If I take part ONLY in my own tone-works I play for nothing; & if I play a concerto as well I ask a lowered fee—200 dollars instead of 300, or 350, or 550 & the like. And I feel so much more comfy that way—for I am sure that my concerto-playing (however flaw-ful ((imperfect)) it may be) is worth 200 to the tone-show-giving body ((concert-giving society)), whereas I never felt that my playing was worth 300 or 500 dollars. Now the whole thing is just-right: They are doing me a kindness, in forth-playing my wretched tone-works; & I am doing them a kindness, playing a concerto; & the listen-host pays the 200 dollars to 'be there' (I will not say 'to hear it', for I am not sure they care for what they 'hear' from me; but I am sure they like to 'be there'.)

Between March 17 & June 15 I will have had:
MARCHING SONG OF DEMOCRACY (BAND), once
SUITE 'IN A NUTSHELL', twice
DANISH FOLK-MUSIC SUITE, twice
YOUTHFUL SUITE, once
ENGLISH DANCE, once
TO A NORDIC PRINCESS, once
COUNTY DERRY AIR (1920 setting), twice
RECESSIONAL,[1] ENGLISH GOTHIC MUSIC (Alleluia psallat, Beata viscera), each once
CHOSEN GEMS for band or wind groups[2] (13th year-hundred English, 15th y-h Burgundian, 16th y-h Spanish, 17th y-h English, & so on) once or more
CHILDREN'S MARCH, piano & band, many times
COLONIAL SONG, twice
SPOON RIVER, sundry times
ELLA'S 'LOVE AT FIRST SIGHT' chorus,[3] once
THE LOST LADY FOUND chorus, twice. And many shorter & older works.

Kipling's RECESSIONAL was so sweetly sung, in a small college

---

[1] A Kipling setting sketched in 1905, completed in 1929.
[2] Grainger's collection of his arrangements for smaller ensembles, most dating from the 1930s and 1940s.
[3] Melody and words by Ella Grainger, with harmonization by Percy Grainger, for unaccompanied mixed chorus with soprano solo, published by Schirmer in 1946.

town,[1] that I almost wished I was dead & it sung over my grave! The YOUTHFUL SUITE was quite bearable to listen to—true-to-type ((typical)) of my half-grown-up tone-mind around 1898–1902. But the wonder of these last months was the forth-play-ment ((performance)) of TO A NORDIC PRINCESS & ENGLISH DANCE by handsome, witty & charming Russell Ames Cook (New Englander) & his lovely-looking sweet-hearted Danish-American wife (she did not take part in the tonery ((music)) itself, but I cannot think of them apart; they are a team) at Portland, Maine.[2] It is beyond me to fathom how R.A. Cook could get a play-for-the-love-of-it ((amateur)) wind-&-string-band ((orchestra)) to play such works as TO A NORDIC PRINCESS & ENGLISH DANCE. But it is a fact that such a body of tone-lovers, so led, is much more hope-fulfilling ((satisfying)) to listen to in such works than would be the 'world's finest wind-&-string-band' ((orchestra)) with one rehearsal & a less noble & less keen time-beater ((conductor)). This way it was just-right, for my ears. What a glory-ful ((glorious)) organ, up in Portland! And how stunningly played! I dont give a fig for a wind-&-string-band without an organ. Fancy wasting the tune-line powers of part of a wind-&-string-band in forming chord-backgrounds to the tune-voices! To score for wind-&-string-band without organ is to misunderstand the whole way-things-are in the white man's tonery. I find the NORDIC PRINCESS an utterly well-sounding piece, from first to last. To start with a smallish body of single tone-tools ((instruments)) (backed by harmonium) & to work up bit-by-bit to full wind-&-string-band (backed by organ) is such a sound & straight-forward a line to take—I cannot think why it hasnt been done often. As for the ENGLISH DANCE; it has all its old spell, for me. I love such surging, swirling tonery, & Russell Ames Cook gave himself to it with spirit-lit-ness ((inspiration)) & mastery. The quick-changing chords sounded much clearer to me this time than when I last heard it—at Bournemouth, 1936. I dont say that the scoring is all it should be—I never had, & I never will have, any real gift for scoring (may be it would have been better if I had been at-rest-set ((content)) just to mind-birth the notes, chords & form of my tonery ((music)), hiring some in-the-know scorer to do the scoring?). And it may be that the well-deeming-ness ((approval)) with which

---

[1] In Eureka, Illinois, on 26 Apr. 1949. Griff Lathrop conducted the Eureka College Choir.

[2] Russell Ames Cook (*c*.1888–*c*.1965) conducted the symphony orchestra in Portland and also lectured in New York. His wife Clara was a pianist and organist. The concert of 24 May 1949 featured an all-Grainger second half; before the interval Grainger played the Tchaikovsky Piano Concerto No. 1.

I nowadays listen to my things is just the blunt-minded-ness & dont-caring-ness of old age. In either case I am alike well-pleased. For what is the real urge behind all this hearing & testing of one's tonery—is it not the longing TO BE DONE WITH IT ALL? I was tone-happy in my late teens & early manhood—when I merely mind-pictured my tonery without putting it to the test of forth-play-ment ((performance)). And it is that happiness I want to sink back into. I shall be glad when the last rehearsal, the last tone-show, is over & when tone-wrighting ((composing)) for me again means nothing but the shaping of tone-thoughts & the writing down of them. That is my real job, after all. Just now my main job is the reading thru (for mistakes) of HILLSONG II (24 winds) score & parts. The score has been glory-fully hand-written by a work-for-pay copy-er (I paid over 200 dollars for it) & from his hand-writ on see-thru-able paper the printed copy will come about—by round-about ways. It gives me unspeakable at-rest-ness ((contentment)) to see this best-loved work next-door to being forth-printed ((published)).[1] And as I con its pages I am well-pleased to think that it is honor-tokened ((dedicated)) to Balfour Gardiner. For—talking of 'ME' & 'MINE'—what could ever be closer to me (more 'MINE') than his top-rung choir-piece 'AN OLD SONG RESUNG'[2] (Masefield)—out-chosenly ((especially)) the setting of the words 'Her merry men were cheering, hauling on the brails' & 'pulling claret bottles down, and knocking off their necks, The broken glass was clinking as she sank among the wrecks'. Is this not a godlike summing up of our whole time-stretch ((period)), & of the state of the British World-realm? As I look at Balfour's noble side-face color-photo, done for my past-hoard-house ((museum)), I see the very match to this lordly tonery. Love to you all; I wanted you to know how thoroly happy my art-life is, these days. Percy.

AFTER-WRIT ((Postscript)) (June 11, 1949). A little while ago I bought a really good tone-disc-player ((gramophone player)), & on it I have been playing thru, many times, all sorts of disc-takes ((gramophone records)) (mainly over-the-air takes) of my tone-works—things such as Leslie Woodgate's 1936 BBC All-Grainger tone-bill-of-fare ((programme)),[3] Stokowski's Hollywood forth-playments,[4] Kipling Jungle

---

[1] The score was published by the Leeds Music Corporation, New York, in 1950.

[2] For unaccompanied four-part chorus, published in 1920.

[3] Broadcast on 5 Nov. 1936, directed by Quilter's former secretary Leslie Woodgate (b. 1902), then BBC chorus master.

[4] Probably of the concerts featuring Grainger's works on 15 July 1945 and 21 July 1946.

Book Cycle in Chicago (1942),[1] London forth-playments of 1948,[2] & the like. And I feel very angry as I real-see ((realise)) that all my worrying over my scoring-weaknesses, & my plans for re-hearing & re-scoring of sundry works (such as 'The Bride's Tragedy'), has been quite needless & a waste of time—& a silly lack of self-trustingness. There is one flaw in most tone-discs ((records)) of my tone-works (whether time-beaten by me or by others): they go too slowly. But by tuning my disc-player up one half-tone, or one whole-tone, the right speed is gained & the tonery ((music)) sounds all the brighter & better for being raised a bit in pitch. After again-&-again hearings I now feel sure that the scorings of all these pieces (March. S. of Democr., Hillsongs, The Brides Tragedy, a.s.o.) is quite qood enough (as good as Brahms's scoring of his 'Harz-Reise' Rhapsody for she-low-voice ((contralto)) & string-&-wind-band ((orchestra)),[3] for sample). From now on I shall worry no more about my scorings, but shall just forth-print everything more or less as it stands, & not mind if a few flaws are left for younger tone-men to grapple with ('other little children will draw my boats ashore'—Robert Louis Stevenson). Also with new tone-works: I will trust my scoring-witfulness rather than distrust.

I have also been going over Cyril's FESTIVAL OVERTURE as played in Bournemouth by Richard Austin in 1946. And for the life of me I cannot see what Cyril himself, & Robert Elkin,[4] & others, have against this piece & its scoring. I can only hear that it is a piece of stunning over-soul-ship ((genius)); highly self-ful & first-hand-y ((original)), full of the most telling change-shocks ((contrasts)), & LOVELY, LOVELY thru-out. It is the damnable twistedness & unfairness of English-speakers anent their own tone-art (a match to that silly wish to 'preside over the liquidation of the British Empire') that is guilty in this matter, & I have no forgiveness or thole-hunger ((patience)) for such nonsense. I am jolly glad that I have lived long enough to see a younger batch of time-beaters ((conductors)) arise who are more friendly to my tonery than their fathers were & that I can now wash my hands of the whole dirty business. Percy.

[1] Performed on 5 Feb. 1942 by the choir and chamber orchestra of the Gustavus Adolphus College of St Peter, Minnesota. On 4 Dec. 1941 Grainger heard Adolph Nelson (c.1899–1979) rehearsing the cycle at the college and wrote in his diary, 'I guess the most hopefulfilling rehearsal of my whole life. Nelson goes beyond anything ever witnessed.'

[2] Probably a Promenade Concert of 21 Aug. 1948, in which Basil Cameron conducted the English première of the *Danish Folk-Music Suite*, and a broadcast concert of Grainger's music on 21 Nov. 1948, for which Grainger conducted the BBC Theatre Orchestra.

[3] Op. 53 (1869), based on Goethe's 'Harzreise im Winter'.

[4] Scott's London publisher.

60   *To Ella Grainger*

Mississippi Valley | (La Crosse to St Paul)
Wed. midday, Nov. 23, 1949

Darling Peer,

Of course we are very much in love with each other, & very fond of
each other, & therefore have, on those scores, the best possible reasons
for wanting to be close to each other & never sundered, if we can help
it. But even if those reasons were lopped away, it seems to me we
would be just as much driven into each other's arms by the fact that
we are so alike & so like-minded, *& that all other people are so unlike us as
to make it unthinkable that one could live with them at all.* Let us take all our
best friends in review (blind-seeing our non-friends wholly) & consider
them alongside ourselves, quality for quality, habit for habit, attitude
for attitude. (In this review I am not seeking to stress our superiority,
only our unlikeness.)

Creativeness. Most of our creative friends are creative in only one art:
   Wildenveys, Roger, Balfour, Miss Morgan, Emile Walters, Delius,
   Frederiksson,[1] Sandby. Cyril is the only one I can think of quickly
   who is, like ourselves, equally creative in several arts or branches.

Languages. Few learn more than 2 languages & hardly any learn *any new
   languages* after 20. In this only Balfour is like ourselves; he has
   learnt, or nibbled at, Swedish & Spanish, since grown up.

Socialism. (Not to be at all theoretically or practically socialistic in our
   age is to suffer a grave time-lag. It is not a matter of personal
   choice any more; it is a matter of fitness or unfitness.) My being
   able to do socialistic business (a fair lay-round of money) with you
   when I met you got me my wife. My socialistic business with my
   museum, with Stewart Wilson[2] & the Central Music Library, with
   Fred Austin, with Harrogate in 1927,[3] got me my re-entry into
   British & Australian life. Yr relations with Tant,[4] with Mrs Adams
   & yr present old man (in fact, with all yr servants & workers) are
   all socialistic. Cyril's lack of socialism makes him unable to get on

---

[1] Perhaps a Swedish military officer with whom Ella Grainger maintained a correspondence
during her London years.

[2] Perhaps Sir Steuart Wilson (1889–1966), tenor, director of music at the BBC briefly in
1948–9.

[3] = the Harrogate Festival of 24–6 July 1929, at which four Grainger works were conducted by
Basil Cameron.

[4] = Tant Ström.

with Mrs Barham in Pevensey. But Roger & Balfour have some real fund of socialism in their nature & behavior. It was yr socialism that won over Frederiksson to yr side. One cannot (I suppose) call Miss Morgan or Wildenveys or Sandby socialistic? Elsie is, of course; but not Robert (his mother more).[1]

Preservation of figure, hair, etc. In this field many do fairly well—Roger, Cyril, Elsie, Simpson,[2] Miss Morgan, Tant, Sandby, etc. But others (otherwise 'civilised') just simply 'age'—Sladen,[3] Frederiksson, Balfour, Wildenveys. Many of those that dont fatten (like Cyril), wizen instead. To get neither heavier nor lighter (you, I, Roger, Tant) is fairly rare.

Earning increase. Most people who inherit money, or earn it themselves professionally in their young years, come to a prosperity halt fairly early in life & just keep on an even keel financially, or dwindle monetarily. In this class are Balfour, Cyril, Miss Morgan, Wildenveys, Roger, Frederiksson, Bedfords, Margaret Tjader,[4] Austin, Sandby, S. Olsens. Wives that help (with cunning counsel) their husbands to grow rich & increase their riches (like you, Elsie, Tant) are not in this come-to-a-halt financial class, even if you do not earn professionally.

Child-begetting. Aside from the accident of birthing, or not birthing, a child, mankind is divided into child-approvers or not. Balfour was a child-approver when he said of Rolf's wife[5] (before her first child) 'I dont think she's any good.' Tant was a child-approver when she brought up so many children & Gisken[6] when she adopted Hanna. Cyril is quite a father. And it is rare to be so far from child-approving as you, I, Miss Morgan, Roger, my mother are (were).

Internal decorators. Almost all inartistic women, & surprisingly many men, fall into this class:— Cyril, Roger, Balfour, etc. I dont think Tant (in spite of her clever home-building—it is too rooted in *real building*), Wildenveys, Sandby come under this heading. Neither do you & I.

Love worship. With most people real sexlove (felt for a few years in first

[1] Elsie and Robert Bristow, see Biographical Register.

[2] Perhaps Henry Simpson of London, friend of the Bristows.

[3] Douglas Sladen (1856–1947), British historian and prolific author, who had come to know Ella Grainger around 1920.

[4] Probably Marguerite Tjader (Sen.), wife of the explorer and lecturer Richard Tjader (1869–1916).

[5] Gardiner's nephew's wife.   [6] Wildenvey.

grown-up-ness, if at all) soon gives way to family life, or profes-sionalism, or dried-up-ness, or social life, or mercantilism, or house-furnishing. Even Cyril's affection for Marjory[1] must be con-sidered 'family life', I think; I think Balfour has some yearning for love, but he doesnt know what it is, so cannot act on it. To be swayed by true lust in one's sixties (as you & I are) is quite unique. Margaret Tjader Harris[2] seems quite love-swayed.

Art-clique. Most artists have joined some kind of a clique (or group-movement) before they are our age. Cyril is swayed by some period-feeling (art before 1910 appeals to him). Balfour, on the other hand is not clique-minded (as shown by his whole-hearted excitement about the 'Futurists', 1910) only a little out-of-things. Most artists (Roger, John Ireland) are a bit *scandalised* by the state-of-art in their old age. But not at all you & I.

Religion. Hardly anyone can resist the onslaught of religion all their lives. Yr mother, Sisley,[3] Balfour, Elsie did (& you & I, of course). Not Cyril, Sparre Olsen, etc., however.

A niche in society. Most people (to their undoing) drop into this sooner or later, & one wonders why, since they never gain by it but always lose. In the case of real artists, there is no ready-made niche into which they can fit; so it is like wearing ill-fitting shoes. I have always wanted to fit into some niche, & that is why I liked the army as well as I did. You liked studio life in the same way & enjoy the Kurki & Aldridge family backgrounds. But this comfort does not stretch very far, owing to the utter lack of understanding of the art-urge on the part of non-artists.

Professional exotic-seeking. Perhaps one is unjust in saying that men like Robert Louis Stevenson, Colin McFee,[4] Malinowski,[5] Nordoff,[6] Margaret Meade[7] & others take a 'professional' interest (rather

[1] Fellow occultist and Scott's companion from about 1945.

[2] (b. 1901), author and translator, daughter of Richard and Marguerite Tjader (see above). She was one of the last to visit Grainger in hospital, and a friend of Ella Grainger until her death in 1979.

[3] Thomas A. Sisley (d. 1925), Australian artist and teacher. He taught Grainger acting and paint-ing in Melbourne from *c.*1891 and is credited with having introduced him to Nordic literature.

[4] = Colin McPhee (1900–64), Canadian-born American composer and ethnomusicologist. Grainger had recently been most interested in his article 'The five-tone gamelan music of Bali', published in *Musical Quarterly*, 35 (1949), 250–81.

[5] Bronislaw Malinowski (1884–1942), Polish anthropologist. Many of his theories were based upon his experiences of the native peoples of New Guinea.

[6] Paul Nordoff (1909–77), American composer with a pioneering interest in music therapy which he developed through fieldwork in Germany, Finland, and England.

[7] = Margaret Mead (b. 1901), American anthropologist, particularly interested in South-East Asia and the South Pacific.

than a 'personal' interest) in certain exotic lands & people. This may be said if the white man does *not* have sex-affairs with the natives. Lafcadio Hearn[1] in Japan, Pierre Loti & Gauguin in Polynesia had (or seemed to have had) personal love for the nations, & that is what you felt for Ariki[2] & what I felt in Rotorua that time.[3]

The upshot of all these comparisons seems to be that unaging human beings & artists-thru-&-thru (such as you & me) are *helplessly* in the grip of some uncomfortable & unreasoning force, helplessly in the sway of some deep feelings & thereby prevented from *settling down* into some negative comfort or satisfaction that comes over all the others like a blight, preventing them from knowing REAL BLISS or doing undying good work.

Of those I can think of Balfour seems the only one who is still some-what in our own class. His art was always a matter of pure inspiration (even if the inspiration was sometimes a bit commonplace) & his life (despite its placidness & uneventfulness) has some tragic quality in it that proclaims the true artist, the born non-niche-fitter. That is why I could have imagined sharing some part of life with him, if he had re-ciprocated.

As for you & I, we are thrown into each other's arms by the fact that we are both

1   artistic thru & thru
2   non-family-minded
3   on the upward money grade
4   non-niche-filling
5   still purely sex-imbued.

I dont think I have ever met anyone else who was like myself in all these particulars. Therefore my ability to marry Karen or Margot was almost non-existent—however much I may have been attracted by them at times. We cannot help keeping *to our main campaigns* in life, & we cannot very well share our lives with those whose campaigns are hostile (or even just too different) to our own. What slight difference there is between you & me (perhaps merely the difference of he-some & she-some) may be summed up as follows: You are a love-child mov-

[1] (1850–1904), American-Japanese author, from 1896 until his death professor of English litera-ture at the Imperial University of Tokyo.
[2] = Iyemasa Tokugawa.
[3] Grainger's feeling of affinity with Maori and South Sea cultures during his visit of Feb. 1909.

ing towards art. I am an artist moving towards love-child-ness. You need upheartenment towards art. I need upheartenment towards love. And that is what we both get from each other.

 Yr close-knit (to Ella)
  Percy

1950–1961

'My Silly Selfish Self-Indulgence'

61   *To Robert and Elsie Bristow*

[Although Grainger wanted to believe that he belonged to the ageless, that old age which he so feared was slowly creeping up on him. The 1950s would be, for him, a decade of cancers and failing abilities—first physical, then mental—which left him wildly bitter at what he would now never achieve. But, despite frequent bouts of whingeing and self-accusation, he did continue until his final months to promote his music, to lecture and to play in concerts. He also managed to order his Melbourne museum, to tie up loose compositional ends and to make important advances with his 'Free Music' machines. The circle of his intimate correspondents declined markedly between 1950 and 1953 with the deaths of such close friends as Balfour Gardiner, Roger Quilter, and Karen Kellermann. Only his wife, Cyril Scott, Herman Sandby, and Grainger's stepdaughter Elsie Bristow remained to share the more confidential news of his final years.]

In the train, Pa. March 28, 1950

Dear Robert & Elsa,

It was most kind of you both to write me in such a kindly vein about my election to the National Academy of Arts & Sciences.[1] I am surprised that the matter was mentioned in the English press, as I (personally) had never heard of the Academy until they wrote & said that it was proposed to elect me. Even then, I was not going to answer their letter, as I regard such societies as a bit 'shady'. I always think they are just formed by a few ambitious no-goods, who elect each other for the sake of their own aggrandisement & then have to elect a few outsiders (like me) so that the whole thing doesnt look like a put-up job. So I am always afraid of such societies. But Ella noticed the letter lay unanswered & wondered whether I shouldnt answer it. I noticed the names of 2 composers I much admire (Daniel Gregory Mason & Howard Brockway[2]), so said 'yes'. But the whole thing is a kind of fake. The fact is that the real public cares nothing for the

---

[1] = Institute of Arts and Letters.

[2] (1870–1951), New York composer and pianist. He was elected a member of the Institute in 1910; Mason joined in 1938.

243

music of classical composers (such as Mason, Brockway & myself) & these societies are formed to try & lend to us an importance we dont possess—in actual fact.

The only people who seem to really like music such as mine (& that of my fellow composers) are the young high school, college & university students who play & sing in the choirs, bands & orchestras of the educational institutions to which they belong. They are of an age *when they like almost anything*; so it is not unpleasant to work with them. From last Feb to next June I am engaged in a composition-performance-promoting tour, dealing mostly with the young folk I have described. The object of the tour is to bring sales of my music to my publishers—who, otherwise, get disgruntled & let all my music go 'out of print' & stay there. I both play & conduct, but take no fee for so-doing (beyond my railway expenses) in order that the college, etc may spend their money buying my music from my publishers. The average college buys from 50 to 125 dollars of my music, this way, which is encoraging to the publishers when as many as 30 or so towns come into the picture.

We were so very glad to hear, dear Elsa, that you might be able to arrive in Sweden very early in July. We sail on June 20, so ought to arrive in Gothenburg[1] before July 1st. If you are arriving the first week in July perhaps we will stay in Gothenburg until you appear. I may have to dash down to Copenhagen (as soon as we land in Gothenburg) to deposit in the Royal Library, Copenhagen, the gramophone records of Danish folksingers I took 1922–27 & gave to the Royal Library.

These I borrowed (on one last Scand. trip)[2] in order to get them copied at the Library of Congress, Washington, DC. This was done, so I must now return the originals to Copenhagen. So any time you arrive in Gothenburg after about June 28 will suit us splendidly—the earlier the better! If I have to dash down to Copenhagen & back to Gothenburg, it will only take 2 days, & Gothenburg is a *delightful* town for you & Ella to be in for a few days, before proceeding to Stockholm.

Lots of love to you both.

Percy

---

[1] = Göteborg.   [2] During the summer of 1948.

62   *To Elsie Bristow*

April 20, 1951

My dear Elsie,

I am delighted to hear that Robert has wisely induced you to have
your throat examined & that an X-ray is being taken. May it tell good
news! I have always had rather a queer throat myself. I think I told
you that as a child in Australia I had 'sore throat' almost all the time
& was forever being treated for it. It was only when I was about 20, &
started reading MacFadden's 'Physical Strength' (or whatever it was
called)[1] that I veered away from meat, more or less (tho not a strict
meat-shunner till 1924),[2] & lost my everlasting colds & sore throats.
But my throat still feels tight. We are very anxious to hear the verdict
about your throat, dear child.

In one of your recent letters you said that my letters distressed you.
I suppose this means that my rather hyperbolic Australian way of 'laying it on thick' (especially where my own grievances are concerned)
distresses you. In any case I am very sorry if what I write seems upsetting. I think I can explain part of it.

I would not have collected (especially decyphered) folksongs as I
have, or struck out for English-speaking music as I have, or have put
so much 'heat' into music, if I had not taken a rather desperate view
of things from the start. A good sample case was the loss of Cyril's
String Quartet, when he was about 20–22.[3] All we composer-friends
rated this work most highly, I think—the other friends no less than I.
Certainly it had a rare beauty in it & was clearly a work of genius. It
got lost somehow & for me this loss became one of the major sorrows
& tragedies of my life. I begged Cyril to try & write down as much of
it as he could from memory, but he could not remember much of it &
didnt seem much interested. For him it was just a work he had written
& was willing to forget in order to pass on to newer & (if possible) better things. Nor did his other dear friends seem to feel the loss of the
manuscript as a personal & national TRAGEDY, as I did. I am sure
that none of his other friends ever think of the work any more, & if
they were asked to name Cyril's chamber works would be highly likely

---

[1] *Physical Culture Magazine*, by Bernarr MacFadden (1868–1955), American publisher and physical culturist.

[2] See Grainger's article 'How I Became a Meat-Shunner', *American Vegetarian*, 5/4 (Dec. 1946),
4.

[3] i.e. *c.*1899–1901.

to forget it altogether. Yet this work meant a great [deal] to us at the time it was new & has probably influenced all we have written of chamber music ever since.

As for me, I suppose I think of the work every day & always with the same poignance & same sense of PERSONAL LOSS. Who is right in this matter—I who mourn the work un-up-lettingly, or the others who have forgotten it long ago? Esthetically, I am right, of course. For even if my mourning the loss of the work doesnt bring it back MY MEMORY OF IT WILL ENABLE ME TO WRITE SENSIBLY & TRULY ABOUT IT, when I come to write my books on music.

It may be that the only office that art performs in modern life (the only valid excuse for art's existence—the only justification for all the time we all, in one form or another—if it be only reading the newspaper—devote to art, or WASTE upon art) is to make us all more aware of tragedy, sorrows, losses, defeats[1] & thereby make us more likely to avoid wars, strifes, struggles in the future. I can think of no other good reason.

If all this is so, how can I be a good artist (that is: a good mourner for the dead, a good sorrower with the unsuccessful, a good resenter of injustices) unless I am continually on the verge of tears, so to speak. If I didnt 'take things hard' in my own personal life & in my artistic life I would not be able to strike that particular note of tragedy, protest & sorrow that is the hall mark of the art we call 'good' or 'great'. For it is true (isnt it?) that the artists we call 'great' (Bach, Wagner, Tchaikovsky, etc) are more darkmooded, tragic, grouchy & hyperbolic than those other fine geniuses, of a smoother temperament, that we consider, rightly or wrongly, less 'great':—such as Scarlatti, Ravel, Mendelssohn. So I beg you to regard my hyperboles, my grouchiness, my hard-luck-stories as part of my artistic stock-in-trade—almost as part of my 'professional' equipment.

Not that I have anything to grouch about just at present. As a matter of fact I have run into an amazing run of good luck, the last few weeks. I was rather dreading 'THE LADS OF WAMPHRAY' in Peoria, as it seemed to me to be a rather 'unperformable' work, & I had heard from Peoria how much the chorus disliked singing it & how

---

[1] Grainger pursued a different line of thinking, however, when drafting his introduction to his intended autobiography 'My Wretched Tone-Life', on 16–22 July 1951. There he wrote: 'My tone-art is at its best when it has nought or little to do with mankind-some ((human)) stirs, longings & sorrows. My tone-art is at its best when it tallies the streaming, surging, soothing forces of the un-man-th ((non-human)) nature . . . or the wholly un-one-body-some ((impersonal)) trends of mankind-as-a-whole . . .'

much the orchestra hated rehearsing their part, & how apprehensive the choral conductor & the orchestral conductor & the business manager were about the work.[1] Under such circumstances it takes some boldness to go to the town & face the first rehearsals. But for once I acquitted myself thoroly well as a PRACTICAL conductor (the thing I feel it so hard to be). In the first rehearsal I was really inspired (for once) to be rough & confident. So the battle was won right away. Not that the performance was really good. They had practised it so slowly & were like lead, pulling back all the time. But it WAS PERFORMED without mishap & it was shown (at least to me & to Ella) that it is a thoroly effective & likeable piece.

In Ann Arbor William Revelli[2] (who was so against HILLSONG II that he refused it for the 'UNIVERSITY OF MICHIGAN BAND SERIES' publications when Schirmers urged him to accept it) seemed to be quite won over to the work.[3]

And now all my troublesome concerts are over—just a few easy ones left.

But the good luck centers around the FREE MUSIC invention & its progress. Both Ella & Burnett[4] have given me splendid support & the 3 of us have dragged all the worst problems to singular victory at last. Almost every day sees a new problem licked & ABSOLUTELY licked. In the last week the following victories have been won:

1. Utter non-veeringness of paper roll—no more weaving to right or left on the part of the paper roll that will play the music (the veering would cause the holes in the paper roll to play upon the wrong reeds & would make dynamic control uncertain.)

2. New method of cutting holes in paper roll (the holes cut much smaller than the holes in the tracker bar, so that the small holes in the paper always hit PART of the tracker bar holes), IN CASE the victory under No 1 had not happened.

3. Easy & effective way of controlling the sound-strengths ((dynamics)) by the size of the holes in the paper roll—a thin slit for softer notes, a wider slit for louder notes. (There are not many instruments on which the size of the tone is controlled by the notation itself—usually notation & dynamics operate separately.)

---

[1] This performance, involving the Orpheus Club choir and the Peoria Symphony Orchestra of Illinois, took place on 1 Apr. 1951. The conductor of the work in concert was Rudolph Reiners.

[2] (b. 1902), director of bands at the University of Michigan from 1935 to 1971.

[3] Grainger himself had conducted the band in *Hill-Song* No. 2 at a student recital on 4 Apr. 1951.

[4] Burnett Cross (b. 1914), White Plains physicist, who worked at the Teachers College of Columbia University.

4. Synchronisation of the 4 paper rolls (each 36 inches wide) by means of winding all the paper rolls (together about 9 yards in width) on the same axle.

The victory over the paper roll (preventing it from veering) is the most important gain of all.[1] Only this morning (before she went into New York to see the MacArthur parade)[2] Ella sewed on to a long paper roll some window-felt (anti-draught) so smoothly that the paper hangs in beautiful smoothness—the felt is sewn onto the rims of the sides of the paper roll & protrudes beyond the cylinder the paper runs on, thus keeping the paper true upon the cylinder.

If things go on as luckily as this for a few more days WE WILL HAVE A MACHINE READY TO ACTUALLY PLAY 'FREE MUSIC' IN A FEW WEEKS. If the actual musical jobs can start this spring & summer I will soon know whether I can dub the Free Music experiment a success or a failure (what do you think?). That will tell me what line to take in the museum exhibits regarding Free Music models (whether to 'Play them up' or not)[3] & how to write about the whole matter in my books on music. If the experiments didnt work I should have to describe these activities as failures—like so many aspects of my artistic life. But if they succeed as they seem now to promise to do (am I being stupidly hopeful?) I will be able to boast & gloat over them (how clever am I, & why have the other boys been so stupid & stick-in-the mud?) & that will suit my Australian temperament much better, of course.

Tomorrow is the 'PORGY & BESS' concert. I will let you know how it goes.

Yours with great anxiety to hear good throat news,
   Percy

April 24. The Town Hall concert is now over & a rather poor show it turned out to be.[4] Grayson (who did so well in the Porgy & Bess

[1] Grainger and Cross had made great advances in the years 1948–50, leading to the production of the first truly 'gliding chords' on the 'Estey reeds tone-tool' early in 1951. Over the following year they developed the 'Hills and dales' oscillator-player, which could produce a perfect glide, and by Apr. 1952 were building a 'Kangaroo-pouch' machine, which played polyphonic gliding music of irregular rhythms. See plate No. 23.

[2] The New York parade of General Douglas MacArthur, who had just been removed from United Nations' command of the Korean War, drew some seven-and-a-half million spectators and lasted for six-and-a-half hours.

[3] Grainger did come to consider the experiments a success and so did 'play them up' in his Museum exhibits.

[4] This afternoon concert on 21 Apr. 1951 featured the Centenary Singers from Centenary Junior College, Hackettstown, NJ, in association with Grainger and W. Norman Grayson, as pianists. The première of Grainger's arrangement of tunes from Gershwin's *Porgy and Bess* took place as the fourth item. See plate No. 20.

rehearsals you heard) unfolded towards the concert time some rhythmic freakishness that I found impossible to follow accurately. Also he
would skip a bar, now & then. I myself was in very meagre shape, my
slow eyesight leading me to bungle many passages. We gave a really
rotten performance of Daniel Gregory Mason's superb SCHERZO[1] &
the poor man almost got up out of a sick bed to be present. However
we did PORGY & BESS fairly well (it has turned out to be a MAGNIFI-
CENT arrangement) & it seemed well liked, so we repeated it from
'Bess, you is my Woman now' to the end. If it hadnt been for you
(with your discerning remark about 'Bess, you is': 'This is the best
thing in the whole opera, dont you think so?') I might never have
sensed the full value of that duet & I might have neglected to give it
the central place in the scheme of the Fantasy, as I now have. I am
often very dense about artistic & emotional values & need to be
touched off by someone more true-seeing than I am. Thank you,
clever & wise Elsie, for that golden hint!

What a strong Pevensey & Regina[2] flavor the Porgy & Bess Fantasy
has! (In my mind's ear I can hear the sounds of 'Oh, I cant sit down',
as practised by Ella & you—loudening as I approached the Regina
drawing room—the most fascinating musical experience of my life!) If
I hadnt started with that often-repeated, amateur home-music impression of Porgy & Bess the music might never have got under my skin as
it did & I could never have made such a grand arrangement as I have.

Daniel Gregory Mason has written some vocal canons, one of them
to the following verse-lines by Walter Savage Landor,[3] which lines I
think worthy of being written out for you:

I strove with none, for none was worth my strife.
Nature I loved, & after nature, art.
I warmed both hands before the fire of life;
It sinks, & I am ready to depart.

Somewhere in his poems Swinburne mourns the death of his friend
Walter Savage Landor:– 'Back to the flower-town', or something.
'Flower-town' must be Florence (Firenze) I suppose, for Latin L (flora)
is lost after F in Italian.

Now that my concerts are well nigh over I can say, in wonderment
& with thankfulness, that I have not had one single tremor of anxiety
in public playing this season. As Burnett would say: 'Amazing'. Both

---

[1] Op. 22b.
[2] Hotel Regina (London), where the Graingers had stayed during their London visit of 1950.
[3] (1775–1864), English.

Ella & I feel that this is the best artistic year we both have ever had—the widest response, the most hopeful vista for the future.

You write: 'It seems strange that people should want to change each other'. I dont think it strange at all. The things we like in people are largely impersonal. Beauty, cleverness, speed, depth, kindliness, wit, prophetic powers are impersonal enough. It is dead easy to approve of such good (such impersonal) things, so we do so, with great unction. But the moment we strike a personal characteristic that is upsetting or dangerous to the health or welfare of the beloved person (and most personal characteristics ARE dangerous & harmful) we at once disapprove. How can we do otherwise? We cannot applaud the downfall (even to the tiniest degree) of those we love.

No, I havent sent any ANECDOTES[1] to you to type, nor have I written down a single anecdote, alas. I have not had the surplus energy. The fact that this season has been a GOOD ONE artistically has made it also more time-filling. So when I found myself in the train I felt more like sleeping away those hours I had hoped to devote to anecdote-writing. And often, for reasons of economy, I found myself in the write-hostile bus instead of in the write-friendly train. But the anecdotes will be written out & sent (with thankfulness for your generous willingness to type them) in due time.

I am so glad you liked the Cesar Franck Symphony over the air, & felt at home with it. The Flemings[2] are great artists & C. Franck always seems to me one of the VERY greatest of great composers. He seems to me to voice the normal heart of normal mankind. He has some sort of Greek calmness & balancedness 'Sad, but not crushed with sadness' (see Swinburne's poem 'Before the Mirror'—one of his many best).

As regards piano practice: I think I am right in deeming practice of the Bach Preludes & Fugues (especially at a slow speed, with a loud tone & with the metronome) more developing of one's pianism than the playing of piano pieces such as Grieg's & mine. You see, Bach's Preludes & Fugues were written, many of them, for his own family & for his pupils *as study music*. So they fulfil that object wonderfully well, whereas pieces like Grieg's & mine dont, being conceived as music & not as studies. Particularly the 2-part numbers, such as the G minor Prelude in the first book (in which each hand plays a single voice), are

---

[1] Grainger started to write down various anecdotes in Oct. 1949. He continued to do so until Nov. 1954.
[2] = Flemish.

useful in giving one familiarity with keyboard distances, some of the phrases calling for moderate stretching of the hands & fingers. Piano playing hinges largely on a subconscious sense of keyboard distances, & this subconsciousness is specially helped by Bach-practice, I think.

In one of your dear & greatly-prized letters you speak of the times we live in as disquieting & depressing, or words to that effect. I cannot agree. I have never known any times as good as the present ones, from my viewpoint. Each age has to rectify somehow old injustices that have prevailed overlong or have newly sprung up. For instance in the so-called (wrongly-called, I think) 'dark ages' the church had to counteract & morally disqualify strong-arm violence—euphemistically called 'heroism'. In the Renaissance period the right-to-individual-feeling was advanced. In our own age (as I see it) the great contrasts between useless wealth & useless poverty (between individuals, between classes, between nations) had to be—still has to be—evened out. The tyranny of capitalism & the tyranny of trade-unionism (proletarianism) are both of them anti-human & must go. So it is good that the capitalism of Western civilisation is being threatened & that the proletarianism of Russia is being opposed. I cant think of a better solution. But it is essential that the solution be reached without too many wars: for we cannot afford them. (What nonsense I talk. Of course we can afford everything we think is right.)

In one of your letters you say I have been 'lenient' to you. It is very easy to be lenient to those one thoroly approves of. In general it may be said that the very old are inclined to approve of the young. I suppose I *DO* today approve of all you are & do more than I did 20 years ago. Or it may be that life with Robert & life in India have made you more easy-to-approve-of. Certain it is that if I had a daughter of my own I would wish her to be EXACTLY like you in every way—in looks, size, speech-pronunciation, sympatheticness, compassionateness, kindliness, depth of mental perception, speed of mental uptake, athleticness, gaiety, universal helpfulness, way of playing music, way of thinking about the arts & life. Perhaps the greatest contribution to life is to hold up to life a perfect picture of what life should be. That is what is done by approveable you, dear Elsie,

      Your approving
      Percy

I saw the film 'Bitter Rice'[1] & Ella & I saw the film 'Kim'.[2] In

---

[1] 1950 Italian film presenting a sombre account of women working in Po Valley ricefields.
[2] 1950 Hollywood film starring Errol Flynn.

'Bitter R' I was glad to see that the women hadnt shaved their armpits. The French & Italians often show good taste in such matters; for what is 'good taste' but as natural-as-can-be-ness? An old country-man like David Holter has good taste & a good class Australian like old Mrs Eliott has good taste, for both are more natural than the timid middle class. I never liked the novel KIM[1] as much as Kipling's verse & short stories. K's flair for racial types & broad generalisations fitted him marvelously to touch off contrasts in a short story or poem (like THE BALLAD OF EAST & WEST),[2] but handicapped him (I thought) in sustaining a plot or in interesting himself more than superficially in individual lives. But Kipling gained 'status' in writing a novel, just as any silly composer does in writing a symphony.

63   *To Cyril Scott*

Dec 10 & 11, 1951

Darling Cyril,

I want to answer yr very welcome & much-prized letters of Nov 11 & Nov 23. But before doing so I want to say something about yr Piano Sonata, op.66.[3] And that is: How VERY MUCH I enjoy practising it—going back to it after all these years—about 30 years. I like the MUSIC of it so very much. I mean the texture of the harmonies, the voice-leadings, the non-architectural flow of the form, the easy but brilliant pianistic style—so typical of yr incomparable improvisings. I still disap-prove of the things I disapproved of when I first heard the work in 1909: the fact of its being written for that loathesome instrument the piano, the non-polyphonic nature of its tone-thoughts, that it bears a title sullied by use by our enemies the Italians & the Germans (how a Britisher can use a title that has been used by our enemies is beyond my comprehension).[4] I dislike these things as violently today as I did in 1909. Yet I am utterly bowled over by the beauty, the originality & the mental liveliness of the music—in short, by its GENIUS.

---

[1] Pub. in 1901.   [2] Pub. in Kipling's 'year of fame', 1890.

[3] Composed *c.*1904, and published as Scott's Op. 66 in 1909. Grainger, with Scott's collabora-tion, abridged the work and performed it several times around 1909–10 under the title *Handelian Rhapsody*, Op. 17.

[4] For more on Grainger's dislike of 'enemy' work titles and performing instructions, see letter **71**. Scott wrote, in total, three piano, one cello, and two violin sonatas.

About Ella making a score from the parts of your Quartet:[1] We are happy that Elkin likes the idea. But if he intends to bring out the score in miniature size (as most quartets are, I suppose), then there is perhaps no point in Ella writing it on transparent music paper, as a miniature score is usually (I think) written large size on large size music paper (about 11 by 13 & a half, or about 9 and a half by 12 and a half—that is the overall size of the paper, not just the size of the staves or music-lines) & then reduced in size photographically. In that case there is no advantage (either to Ella or Elkin) in Ella writing on transparent music paper—she might just as well write on ordinary music paper. On the other hand, if the score is to be printed about 9 & a half by 12 & a half then there may be an advantage in Ella writing on transparent paper such as the enclosed. Please show the enclosed sheet to Elkins & ask them to kindly let us know

(1) Whether the printed score is to be reduced photographically from Ella's MS or not.

(2) What the size of the printed score is to be.

(3) Whether they would like Ella's MS to be written on transparent music paper such as the enclosed, or on ordinary opaque MS paper. If they prefer ordinary opaque music paper, will they please state what size the actual music part of the page should be—that is, the actual area that the staves & Ella's writing on them should cover.

I am glad to 'stand corrected' in my remarks about your father. (I sometimes think I make the ignorant statements I hazard in order to have my misconceptions set right—as when I wrote in the 'Australian Music News' that Ida Gerhardi & Jelka Rosen quarrelled over Frederick Delius & got a resentful letter from Jelka saying that the curious thing was that she & Ida Gerhardi had never quarrelled over F.D., altho both were in love with him, & that it was very naughty of me to make such misleading statements in print.)[2] All the same, was yr father not a chemist? If so, is it not conceivable that you grew up in some atmosphere connected with medicines & cures—however little your father may have ultimately believed in such things?[3] If he chose

[1] String Quartet No. 2 (1922), eventually published in 1958 by Elkin (London) reproducing Ella Grainger's MS. See letter **70**.

[2] Grainger had written: 'Jelka Rosen and Ida Gerhardi—both in love with him romantically and artistically—quarrelled violently over him, but later made the quarrel up and remained devoted life-long friends.' ('The Personality of Frederick Delius', 24/12 (July 1934), 10–15 (p. 11). Jelka Rosen (d. 1935), eventually Delius's wife, was a painter; Ida Gerhardi, also a painter, had been her friend since childhood.

[3] Henry Scott had been in the shipping business and was also a Greek scholar of note. Cyril Scott records: 'He believed that the secret of good health was frugality and plenty of unviolent exercise.' (*Bone of Contention* (London: The Aquarian Press, 1969), 15.)

to become a chemist is there not some likelihood that he, at one time or another, may have attached some importance to medicines & cures, thereby coming to 'see thru' the limitations of doctors & their methods? As a matter of fact, was there not some basic likeness between his distrust of conventional doctoring & your own? (If a child grew up with me he/she could hardly fail to imbibe some pianistic outlook, however much I may dislike the piano.)

I am not against the idea that the time of year we are born at may affect our type, interests & tendencies. I am only against the idea that I am a 'hoarder' (altho I will not deny that there is likely to be SOME TRUTH in any statement you & my darling mother have made) & that I am especially fascinated by things old. I see no evidence that this is true. As to mother saying that I became really unhappy if any of my old clothes were got rid of in any way I can only say this: You must remember that my mother (not exposed to early German & Scandinavian influences as I was) was a true Anglosaxon & therefore not so saving as I. I can remember the look of bland surprize on her face when I said to her, when I was about 15 or 16: 'There is one thing we must do, mother, & that is to save money all we can.' Never had she heard such an intention from the lips of either an Aldridge or a Grainger! It left her utterly flabbergasted. Amongst Frankfort influences we must not forget Sigurd Fornander. He was more a spendthrift than a hoarder. But being a Scandinavian he kept all the clothes of his prosperous years (1900 to 1918) & they covered him all his lean years (1918 to 1945). When Ella came to White Plains first (1928) there was an old vacuum cleaner that she disliked, because she dislikes vacuum cleaners. But (being a Scandinavian) she did not get rid of it. And when Burnett Cross & I started making our FREE MUSIC experiments we needed a vacuum cleaner to use as air-blower & air-sucker & Ella was able to produce the disliked V.C., thereby saving us delay & expense.

Being an Anglosaxon (without early foreign influences such as I had) mother was subject to 'cleaning up' fits in which my comfortable old clothes were as likely to disappear as my uncomfortable old clothes. I have noticed that men & women of genius are much more fussy about clothes-comfort & shoe-comfort than ordinary mortals. (Ella gets wholly disconsolate if her shoes are tight.) So my only way of safeguarding my comfortable old clothes was to 'crack down' on all giving away, or throwing away, of any of my old clothes whatsoever. In my mid-London period mother suddenly got rid of several volumes of

'The Yachtsman' that I had treasured from my around-10-year-old days & had taken with us everywhere. The reason given was 'lack of space'. But the 'Yachtsman' volumes only took up one quarter of a suitcase & only weighed a pound or so, whereas my father's bound volumes of Italian operas, which were much less interesting to me & also much bulkier & heavier, were never thrown away & are now in the museum.

As you know, I have never been a true musician or true artist, my real leaning being towards soldiering & sailoring & other brutalities such as flagelantism & sadism. And the only thing that reconciled me to the life of a sissy (which is what I consider the life of an artist to be) was the hope that I would be able to express in my arts soldierliness, sailorishness & general brutality as it had never been expressed in music before. From 3 to 12 the rapturousness of my life centered round the Albert Park Lagoon in Melbourne & it was there that the lapping of water along the side of boats started the observations that eventually led to 'Free Music'. But I was able to get to the Albert Park lagoon but seldom, & since I first left Australia in 1895 I have indulged my passionate longing for yachting only once, altho it probably is the keenest longing in my life. So 'The Yachtsman' volumes was a 'surru-gat' [*sic*] for one of the main impulses of my emotional & artistic life & in view of water lapping against the side of boats the fact that my Free Music is largely a tally of the impressions of water lapping against the side of boats my childhood volumes of 'The Yachtsman' can be con-sidered as particularly valuable & desirable for my museum without such an opinion being the result of hoarding or a special fondness for things old. Such an opinion seems to me to be the normal reaction of a cosmopolitanly-trained & historically-minded esthete in opposition to the wild & wicked destructiveness of Anglosaxon life. When I was in Frankfort I heard that someone had preserved in a bottle the water in which Bismark had washed his hands after signing the Treaty of Frankfort[1] & I saw nothing strange in such an act of preservation. I never see anything strange or queer in acts of preservation, whereas all acts of destructiveness (including murder, in which I see NOTHING ATTRACTIVE OR ROMANTIC) strike me as loathesome & feeble.

In the same way as I disliked losing my old comfortable clothes I dislike losing my sweet light American bicycle, which I had in Frankfort, & I held it very much against Miss Permin (who was

---

[1] Signed in May 1871 following the Franco-Prussian War.

looking after the sending of our store[d] furniture & goods from London to USA in 1921) that she allowed it to get lost. It is quite likely that in the whole of Australia there is not such a sweet light bicycle as my 'Hartford' (with wooden handlebars & wooden inner wheel-rims) on which it was so easy to do tricks. It would have been a golden asset to my museum. Thank goodness I made a watercolor painting of this bicycle in Frankfort & the painting is in the museum.[1]

I cannot fathom how you can bring yourself to call me especially fond of things old—I who am so unusually fickle & changeable in my tastes & always some new will-o-the-wisp following.

Now, if I called you & my other European friends fond of things old there might be some justification in it, for you do not seem to change your artistic tastes radically thru life. But my artistic life is a matter of constantly changing attractions & whims—altho I never change my OPINIONS & LOYALTIES. I dont need to. All my opinions (for instance politically) always turn out to be right; so I have no need to change them. With my FONDNESS it is quite different. I believe in spreading my fondness over as many fields as possible, since life is so short & since, as Robert Louis Stevenson says 'the world is so full of a number of things, I'm sure we should all be as happy as kings'. If you want an indication of my constantly shifting & veering tastes just look at the following very incomplete list of my MUSICAL ROMANCES: Bach, 1892; Brahms & Wagner, about 1896; Grieg & Cyril Scott, about 1897; English Scandinavian & Faeroe Island folksongs, 1904; Madame Lineva's[2] phonograms of polyphonic Great-Russian folksongs, 1904; Sandby, 1901; Gabriel Fauré, ab. 1908; South Sea music, 1909; Balakirev, ab. 1910; Cesar Franck, ab. 1912; Negro-American partsongs, 1915; Dett, Guion, J.A. Carpenter, etc, 1915–1922; Delius, 1907; Albeniz, ab. 1910; Oriental & Madagascan music, 1932; Arnold Schoenberg, 1910; Arthur Fickenscher, 1931–45; Gothic Music & other pre-Bach music, 1932; V. Williams, Wm Walton, John Ireland, etc, ab. 1947; Sparre Olsen, ab. 1929; Dag Wirén, ab. 1947.[3] Anent literature also the only things stable in my literary tastes is my love of change: Homer, about 1890; Icelandic sagas & Anglosaxon prose, ab. 1892; Longfellow, ab. 1896; Kipling, ab. 1897; Walt Whitman, ab. 1897; Mark Twain, ab. 1900; Danish authors, 1903–1914; Icelandic sagas

[1] See plate No. 4.
[2] Evgenia Lineva (1854–1919), a pioneering collector of songs from the Volga region, who used the phonograph as early as 1894. Her two-volume study was published in English in 1904. Grainger set two of her tunes for choir in 1934.
[3] (b. 1905), Swedish composer.

resumed, ab. 1897; Anglosaxon verse, 1902–1923; Evald Tang
Kristensen, 1905–1927; Norwegian peasant language & its literature,
1910; Swinburne, ab. 1908. Gaelic begun, ab. 1908; Welsh begun, ab.
1949; South Sea literature (native & European), 1909; Edgar Lee
Masters & Vachel Lindsay, about 1917; Swedish authors (Eva Berg,[1]
Thorsten Johnson),[2] ab. 1945–1950; Modern Icelandic authors
(Laxness,[3] Stefansson,[4] etc), 1935–1951. Where do you get my 'love of
things old' in music[?] I dont much care for Danse negre or Lotus
land,[5] tho they are old. I love your Oboe Concerto[6] & yr 2nd
Quartet, both comparatively newer. If I hear a new piece of yours
today, I fall in love with it, that is love of the new, I suppose. But if I
like it equally 10 years from now, what does that constitute—a love of
the old? If I make a new machine today & I make a watercolor painting of it, or have it photographed, does that constitute a love of the
new, or a love for things old, according to you. Must I, in 10 years,
turn my back on something that is new now & which I like now, in
order that I shall then (10 years from now) be said to be 'attaching
especial importance to things old'? How you can call a man especially
fond of things old when all his life he has played new composers &
new music, has always enthused for new & iconoclastic developments
in music (like your Piano Sonata & Schoenberg's 'Fuenf Orchester-
stuecke') & has spent his whole musical life earning money so that he
can afford to try to overturn the existing order of music & to usher in
a wholly new musical system, is beyond me.

To me, as an Australian, it seems especially insulting to be dubbed a
lover of things old—or of things new, for that matter. All suggestion
that one lolls over on one side & doesnt keep a middle course is naturally insulting to an Australian; any suggestion of specialisation is naturally insulting to an Australian.[7] You who come from over-populated
countries do not seem to mind being considered specialists. In over-
populated conditions of life it is perhaps not unnatural that each man
should be somewhat of a specialist. But in a large & empty land like
Australia it seems almost needful that each man shall spread himself
over many tasks & be an 'all-round man'. At any rate, that is the one

---

[1] (b. 1904), novelist.

[2] Probably Thorsten Jonsson (b. 1910), Swedish journalist and novelist, from 1943 a correspon-
dent, then literary critic, in New York.

[3] Halldór Kiljan Laxness (b. 1902).   [4] David Stefansson (b. 1895).

[5] Scott's piano pieces of 1908 and 1905, respectively.   [6] Concerto for oboe and strings (1948).

[7] Grainger's views about this 'middle course' are best expressed in his article 'The Specialist &
the All-Round Man' in *A Birthday Offering to [Carl Engel]*, ed. Gustave Reese (New York:
G. Schirmer, 1943), 115–19.

thing I want to be—a BALANCED all-round man, Saint Paul's 'All things to all men'. I know that I dont have much talent for music (I have a bad ear, I have no gift for creating melody, I have no sense for tone-color) or indeed for anything. And I dont mind that. I dont think it any disgrace not to do some special thing well, as long as I can acquit myself reasonably well as an all-round man, able to do fairly well in the arts, able to earn fairly well, able to speak many languages fairly well, able to understand all the races of mankind fairly well, able to understand the general trend of humanity fairly well & above all ABLE TO UNDERSTAND WHERE WE ARE HEADING FOR? (Do you remember Bernhard Scholz's[1] 'Wohin treiben wir?').[2] My reason for being interested in the art of the past (for instance, Icelandic sagas) is because I hope that they will in some way equip me to understand the future. The one thing I want to avoid is being 'tendenziös'.[3]

By the way, if Ella writes out the score of your Quartet, who is going to write out the parts? Would Elkin provide the parts if Ella provides the MS of the score? Or should we write out the score in such a way that both the printed score & the printed parts could be printed from the same MS score—not drawing the barlines down thru the 4 staves at first (until parts are done) & then drawing the barlines thru the 4 staves before the score is printed? It would depend largely on the turning-pages problem, in the parts—on whether we could find places, in each part, where the parts turn conveniently at the ends of score braces. I will let you know when I have looked into the parts from this view-point.

Yes, please kindly wear the suit for a few weeks before kindly sending it to me—so it has a lived-in look.[4]

Love to you both from Ella & me

Percy

---

[1] (1835–1916), director of the Hoch Conservatory in Frankfurt from 1883 to 1908.

[2] = to where are we drifting? (German).

[3] = biased (German).

[4] The suit was to dress Scott's papier-mâché dummy in the Grainger Museum. Scott's, Quilter's, and Gardiner's dummy presentation there was modelled, even in bodily position, on plate No. 12, with Gardiner substituting for Grainger.

64   *To Herman Sandby*

White Plains, 25th Oct. 1952.

Beloved Herman,

We are terribly sorry to know that Alfhild is in hospital, but hope the rest will benefit her greatly. Too bad about your nice dog being bitten. Boxer dogs are swine.

We went to the Danish Radio Orchestra concert here[1] & I was amazed at the superb perfection of the orchestra. Jensen[2] is a capable conductor, but without charm or talent. The program was without heart-throb appeal, except the Grieg Symphonic Dances, which have all the *sadness* that is the hallmark of true genius. The Carl Nielsen 4th Symphony[3] is totally without *sadness* & therefore without genius. Your music has always been chock full of sadness & therefore it has true genius. Life is so cruel, so unjust, so precarious & so dangerous that only utterly heartless people can go thru it without feeling full of sadness. A composer who does not feel & cannot express sadness, is a brutal swine, & that is just what Carl Nielsen is. It is a class matter. All these low class swine (like C.N.) who *rise socially*, thru their art (the same with Sibelius) are *so full of their social victory* that they fail to see the sadness of life. I hate all artists (like C. Nielsen, Knut Hamsun,[4] etc.) who make the astounding discovery that 'life is vital'. I hate all 'strong men'. I like sinful men (like in the sagas), weak men, (like in J.P. Jacobsen, J.V. Jensen,[5] & Thor Johnson) & dream-smitten men (like Walt Whitman, Kipling, Swinburne). But not strong men. Uha, Uha.

The world is divided chiefly into 2 types: workers & parasites. The peasants & the geniuses work. The middle class just *feed on the produce of the workers*, like a great fat man being carried by a weak little man. I understand perfectly why the Americans (& other 'white collar' middle class people) like C. Nielsen, Sibelius, V. Williams, etc. The middle class hate Jazz, because it is the music of love and youth. They hate 'nature music' (like yours, Delius's) because they hate & fear nature!

---

[1] The concert took place on 15 Oct. 1952 in the Carnegie Hall. The programme consisted of Dvořák's *Carnival Overture*, Op. 92, and Stravinsky's *Firebird Suite*, as well as the works Grainger mentions.

[2] Thomas Jensen (1898–1963), Danish conductor, best known for his performances of Nielsen's and Sibelius's works.

[3] 'The Inextinguishable' (1914–16).

[4] Penname of Knut Pedersen (1859–1952), Norwegian author. He had gained the Nobel Prize for literature in 1920.

[5] (1873–1950), Danish author.

They like 'Symphonic music' (C.N., Sibelius, V. Williams) because it glorifies the middle-class ideal—which is war, profit, monopoly, competition, victory, anti-nature.   Love from Percy.

65   *To Ella Grainger*

[In June 1953 Grainger was diagnosed as suffering from prostate cancer.[1] He was to enter the Mayo Clinic in Minnesota for treatment at the end of July, but after much debate decided to have the operation performed in Denmark by his friend Cai Holten. This operation was not successful, however, and Grainger was to endure several operations over the following years as the cancer gradually spread through his body. His moods changed and, with fewer concerts, money was often short. America, too, he considered a different country from the one that had captivated him forty years before, but it was now too difficult for the Graingers to leave.]

July 17, 1953, St Paul RR station | morning 9.15

Can't you help me? Here I am, worrying myself ill (if ever a man did) & I'm sure you could rescue me from the whole thing. I am not worried about my health (if I should die it would probably be the best thing that could happen to me). I am not worried about my arts, for I feel I could master them (more or less) *if I ever got round to them*. I am not worried about our happiness, for there, again, I feel we could achieve happiness if we only had *time*. But I am worried to death financially. I can only see that we are 'bleeding to death financially.' The silly trips to Florida & Toronto, my silly selfish self-indulgence with my inventions, our silly big window—we are building up no future with these things! And what does it mean? That I have to go on giving concerts (which also means endless letter-writing) to fill out the gaps caused by our silly outlays.

When a man 'finances' a woman he would divide the money he could spend on her into 2 halves: the first half to build up her investments, the 2nd ½ for her living expenses. But if they live together (share house together) the investments are going to be neglected & the momentary expenses favored. That is why I wanted you to live in Paris; so that the investment side could have been properly attended to *& your tile books published within a few years*. Now (with travelling expenses

[1] See John O'Shea, *Music & Medicine: Medical Profiles of Great Composers* (London: J. M. Dent, 1990), 210–16.

raised) it has grown into a nightmare of 'bleeding to death'. 2 tickets to Australia, if we go there. 2 tickets to Rochester,[1] if we go there. 2 tickets to Denmark, if we go there. And what is gained by it? If we both go to Australia, & you go on tour with me, the earnings are partly eaten up by double travelling. If you stay in Melbourne, or Sydney or Adelaide, while I wander around, it is just like not going to A, in the sense that we are separated anyhow. If you go to Rochester & they kill me, what good is it yr being there? There is no point in seeing me dead. The same in Denmark. It is no use lovers being together during convalescence periods—is it? Lovers should reserve their *happy* times for each other, not their sick bouts. I even go so far as to say that if one of 2 lovers becomes an invalid, the hale one should leave him. Love is a *healthy* job. (But if that sounds harsh, I will not say it; for harshness is the last thing I have in mind.) I do not think I am going to die, & I do not think I am going to be an invalid. But I *do* think our financial future should be given our best attention. I am wriggling out of possible unholy expenses in Rochester because I dont like 1) buying a pig in a poke, 2) because I dont like being made a fool of, 3) because I do not want to be cured à la ameriquain, 4) because I do not want to have to thank detested America for either my life or my health. But if I now go to Cai Holten[2] instead (because he is a friend & because it is cheaper) do not let us waste the financial advantage by buying 2 *steamer* tickets (unless you wanted to go to Sweden at that time anyway). It might be easier to try to get a 3rd class ticket for one alone (in a cabin with other men) for as near (soon) a date as possible, so I could have the Aarhus treatment early August & be back here in time for Puerto Rico (Sept 21) or for the Canadian–midWest dates (Oct 5–12) at any rate.[3] If you dont want to stay in White Plains (August–Sept) you can take a holiday elsewhere. When I go to Australia (Jan 22) let it, again, be a real business trip, either just for the museum (3 months there?) or for the ABC tour & museum (5 months?)—with only one person's ticket involved. You could go to Sweden when I go to Australia & I can join you there after Australia—by boat from Australia to Europe (with meeting in Sweden mid-1954). If I did that kind of a trip to Australia I would try to avoid seeing my kin altogether (which I couldnt if you were with me) or see

---

[1] In Minnesota, to the Mayo Clinic.

[2] Karen Kellermann's brother, a surgeon in Aarhus.

[3] These engagements had to be cancelled, as Grainger's recuperation took much longer than he had anticipated.

them very briefly. Perhaps I would not go to Adelaide at all! That way the health-job would be done by mid-Sept, then you & I would be together here late-Sept, Oct, Nov, Dec, Jan before being parted when I go to Australia. Then, when we meet in Sweden, mid-1954, all my immediate *duties* will be behind me (with less expenses incurred) & we would be able to give ourselves up to holiday-making, or to art, or to a nice rest.

There are many excellent things about marriage—the best being that the outside world has no right to interfere! The worst habit connected with marriage is a concentration on *duties*, instead of on pleasures. But there is no need for this. You & I can make an iron rule:— always to *concentrate jointly* on pleasures, but to accomplish duties *singly*. Let me go alone to Aarhus & make it as much of a flying trip as I can. (Even in Aarhus they would rate one richer & charge one more if 2 turn up. Alone, I can pull the poor mouth & get things just as cheap as possible). The Australian trip we can discuss when we meet, 10 days from now. But the Danish trip should be acted upon at once, &, if you agree to my Denmark-alone proposal, go to the Scandinavian lines at once & try & get me a 3rd class (or other class if 3rd is un-get-able) *round trip* getting back here in time for Puerto Rico Sept 21, or at least for Canada (Oct 5). It is no use getting cured (at R'chester or Aarhus) if one has no money afterwards to enjoy one's health with. And I beg you to cooperate with me in helping me to cut down such expenses as are connected with me. You have seen that I do well in cheap trains, cheap meals, cheap hotels. If I should be unlucky enough to die, I dont want you to sit there financially ham-strung by my illness-treatments. If I recover my health (which I expect to do) I want us to have plenty of money for our *older* old age. It can all be done. But we mustnt throw the money away in travelling or treatments just when expenses are on a high period. Dont you agree? Let me hear to Kansas[1] what you feel.

Eagerly to upbuild
Percy

---

[1] Grainger was engaged for a summer concert course at the University of Kansas, 22–6 July 1953.

66   *To Kaare K. Nygaard*

March 5, 1954

Dear Kaare,

We hope that you & Ella are having a lovely time & a lovely rest.

I do not know how to answer your unbelievable letter of Feb 17, because I am torn between 2 feelings: the one, to bask in the sun of your generosity & 'fatherly' helpfulness (I have never encountered fatherliness to the degree I have in Scandinavia, & I think fatherliness & motherliness the most wonderful things in the world); the other, to try to behave not wholly miserably & unfairly to a fellow Nordic (using the term in the English sense & not in the Scandinavian sense of 'nordisk').[1]

I am constitutionally sensitive (happily sensitive, I mean) to being at the receiving end of generosity because of my early impressions of life. From the age of 7 to 18 I always saw my mother, handicapped by neuralgia & other ills, struggle to earn the living for herself & myself. It always seemed to me, in those years, as if a little money would cure all our ills. So I acquired a fixed idea that to earn money & to save money was my only duty in life. At the same time I always had the greatest difficulty in earning. Altho I knew that I couldnt earn a living for us both by composing, composing was the only thing I wanted to do. However, I gradually increased my control over myself, so that by the age of 25 I had almost ceased to compose, & have never seriously composed since. But life without composing is a misery to me, & this misery continued up to the last few years. It is only in the last 3 or 4 years that I could call my life happy, as a musician. In my years of 'earning' I acquired about 9 dependants, who gradually died off, or became provided for. But even my love for those 9 people was always darkened by economic fears, uneasiness, etc. I was not cut out to be a 'provider'; I was cut out to be a composer. In my musical life— whether as a pianist, teacher or composer—I have always met with considerable hostility or opposition (except from individuals such as Grieg, Cyril Scott, Sargent,[2] Richard Strauss[3]). Of this hostility I will

---

[1] i.e. in the broader racial sense, not the narrower geographical sense of being from one of the countries of Scandinavia.

[2] Artist John Singer Sargent, rather than Malcolm Sargent (1895–1967), although in 1929 the latter did record Grainger's *Youthful Rapture*, with the cellist Beatrice Harrison, and occasionally conducted his works in concert.

[3] Strauss had in 1911 been one of the earliest Continental conductors to programme Grainger's folksong arrangements.

only mention 2 aspects: No major composition of mine has ever been performed in any capital of the world (London, New York, Berlin, Melbourne, Oslo, Copenhagen, etc) unless I financed the performance myself. In spite of the fact that I have provably invented most of the formulas of modern music used by Schoenberg, Cyril Scott, Stravinsky, Gershwin (such innovations as discordant harmony, irregular rhythms, large chamber music, wordless singing, gliding tones, etc) I have yet to ever see my name mentioned in connection with any of these innovations. And altho last year I topped the Schirmer composers on television, & altho for many years 'Country Gardens' was Schirmer's 'best seller' my 70th birthday passed without any mention anywhere or any performance of any work of mine. Also, in spite of Grieg's clearly expressed opinion about my playing of his music (an opinion I do not agree with) I have never found a gramophone company willing to record my playing of the Grieg concerto, even when I offered to play my part for nothing.[1]

I mention these things so that you may imagine with what thankfulness & happiness I read of your wish to be my benefactor. I am SURE that you consider me a sincere (even if an unsuccessful) artist & that you concur wholly or in part with Grieg's good opinion of me as a musician. And to receive a GREAT GIFT from you can only be balm to my soul. I am so entirely humbled as a professional musician, so entirely without RIGHTS & hopes, that I am most perfectly prepared to receive a great gift at your hands with prideless joy & exultation. (Like a dear old German friend I had in Frankfurt, who by his lithography had become a millionaire before the first German war. When I visited him in 1923 he was overjoyed if one brought half a quarter of a pound of butter: 'Ei, was hat man doch hier.'[2]) On the other hand, why shall I, a Nordic, behave so badly to you? For whatever is done for us by the Jews, the Germans, the Italians, & by miserable business people, we pay thru the nose, or at least we pay. But when an angelic Nordic does something superlative for us (such as SAVING OUR LIFE) shall we pay nothing? Is it right towards our race that we IMPOVERISH EACH OTHER by taking time, genius, skill & worry FOR NOTHING?

---

[1] This is surprising, given that at Grainger's very first recording session, in London on 15 May 1908, the cadenza from its first movement had been recorded. Live recordings were made of Grainger playing this concerto in 1945 (Hollywood Bowl, with Stokowski), 1956 (Southeast Iowa Symphony Orchestra, with Richard A. Morse), and 1957 (Aarhus Municipal Orchestra, with Per Dreier). In 1921 he also recorded the work on Duo-Art piano rolls, with modified piano accompaniment.

[2] 'Ah, but what have we here.' (German.)

I have been such a pest to you, coming again & again with everlasting new troubles. And you are not merely a 'professional' healer—just as I am not merely a 'professional' musician. You would not be able to do the wonderful cures you do for us all if you did not TAKE US TO HEART, if you DID NOT WORRY about us! And your good deeds are tangible. I might easily be dead today if it were not for you. There is no questioning the advantage of being alive, as the advantage of my composing a piece can be questioned. Being alive, I can put my museum in shape, can finish my unfinished compositions (such as they are), can record my piano playing (such as it is), can bring my FREE MUSIC to a successful conclusion. Are these things worth nothing[?] I pay for the music paper I write on. I pay for the miles I travel by train or bus. I pay my income tax (& quite willingly). Shall I not pay for my life? What is to become of us 'poor Nordics'? We want to do everything for nothing & everybody (non-Nordic) WANTS us to do it for nothing. It is perfect. Everybody is pleased. But I cannot help feeling it is unfair & mean to our wonderful race—which is the only race that has the future of mankind BURNINGLY at heart. Any money paid to you, or to me, is, after all, paid into the account of the future of mankind. Will you not let me pay a fair sum into that account?

Your greatly honored

67   *To Wilhelm Munthe de Morgenstierne*

[Grainger's promotion of things Nordic was finally acknowledged in 1954 by the award of Norway's Saint Olav medal. His work had come to the attention of the Norwegian embassy through his participation, despite illness, in a Norwegian concert in New York on 31 October 1953.]

7 Cromwell Place | White Plains, New York
5th November, 1954

Your Excellency,

I am most grateful to have your kind letter of 24th September.

It was extremely gracious of His Majesty the King of Norway[1] to confer the Saint Olav Medal[2] upon me. I wish you would be so good as to convey to His Majesty how highly I prize this very great honor.

---

[1] King Haakon VII (1872–1959), who had reigned since 1906.
[2] An award, in civil and military divisions, founded in 1847 by King Oscar I.

Your Excellency's letter, the medal, the insignia of the decoration, together with the accompanying diploma were handed to me by the Royal Norwegian Consul General at New York, whose kindness and hospitality made the occasion a very happy one for me.

I am so glad that you feel I have merited the great honor conferred on me. My relations with the music of such inspired Norwegian geniuses as Edvard Grieg, David Monrad Johansen[1] and Sparre Olsen have been the happiest part of my musical life. The originality and daring of Grieg's harmonic innovations have proved highly fructifying to progressive composers in many parts of the world—composers such as Cesar Franck, Debussy, Ravel, Delius, Cyril Scott, Sibelius, MacDowell,[2] Gershwin, Albeniz, Puccini—and I have always felt it to be a high privilege to be able to try to make better known in various countries the less familiar achievements of Norwegian creative musical genius.

Of late years my activities in this direction were curtailed by illness. But my wonderful Norwegian friend in White Plains, Dr Kaare Nygaard, by his unique skill and generosity has now restored me to health, and I hope that a good measure of that restored health may be applied to spreading the gospel of Norwegian music.

Again thanking Your Excellency for your kindness,

I remain,

Yours very truly,

Percy Grainger

68   *To Benjamin Britten*

[Grainger was ignored rather than acknowledged by most of the younger generation of British composers. To them he was eccentric, rudely colonial and even embarrassing with his multiplicity of enthusiasms. Benjamin Britten was one of the few who recognized Grainger's genius as a setter of folksongs and acknowledged a compositional debt to him. The two composers corresponded occasionally, and finally met in 1958.]

---

[1] (1888–1974), whose works continued Grieg's lyrical line of national composition.

[2] Edward MacDowell, the American composer, was, like Grainger, fascinated by Nordic legends and customs. His Third Piano Sonata ('Norse', of 1900) and Fourth ('Keltic', of 1901) were both dedicated to Grieg.

7 Cromwell Place, White Plains, NY, USA | Feb 2, 1955

Dear Benjamin Britten,

Last night my wife & I heard Malcolm Sargent & the Philadelphia Orchestra play your entrancing VARIATIONS & FUGUE ON A THEME OF PURCELL.[1] Strangely enough, I have never heard this inspired masterpiece before & was completely 'bowled over' by it, by the utter originality of all its musical thoughts & orchestration & the tellingness of it all. It certainly is the most brilliant score ever penned in its field. And I think the brilliance comes from the vitality of the intervallic thinking rather than from mere scoring. I particularly love the brooding sonorousness of trombones & tuba with cellos, etc. I think the performance must have been a particularly perfect & inspired one. Certainly the piece was accorded a frantic ovation, as nothing else on the program was. Please dont bother to answer. A thousand thanks for a great treat.

Ever admiringly, Yours

69   *To Richard Fowler*

[Despite continuing health problems Grainger did return to Australia for the last time between September 1955 and June 1956. There he and his wife worked tirelessly to put in order the materials he had been sending to his Museum for the last seventeen years, and, with the Museum's curators, the Fowlers, to prepare it for opening to the public. His visit was clouded, however, by deepening feelings of rejection by his homeland.]

Sept 12, 1956

My dear Richard,

Thanks for your welcome letter of 2/7/56. I would have answered long before, but have been very crowded with things. I have done quite a lot of concerts & had a spate of music to prepare for such concerts & for our coming European trip (we sail for England early Jan I suppose). Also I have been in bed with lumbago (too much music-machine lifting?), but that is all cured now.

I have altered our address books—Railway Parade to Kelvin Grove. Isnt it queer, that whenever a change is made it is for something racy

---

[1] = *The Young Person's Guide to the Orchestra* (1946).

or poetic (such as Railway Parade or Tailem Bend) to something more commonplace?

We hope that Dorothy, John, Margaret & yourself are all very well. And we hope that the preparations for 'public access' will not be too tiring & bothersome. At this stage we must (I feel) not make too many demands upon ourselves re the museum. After all, it is only a personal record which is in process of being worked out. In the mean time we are letting the public see how we are getting along.

Miss Halkyard[1] was very kind in wishing to help. She is a close relative of one of my mother's and father's earliest & closest friends in Melbourne & as such she is naturally very interested in the museum & was very helpful to us in many ways. She also kindly expressed her willingness to dust some of the slanting music-racks in the pre-opening days. But as soon as the opening happens, & from then on, I think it very essential that nothing should happen at the museum except as planned by Dorothy and yourself & requested by you both. No division of initiative, in other words. Also, I think the museum should not be opened except as arranged or approved by you, with due regard for the wishes of the conservatorium, of course. In other words, there is no hurry or urgency. You & your family, Ella & I, all worked very hard at the museum during the months we were in Melbourne. We should all of us (I feel) take a long rest from museum matters—except such details as you may feel should be considered in connection with the opening.

How did your father's tablet turn out?[2] Were you pleased with it?

There are a few matters of SAFETY that I neglected to attend to before leaving. There is no hurry about them, but I suppose they should be considered amongst the things first to be thought about.

1. DELIUS PICTURES,[3] on the walls. I think they are hanging from curtain chord which should be changed to wire.

2. At the end of the ALDRIDGE FAMILY division (before the LONDON ROOM) there were a few photos standing on the floor—one of Leslie Aldridge & perhaps a colored one of Leslie & Georgie Aldridge.[4] These should be hung somewhere safer than the floor, I suppose.

---

[1] Probably Cora Halkyard, granddaughter of Captain and Mrs Isobella Black, who still lived at the family home 'Barone' in Brighton which Grainger had visited as a child.

[2] James MacKinnon Fowler had died in 1940. Grainger had subsidized the publication of his volume *False Foundations of British History* in 1943.

[3] Including Jelka Delius's portrait of her husband, which Grainger had acquired in 1948.

[4] Grainger's cousins, children of Rose Grainger's elder brother James Henry Aldridge.

3. LEAKAGES UNDER THE GIRDERS, particularly near my father's pictures (watercolors), the pictures of my grandparents, my mother's photos, etc. If these places leak perhaps the pictures could be moved to somewhere safer?

4. WATERCOLOR PAINTING OF MY MOTHER, by me, Frankfort, about 1896–7.[1] The original has plenty of salmon pink in it. The face is side or three-quarters & I think my mother seems seated at a table. I think it is my only watercolor portrait of my mother. The number is 70–1. The original is in those wide shallow drawers in the (Pengelley) document or picture case, with the insertable wooden front. Probably the drawer is marked 'Rose G'. I thought I took Mr Lewis's color negative with me, to have it enlarged here. But I cant find a trace of it. A copy of Mr Lewis's original is in that yellow-wood letter-size small upright cabinet that faces the door in the north store room. But this negative is not as good to mark enlargements from as Mr Lewis's original color-neg. Do you think that Mr Lewis could make another color transparency from this watercolor? And kindly send it to me here? (When Mr Lewis has a stray color film left, of course.) If so, will he very kindly make the transparency (make the copy) AT THE MUSEUM? I DONT WANT THE ORIGINAL WATERCOLOR TO BE TAKEN OUT OF THE MUSEUM.

We hope that dear Dorothy's neck has been behaving well & that she feels well in general. The Melbourne months (in spite of all that terrible walking) seem to have had a splendid effect upon Ella's & my health. For our condition has been marvelous since we got back.

Just at present I feel knocked out by excitement. Our FREE MUSIC machine is in such a terribly exciting stage of its unfoldment that I feel quite woosey.[2] And so is the rescoring work I am doing on my MOWGLI'S SONG AGAINST PEOPLE (Kipling Jungle Book) for mixed chorus & chamber music, which is one of the pieces programmed by the Aarhus (Denmark) people for my concert there Feb 25.[3] I have always been like that. As soon as I get time for really interesting work, & particularly if I respond well to the possibilities, my body feels knocked out & I seem to myself little better than a nit-wit. But what a

[1] See plate No. 3.

[2] Grainger was by this time increasingly interested in applications of electronic technology to his Free Music machines. In the following year he attended a seminar on electronic music synthesis at The Juilliard School.

[3] Grainger's programme also included his *Country Gardens* and *Ramble on Love* paraphrase (solo items), Grieg's Piano Concerto and the Danish Folk-Music Suite. The Aarhus Municipal Orchestra was conducted by Per Dreier. These non-vocal items were included on a Vanguard recording which was manufactured, but not released.

wonderfully blessed condition that is—when one's interests, opportunities, experiences so far outstrip ones powers that one's carcase is left in a swoon on the road, so to speak.

Give our love to Dorothy & the dear children. Please remember not to overdo efforts at the museum. When one has a double job one mustnt let oneself be dragged into too much.

Please forgive this very hazy letter. I will try to be more sensible another time.

A splendid record has been made of ARNOLD SCHOENBERG'S 5 PIECES FOR ORCHESTRA, op. 16, with Rafael Kubelik conducting the Chicago Symphony Orchestra: Mercury Classic, MG-50024. There are the pieces that altered the whole face of modern music. And how really LOVELY they are. I heard them London 1912.[1] Since then have never heard them, or heard of them being recorded. Can you get these in Melbourne? If not, shall I send them to the museum from here (so you can use them on your series)?

Love to you all
Percy

70   *To Cyril Scott*

Nov 8, 1957

Dearest Cyril,

Thanks for your last letter, containing answers to 2 questions about your Quartet. I think we now have all the information we need & that Ella & I can go thru all the Quartet material we have & thoroly scour her MS of possible errors before sending off copies to you & Elkin.[2]

I came home from the hospital yesterday after the operation of removing the testicles.[3] It is a comparatively slight operation leaving next to no pain behind it & next to no worn-out-ness. All the same I felt it to be very shameful that I had been flouting the advice of such a

[1] Two days after their London performance Grainger had written: 'we heard 5 orchestral pieces by *Arnold Schönberg* the Viennese composer. He is *excellent*, dear. Hear something of his if you in any way can. He is the greatest revolution I have witnessed. He opens great and rich free-doms for all of us composers.' (5 Sept. 1912, to Karen Holten (Kellermann), in Dreyfus (ed.), *The Farthest North of Humanness*, 465.)

[2] Scott dedicated his String Quartet No. 2 to the Graingers, in appreciation of their efforts in bringing the work to publication.

[3] This bilateral orchiectomy was carried out by Nygaard at the White Plains Hospital on 30 Oct.

very dear & clever friend as yourself—the more so since all my sympathies are with the saltless, meatless, knifeless method—not knowing
anything about it one way or another.

But there is just one thing I could not bring myself to do—to be
rude to such a sweet & sensitive man as Dr Nygaard. And I cannot
help it—I would feel it rude to say to him 'I know of a man in New
York who has cured even cancer by less drastic means'. It would be as
bad as when that nasty unkind German-American critic said to me, in
1916 or 1917, a day or so before Howard Brockway's first concert of his
exquisite settings of Kentucky folksongs:[1] 'But this is the REAL
THING'—meaning that my folksong settings were not the REAL
THING.

And then there is the question of the get-at-able-ness of Dr
Gerson[2]—with a life such as mine. This winter I am booked (self-
booked, even) for about 10 or 12 concerts situated in Michigan, North
Carolina, Texas, Cincinnati, Wisconsin, California, etc. If I am taken
with cramp on these trips I am fairly sure of getting help from some
friend of Dr Nygaard or the Mayo Clinic. And if I went on a saltless
diet (which I would be delighted to do—I read about salt & cancer in
Sir Arbuthnot Lane's[3] books 50 years ago) how would I carry it out on
the trains?

If Dr Gerson is 'successful' with his methods I suppose being treated
by him would be as disagreeable as being treated by any other 'successful' man. It is the success that is frightening. If Dr Gerson is an
'original' man I suppose he has everyone against him (as I have, let us
say) & if one went to him one would catch some of the cruelties &
hardships that society always (if it can) doles out to the 'originals' &
their followers. As far as I know I am the only composer who investi-
gated the possibilities of 'tuneful percussion', guitars in chamber music,
etc. No one will touch any of these things altho they are quite practical & effective, as I think. Sandby has just written me of his pleasure
in hearing my short pieces so often in Denmark. And that he had
given my MARCHING SONG OF DEMOCRACY to the Radio people in
Copenhagen. But they only say 'the vocal parts are too difficult'. Yet
you think I am a master of choral treatment. Shall I go thru this all
over again in my health life—something that doesnt mean much to

---

[1] *Twenty Kentucky Mountain Songs*, published in 1920.

[2] Perhaps Dr Martin J. Gerson of Park Avenue, Manhattan.

[3] (1856–1943), leading British surgeon, author of such books as *Secrets of Good Health* (1927) and
New Health for Everyman (1932).

me? Nevertheless I feel (as I said) deeply shamed that I was not brave enough to follow your advice about my health.

I shall let you know how I shape. So far I feel very well. But I have no confidence. A thousand thanks again for your PASSIONATE concern about my health.

Lovingly
Percy.

71   *To Thomas Armstrong*

7 Cromwell Place, White Plains, NY, USA | Oct 17, 1958

My dear Tom,

I note that your dear letter of 25 Sept,[1] about the Frankfurt group, was posted by sea-mail, ordinary post, & did not reach me here till about a week ago. During the week since it arrived I have been finishing score & parts of my KIPLING 'JUNGLE BOOK' CYCLE, which is urgently needed in Sydney[2] & which I had promised. It is now off & I can attend to the Frankfurt group information. You mention your talk to be 'in a few weeks time' & I hope I am not going to be too late with this letter. I will write a mere outline today & post it today, & send you a more detailed account in a day or so. For speed's sake I will write in the 'it is' style & not in the 'it seems to me' style.

Why the English composers (O'Neil[l],[3] Scott, Gardiner, Quilter) went to Frankfurt I dont know,[4] for I am not aware that Knorr had any famous pupils before the above quartet.[5] As for myself I went to F. to study with Madame Schumann,[6] but she died a few weeks after

[1] Armstrong was seeking information for a paper on 'The Frankfort Group' which he was presenting to the Royal Musical Association in London on 17 Nov. 1958. That paper was published in the *Proceedings of the Royal Musical Association*, 85 (1958–9), 1–16.

[2] Sir Bernard Heinze intended to conduct the augmented eleven-item cycle. Grainger had hoped to go to Australia in 1959 to hear the performance and then to work in his Museum in Melbourne, but was insufficiently well to travel.

[3] Norman O'Neill (1875–1934), English musician studying in Frankfurt between 1893 and 1897, recognized as the fifth member of the 'Group'. He became best known as a composer of incidental music and as Treasurer, from 1918 until his death, of the Royal Philharmonic Society.

[4] The Hoch Conservatory was very popular among British music students at this time. Of the 257 students enrolled for the 1895/6 academic year 36 were British (including 3 from Australia and 2 from New Zealand). Fourteen Americans were also enrolled.

[5] Grainger fails to mention the composer Hans Pfitzner, who had studied under Iwan Knorr (1853–1916) in Frankfurt during the mid–late 1880s.

[6] Clara Schumann (1819–96), German pianist and composer, wife of Robert Schumann. In 1878 she had been appointed principal piano teacher at the Hoch Conservatory. She died on 20 May 1896, nearly a year after Grainger's arrival in the city.

my mother & I arrived in F. So I was advised to go to the Con. (conservatorium). That was the summer of 1895. Scott was in England at that time. He had been in F. for a year or so before that & was beloved & famous in F. for his prettiness (he was about 12 when there, I suppose) & his delightful playing and charming manners. There was a very artistic family called KLIMSCH[1] who loved & admired Cyril very much on his first visit to F. They were never tired of talking about him. Karl Klimsch was about 60, retired from founding one of the world's finest lithographic businesses. He was an amateur painter & composer, the only man I ever learnt anything from as a composer. The daughter ('Butsie')[2] was a nice pianist, had been very fond of the erstwhile Cyril. Cyril, Butsie & I met accidentally one day (1896) & Butsie said to Cyril 'Percy has just written a Piano Concerto'. Cyril said to me 'Do you know anything about musical form?' I said 'No'. Cyril said 'Then you cant call it a Concerto'. (He was 17 then).[3] He & a friend were walking along the 'Promenade' & the friend was talking a lot, Cyril whistling & not paying much attention. Creichton[4] said 'Are you listening to what I am saying?'. Cyril said 'Go on with your childish prattle. Your babbling helps me to think'.[5]

Cyril had written a heavenly string quartet. Old Mr Klimsch wanted Cyril to hear it played & arranged for it. Afterwards Mr K. pointed out what was ineffective or faulty & produced a quartet of Beethoven's. 'Now you will hear how a quartet OUGHT TO BE.' Cyril went to listen in the next room & was discovered there asleep by Mr Klimsch when he went to 'rub it in'.

Cyril, appalled by the old-fashionedness of my Piano Concerto & other compositions asked me 'Dont you like modern harmonies?' 'What do you mean by MODERN harmonies?', and he played me the opening of Grieg's Ballade[6] & the opening of Tchaikovsky's Air & Vars.[7] I was bewitched & became a modernist over night. (I was 13 or

[1] Headed by Karl Klimsch (1841–1926), a printer by trade.
[2] = Pauline Schumacher (née Klimsch) (c.1878–c.1970).
[3] The joltiness from section to section of this letter arises partly because Grainger lifted passages directly from his autobiographical writings of the late 1940s and early 1950s. Grainger has e.g. copied (with minor changes) this trivial story about 'childish babbling' directly from an entry in his 'Anecdotes' dated 13 July 1953.
[4] Walter Creighton, 'a very handsome tall friend of Roger Quilter's'.
[5] Grainger's point in telling this story is explained in his 'Anecdotes' entry 423–26: 'such things were said by Cyril in a graceful laughing way, almost as if it were a quotation. All the same, Creighton held it against Cyril. Genius always knows how to get itself disliked.'
[6] Grieg's Ballade (1875–6) for solo piano, written in the form of variations on a Norwegian melody.
[7] Perhaps his Theme and Variations, Op. 19 No. 6 (1873).

14.) In 1898 we were together in Knorr's composition class. The task was to write Theme & Vars for string quartet. One of my vars was 'der pfeifender Reiter'.[1] My mother & I had been bicycling in the woods south of Frankfurt. I heard a rider whistling as he rode thru the wood, it fascinated me & I wrote a variation on it. When Knorr saw it he applied his sarcasm. 'This is important. You must hear it played' which I thought very kind of him. He told the whole staff they must come & hear it—that they would laugh themselves to death. And they did.[2] They simply squirmed with laughter. But Cyril (in spite of his admiration for Knorr) came over to me & said 'I see nothing to laugh at. I think it is effective & most original'. That is when our real friendship started. That is how Cyril championed us all. In my Museum I have postcards from Cyril to Balfour urging B. to concentrate on composing & not on Oxford, as Oxford does not seem to lead you to music.[3] When Frederick Austin came to London to give his first song recital C. wrote to all sorts of people, saying how gifted Austin was & urging them to go to Austin's concert. Cyril was a great championer of talent.

Knorr was very sarcastic & was supposed to be very clever. At the beginning I liked him very much, so much so that I used to wait with my bicycle for him to pass where we lived in order to accompany him to the Con. I used to do some simple tricks on my bicycle. He said 'It is a pity you are not equally skilful at counterpoint'. (I feel that counter-melodies are one of the assets of my music. Strange that my composition teacher saw not sprouting countermelodies in me.) Around 1897 I experimented a lot with whole-tone harmonies. When Knorr saw it he said 'I dont know what all this super-chromaticism is good for'. I didnt think it a clever name for whole-tone harmonies. So I began to think him silly. And when I took him some songs with Kipling words & he said 'The music is crazy & the poems are crazy too,' I felt I had enough & refused to go to further composition classes,[4] altho my mother had paid for the classes & we were so poor—never knew where food would come from more than a few days ahead. Cyril paced up & down in our room urging me to go back to

[1] = The whistling rider (German). The twenty-page MS, now held in the Grainger Museum, is dated Apr. 1898. On its envelope is written the comment '1st modern Grainger tone-piece'.

[2] The quartet was performed in the Conservatory on 8 June 1898.

[3] Gardiner studied in Frankfurt in 1894–6 and 1900–1. In between, he studied at Oxford, scraping a degree with fourth-class honours in *literae humaniores*. One of his student friends at Oxford was Donald Tovey.

[4] Grainger's rift with Knorr can be dated to the 1897–8 academic year.

Knorr & appealed to my mother for her to urge me to go back. But my mother was not an urger. Altho Cyril championed me he still believed in Knorr. All the boys but me did.

The Boer War was on & the Germans were full of hate for the British.[1] My mother earned our living teaching English. A middle-aged man, on concluding a set of lessons said to my mother on saying good-bye: 'I hope as many as possible of your people in Africa get killed.'[2] But even this sort of behavior did not embitter Cyril or make him war-minded. 'All I mind', he said, 'Is that such fine young men get killed'.

My father (in Australia) wrote to a friend 'the boy (me) is getting too Teutonic. I must send him some Kipling to tickle up the British lion in him.'[3] And it did. I not only set all sorts of Kipling poems to music but I began to take a chauvinistic view of music (which I still have) such as being unwilling to use titles (symphony, sonata, cantata, etc) hallowed by German, Austrian, Italian & other foreign usage, or expression marks such as crescendo, staccato. That was the origin of my 'louden', 'short', etc.

But I couldnt get my English (or Danish) friends to follow me in my chauvinism, or anything else extramusical, tho they were willing enough to copy my musical innovations: irregular rhythms, unresolved discords, gliding tones, ending on discords, large chamber-music (I am enclosing, or sending separately, some descriptions of these innovations.)

My mother used to say that if she were a young woman Balfour Gardiner would have been the most attractive to her of my composer-friends. Walk[ing] along the Eschersheimer Landstrasse[4] one day, about the turn of the century, he said to me 'Cyril thinks you a genius, but I see nothing in your music to justify such an opinion'. He was very outspoken, but a true friend & the kind of animal the world should be full of. I think one of the most remarkable things about him was the way he was tied to countrifiedness. Of all his works I think the STRANGER'S SONG (hangman's) touches me the most. The feeling for the yokel to be hung for stealing sheep, & the feeling for the sailors dead in NEWS FROM WHYDAH & the young men in AN OLD SONG

---

[1] A fuller version of this story, dating from 'around 1899', is found in 'Anecdotes', 423–31.

[2] The deterioration in relations between Britain and Germany over the situation in southern Africa can be dated to Jan. 1896, when the Kaiser had sent Paul Kruger, president of the Transvaal, a telegram congratulating him on the defeat of the British in the Jameson Raid.

[3] Grainger probably received his first books by Kipling in late 1897.

[4] See plates Nos 1 and 2 for Grainger's paintings of Frankfurt from the 1890s.

RE-SUNG (pulling claret bottles down & breaking off their necks). And I think the Weltschmerz in PHILOMELA[1] a world's wonder. The account of B.'s music study that was reprinted in the Memorium [*sic*] concert program[2] is a marvel of truth regarding the feeble way composition was taught at the Frankfurt Con. Of Roger Quilter's songs Cyril always said that he LIKED them so much more than their importance perhaps justified.

In other words it is not so much the Frankfurt group as the CYRIL SCOTT GROUP. He was a true leader & benign to us all in one way or another.

It is in his grandly flowing form & bewitching melody that I always think him a great genius. As for me, I think my melodic invention is poor, my orchestration clumsy & uninspired & my choice of subjects unpleasing. But as an innovator (irregular rhythms, etc) I think I am first class & that no one has given me credit for these things I consider very unfair to Australia.

[18 October 1958]

Norman O'Neil[l] I never knew well—either as a person or as a composer—I am sorry to say. His time at F. must have been several years before mine altho he probably came to F. occasionally while I was there.

As I think of the other ones (Scott, Quilter, Gardiner & myself) & seek to find a characteristic that marks our group off from other British composers it seems to me that an excessive emotionality (& particularly a tragic or sentimental or wistful or pathetic emotionality) is the hallmark of our group. When Cyril returned to F. in 1896 the books & pictorial art we got to know thru him were the plays of Maeterlinck[3] (to which he wrote several overtures in those early days), the poems of Stefan George & Ernest Dowson, Walt Whitman, Aubrey Beardsley. One of the greatest achievements of Scott's life as a composer is his setting of FAIR HELEN OF KIR[K]CONNEL for baritone & orchestra, composed 1900. This I consider one of the greatest ballads ever written. A few years later came LA BELLE DAME SANS MERCI,[4] of a somewhat similar nature. Before 1900 was SAENGE EINES FAHRENDEN SPIELMANNS, for voice & piano (words by Stefan

---

[1] Setting of a text by Matthew Arnold, for tenor, women's voices and orchestra, completed in 1923. The work was first performed on 4 May 1955.

[2] Held at London's French Institute on 23 Apr. 1951.

[3] Maurice Maeterlinck (1862–1949), Belgian man of letters and Nobel prize-winner in 1911.

[4] For baritone, chorus, and orchestra, composed in 1915–16.

George)[1] & around 1911 came AN OLD SONG ENDED.[2] (I have chosen nothing but early or fairly early works, when the F. influence, active or passive, might be at its strongest). All these works are informed with some agony which I would be inclined to attribute to German influence. All we 4 composers spoke German as fluently as English—tho not necessarily gramatically. I think it might be true that the exagerated tenor of German emotionality had had some influence on us all 4. The influence, if any, lay in the willingness to take such emotional views of things. The feelings themselves were typically English in their wistfulness & patheticness. Perhaps it might be true to say that we were all of us PRERAFAELITE composers.[3] The 4 works of Cyril's I have mentioned above were quite prerafaelite.[4] And my own music has certainly always been prerafaelite since I was a boy in Australia, where (at the age of 9 to 11) I discovered the Icelandic sagas & the Anglosaxon Chronicle & found I liked them better than any other literature. Under 'prerafaelite' I understand art which takes a CON-SCIOUS charm from what is archaic, an art in which KNIGHTS or heroes are always present. And what musical medium could provide the agonized emotionality needed? Certainly not the 'architectural' side of music & not the truly English qualities of grandeur, hopefulness & glory so thrilling in Elgar, Parry, Walton, Vaughan Williams & other British composers. I think the answer is 'the CHORD'. The chord has the heartrending power we musical prerafaelites needed. Based on Bach, Wagner, Skriabine, Grieg & Cesar Franck, Cyril, Balfour & I became chord-masters indeed. If we want an example of the magical power of Cyril's chord-skill examine his treatment of ALL THROUGH

---

[1] = Songs of a wandering minstrel. It was through his settings of these George texts that Scott first came to know George personally.

[2] A setting of words by the Pre-Raphaelite figure D. G. Rossetti.

[3] Reference to a group of young British painters who banded together in 1848. They looked to 14th- and 15th-cent. Italian art for inspiration in developing an alternative to prevailing Royal Academy styles. In his paper Armstrong concluded about the Group: 'They were in a sense belated pre-Raphaelites, and anybody who has had the privilege to enter the house of Cyril Scott will have realized at once from the whole decor that the influence of William Morris, Rossetti, and the pre-Raphaelite movement, was an all-powerful one. The movement had affected Continental musicians at an earlier date: it had had a powerful influence upon Debussy, for instance, but this influence had passed from the European scene long before the Frankfort Group reached maturity as composers. By the first decade, when these musicians were active in their London careers, the pre-Raphaelite movement was a thing of the past, and in this respect the work of the Frankfort Group was not truly contemporary.' (pp. 15–16.)

[4] In his *My Years of Indiscretion* (London: Mills & Boon, 1924), 25, Scott wrote: 'My ideal was to invent a species of Pre-Raphaelite music, to consist mostly of common chords placed in such a way as to savour of very primitive church music, thereby, as I thought, reminding its listeners of old pictures.'

THE NIGHT in his British Folksongs.[1] If the chord gave us human unity, irregular rhythms gave us the tally of English energy—that is, in fast tempos (at slow tempos irregular rhythms are, of course, hardly distinguishable from regular ones). It will be seen from the sketch of the 1900 TRAIN MUSIC SKETCH[2] how early I was in that field, about 10 years before the almost identical irregular rhythms in SACRE DU PRINTEMPS.[3] If you have time I wish you would read thru the pages I sent yesterday about innovations, Wenlock Edge,[4] large chamber music, etc. I think it is a shame that credit should go to the conceited Continent for innovations created within the British Empire.[5] I think my best compositions, from my standpoint, are Hillsong I & Sea-song sketch of 1907. I rate them as follows: Cyril as the great composer, great melodist, etc. Balfour for his social justice in music. Quilter for his loving expression & normalness in music. Myself as innovator. I was talking to Balf. about creating new types & mediums in music & he said 'Creating new mediums isnt as important as creating perfect music with the mediums that exist'. Please forgive my disconnected thoughts, poor typing, feeble reasoning. I am not very well.

72   *To Thomas Armstrong*

7 Cromwell Place, White Plains, NY, USA | Oct 21, 1958

My dear Tom,

It is not true (what I think many musicians believe) that Cyril began composing with small pieces & only later turned to larger forms. Ever since I have known him (1896) his most natural & prolific expression was in the larger forms—MAGNIFICAT, 1st SYMPHONY, Piano & string QUARTET,[6] 3 SYMPHONIC DANCES,[7] AUBADE[8] & several Maeterlinck OVERTURES.[9] The Magnificat is one of the most

[1] Scott's arrangements of eight traditional British songs date from 1921–6.
[2] Grainger's sketch was dated 10 Feb. 1900. In Feb. to May 1901 he worked further on versions called *Charging Irishry—Train Music Style* A and B, both for orchestra, but these scores were not completed. See Grainger's further comments in letter **72**.
[3] Stravinsky's *The Rite of Spring*, composed in 1911–13.
[4] Vaughan Williams's *On Wenlock Edge* of 1909.
[5] Armstrong quoted most of these last three sentences directly in his article (p. 6).
[6] Probably the Piano Quartet in E minor, composed in 1903.
[7] From Scott's original Symphony No. 2, of 1903.   [8] For orchestra, of 1911.
[9] Scott wrote at least three overtures on Maeterlinck texts around 1912, but withdrew two of them.

magnificent cantatas (if that is the right term): the choral writing almost Handelian in its trenchant manliness, the orchestra brilliantly offsetting the voices, & the musical form unfolding itself with inspired urgency. Of course it has never been heard—Cyril would see to that! Cyril is interested only in his own progressiveness, for his own genius, perfection he has no stomach. The Magnificat is refreshing & virginal like a Botticelli. His 1st Symphony had much the same quality. It was performed by de Haan in Darmstadt the middle of February, 1900. The afternoon before the 1st rehearsal the copyist (in Frankfurt) got ill, with a lot of orchestral parts still not written. So Cyril & I spent the whole night writing the missing parts. During the performance of the Symphony I was standing at the back of the stalls. I heard one working man say to another, in their dialect: 'Des solle de Englander de Bure emal vorspiele; dann laufe sie bis zum Equarte erauf' [*sic*] (The English should play that to the Boers; then they'll run away up to the Equator.) A few days later (than the Darmstadt performance of Cyril's Symphony) my mother (very ill) [and I] were in an Italian train between Genoa & San Remo—very jolty. There & then I wrote my first sketch for my TRAIN-MUSIC. I enclose the sketch of the orchestral score, written in 1901. (Did I send this already?) But before the Italian train I had done many studies for irregular rhythm. In 1899 I got Roger Quilter & others to read biblical & other prose aloud to me & I would write down what I thought the rhythms were. The interesting point about these irreg. rhythms was not that I evolved them, but that almost every composer in the early 20th century took them up—for a time. But I didn't do them 'for a time', but for my whole life, showing that they were really part of me. About 1908 Cyril wrote to me saying he had heard my irreg. rhythms so long & so much that he felt he could not compose without them & would I mind if he adopted them.[1] I said not at all as long as it was always stated that it was an Australian invention. This acknowledgement was never made, of course, no one will give Australia credit for anything in music.

I think Roger Quilter's most important work[s] are the 3 ENGLISH DANCES.[2] They remind me of something with Knorr. I was passing Knorr's room one day & heard the most manly & rich-sounding music, played by violin, cello & piano—a kind of new Schumann. It turned out to be something of Roger's.

Knorr had been a friend of Tchaikovsky's I think. He was very

---

[1] In his Piano Sonata No. 1, first drafted in 1904.   [2] For orchestra, of 1910.

insistent that Tchai. had NOT committed suicide. I think he swayed his pupils. In the instrumentation class he urged us to take Tchai as our guide, to begin with. After the class I spoke to him privately, saying I didnt like the sound of T's orchestration—couldnt I take Bach as model instead. But what Bach writes is not orchestration, said Knorr. But I hear it on the orchestra & it sounds perfect to my ears. Such things did not make me popular with Knorr, of course. The English boys liked Tchai, Bizet, Bach, Wagner. But my taste ran to Bach, Brahms, Wagner. The one thing we were all united on: We all hated BEETHOVEN.[1]

Best greetings, *Percy*

73　　　　　　　　　　　*To Ella Grainger*

Chicago—to New York, Oct. 19, 1959

My own hearts-dearest, bewitching Ella,

Let it be admitted: I like train-travelling (just as much as I hate motoring) & I like concert-giving (& would like it still much better if the pieces I play were not so fiendishly difficult). I like the streams & the trees as they pass by, I like the shaking of the train; and I like the surging sounds (the overflow of richness) that comes from the choirs, orchestras, bands & the general feeling of victory that goes with a successful concert. And this was a successful concert indeed, with (it seems) the biggest audience they've ever had—at any rate, a sold out house. And so many people remembering you & the bells, the 'Wamphray' ballad & the Danish suite. All this appeals to the vulgar & gloating side of my nature, and puts to rest my anxieties & craven fears.

Let us begin at the beginning. The trip in the 'Commodore Vanderbilt' was comfy enough, with a whole seat to myself. But in the night, while lying along the seat, I managed to fall off the seat, falling with my forehead onto one of the metal handles of my music-case, I suppose. Result: a smallish bleeding scrape on the forehead. So I sup-

---

[1] Grainger's private writings from his Frankfurt and early London years do not bear out this statement. In the draft of a letter to Dr Henry O'Hara of Melbourne at New Year 1897, e.g., Grainger wrote: 'I am now practising the first movement of Beethoven's 4th [*sic*] Concerto in C minor, a very difficult thing & beyond me in technique, but it is splendid practise. . . . Concertos are lovely things to practise, & Beethoven was such a master at them, for instance his glorious E♭ major a real masterpiece of composition.'

pose I must try to spend my nights on the train sitting up, leaning back & getting the most out of the slant of the 'reclining' seat.

The 'Commodore' got in an hour late, but Rudy[1] & Marguerite were waiting for me. She drove me to their house, but he had to teach & rehearse until nearly 10 in the evening. Beautiful dark repose in the house for 2 days & lots of good food, yoghurt, oatmeal, noodles, etc. Nevertheless, 2 terrible days, with all the passages so carefully practised in White Plains fading into utter oblivion—the chromatic thirds in the Concerto[2] melting away from me, & the simplest tasks of memory failing. Reasonableness, under the circumstances, says: 'Cancel the appearance before worse happens'. But I am unreasonable; my wish to earn a little money & my longing to triumph are too strong. So Friday & Saturday were spent in wretchedness, with constant practising to the limits of powers of hands and arms.

Sunday (the concert day) I was dressed & shaved early, but the others arose at normal hours & we did not start the motor trip to Peoria (3½ hours?) until nearly 9.00. I shall try to make that my last long motor trip I ever take. Rudy drives well, the toll-ways are fine & rather empty, on a Sunday morning; but the inherent danger in the whole thing is too great & one is a dullard to do such a trip the wrong way (motor) when the right way (train) is available & offers every possible betterness. Still, Rudy was considerateness itself, & is in all ways a sweet, kindly man except (of course) in his attitude towards socialism.

Of course I dreaded to open my desk-roller suitcase & find something essential shaken loose. But no! Burnett's good workmanship had held its own, & the attitude of the orchestral man & others (even the women) was benign towards the roller.[3] By about 1.00 (midday) we were rehearsing the concerto & a more alarmingly incompetent rehearsal I have never in my life played—chromatic thirds collapsing, wrong basses & general 'turgidness' (quoting Charlesworth of Toronto[4]) galore. Even the simplest chords of the slow movement bristled with mistakes. But I stuck to my guns, & by the end of the rehearsal my dispair was sprinkled with hopefulness. At about 2.30 I rehearsed the choirs (250 voices),[5] about whom I had been told only bad reports—just as the last time in Peoria with the 'Wamphrey' bal-

---

[1] Dr Rudolph Reiners, conductor of the symphony orchestra in Peoria, Illinois. See letter **62**.
[2] Grieg's.
[3] Performer-controlled device which presented the musical score continuously, without having to turn pages.
[4] Hector Charlesworth (1872–1945), Canadian music critic from 1904 until his death.
[5] The massed choirs of Manual, Peoria Central, and Woodruff High Schools.

lad. I had been told that the orchestra drowned the chorus, that the middle-voices could not be heard—so strong is the German prejudice against all *sung* music! Sometimes I feel very helpless with large bodies of voices, at other times I feel gently persuasive. Yesterday was one of my 'gifted' days, with everything falling into place without talky-talky. It did my soul good to hear the sweet, rich sonorities of 'Ye Banks' & 'Harvest Hymn' after the thin, harsh, 'karg'[1] sonorities of the Beethoven 5th Symphony, rehearsed earlier. The Beethoven is full of lovely & telling musical 'ideas', transitions, themes. But on an amateur orchestra it really is a corker for poverty-stricken & meagre sound. Not that Rudy is cool to my music—he says only nice things about it. After packing up the desk-roller (such chores offer me relished relief) we were whisked off to the buffet supper where I was given a glorious plate of fruit salad, milk, etc. Then early to bed (with wet-proof plastic) & up at 5.30 this morning to catch the train to Chicago & New York. Of course, you should auðvitað[2] have been there.

Rudy's wife Marguerite is quite a nice woman & seems to find great satisfaction in her children (2 boys, one girl), 2 of whom are married & the 2nd boy around 19. The married girl lives very close at hand and keeps popping in. They try & save the girl all heavy jobs (such as laundry) as I think she is expecting a baby. Some years ago Rudy told me the girl is onormal skapt—hon har manliga organer såväl som kvinnliga,[3] or something like that. So I suppose the mother wears herself out to save the daughter. Or is it just American to wear oneself out? Take Sunday. At about 7.00 (morning) she & the girl go to Mass (Catholic). Then home & make breakfast & sandwiches. Then 3½ hour motoring to Peoria. All sorts of activities in Peoria. At about 6.00 buffet supper. Then she is driven back to Chicago, as she [is] to review a book for some book club the next morning (Monday). You & I are lucky that our arts, as well as our lives, are not cluttered up with needless appointments that just dissipate one's energy & inspirations. I think you & I are very alike in our arts. A sweet repose hovers over most of your tiles (especially those of late years) & their mood is very akin to the mood in my *Love Verses, Early one Morning, Irish Tune, Ye Banks, Australian Up-country Song*.[4]

It is glorious when 2 artists are mated in wedlock, but heavenly when the moods of their arts are akin. I feel so unspeakably supple-

---

[1] = barren (Swedish).   [2] = naturally (Icelandic).
[3] = created abnormal—she has male organs as well as female (Swedish).
[4] For unaccompanied five-part chorus, composed in 1905 and 1928, later scored for band.

mented by your poems, paintings, compositions, & I am deeply enriched by this like-moodedness in our arts. Much as I enjoy & admire almost all art in some way or other, there is not much art that I would feel supplemented by. Not much art that I feel is *akin* to my own. I think both you & I are unusually gentle & subtle & therefore I consider it a miracle of good luck that we met and wedded. I am so endlessly thankful to my darling wife.

Percy.

74   *To Elsie Bristow*

[By 1960 the cancer was slowly spreading to Grainger's brain. His mind would wander and unexpected associations would crop up in his conversation and correspondence. His final professional appearance was on 29 April 1960 at the Dartmouth Music Festival in Hanover, New Hampshire. He managed to give a lecture-recital on 'The influence of folk-song on art music' in the morning, but could not concentrate adequately when called on to conduct *The Power of Rome and the Christian Heart* in the afternoon. On the final envelope in his vast programme collection, stretching back to the mid-1890s, Grainger simply wrote: 'Here was *Percy's last concert,* 1960. Oh so nice at morning Recital, the[n] a "fiasco" with Band in the afternoon—*also nice.*'[1]]

White Plains, NY, August 10, 60

Dearest Elsie,

Do you have a record of Peter Pears[2] singing Benjamin Britten's setting of the English folk song O WALLY WALLY[3] on one side & my setting of 6 DUKES WENT A-FISHING[4] on the other side, Benjamin Britten accompanying both (His Masters Voice, DA 2032)?[5] As it is a 78 revolutions per minute disc it must be an old record—but none the worse on that account. Their rendering of 6 DUKES is sweet & lovely, but it is the B. Britten setting of O WALY WALY that we have fallen in love with. Britten's chords are tragic & inspired. If you dont have this disc, try to get it. If you cant get it, we will try to make a copy of it here for you.

I wish you would buy yourself THE PENGUIN BOOK OF ENGLISH

---

[1] See plate No. 24.
[2] (1910–86), English tenor and leading interpreter of Britten's vocal music.
[3] = 'O Waly Waly'.
[4] Grainger had collected and set this Lincolnshire tune in 1905–6.
[5] This recording dates from 1950.

FOLK SONG, edited by Vaughan Williams & A.L. Lloyd,[1] so we have it in Pevensey & can discuss its contents by letter. It has a lot of complete texts of texts that I collected incompletely (owing to my singers not remembering the complete texts). The book costs 95 cents in USA. Tell me the English price & I will refund.

I have delayed writing you for a week or so as I wanted to give you Dr Nygaard's verdict on my health, my prospects of accompanying Ella to Europe, etc. Unfortunately, the verdict is bad. I think Dr Nygaard does not think it will ever be safe for me to travel to Europe or Australia. He says that chilliness & damp air is so bad for my bursitis.[2] I said to him: 'But it was cold enough in Rochester, Minn. & I took no harm from it'. To which Nygaard said 'But if you had got bad you would have had the best doctors in the world to turn to'. Which is all quite true. But Americans & Scandinavians feel the cold so much, whereas neither Ella nor I do.

Dr Nygaard is very pleased with my having put on 2 or 3 pounds of weight; and I am eating tremendously. But it seems as if I will have to wage a long battle with the bursitis. And what a prospect:—To have to live & die in America. Never to see you & Robert in Southolm. Never to see England, Australia, Scandinavia, Holland again. It seems to me that if the bursitis is held in check while in America one might well risk a 4 or 5 day sea trip to England. When the bursitis was at its worst, a few weeks ago, Dr Nygaard advised me never to put up with pain but always to take a pain-killing pill—because pain is always bad for the whole system & the pills he gave me are quite harmless. So I took pain-killers 3 or 4 times, spread over a few weeks. And HOW WONDERFULLY NICE THEY ARE! A heavenly balminess sinks down upon one & one feels so fresh & free the next day. Never the less, I am dead against anything that could develop into a habit. So I have not taken any pain-killer for about the last 2 weeks. And I will repeat what I always say: That artifice is always superior to naturalness. It is much pleasanter to be ill-ish, have pain, & banish the pain with a pain killer than just to be dully well & have neither pain nor pain-killer. I suppose that is what Whidgee feels about molting. It must be a sort of delicious agony.

How very nice that the Wiltons are to be with you. Wouldnt it be delightful if they decided to live in Pevensey!

Is it really true that Robert has won the Battle of the Meadows? How splendid of him. Lots of love to you both—also to the Wiltons.

[1] (Harmondsworth: Penguin, 1959).   [2] Inflammation of the joints.

I have been working at COLONIAL SONG—a few revisions of orchestration. Dont you think that F. Fennell's[1] recording of C.S. is wonderfully fine—so rich & glowing. He is a wonder.

I have been working at the MSS of Cyril's *'Fair Helen of Kirk[c]onnel'* which he wrote for baritone voice & orchestra in 1900, & which he 'titivated' (brought up to date) in 1958—he making his 'face-lifting' & I writing down what he approved of. This piece is one of the wonders of music & I hope we will be able to leave it in a perfect & practical form.

Love from Percy.

75　　　　　*To Robert and Elsie Bristow*

Tuesday, Dec. 22, 1960

Dear Robert & Elsa,

I am writing to you both, not that I have anything interesting to say, but because Ella & I agreed, the other day, that nothing could be so nice as to write to you both, even so.

I had about 3 weeks in the hospital[2] & I must say it was purely damnable in every respect, to be there for the cause for which I was there—the cause for which I was there was hallucinations—making me believe I was in a different part of the world to which I am, in a different part of the hospital. Of the workers (nurses, etc.) I could understand & be understood by

the Americans—completely

the Latin Americans—often quite well

the American Negroes—hardly at all

By day all was fairly all right, for people were moving about. At night everything was enraging, for my right foot was fastened to the end of the bed & often there seemed no way of getting hold of anyone—if one wanted the urine-bottle for instance. There was a barrier on one side. It is infuriating to have one's foot tied to something, or to have one's middle made fast to something, as I often was. Sometimes I tore the fastenings apart & at other times I cut them with my razor blade. When Ella was there it was heavenly, of course. But she couldnt be

[1] (b. 1914), American band conductor, founder of the Eastman Wind Ensemble in 1952.
[2] White Plains Hospital.

there all the time & never at night. To go thru the whole night in terror was of course sheer torture.

They took me to the hospital because of a very sharp pain I sudden[ly] had here one evening. They did not know whether the pain was a broken bone, or just a split bone. Luckily it was only a split bone. Had it been broken I would have had to be there for 6 months. As it was they let me come home, if I was awfully careful, which I have been, as you may imagine. Now I have the boon of being home & it is quite silly, the sort of things one's delight centers upon. One of my unreasoning joys is oatmeal, without either salt or sugar. It is so acutely 'grainy'. And when one thinks how it has been the main food of our race for so many hundreds of years it is quite poetic. It figures in the *Eyrbvgja Saga*.[1] It is mentioned by Ivar Aason[2] ('a woman who cannot cook an eatable porridge'). It is the only dish mentioned in the Scottish joke 'Does a man get tired of his feed?' And so on. In my childhood porridge was apt to have lumps in it. Now it never has. But then that may be because Ella is a porridge-virtuoso.

There is something very final about old age that is nice. A few years ago if someone mentioned 'The Warriors' it conjured up potential *future* performances. Now it means only Waco, Texas about 7 years ago. If Hillsong II is mentioned it means only Oberlin Ohio about 10 years ago.[3] All the same: I wish I were walking along the stretch of road from Holtom's Corner to Southolm.

Love & thanks
Percy

76　　　　　　　　　　*To Robert Bristow*

Jan 12 1961

Dearest Robert

That was a surprise indeed! I had already gone to bed (at about 7.00. For I wake at about 4.30 or 5.00 in the morning) & was awakened by Ella to say good evening to Margarite Tjader[4] (part Swedish

[1] = *Eyrbyggja Saga*, 13th-cent. Icelandic saga.
[2] (1813–96), Norwegian linguist who constructed Landsmål (New Norwegian).
[3] Grainger had guest-conducted the Oberlin Symphony Band in *Hill-Song* No. 2 on 14 Jan. 1951.
[4] Probably Tjader Harris.

& part American: and very like Elsa in voice, looks, etc.) 'But she looks very like Elsa', I said to Elsa[1] (for my eyesight is very failing).

All the same, I think it very wrong that you should be left without wifely ministrations right in the middle of the winter. But I am glad you are having nice weather in Pevensey just now. I think Elsa is looking very well—just the same as 10 years ago. That is a great achievement.

The hallucinations are very trying. By dint of tearing at a leather fastening; by dint of cutting thru a leather fastener with a razor blade one cuts oneself somewhat loose, only to find oneself on the same floor one began on. One expected to find one half a floor lower! And by seeing double one sees all sorts of queer sights & combinations. The main thing to remember [is] that it is *unreal* what one sees. I have been trying to write score for several days. But I have not succeded yet.

At any rate, we think it most unusually generous of you to let us have this glimpse of Elsa in mid-winter. We only wish you could have come along with her. But we realise that you have done so much already & we are so very very grateful.

Lots of love from Ella & Percy[2]

[1] = Ella.
[2] This was one of the last letters written by Grainger. He died in White Plains Hospital on 20 Feb. 1961.

Index

296

299

Index

Index

Vandals 44

Van Gogh, Vincent 225

Vatnsdaela Saga 201

Vaughan Williams, Ralph xii, xxvi, 8, 102,
149, 172, 221, 225, 228, 256, 259–60, 277,
278, 284
  letter to 221–4
  An Acre of Land 222
  Ca' the Yowes 222
  Fantasia on a Theme of Tallis 103
  Fantasia on Greensleeves 222
  Job 176, 222
  On Wenlock Edge 222, 278
  Serenade to Music 222
  Symphony No. 1 ('Sea') 222
  Symphony No. 3 ('Pastoral') 103, 222
  Symphony No. 4 222–3
  Symphony No. 5 222
  Symphony No. 6 222
  Wasps, The 222

Verdi Giuseppe 226

'Vermlandsvisan' 201

Viaud, Julien (Pierre Loti) 68–9, 240
  Marriage of Loti, The 69

Vienna 199, 226

Vienna Awards 169

Vikings 42

Vinita (Oklahoma) 174

Visby 201

Vogt, Augustus Stephen 19

Volkert, Charles G. J. 57

Waco (Texas) 286

Wagner, Richard 30, 33, 118, 136, 172, 183,
211, 222–3, 225–6, 246, 256
  Parsifal 103
  Ring cycle 212

Walmsley, Alfred 131

Walters, Emily 237

Walton, William 8, 228, 256, 277
  Viola Concerto 175–6

Warlock, Peter, *see* Heseltine, Philip

Washington, D.C. 141
  Library of Congress 25, 112, 244

Waterville (Maine) 41

Wausau (Wisconsin) 161, 165

Weinberger, Jaromir ('Schwanda') 206

Wellington 72, 129–31
  Apollo Singers 131
  Harmonic Society 131
  Symphony Orchestra 130

West Point (Virginia):
  Band xvii, xxv, 199–201, 208, 209

West, Velma 100

West Virginia 14

White, Maude V. 229

White Plains xi, xv, xvii, xxi, xxiv, 3, 51, 54,
56, 60, 62, 109, 155, 170, 171, 190, 198,
202, 204, 214, 219, 272, 278, 283, 285
  Country Trust Co. 56
  Hospital 270, 286, 287

White, Temple 131

Whitman, Walt xiii, 1, 23, 29, 30, 38, 40, 116,
121, 179, 220, 256, 259, 276
  Leaves of Grass 121

Wiesbaden 51

Wildenvey, Gisken 100, 237–8

Wildenvey, Herman 100

Wilhelmj, August 21

Willaert, Adrian 207, 216

Wilson, Steuart 237

Wirén, Dag 256

Wisconsin 271

Wodson, Henry 214

Wolfe, James 47

Wood, Henry 225

Woodgate, Leslie 235

Woodside, Christine 97

Worcester Festival (Massachusetts) 109

Worcester medieval harmony, 149

Work Projects (Progress) Administration (WPA)
204

Yachtsman, The 255

Yasser, Joseph 186

Yeats, William Butler 46